THE NOBEL PRIZE WINNERS

Literature

THE NOBEL PRIZE WINNERS

Literature

Volume 1
1901–1926

Edited by
FRANK N. MAGILL

SALEM PRESS
Pasadena, California   Englewood Cliffs, New Jersey

Library of Congress Cataloging-in-Publication Data
The Nobel Prize winners: literature/edited by
Frank N. Magill. p. cm.
  Includes bibliographies and indexes.
  Contents: v. 1. 1901-1926—v. 2. 1927-1961—
v. 3. 1962-1987.
  ISBN 0-89356-541-5 (set)
  1. Authors—20th century—Biography. 2. No-
bel prizes. 3. Literature, Modern—20th century—
History and criticism. 4. Literature, Modern—20th
century—Bibliography. [1. Authors. 2. Nobel
prizes. 3. Literature, Modern—20th century—
History and criticism.] I. Magill, Frank Northen,
1907-
PN451.N63 1988
809' .04—dc19   88-6469
[B]   CIP
[920]   AC
ISBN 0-89356-541-5 (set)
ISBN 0-89356-542-3 (volume 1)

PUBLISHER'S NOTE

THE NOBEL PRIZE WINNERS: LITERATURE is the inaugural set in a projected series which will cover the Nobel laureates in all award areas: Literature, Peace, Physics, Chemistry, Physiology or Medicine, and Economic Sciences. Aside from the Nobel Foundation's own publication, *Les Prix Nobel*, issued annually to document the award ceremony and speeches for that year in all award areas, the present reference set is one of the few which offers comprehensive coverage of the laureates as well as the speeches and commentary attendant on the Nobel Prize; in addition, the series is designed to provide that information by all the subject areas (for example, literature, peace, physics) to facilitate access by library users.

Volume 1 opens with a substantial history of the Nobel Prize in Literature by the Associate Editor of the journal *World Literature Today* (formerly *Books Abroad*), William Riggan, who has made the Nobel Prize in Literature one of his specialties. In his "History and Overview" of the literature prize, he covers the "'gold standard' against which all other awards . . . are measured," beginning with its birth in Alfred Nobel's bequest in 1895 and continuing with the award's administration by the Nobel Foundation and the Swedish Academy, selection procedures and criteria, the ceremonies, the award itself, and finally a detailed examination of past literature laureates in historical perspective.

Following Mr. Riggan's essay is a time line which lists, in tabular form, core data about the Nobel laureates in literature: names, dates (of birth and death as well as award years), nationalities, and the literary genres with which the laureates are most closely identified. The articles are arranged chronologically, starting with Sully Prudhomme, the recipient of the first award in 1901, and ending with Joseph Brodsky, the winner in 1987. For years in which the prize was awarded to two laureates (1904, 1917, 1966, and 1974), a separate article was prepared for each laureate; their order is alphabetical within the sequence (hence, for 1974, Eyvind Johnson appears before Harry Martinson).

Each article is preceded by a display page listing the laureates in the other disciplines for the same year, to provide the reader with some historical perspective. There follows a photograph of the laureate on the left-hand page facing the opening of the article.

The articles themselves, averaging 3500 words in length, follow a standard format that enables the user of this reference set to find information quickly: Ready-reference listings at the top of each article give the laureate's name, place and dates of birth and death, language(s) in which he or she wrote, and principal genres. A synopsis of the laureate's impact on literature appears in italics and indicates the prizewinner's "Nobel worthiness"; this statement may take its cue from the Nobel Foundation's official award citation but deliberately does not duplicate that citation—rather, it speaks from the late twentieth century perspective.

The text of each article is broken into sections as follows. *The Award* covers three areas: the "Presentation," a synopsis of the main points made by the presenter of the award, often the Swedish Academy's Permanent Secretary; the "Nobel Lecture," an overview of the laureate's Nobel lecture, acceptance speech, or other response to having won the prize; and "Critical Reception," a survey of responses to the Academy's choice garnered from the international press, scholars, and other communities. A *Biography* briefly sketches the salient events of the laureate's life, while *Literary Career*, constituting roughly one-third to one-half the length of the entire article, traces the development of the laureate's literary production, with reference to key works. Finally, the *Bibliography* divides itself in two: the "Primary Bibliography" lists the laureate's principal works through 1987, by genre; the "Secondary Bibliography" is annotated to provide readers with criteria for choosing sources for further study.

A combined author/title index serves also to help the user of the set interested in locating all laureates from a particular country and all laureates who worked in a particular genre. For those wishing to refer to a complete alphabetical list of the laureates, one is located in the front matter of each volume. Finally, all articles, written by experts in their respective fields, are signed by their contributors; a complete listing of contributors and their academic affiliations appears in the front matter to volume 1.

ACKNOWLEDGMENTS

The following individuals and organizations were instrumental in the preparation of *The Nobel Prize Winners: Literature*; without their dedication and high standards the compilation of this reference work would not have been possible: The Nobel Foundation, especially its Information Secretary, Mrs. Birgitta Lemmel, for providing historical and current information and photographs; Mr. William Riggan, Associate Editor of *World Literature Today*, for his expertise and editorial guidance; our contributors, for their devotion to their disciplines and to the dispersal of high-quality information to the public; and the research, editorial, and production staffs of Salem Press.

Photographs of the laureates are reprinted with permission from the following sources: The Nobel Foundation, for photographs appearing on pages xxi (Alfred Nobel), 32 (Sully Prudhomme), 42 (Theodor Mommsen), 54 (Bjørnstjerne Bjørnson), 66 (José Echegaray y Eizaguirre), 76 (Frédéric Mistral), 86 (Henryk Sienkiewicz), 98 (Giosuè Carducci), 120 (Rudolf Christoph Eucken), 132 (Selma Lagerlöf), 144 (Paul Heyse), 158 (Maurice Maeterlinck), 170 (Gerhart Hauptmann), 182 (Rabindranath Tagore), 194 (Romain Rolland), 206 (Verner von Heidenstam), 218 (Karl Adolph Gjellerup), 228 (Henrik Pontoppidan), 240 (Carl Spitteler), 266 (Anatole France), 278 (Jacinto Benavente y Martínez), 290 (William Butler Yeats), 302 (Władysław Reymont), 314 (George Bernard Shaw), 326 (Grazia Deledda), 336 (Henri Bergson), 348 (Sigrid Undset), 358 (Thomas Mann), 382 (Erik Axel Karlfeldt), 394 (John Galsworthy), 404 (Ivan Bunin), 418 (Luigi Pirandello), 434 (Eugene O'Neill), 446 (Roger Martin du Gard), 458 (Pearl S. Buck), 468 (Frans Eemil Sillanpää), 478 (Johannes V. Jensen), 488 (Gabriela Mistral), 498 (Hermann Hesse), 510 (André Gide), 522 (T. S. Eliot), 534 (William Faulkner), 546 (Bertrand Russell), 558 (Pär Lagerkvist), 570 (François Mauriac), 582 (Sir Winston Churchill), 594 (Ernest Hemingway), 608 (Halldór Laxness), 620 (Juan Ramón Jiménez), 632 (Albert Camus), 644 (Boris Pasternak), 656 (Salvatore Quasimodo), 666 (Saint-John Perse), 678 (Ivo Andrić), 690 (John Steinbeck), 702 (George Seferis), 726 (Mikhail Sholokhov), 738 (Shmuel Yosef Agnon), 750 (Nelly Sachs), 762 (Miguel Ángel Asturias), 776 (Yasunari Kawabata), 788 (Samuel Beckett), 800 (Aleksandr Solzhenitsyn), 816 (Pablo Neruda), 828 (Heinrich Böll), 840 (Patrick White), 850 (Eyvind Johnson), 862 (Harry Martinson), 874 (Eugenio Montale), 884 (Saul Bellow), 898 (Vicente Aleixandre), 908 (Isaac Bashevis Singer), 922 (Odysseus Elýtis), 932 (Czesław Miłosz), 942 (Elias Canetti), 954 (Gabriel García Márquez), 966 (William Golding), 978 (Jaroslav Seifert), 990 (Claude Simon), 1002 (Wole Soyinka), 1018 (Joseph Brodsky); the United States Library of Congress, for photographs appearing on pages 108 (Rudyard Kipling), 254 (Knut Hamsun), and 370 (Sinclair Lewis); and The Bettman Archive, for the photograph of Jean-Paul Sartre appearing on page 712.

CONTRIBUTORS

Patrick Adcock
Henderson State Unversity

Stanley Archer
Texas A&M University

Bryan Aubrey
Maharishi International University

Peter Baker
Southern Connecticut State University

Thomas Banks
Ohio Northern University

Thomas F. Barry
University of Southern California

Mary G. Berg
Center for Literary Studies
Harvard University

Clifford Albrecht Bernd
University of California, Davis

Marilyn Johns Blackwell
Ohio State University

Gerhard Brand
California State University, Los Angeles

Susan Brantly
University of Wisconsin-Madison

J. R. Broadus
University of North Carolina at Chapel Hill

Carl Brucker
Arkansas Tech University

Rosemary M. Canfield-Reisman
Troy State University

William Condon
University of Michigan, Ann Arbor

Deborah Core
Eastern Kentucky University

Liselotte M. Davis
Yale University

Frank Day
Clemson University

John Deredita
Independent Scholar

Giuseppe Di Scipio
Hunter College
City University of New York

Bruce L. Edwards
Bowling Green State University

Thomas L. Erskine
Salisbury State College

Clara Estow
University of Massachusetts at Boston

Thomas H. Falk
Michigan State University

Edward Fiorelli
Saint John's University, New York

Howard L. Ford
North Texas State University

Robert J. Forman
Saint John's University, New York

Robert J. Frail
Centenary College

Lawrence S. Friedman
Indiana University and Purdue University
at Fort Wayne

Ronald H. Fritze
Lamar University

Dana Gerhardt
Independent Scholar

NOBEL PRIZE

Steven L. Hale
Berry College

Fred R. van Hartesveldt
Fort Valley State College

Terry Heller
Coe College

Loretta Turner Johnson
Mankato State University

Steven G. Kellman
University of Texas at San Antonio

Jerzy Kolodziej
University of Tennessee, Knoxville

Paula Kopacz
Eastern Kentucky University

Leon Lewis
Appalachian State University

C. S. McConnell
University of Calgary

Martha Manheim
Siena Heights College

Thomas Matchie
North Dakota State University

Jonathan Mayhew
Purdue University, West Lafayette

Vasa D. Mihailovich
University of North Carolina at Chapel Hill

D. Gosselin Nakeeb
Pace University

Greg Nehler
Indiana University, Bloomington

George O'Brien
Georgetown University

Michael C. O'Neill
Wilkes College

Robert M. Otten
Assumption College

Robert J. Paradowski
Rochester Institute of Technology

René Prieto
Southern Methodist University

Charles Pullen
Queen's University, Ontario, Canada

William Riggen
World Literature Today
University of Oklahoma

Carl E. Rollyson, Jr.
Bernard M. Baruch College
City University of New York

Joseph Rosenblum
University of North Carolina at Greensboro

Robert L. Ross
Independent Scholar

Sven H. Rossel
University of Washington

Murray Sachs
Brandeis University

Per Schelde
York College
City University of New York

June H. Schlessinger
North Texas State University

George C. Schoolfield
Yale University

R. Baird Shuman
University of Illinois at Urbana-Champaign

Marjorie Smelstor
Ball State University

D. P. Smith
United States Naval Academy

James E. Smythe
Pepperdine University

Tuula Stark
University of California, Los Angeles

S. J. Stearns
College of Staten Island
City University of New York

NOBEL PRIZE

Paul Stewart
Southern Connecticut State University

Jean Thorleifsson Strandness
North Dakota State University

Paul Stuewe
Independent Scholar

James Sullivan
California State University, Los Angeles

Charlene E. Suscavage
University of Southern Maine

Roy Arthur Swanson
University of Wisconsin-Milwaukee

Thomas J. Taylor
Purdue University, West Lafayette

Anne R. Vizzier
University of Arkansas, Fayetteville

Ingrid Walsoe-Engel
Yale University

Harry Zohn
Brandeis University

CONTENTS

ALPHABETICAL LIST OF NOBEL PRIZE WINNERS

NOBEL PRIZE

NOBEL PRIZE

THE NOBEL PRIZE WINNERS

Literature

ALFRED NOBEL

THE NOBEL PRIZE IN LITERATURE
History and Overview

Three comments that appeared in *The New York Times* within eighteen months of one another in 1982-1983 illustrate a number of widely held conceptions and misconceptions concerning the Nobel Prize in Literature. Harriet Zuckerman of Columbia University, though subsequently turning her attention to the prizes in science, wrote on January 2, 1983: "The unique prestige of the Nobel is symbolized by its use as a kind of gold standard against which all other awards . . . are measured. . . . Not least among the unintended social consequences of the Prize is the sort of prestige assigned to laureates. They become socially defined as seers and sages." Critic John Leonard, reviewing Günter Grass's novel *Headbirths* for the March 14, 1982, edition of *The New York Times Book Review*, noted, "When the gnomes of Stockholm get around to giving [Grass] his Nobel Prize, they should give one as well to his admirable translator, Ralph Manheim." And Roger Straus, publisher (as president of Farrar, Straus and Giroux) of 1983 laureate William Golding, responded on October 7, 1983, to the unprecedented public criticism of Golding by a selection committee member: "[The Academicians] have their own screening committees and one never knows how names get on there. . . . There is no way you can nominate writers."

First, the Nobel Prizes have become not only synonymous with excellence, a "gold standard" against which all other awards in any field of endeavor are measured, but also emblematic of outstanding accomplishment per se—"the ultimate prize," in the words of Richard Kostelanetz in *The New York Times Book Review* (September 27, 1981): "Of all the world's literary prizes (whose numbers seem to increase each year), none is quite so famous, remunerative or incomparably prestigious as the Nobel Prize in Literature. Awarded annually since 1901, it is the granddaddy of such prizes." Architects, musicians, entrepreneurs, even athletes—all have been lauded at one time or another in print and over the airwaves as deserving of the Nobel Prize in their respective profession or subspecialty, meaning simply that they are among the very best in the world at what they do. Oddly enough, however, the Olympian aura of the prizes does not extend to the committees and individuals charged with the responsibility of making the annual selections, at least in literature and peace. Cynicism and invective are common threads in each year's critical reaction to the prize announcements in these areas and in the occasional retrospectives or analyses that take a longer view of the literature award's history, as in Leonard's reference to the "gnomes of Stockholm" and in George Steiner's front-page essay in the September 30, 1984, issue of *The New York Times Book Review*: "The Scandal of the Nobel Prize," with its references to the "patrician parochialism of the self-perpetuating selectors," to "obscurity and caprice," to "petulance" and "willed ostracism." All too often, though, such attacks lose much of what merit they may possess through incomplete information, misunderstanding, or unfortunate ignorance. Mr. Straus, for example, whose firm publishes a goodly number of the authors honored by the Nobel in recent years (including Isaac Bashevis Singer, Czesław Miłosz, Elias Canetti, and Joseph Brodsky), was dead wrong in his remarks regarding the supposedly secret nomination procedure; and virtually every commentary on the prize's history indulges to a degree in some variant of the "Where's Tolstoy?" litany, citing major twentieth century writers not honored by a prize and derisively lining them up against such recipients as Rudolf Eucken and Pearl S. Buck—but without bothering to consider such details as posthumous fame, changing tastes, evolving interpretations of the Prize charter, and the nature of that charter itself. What follows in this introduction and in the individual essays of this book will perhaps serve in at least some small measure to remedy this situation and to clarify the choices and omissions that mark the more than eighty awardings of the Nobel Prize in Literature.

The Nobel Will
    The 1893 will drawn up for the Swedish dynamite inventor, munitions magnate, entrepreneur, scientist, philanthropist, linguist, and amateur writer and social activist Alfred Bernhard Nobel (1833-1896) made only a general reference about rewarding "the most important and original discoveries or the most striking advances in the wide sphere of knowledge or on the path of human progress." The final will of November 27, 1895, however, stipulated that one of five annual awards for "those who, during the preceding year, shall have conferred the greatest benefit on mankind" was to be given to "the person who shall have produced in the field of literature the most outstanding work of an ideal tendency" and that this prize be distributed by "the Academy in Stockholm." Nobel's wish to promote the cause of letters, wrote Academy member Anders Österling in his 1950 book *Nobel: The Man and His Prizes*,

> was inspired, first and last, by his own interest in literature, which had been developed in his earliest youth and was later stimulated by his continued language studies. He not only read but mastered five languages, including Russian; his poems in English, written in his late teens and still preserved, show an astonishing mastery of poetic diction and an unmistakably poetic instinct. Throughout his life, Alfred Nobel gave serious attention to literature and, as far as his absorbing and hectic existence permitted it, kept in touch with the literary developments of his time.

In the awarding of all the prizes, moreover, the will stipulated that "no consideration whatever shall be given to the nationality of the candidates, . . . the most worthy shall receive the prize, whether he be a Scandinavian or not." All in all, an odd combination of specificity and vagueness, of grandiose vision and eccentric impracticality, which created several thorny problems of both the immediate and the enduring kind: the definition or delimitation of *literature*, the restriction of *work* to a single opus or its expansion to encompass the entire oeuvre of a lifetime, the literalness with which the "preceding year" stipulation should be taken, the meaning of *ideal* and of the phrase "benefit to mankind." In addition, the "Academy in Stockholm," like other institutions designated in Nobel's will, had not been consulted beforehand for either advice or assent and thus required lengthy consultations with Nobel's executors, heirs, and intimates as well as among its members in order to begin sorting out such questions before deciding whether to accept their testamentary charge.

The Swedish Academy

The Svenska Akademien itself was founded in 1786, under the reign of King Gustaf III. Although based on the model of the Académie Française, the Swedish Academy is composed of only eighteen members instead of the former's forty—reputedly because Gustaf preferred the resonant sound of "En av de Aderton" (One of the Eighteen) to that of all other possible numbers, particularly the pinched nasal tones "En av de Fyrtio" (One of the Forty). The Academy's principal duties were originally the promotion and preservation of Swedish language, literature, history, and culture; since 1893 it has also published and periodically updated the *Svenska Akademien ordbok* (dictionary of the Swedish Academy). The organization awards numerous grants and scholarships to individuals, to journals, and to groups, with the total annual amount allocated for such awards, philological work, magazine publication, and research roughly corresponding to that of three Nobel Prizes.

According to Lars Gyllensten, Chair of the Nobel Committee for Literature of the Swedish Academy, members of the Academy, who are elected by the group itself for life and occupy specific numbered "chairs" within the organization, are drawn "from Swedish cultural life and the humanities"; approximately half are themselves writers, the others being elected on the basis of their "literary leanings and expert knowledge of the Academy's various spheres of responsibility." The organization "is not subordinate to any state or other authority. The governing body consists of a Director (chairman) and a Chancellor (vice chairman), who are elected for six months at a time, and of a Secretary, who usually remains until the age of 70—all of them members of the Academy. The Academy meets weekly and conducts its business in its own premises on the upper floor of the Stock Exchange (from the 18th century) in the old part of Stockholm."

Within a month of Nobel's death on December 10, 1896, the Swedish

Academy was informed of the task entrusted to it by the magnate's will. There was evidently considerable hesitation and even reluctance among the members to assume this new responsibility, which some believed would so increase the Academy's work load as to force that body to neglect its traditional duties. That a majority of the Academicians did in fact ultimately vote in favor of acceptance was doubtless the result of the persuasive force of the group's Permanent Secretary at that time, Carl David af Wirsén, who argued:

> If the Swedish Academy refuses to assume this responsibility, the whole donation will be forfeited as far as literary awards are concerned, and by that very act the leading men of letters throughout Europe will be deprived of the opportunity to enjoy the financial rewards and the exceptional recognition for their long and brilliant literary careers which Nobel had in mind. A storm will blow up, a storm of indignation. The Academy's responsibility is great; if it definitely rejects the task, it will suffer sharp reproaches; in these reproaches may join future generations of our eighteen members who are to succeed us and who may find it strange that for reasons of personal convenience the members of today deliberately declined an influential role in the world of letters. The task is said to be foreign to the true purposes of the Academy. The work will, no doubt, be both new and arduous, but it can hardly be called foreign since it is of a literary character. A body that is to judge the literature of its own country cannot afford to be ignorant of the very best produced abroad; the projected prizes are to be given to the best living writers anywhere, and, consequently, as a rule, to the very men whose work ought to be familiar to the Academy members anyway.

In early 1897, the Nobel Foundation was established in Stockholm to administer the huge sum made available from Alfred Nobel's estate for the five prizes (physics, chemistry, physiology and medicine, peace, and literature; the prize in economics was added in 1968 by the Bank of Sweden "in memory of Alfred Nobel") and to coordinate the judging and presentation of the awards. Though managed by a board of directors elected by the prize-granting institutions, to which it is responsible, the Foundation has no involvement at all in the deliberations and choices of those organizations; and though the Chairman and Deputy Chairman of the board are appointed by the government, the Foundation functions without government intervention or supervision except for enforcement of the fundamental legal statutes which apply to all private foundations.

Following acceptance of Nobel's charge, and with the Foundation in place, the Swedish Academy, like its counterparts in the other four fields—the Caroline Medico-Surgical Institute (physiology and medicine), the Royal Academy of Sciences (physics, chemistry), and the Norwegian Nobel Committee (peace)—began to draw up formal guidelines and regulations detailing the procedures by which it would carry out the work of assessment and selection, submitting its final proposals to the Foundation in early 1900. In December of that year, shortly before the prize machinery was set in motion, the Academy Director Esaias Tegnér delivered an address which became something of a program declaration regarding the organization's approach to its new duty. He emphasized that the task was one which the Academy did not take lightly, one which it in fact could not shirk, since the donor's millions had been given not to the Academy itself but to all mankind as represented by its foremost writers. His fervent hope was that a prize of such magnitude would in any event "have the effect of making a good piece of work known in much wider circles than would otherwise have been the case—and that it would be an excellent piece of work, if not in every instance the best available for a prize, he felt could be taken for granted." Tegnér foresaw the difficulties involved but pointed up as well the Academy's uniquely favorable position for accepting a task such as that assigned it by Alfred Nobel's will:

"The Swedish Academy," [Tegnér] proceeded, "certainly does not cherish the illusion that even once it may be able to award a prize in such a way as to escape criticism. Nay, it anticipates with certainty that such criticism will often be merited. But it consoles itself with the assurance that in the whole world there is no other institution which would not meet the same fate. . . . If there are drawbacks to being a small nation situated on the outskirts of the civilized world, there are also certain advantages. And when it is a question of a responsibility like this, a few of them become clearly evident. A person living on the border of a province is better able to decide which peaks inside it are the highest than an observer standing amidst the mountains themselves. In a different sense, this is also true of us. And in the fact that we are a small nation we have, in a way, a safeguard against partiality which the big nations lack: we shall less often be able to appear as contenders for the prize ourselves."

Selection Procedure

The final proposals submitted by the Swedish Academy and approved by the Nobel Foundation in the spring of 1900 placed primary emphasis on the matter of nomination procedures, including the question of eligibility to propose candidates for the literature prize. Österling explains the difficulties involved:

In the case of the Swedish Academy the problem was all the more complicated as there were no other institutions of the same type anywhere in the world, except the French and Spanish academies. It would obviously have been unfair to limit the nominating rights to these two bodies, and it would have been equally inappropriate to grant such rights to any institution as a body, since the Academy's freedom of action might thereby be hampered by overwhelming external pressure. It was therefore proposed that the right to nominate candidates should be granted to the individual members of such institutions and not to the institutions themselves. The Academy felt, it was further stated, that by distributing the nomination rights so widely, it had tried to make sure that proposals could be made by duly qualified persons in all parts of the world and that no domestic or foreign literary organization of any importance should have cause to complain that the rights and privileges of its members had been slighted. The proposed text for the special statute was formulated as follows: "The right to nominate candidates for the Prize in Literature is granted to members of the Swedish Academy; and of the French and Spanish Academies which are similar to it in character and objectives; to members of the humanistic sections of other academies, as well as to members of the humanistic institutions and societies as enjoy the same rank as academies, and to university professors of aesthetics, literature, and history."

The statute was altered in 1949 to broaden the range of groups regarded as competent to make nominations. The field, according to Gyllensten, now includes "members of the Swedish Academy and of other academies, institutions, and societies similar to it in membership and aims; professors of languages or in the history of literature at universities and university colleges; Nobel laureates in literature; and presidents of authors' organizations which are representative of the literary activities of their respective countries." Gyllensten continues:

In order for anyone to be considered for a Nobel Prize, he or she must be proposed as a candidate for the prize by someone qualified to make such a proposal. . . . Nominations must be sent in writing to the Swedish Academy or its Nobel Committee before the end of January of the year in which the award is made. The reason for a nomination should be stated, but detailed analysis is not necessary. A person who has once been proposed for a Nobel Prize is not automatically regarded as a candidate in following years but can be proposed again. Also, the Nobel Committee or the Academy can, if it sees fit, reconsider a previously proposed name, if this is not among the nominations from outside. Applications to receive a prize are disregarded.

In order to stimulate nomination, the Nobel Committee during the autumn sends out reminders or invitations to nearly 600 persons within the groups having the right to nominate candidates. The Committee endeavours to distribute such invitations all over the literary world and to vary the recipients each year. This procedure does not mean that others who are entitled to submit proposals do not have the right to do so—this right holds good even if no special invitation has been received.

Such letters of invitation are courteous but brief and to the point, as in the following example, directed to the Dean of the College of Arts and Sciences at the University of Oklahoma and dated November 13, 1984: "Every year we address ourselves to a random selection of universities all over the world to remind them of the right for all professors of literature and modern languages to propose candidates for the Nobel Prize in Literature. This right is however permanent and is not dependent on the receipt of such an invitation. Enclosed you will find a number of invitations, which we ask you to distribute to those members of your staff whose particular field of interest is modern literature (i.e. works by authors now living). Sincerely yours, Lars Gyllensten, Chair of the Nobel Committee of the Swedish Academy." The text of the actual invitation enclosed with the letter reads: "On behalf of the Swedish Academy, the undersigned, members of the Nobel Committee, have the honour of inviting you to nominate a candidate for the Nobel Prize in Literature for the year 1985. A brief statement of the reasons for the nomination is desirable though not essential. In order to receive consideration during the coming year the nomination must reach the Nobel Committee not later than February 1st, 1985. Out of consideration for the nominees it is requested that their names should not be made public. All communications should be addressed to: The Nobel Committee of the Swedish Academy, Börshuset, 111 29 Stockholm."

The Academy receives between three and four hundred nominations each year prior to the February 1 deadline, according to Gyllensten:

> Many of the proposers nominate the same candidates, so that the number of suggested prizewinners is much smaller than the number of proposers—of recent years, the number of nominees has usually amounted to 100-150. Of these, only a few are new names which have not been proposed before—about a dozen. It does not occur that a candidate of any literary importance is proposed who is unknown to the Academy or the Nobel Committee. The names of the more important ones are sent in year after year. It is very unusual for anyone who has been proposed for the first time to receive the prize. As regards appraisal of the most qualified candidates, there is a clear consensus of opinion between many of the proposers from different parts of the world.

Organization

In setting up a mechanism whereby it might handle the nominations most efficiently, the Swedish Academy established, prior to the very first prize, the above-mentioned Nobel Committee, which consists of five regular members and may also include one or more co-opted members appointed by the Academy. Committee members are elected for three-year terms, receiving a yearly honorarium of approximately $1,200 (otherwise the Academicians receive no salary or stipend for their Academy work) and may be reelected without restriction; Österling, in fact, served on the panel continuously from 1921 until his death in 1981 at the age of ninety-seven. The Nobel Committee, writes Gyllensten (himself a member since the mid-1970's), is responsible for the adjudication work necessary in dealing with the questions concerning the Nobel Prize in Literature. . . . This work goes on all the time, the whole year round. It is the Committee which gathers in the nominations from outside, supplementing the list if necessary, and which sees to it that the merits of the nominees are scrutinized sufficiently to give the [Academy] a solid basis for its opinion. . . . The Committee is aided in its work by a secretary (the head librarian of the Nobel Library) and a literary scholar engaged as professor at the Academy. . . . The Nobel Committee's adjudication work is of course decisive for the Academy's choice, but this work is done in continual contact with the Academy as a whole and during discussions which can be carried on all the year round in connection with the Academy's regular meetings each week.

Assisting the Academy and the Nobel Committee in their work is the Academy's Nobel Institute, which includes the Nobel Library, housed in the Academy's premises in the Royal Stock Exchange. The Library maintains a large collection of Swedish fiction, poetry, drama, essays, and criticism for use in the Academy's regular activities, and also procures some 1,500-2,000 books annually in modern literature from throughout the world, in accordance with each year's list of Nobel Prize candidates. The total collection numbers approximately 150,000 volumes, making the Nobel Institute "the largest library in the Nordic countries as regards modern literature," notes Gyllensten. Moreover, "It is available to the public and is part of an interurban library service together with other public libraries. It is financed, however, entirely by private means from the Nobel Foundation and the Academy, without state or municipal grants. In addition to the head librarian and his assistants, the previously mentioned literary scholar works at the Academy's Nobel Institute."

All candidates proposed prior to February 1 by eligible individuals or organizations are placed on the year's list of nominations by the Nobel Committee, which may not exclude anyone so proposed. "This list," explains Gyllensten, "is put before the Academy as a whole during the first days of February. The Academy can then add new names, if necessary supplementing with those which for some reason, perhaps mere chance, have not been included. Nowadays the Academy, as well as the Nobel Committee, is more active in making such nominations than it was in the early days of the prize, when the members thought they should be very restrictive with their own proposals." All nominees on the supplemented list are appraised by the Academy, but "for one reason or another, many are unthinkable as Nobel laureates—perhaps because their production must be regarded as scholarship without the stipulated literary qualities, perhaps because their work, even if it does belong to literature, is far from having the necessary weight or quality, perhaps because they have obviously been proposed on grounds other than factual or literary ones (in some cases political, provincial, ideological and other motives appear as the decisive ones for the nomination in question)." The remaining names are then turned over to the Committee for thorough scrutiny. Gyllensten outlines the procedure at this stage of evaluation as follows:

> [The candidates'] works are procured in the original or in translation, if they are not already in the library. In cases where there is a paucity of translations and where candidates write in a language unfamiliar to the Academy's members or the experts, sample translations can be commissioned. With the aid of reference books, magazines, critical or scholarly reviews of literature etc. the Nobel Committee and its assistants familiarize themselves further with the nominees and their position in the literary world. Experts within or outside the Academy, at home and abroad, are commissioned to submit reports. Sometimes such assignments are given to individual writers, sometimes they are extended to include specific language areas or countries and certain literary schools or genres etc. Several investigations are made concerning most of the candidates of any importance and extensive information is collected about them. At the same time, the members of the Committee themselves read as much as they can of the candidates' works in the original or in translation and recommend books for the other members of the Academy to read.

Criteria

Several factors pertaining to Alfred Nobel's will must be considered by the Committee and subsequently by the Academy as a whole in weighing each year's candidates: the nature of "literature," the "work" to be recognized, the "recentness" of that work, its "benefit to mankind," and the extent to which it reflects an "ideal tendency." Österling points out that in 1900 the original Committee decided that "under the term 'literature' shall be comprised, not only belles lettres, but also other writings which, by virtue of their form and method of presentation, possess literary value"; hence the subsequent selection of such laureates as Henri Bergson (1927), Bertrand Russell (1950), and Winston Churchill (1953), although the Academy has adhered to a more purely belletristic line since Churchill's award. The will's stipulation that the prizewinners must have rendered their noteworthy service "during the preceding year," Österling writes, "is interpreted to mean that 'the awards shall be made for the most recent achievements in the fields of culture referred to in the will, and for older works only if their significance has not become apparent until recently.' The purpose of the new phrasing was, obviously, to clarify in a legally proper way the testamentary requirement which, in most instances, it would have been impossible to interpret in any other way." Gyllensten reasons:

> Literary works in particular often do not acquire their full importance until they are seen as a life's work or parts of a whole, as distinct from more ephemeral lucky shots in the literary market. This is also the background to the fact that many laureates receive their prize when they are well up in years and the great-

ness and creative context of their work is clearly apparent or when their significance to the age in which they live begins to be discerned. The insistence on
topicality and on the benefit to mankind implies, however, the condition that
what is to be rewarded shall still be a vigorous and fruitful literary creativeness
on which the prize and its prestige can be expected to have a stimulating effect.
This point of view has explicit support in what is known of Alfred Nobel's
intentions with his donation.

The statutory regulation that the prizes be given for *a work* or *a writing*
posed no dilemma for the prize-granting institutions in the sciences and
medicine, "but for the Swedish Academy it has been much more difficult to
observe," Österling says. "Usually the literary awards have been given for an
author's entire production, without specifying any particular work. At times
it has been done, however, 'with special reference' to a particular book, as in
the case of . . . [Knut] Hamsun's *Growth of the Soil*, . . . [Thomas] Mann's
Buddenbrooks, [John] Galsworthy's *Forsyte Saga*, and [Roger] Martin du
Gard's *Les Thibault*." The condition that the prizes benefit "mankind" has
been taken at least since World War II as an enjoinder to look beyond the
somewhat limited geographic and cultural views of Nobel's day, to adopt a
more "universalist" outlook, to take into account what is being offered by
civilizations other than those of Scandinavia or Europe or North America,
and to honor their outstanding achievements too. Lastly, the will's directive
that the prize in literature honor the person who has produced the most outstanding work "of an ideal tendency" has caused much perplexity over the
years. Gyllensten explains:

> Just what Alfred Nobel intended is not clear. With the knowledge we have of
> his person and life, and of what he has expressed about his general outlook and
> aims, the words "of an ideal tendency" have been taken to mean a striving for
> the good of mankind, for humaneness, common sense, progress and happiness.
> The fundamental idea has been interpreted as applying to literary achievements
> with constructive aims. All the same, there have sometimes been violent dif-
> ferences of opinion as to what was intended by "ideal tendency" in the strict
> sense. When considering the candidates nowadays, this expression is not taken
> literally. It is realized that on the whole the serious literature that is worthy of a
> prize furthers knowledge of man and his condition and endeavors to enrich and
> improve his life.

Selections
    Once its studies and preliminary discussions are completed—usually by
early summer—the Nobel Committee submits to the full Academy a ranked
listing of the candidates it deems most deserving of full consideration in the
current year, together with information on the nominees' principal works,
suitable secondary-source materials, and available reports by Committee

members and/or outside specialists. This short list usually contains five names but may run longer. The Academy is in no way bound by the Committee's recommendations and may alter or add to the list as it wishes. Upon receiving the short list, the Academy begins its deliberations, which occupy the major portion of time at the group's weekly meetings until a decision is reached—usually by mid-October in recent practice. All nominations, investigations, deliberations, and pollings are confidential, and only the final choice is made public, at a time fixed by the awarding institution; this has come to be at noon on the second Thursday of October. "In order for the voting within the Academy to be valid," Gyllensten notes, "it is required that at least twelve members shall take part and that a candidate shall receive more than half of the votes. The choice is made by secret ballot in writing. As a rule, all members of the Academy take part in the voting; if one or two cannot be present, they send in their ballot papers. Usually the result is apparent after lengthy discussions and scrutiny, so that a large majority, or all, can agree on the prizewinner. No reservations concerning the majority's decision may be expressed, still less made public." Academy guidelines in fact stipulate that any member who breaks this confidentiality may be expelled, yet the vehement public protests by Academician Artur Lundkvist in 1983 over the selection of William Golding passed with no visible punitive action, only a mild rebuke by the Permanent Secretary.

The awards, moreover, cannot be appealed against. In addition, Gyllensten notes, the following regulations apply:

> All prizes may be shared jointly by more than one person (a maximum of three). . . . The literary prize, however, is shared very seldom, as literary achievements rarely show the kind of affinity which often justifies a division of the scientific prizes. . . . A prize can be withheld and awarded the following year. Prizes may only be given to persons, except the peace prize which may also be given to an institution or a society. A deceased person cannot be put on the list of candidates for a prize, but if someone dies after having been chosen a prizewinner and before the prize has been presented, the prize can nevertheless be given. This is the exception, however. Any criteria other than actual merit may not be observed when the decisions are made—in other words, no regard shall be paid to race, sex, nationality etc.

Presentation

Once the final vote has been taken, the Academy notifies the new laureate (usually by telegram or phone), announces the decision publicly, and issues a brief citation which is later printed on the Nobel diploma presented to the prizewinner by the King of Sweden at the official award ceremonies on December 10, the anniversary of Alfred Nobel's death. Responsibility is then passed to the Nobel Foundation for issuing invitations to the recipient and his or her family and for arranging the round of festivities held in conjunction with the presentation ceremonies. The Academy does host a luncheon in honor of the laureate, however, and also sponsors the Nobel lecture that most recipients consent to give, generally on December 8 or at another time shortly before or after the award presentation. Gyllensten notes, however, that "it is a rule for [the Nobel lecture] to be given by the prizewinners in the other spheres, but not always in the case of the literature prize. If the lecture is not held, the prizewinner writes an essay or an article which the Nobel Foundation issues in its publication *Les Prix Nobel.*"

The award ceremonies themselves are a gala event on a grand scale, and the only major state occasion left in Sweden. A festive round of receptions, parties, and banquets culminates in the full-dress presentation ritual held at the Stockholm Concert Hall for winners in five of the six categories (the Peace Prize ceremony is held simultaneously in Oslo). The proceedings begin promptly at 4:30 in the afternoon, when wintry darkness has already fallen. Royalty and an exclusive guest list of approximately 1,700 attend in white tie and formal evening wear and outfitted with all manner of orders and regalia, even exotic ambassadorial garb and native costumes. Royal trumpeters, orchestral tributes, festive speeches and pronouncements, eloquent toasts, exquisite cuisine, and elegant ballroom dancing add to the celebratory air, as do the legions of uniformed honor students who serve as guides and aid in security, as the proceedings spill over into the vast gray stone Municipal Hall (modeled on Venice's Ducal Palace) and continue long into the next morning. In recent years, television has carried the ceremonies either live or in delayed broadcast to a worldwide audience as well, fully in keeping with the international spirit of the benefactor's original conception.

The Award

The prize money itself is almost as grandiose as the surrounding pomp of the ceremonies, with each 1987 individual award worth approximately $340,000—the most lucrative accolade in any of the fields represented. (In literature, the closest competitors, such as Italy's Feltrinelli Prize and the Spanish-speaking world's Cervantes Prize, have values of "only" $80,000 or $90,000 each, depending on prevailing exchange rates.) The gold medal (bearing Alfred Nobel's likeness) and the award certificate are included as well. Peter Dragadze outlines the financing of the prizes as follows:

> In his will, Nobel provided that his fortune be invested in a fund composed of stable securities. This meant that Nobel's interests in the Nobel companies throughout the world were capitalized. Around 32 million crowns (300 million crowns in today's currency, about $68 million) were placed in the fund. The Nobel capital was invested in so-called gilt-edged bonds. An active administration of the Nobel capital has been carried on since 1953, when changes were made in the regulations governing the Foundation. Since then the value of the capital has been preserved and even increased, in spite of continuing inflation. The

capital today [1980] is over 200 million crowns, of which the book value consists of 46.6 percent fixed interest investments, 41.4 percent shares, and 12 percent property holdings. [Nobel Foundation Executive Director Stig] Ramel represents the board that outlines financial policy.

About 5 percent of the Foundation's shares are in the American market, in good, middle-size companies that have done very well during [times] when the blue chips have been very much out of favor. . . . The first prizes distributed in 1901 amounted to about 150,000 crowns each. In 1968 the prizes reached the 350,000-crown mark, and in 1978 each award came to 725,000 crowns [approximately $180,000]. Of the yield on the main fund, 10 percent accrues to the principal, while 22.5 percent goes to the prize committees to pay the enormous expenses, which include hundreds of employees evaluating all suggestions coming in as nominations. The remaining 67.5 percent is reserved for the Nobel Prizes themselves.

History of Selections

Through 1987 a total of eighty-four laureates in literature have been named since the first Nobel Prize was awarded in 1901. In seven different years (1914, 1918, 1935, 1940-1943) no award was made, and on four occasions (1904, 1917, 1966, 1974) the prize has been divided between two recipients. France leads among individual nations with a total of thirteen winners, including the very first selection, the poet Sully Prudhomme. The United States follows with ten, including three naturalized citizens (Singer, Miłosz, Brodsky) and not counting one expatriate (T. S. Eliot). Great Britain boasts eight honorees, also including three nonnative citizens (George Bernard Shaw, Eliot, Elias Canetti), and is trailed in order by Sweden (seven), Germany (six, though only two since 1912 and excluding the expatriate Hermann Hesse), Italy (five), Spain (four), and the Soviet Union (three, not counting émigrés Ivan Bunin and Brodsky), Norway and Denmark (three each), five countries with two apiece—Poland (not counting the expatriates Singer, Miłosz, and Shmuel Yosef Agnon), Switzerland, Ireland, Chile, and Greece—and twelve countries claiming a single winner each: Belgium, India, Finland, Iceland, Yugoslavia, Israel (the immigrant Agnon), Guatemala, Japan, Australia, Colombia, Czechoslovakia, and Nigeria. Only four recipients (Rabindranath Tagore, Yasunari Kawabata, Patrick White, and Wole Soyinka) are not native to Europe or the Americas; only six (Selma Lagerlöf, Grazia Deledda, Sigrid Undset, Pearl Buck, Gabriela Mistral, and Nelly Sachs) are women. The laureates' age at the time of selection has ranged from forty-two (Rudyard Kipling) to eighty-four (Jaroslav Seifert), with an average of about sixty. Only one award has been presented posthumously (to Erik Axel Karlfeldt, in 1931), although several laureates have been unable to receive the award in person because of problems of a political (Boris Pasternak, Aleksandr Solzhenitsyn) or medical (Vicente Aleixandre, Jaroslav Seifert) nature. The prize was refused outright by Jean-Paul Sartre in 1964 and declined rather more reluctantly by Pasternak in 1958. Forty-three of the recipients have been primarily or exclusively writers of prose fiction, twenty-one principally poets, and seven dramatists, while six others have excelled in two or more of these genres (such as Pasternak and Samuel Beckett); five have been writers of a nonbelletristic nature—historians, philosophers, critics. Some have produced enormous bodies of writing that stretch to several dozen volumes; others' collected works scarcely fill more than a single large tome or two. Some are still among today's most widely read and most influential authors, whereas others are no longer even recognized by name, much less read or studied.

In short, no clearly definable pattern of any kind emerges from the list of the Nobel laureates in literature. A disproportionate bias toward European and American writing is readily discernible over the first eighty-seven years of the prize's history but shows every indication of breaking down as time has passed, with three awards since 1968 (Kawabata, White, Soyinka) to writers of non-European-American origin. No country has ever been honored twice in succession, but several have produced winners at only a two-year interval (Germany, Great Britain, the United States), largely discounting any theories about "rotation" or "distribution" of the award. Although fiction writers have garnered more than twice as many prizes as have poets, the latter are represented in a proportion far greater than their share of the worldwide reading audience, revealing that, if anything, the Academy's bias through the years has been in the poets' favor. The number of women recipients is decidedly low and, one could well argue, extremely unrepresentative of the range and quality of women authors in the twentieth century; the fact that only one woman (Sachs) has been honored since 1946—and had to share the prize at that—is, unfortunately, the most telling single statistic one can derive from the table of winners. Sporadic indications of "balancing" attempts of an ideological (Camus/Sartre) or political (Sholokhov/Solzhenitsyn) kind, of infatuation with a particular region (Germany with four awards between 1902 and 1912, the United States with three between 1949 and 1962, France with four between 1952 and 1964), or of favoritism toward a specific genre (fiction between 1964 and 1974, poetry between 1956 and 1963) can be noted but seem the exception far more than the rule in every case, more chance occurrence or coincidence than evidence of intent or design, more short-term trend than monolithic or persistent single-mindedness of purpose.

The last point above should be apparent as well upon reflection about the nature of the literary prize-granting body itself: a continually changing group of eighteen individuals, usually of quite independent minds and tastes and often of strong temperament despite the stereotype of Nordic taciturnity, whose group dynamics evolve constantly as members come and go and as positions on the all-important Nobel Committee and in the Secretariat change every few years. Some commentators, including current Academy member Kjell Espmark in his 1986 book *Le Prix Nobel*, even choose to discuss the history of the prize selections in terms of discrete periods demarcated at least in part by the terms of office of the Nobel Committee chairman or the Permanent Secretary: a "Wirsén Epoch," the "Hjärne Years," or the "Österling Era," to name but three with distinctly different orientations. (More on this is discussed below in an overview of the actual selections.)

What is most evident from the list of recipients, however—and the one point made by virtually every critic who has uttered a word of opinion on the Nobel Prize, whether pro or con—is the large number of twentieth century "classics" *missing* from the slate. The litany invariably begins with Leo Tolstoy, Franz Kafka, Marcel Proust, and James Joyce; usually continues with Thomas Hardy, Joseph Conrad, D. H. Lawrence, Rainer Maria Rilke, Émile Zola, August Strindberg, Henrik Ibsen, Osip Mandelstam, Maxim Gorky, Bertolt Brecht, Robert Musil, Ezra Pound, Virginia Woolf, Vladimir Nabokov, and W. H. Auden; and frequently includes more specialized favorites, such as Hermann Broch, Hugo von Hofmannsthal, Paul Valéry, Federico García Lorca, Paul Celan, André Malraux, Yukio Mishima, Jun'ichirō Tanizaki, Paul Claudel, André Breton, and Nazim Hikmet. The writers in the first two sets are fixed within the canon of modern Western literature, and Academy members of today readily admit that these names as well as many of those in the third group outshine authors actually chosen in years gone by.

For some of the omissions there simply is no explanation other than contemporary taste or mere chance. For many of the uncrowned, however, the reasons for exclusion are quite simple. Tolstoy, for example, was not even nominated for the very first award—remember that at that time the Academy and its Nobel Committee did not supplement outside nominations with proposals of their own—and so, by the strict rules then in force, could not be considered. When outsiders did nominate him in succeeding years (until his death in 1910), his candidacy foundered on two points: He had by that time denounced his masterful novels and stories of earlier decades and had long since turned to writing educational and religious tracts and preaching a kind of fundamental anarchism that was the very antithesis of Nobel's prescribed "idealism" and "benefit to mankind," no matter how liberally defined; he also refused to have anything to do with such niceties as literary prizes and would certainly have refused a Nobel, even had it been offered to him. The Tolstoy of the first decade of this century was simply no longer the Tolstoy of *Sebastopol*, *War and Peace*, and *Anna Karenina*; that earlier Tolstoy would have been a splendid laureate as late as 1880, but the Academy's grounds for passing him by in the 1900's were sound in terms of their charter.

Proust and Kafka present a different and more frequently encountered case, for both died before achieving anything remotely approaching the fame their work has been accorded posthumously. Much of Kafka's writing had not even been published by the time of his death in 1924 and, as is now well-known, was saved for posterity only by Max Brod's refusal to burn all the author's papers as instructed; and Proust had enormous difficulties in getting his *Remembrance of Things Past* published, ultimately financing much of it himself only a few years before his death in 1922. To have crowned either writer with the Nobel laurels would have required a prescience bordering on the supernatural.

Joyce's case was somewhat similar in that the culmination of his literary art, *Ulysses,* though originally published in 1922, was not fully explicated and understood until the decade following his death in 1940; he was unfortunately too much ahead of his time in a quite literal sense and was never even nominated for the Nobel (though his name was invoked in such later prize citations as that for Faulkner in 1949). A relatively early death probably robbed García Lorca and Lawrence of the prize as well, and Mandelstam perished in Joseph Stalin's gulag long before the bulk of his work was made known through the prodigious memory and determination of his courageous widow Nadezhda. More poignantly if less cruelly, Valéry, denied the Nobel in the 1930's because of what the Academy then considered the extreme difficulty and rarefied nature of his poetry, was by all indications the solid choice for the 1945 award but died on July 20 of that year before the autumn's voting began.

The "idealism" qualifier worked against several of the other big names mentioned above: Zola because of his "crudely cynical naturalism," Ibsen because of his "negativism," Hardy because of the "lack of religious and ethical substance" of his heroines, Strindberg because of his "immorality and vicious iconoclasm" (directed toward the Academy, among many other targets, it might have added). Gorky came within a vote or two of winning the 1928 award over Undset, losing out principally because of reservations by several Academicians about the "crudity and squalor, the naturalistic bestiality" of much of his work. Pound's flagrant anti-Semitism and virulent attacks against the Allies during World War II killed what otherwise was a strong candidacy in the 1950's that even his mental illness per se would not have affected (to judge from comments by Dag Hammarskjöld and Anders Österling, as reported by Espmark).

1901-1911

The "Wirsén Epoch," spanning the first eleven prizes, has been accorded very harsh treatment by critics over the decades. In all fairness, this could also be deemed the most difficult period by far, since the task itself of selecting laureates in literature was wholly new and uninvited, the machinery newly devised and untested, the criteria vague and ill-defined, and the pressures from colleagues at home and abroad enormous for turning the prize in this or that direction. It was perhaps inevitable that a cautious and conservative approach be adopted by the Academy in the early going, that Nobel's expressed wishes be adhered to in reasonably strict fashion, and that compromise mark many decisions on procedure and final selections of winners.

The dozen laureates of these eleven years probably deserve their retrospective designation as the blandest and least distinguished such group in the entire history of the Nobel Prize, all the more so in the light of the luminaries not chosen, as indicated above. "Sully Prudhomme, Mistral, Echegaray, Eucken, and Heyse are now generally considered unworthy of the prize," Espmark writes, "and in the case of Heyse the Committee is guilty of one of its major gaffes of all time; in saluting him as the greatest German lyric poet since Goethe and as the creator of the new modern psychology, it betrayed a total lack of understanding of the development of literature after Nietzsche." Eucken is also commonly dismissed today as a nonliterary figure who would (and should) never have been seriously considered except as a compromise choice in the bitter 1908 fight between proponents of Selma Lagerlöf (who triumphed the following year anyway) and advocates of Algernon Charles Swinburne, who had the backing of Wirsén himself and two other Committee members but not a clear majority of the entire Academy. Theodor Mommsen, too, is viewed as an interloper among the literary figures, though his history of Rome was admired for years as a standard-setter in style and scholarship. Bjørnstjerne Bjørnsen is seen as a mediocre substitute for Ibsen or Strindberg, and general enthusiasm for Giosuè Carducci and Lagerlöf is not to be found. Maurice Maeterlinck is viewed as a better choice for his role in establishing Symbolist drama in Europe, but his work does not speak to subsequent generations. The sole undisputed selection from the Wirsén years in terms of literary merit is Rudyard Kipling; his work is rooted in a historical period but has transcended it to remain vital for the ages. Both an international jury of three hundred literary experts polled in 1951 by *Books Abroad* and a 1967 symposium of fifteen scholars in that same journal (called by Espmark the finest group of essays anywhere on the prize's history) cite Kipling's selection with strong approval.

1912-1921

The period from 1912 to 1921 was marked by what Espmark labels "a prudent shift in orientation," attributable in considerable measure to the election of the poet Erik Axel Karlfeldt as Permanent Secretary and the ascendancy of the historian Harald Hjärne to the chairmanship of the Nobel Committee. The first two choices of this period indicated just how bold the shift was to be. In selecting Gerhart Hauptmann in 1912, the Academy went directly counter to its predecessors' outright rejection of "naturalism of the lowest kind," as Wirsén had characterized Hauptmann's work during the debates of 1903, and now found the German's dramas to possess "a most impressive realism . . . of astonishing power. . . full of the most refined poetry." The 1913 award to Rabindrinath Tagore was even more remarkable in its bold venture well beyond the confines of European letters, although the records now indicate that the choice was based not so much on the "Indianness" of Tagore's work (despite the fact that one juror, Esaias Tegnér, could read him in the original Bengali) as on its perceived compatibility with certain Western ideas and with at least two important features of Nobel's testamentary directive. Espmark explains:

> The work of Rabindrinath Tagore was examined on the basis of *Gitanjali*, which had just appeared; the author's participation in the translation of this book into English permitted "its assimilation into an original work." The highly sympathetic reaction which it evoked offers the opportunity to underline discreetly a certain unity of perception with the preceding period. In regard to Tagore's religious ideas, one notes "a sort of esthetic theism": "his faith is not of that pantheistic and in fact abstract variety which generally characterizes traditional Indian writers." Moreover, his mysticism accords well with Nobel's demands, since Tagore "appears to be hearing the voice of nature in his extremely passionate faith in noble ideals of secret origins." Also, the Committee wishes to express "an interest for the future career of this remarkable Indian poet."

Incredible as it may now seem, Tagore's principal competition in 1913 came from the positivist intellectual historians Émile Faguet, Hippolyte Taine, and Joseph Ernest Renan. One of the strongest voices promoting Tagore was the 1916 laureate himself, Nobel Committee member Verner von Heidenstam, who invoked the patronage of the great Johann Wolfgang von Goethe and characterized the Indian as "unrivaled among the living poets" of the day. His reputation has perhaps declined over the decades from that lofty plane, but his place among the laureates continues undisputed.

Heidenstam is viewed with considerable reservation by posterity, as are Karl Adolph Gjellerup and, to a lesser degree, cowinner Henrik Pontoppidan from 1917. Spitteler is dismissed as an unfortunate anomaly, "a tragic dinosaur exhumed from the past," and has been defended only rarely (for example, by George Steiner). Knut Hamsun has held up well among later analysts, despite the stain of his pro-Nazi remarks during World War II (which, if the Pound case is indicative, would likely have eliminated him from consideration had he not received his award before the war), and is generally viewed as the only truly international figure among the Scandinavian recipients of the prize. Romain Rolland has lapsed into relative obscurity nowadays (except in the Soviet Union, where he has long been the most revered of French writers), but in 1915 his literary distinction and passionate idealism in the cause of peace made him a perfect laureate in regard to Nobel's intent. Among the worthies who received strong backing and came close to victory during these years were Spain's Benito Pérez Galdós in 1915 and Denmark's great critic Georg Brandes in 1917-1920.

1920-1929

The 1920's, with Karlfeldt continuing as Permanent Secretary and Per Hallström replacing the deceased Hjärne in 1922 as chairman of the Nobel Committee, are judged quite favorably on the whole by later commentators. The decade proved to be one of greater experimentation and generosity in interpreting the terms of Nobel's will, and also one with something of a nineteenth century cast of mind that extolled the "grand style" of writing represented by Goethe and, in his prime, Tolstoy. Only a broader view of "idealism," for example, could have admitted Anatole France and George Bernard Shaw, and several of the honorees of the 1920's evince a "grandly" descriptive style of writing, particularly Thomas Mann (though the Academicians vastly preferred his early work to *The Magic Mountain* (1924) and in fact specifically cited only *Buddenbrooks*, published in 1901). William Butler Yeats and Mann are two of the century's towering figures by any standard, and both, happily, enjoyed many fruitful years after receiving their awards—all too seldom the case, sad to say. Shaw and France have their detractors but also are deemed eminently worthy of the prize by most. Henri Bergson's seminal role in criticism and cultural history makes him a deserving choice as well in the eyes of commentators, though the fact that he was not a creative writer in the true sense diminishes his fitness as a laureate in some minds. Critical opinion is decidedly more mixed in regard to the prizeworthiness of Jacinto Benavente y Martínez, Władysław Reymont, and Sigrid Undset and seems to be on the wane in each case, paralleling the course of these writers' international reputations in general. Grazia Deledda is the one laureate of the 1920's who is now viewed with virtual unanimity as undeserving of the Nobel. Among the closest of the also-rans during the decade are Thomas Hardy, barely outpointed by the younger Yeats in 1923; the Danish poet and later winner Johannes V. Jensen, bested by Shaw for the delayed 1925 crown; Maxim Gorky, rejected in the later ballots of 1928 and 1929; and Stefan George, who lost to his countryman Mann in 1929 as too "esoteric and obscure" a writer to merit the laurels.

1930-1939

The 1930's represent a serious regression in quality, it is generally agreed now, and have sparked severe criticism for many of the choices made and not made. European politics overshadowed the era and unfortunately many of the Academy's decisions as well, it would appear from Österling's survey and Espmark's examination of the records. Two exceptions save the decade from complete ignominy: Luigi Pirandello and Eugene O'Neill, without both of whom twentieth century drama in the West is unthinkable. Sinclair Lewis has had defenders and detractors in roughly equal measure, with both sides noting that, whether deserving or not, he was simply not the best American writer at a time when the Academy was obviously ready at last to bestow their crown on a representative of American literature; most would have preferred the man Lewis beat out for the honor, Theodore Dreiser, who ultimately fell victim to the "idealism" factor in the final deliberations. The selection of Karlfeldt, representing a "small exception" and intended to honor posthumously one of the Academy's own (he had refused candidacy on several occasions during his twenty-year tenure), is usually attacked as contributing to the overrepresentation of Scandinavians among the laureates rather than for any perceived inferiority in his writing as such. Ivan Bunin and Roger Martin du Gard have small pockets of admirers among the specialists but are largely ignored or downgraded by others, including the polled experts in 1951 and 1967. Frans Eemil Sillanpää finds no defenders outside Finland and precious few even there. John Galsworthy is dismissed as not at all worthy of the honor, and Pearl Buck holds the dubious distinction of being the worst choice ever, in the view of many critics both within and outside the Academy. Among the sterling crew of rejected or excluded authors during the decade: Antonio Machado, Miguel de Unamuno y Jugo, Virginia Woolf, Constantine Cavafy, Fernando Pessoa, Karel Čapek, and Benedetto Croce, as well as Valéry, Claudel, George, García Lorca, and the future recipients Eliot and Hesse.

1944-1964

The twenty-year period from 1944 to 1964 is widely acknowledged as the grandest ever in the Nobel annals, particularly the 1946-1953 stretch, honoring such magnificent "innovators" (Espmark's label for the entire era's recipients) of lasting merit as Hermann Hesse, André Gide, T. S. Eliot, William Faulkner, François Mauriac, and Ernest Hemingway. Comparable admiration is accorded such subsequent choices as the equally innovative and pioneering Albert Camus, Boris Pasternak, and Saint-John Perse; less widely read but nevertheless esteemed by critics and native readers are Johannes V. Jensen, Pär Lagerkvist, Juan Ramón Jiménez, Salvatore Quasimodo, Halldór Laxness, George Seferis, and Ivo Andrić; and Jean-Paul Sartre continues to attract heated argument both for and against his selection and subsequent refusal. Gabriela Mistral's enshrinement is celebrated more for the recognition it finally brought to Latin America than for the intrinsic merit of her own poetry. John Steinbeck's reputation has sagged badly in comparison to the other laureates of these years, though he maintains some enthusiastic supporters, particularly for the social content of his work. The greatness of Bertrand Russell and Winston Churchill in philosophy and in politics respectively is beyond dispute; only the appropriateness of their receiving the Nobel in *literature* is questioned. (Churchill, when informed that he had won the

Nobel, reportedly bellowed, "In what? I hope it is not for *peace!*") In many cases during these years the selection was not nearly so obvious as one might now suspect, but in fact served to "discover" or "rediscover" a writer of singular merit whose work had not received its due attention, in the minds of the Committee and the Academy. William Faulkner's reputation was in eclipse (except in France and Scandinavia) at the time of his award, for example, but the renewed interest generated by the prize rescued his work for readers worldwide. Pasternak, Lagerkvist, Laxness, and Andrić gained international audiences through the fame attendant on their prizes, and the renown of Hesse, Gide, Eliot, Mauriac, and Camus was solidified by their selection.

1965-1987

The late 1960's and the 1970's are more uneven in quality, by general estimation, as the Academy began alternating irregularly between an adventurous advocacy of pioneers and a "safer" course of more conservative choices reminiscent of the prewar years. Mikhail Sholokhov, though a fine storyteller, is at best anachronistic in the 1960's following the work of Faulkner, Gide, *et alia*; moreover, the long-running controversy about the authenticity of his best work, *And Quiet Flows the Don*, has diminished the luster of his crown even more, except in Soviet circles. The Agnon/Sachs shared prize in 1966 has found few enthusiastic or convincing advocates of either laureate. Miguel Ángel Asturias and Yasunari Kawabata were better and more adventurous choices, as the Academy reached out once more beyond the European-North American orbit to recognize entire literary traditions— the emergent Latin American "boom" and the elegant "classical" strain of Japanese literature—through individual representatives; specialists sometimes dispute the selection of these two individuals, preferring Jorge Luis Borges to Asturias, for example, but without denigrating the literatures they embody.

The choice of Samuel Beckett compares favorably with those of the early postwar years in honoring a daringly imaginative innovator—and this time one gifted in two genres and in two languages, to boot. The worthiness of the next three recipients is generally acknowledged but often is overshadowed by the apparent ideological coloration of the choices: rightly or wrongly, Aleksandr Solzhenitsyn's Nobel continues to be seen by many as a "corrective" to the earlier selection of Sholokhov and to honor the courage of the author of *The Gulag Archipelago* more than the literary talent of the author of *One Day in the Life of Ivan Denisovich* and *The First Circle*; Pablo Neruda's prize was viewed in large measure as a swing back in the opposite direction, as much a stamp of approval for the leftist cause he embraced both in this native Chile and abroad as for his poetry; and in 1972 the pendulum seemed to go back in a more conservative direction, as the Academicians opted for the safe and sensible Heinrich Böll rather than the flamboyantly innovative (and socialistic) Günter Grass in order to pay tribute to German literature's resurgence after the war. The jury is still out on Patrick White but appears more indifferent than impassioned for or against. Eyvind Johnson and Harry Martinson have had the same disgruntled reception outside Scandinavia as was accorded most of their Nordic predecessors, the prize becoming more a millstone around their necks than an ennobling ornament. Eugenio Montale's and Vicente Aleixandre's Nobels are lauded by specialists but have not noticeably increased their fame beyond these circles. In the awards to Saul Bellow and Isaac Bashevis Singer, conversely, the Academy again crowned popular and already acclaimed authors, both rather safe and conservative in their way, almost as if to counter criticism about the "eccentricity" of each preceding year's choice.

With Odysseus Elýtis, Czesław Miłosz, and Elias Canetti, the tide shifted yet again, once more singling out writers of outstanding merit who had received little or no previous recognition and creating a worldwide audience for them—particularly Miłosz—virtually overnight. Back once more to "popular" selections in 1982 and 1983, though the critical reaction to Gabriel García Márquez's prize was far kinder and more enthusiastic than was that to William Golding's. Jaroslav Seifert was applauded by the few who knew him, and his work shows signs of gaining more international recognition, like that of Elýtis, but it is still too early to know with assurance if this will in fact be the case. Claude Simon's award was not received kindly in most quarters, and there is little evidence as yet that it will widen his readership beyond a limited circle of specialists in French fiction. Wole Soyinka was roundly hailed as the first African laureate and as the first black writer to be honored, but critical voices have been raised by Africans and non-Africans alike regarding the quality, influence, and representativeness of his work, which includes poetry, fiction, drama, and criticism, and is often oriented as much toward Western modernism as toward indigenous African themes and forms. Joseph Brodsky's selection, finally, has been acclaimed virtually throughout Western Europe and the Americas, but only with great reservations and even bitterness in Eastern Europe and the Soviet Union; if the choice of a modern-day poet can be called "safe" or "popular," then this classically inspired, virtually bilingual heir of John Donne and W. H. Auden, as much as of Osip Mandelstam and Anna Akhmatova, is such a choice. He is also the youngest since Camus and thus should continue producing poetry and essays for many years, if his sometimes fragile health holds up.

As for living writers not honored in recent years, though frequently bruited as leading contenders, the list includes (in no particular order): Grass, Graham Greene, Nadine Gordimer, Milan Kundera, Max Frisch, Camilo José Cela, Yasushi Inoue, Octavio Paz, Carlos Fuentes, Mario Vargas Llosa, Joyce Carol Oates, Thomas Bernhard, Yashar Kemal, R. K.

Narayan, Anthony Burgess, and V. S. Naipaul. These are but the obvious and semiobvious choices. If anything, the history of the selections does not lend itself to easy predictability as to where future decisions will lead: popular writers or obscure ones, safe writers or pioneers, more Western Europeans and Americans or more forays into "exotic" literatures. The fun is in the anticipation and the uncertainty.

Conclusions

The foregoing series of names can mean whatever one wishes it to mean. It provides at least some justification for any of several summary judgments ranging from Steiner's hostile dismissal ("Is it possible to take seriously an institution and procedure that passes over the majority of the greatest novelists and renewers of prose in the modern age?") to Richard Kostelanetz's genial but qualified approbation ("The record of Nobel selections is credible, even if arguable"). Österling's summary at mid-century remains relevant even today:

> It could be objected that a number of equally significant names are conspicuous by their absence . . . and it is not to be denied that the history of the Nobel Prize in Literature is also a history of inexpiable sins of omission. But even so, it may perhaps be said that the mistakes have been comparatively few, that no truly unworthy candidate has been crowned, and that, if allowances are made for legitimate criticism, the results have reasonably matched the requirements and difficulties of an almost paradoxical assignment.
>
> Just as there are older prizewinners in whom a younger generation can take only a slight interest, so there are recent winners who, to the older people, would have seemed unthinkable. The coming of new generations, with inevitable changes in literary tastes, must obviously be reflected in the history of the Nobel Prize, and all the more clearly as time goes on. But under any circumstances it would be presumptuous to expect the Nobel Prizes to exercise any kind of guiding influence on the direction of literary progress. This has so far followed its own course, independently of the prizes, and will continue to do so in the future.

To point up the unique difficulties in choosing each year's recipient of the Nobel Prize in Literature is not to offer any apology for past choices but rather to state what should be readily apparent upon serious reflection. The criteria for assessment here "are necessarily more varied and often, too, more contradictory than in the case of medicine and other natural sciences," writes Gyllensten, himself both a teaching physician and a novelist, and those criteria are also more readily discernible—and therefore disputable—by the layperson than are those for the exact sciences. Gyllensten continues:

> A literary work has its roots in the traditions and the cultural setting of the age and country in which its author lives. The work reflects this background

and acquires its full richness only through this interplay and only in those readers who are, or can put themselves, in sympathy with it. Literary works are
more or less bound to the literary environment in which they are created, and
the farther away from it one is, the harder it is to do them justice.

The task of awarding the Nobel Prize in Literature involves the obligation of
trying to find methods for keeping oneself *au fait* with what is happening in literature all over the world and for appraising it, either on one's own or with the
aid of specialists. Finally, the prize awarders must try to familiarize themselves
with the works of most value, directly or via translations, and to make a careful
assessment of their quality with all the viewpoints conceivably necessary for a
reasonable evaluation. It is obvious that no hard and fast criteria for such an
appraisal can ever be laid down. One must accept a kind of pragmatical procedure and look to the fundamental idea in Alfred Nobel's will as a whole: it was
a matter of encouraging science and literature and of disseminating them in an
international perspective for the benefit of mankind, but not of handing out
empty status rewards.

Whatever posterity may reveal about a particular prizewinner, it is clear
that the Academicians take their year-round labors seriously, as it is hoped
that this introduction has indicated. Kostelanetz concurs in this opinion.

What can be said about the Nobel is that it is a good prize, if not the best.
From the beginning it has been a universal prize rather than a purely regional
or national one. Its annual selection process is elaborate, and its ongoing
committee keeps track of writers' career over many years, while paying attention to the adequate distribution of Prizes among various nations. To these factors must be added the undoubted independence and integrity of the procedure, along with the rigor of the commitment to secrecy.

The annual shots fired by critics and journalists at the Academy's choices
thus are often as ill-considered as they are unoriginal; this is perhaps natural—as Österling notes, "The general public naturally does not like to be
surprised by names it has never heard of before"—but it is an equally regret-
table reaction, totally alien to the spirit of the prize selections. Current fame
is not a major criterion. Quality is. The Nobel Prize in Literature is not
intended merely to echo and confirm popularity. It may also attempt to point
out talent not yet recognized by most of the world's readers and critics. It
may educate the many as it celebrates the one.

Selected Readings

De Mirjian, Arto, Jr. "Who Wins the Nobel Prize in Literature?" *Publishers
    Weekly* 200 (September 27, 1971): 152-155. Evenhanded treatment, includ-
    ing basic information on the history of the prize, the selection procedures,
    a list of winners through 1970, and a few standard criticisms of choices and
    omissions.

Dragadze, Peter. "The Nobel Prize." *Town & Country*, November, 1979: 198-202, 243-245. Interesting article which goes beyond the basic history-and-procedures approach of most such pieces to give information on the award ceremonies and management of the Nobel funds as well as on Alfred Nobel himself.

Espmark, Kjell. *Le Prix Nobel: Histoire intérieure d'une consécration littéraire*. Translated by Philippe Bouquet. Paris: Balland, 1986. (Original Swedish edition published in 1986 by Almqvist and Wiksell in Stockholm.) An excellent, thoughtful, balanced, thoroughgoing, and candid examination of the literary Nobel's history, drawing on the Swedish Academy's official records of deliberations which have thus far been opened to public scrutiny, and also addressing many of the criticisms leveled at the Nobel choices over the years. Espmark is one of the newest and youngest members of the Academy and a noted writer and critic.

Foyen, Lars. "Picking the Nobel Writers." *Dallas Morning News*, October 8, 1987: 44A. Well-informed though brief survey of the prize selections, based on a reading of Espmark's book.

Gyllensten, Lars. *The Nobel Prize in Literature*. Stockholm: The Swedish Academy, 1978. Straightforward factual presentation of the Swedish Academy's organization and selection procedures, including names and dates of service of current Academy officers and Nobel Committee members. Gyllensten is a former Permanent Secretary of the Academy and current Chairman of the Nobel Committee for Literature.

Kostelanetz, Richard. "The Ultimate Prize." *The New York Times Book Review* 86 (September 27, 1981): 3, 31-32. Largely positive assessment of the prize selections and procedures, with much information on both. Valuable also for the comments elicited from Anders Ryberg, secretary to the Nobel Committee, and from Academy members Östen Sjöstrand, Artur Lundkvist, and Ulf Linde.

"Nobel Prize Symposium: A Petition to the Swedish Academy." *Books Abroad* 41, no. 1 (Winter, 1967): 5-45. Collection of essays on the history of the Nobel selections, both in general and in specific linguistic and geographic areas. Termed by Espmark the best single set of articles on the prize and referred to frequently in the closing chapters of his book.

Österling, Anders. "The Literary Prize," in *Nobel: The Man and His Prizes*, by H. Schück et al. Norman: University of Oklahoma Press, 1950. (Revised and enlarged editions published in 1960 and 1972 by Elsevier in New York.) The book covers the history and procedures of all the prize-granting bodies and their selections from 1901 to 1950 (and later in the updated editions). Österling does not draw directly on the official records of the debates, since these had not yet been opened to public view, but outlines the reasons for various choices and omissions in more general terms than does Espmark. The style is urbane and gracious. Österling served on the Nobel Committee for most of his sixty-two years (1919-1981) as an Academy member.

Ratcliffe, Michael. "The Literary Referees." *Sweden Now*, no. 5. (1983): 18-21. Uneven discussion of the prize selections and omissions, vacillating in tone between the sympathetic and the snide. Includes a few "man-in-the-street" comments from the author's visit to Stockholm.

Riggan, William. "The Swedish Academy and the Nobel Prize in Literature: History and Procedure." *World Literature Today* 55, no. 3 (Summer, 1981): 399-405. The article on which the foregoing essay is based.

Steiner, George. "The Scandal of the Nobel Prize." *The New York Times Book Review* 84 (September 30, 1984): 1, 38-39. Strong attack on the prize selections and omissions. Guilty of a few small factual errors and shows some unfamiliarity with the prize guidelines and procedures as well.

Tuohy, William. "Nobel Prize—It's No Short Story." *Los Angeles Times*, August 10, 1981: 1, 4. Informative on the history and procedures of the prize and basically neutral in tone. Better than most such "service" pieces that frequently appear in the daily press around Nobel announcement time.

Vaillancourt, Dan. "The Nobel Prize for Literature: Alfred Would Be Proud." *Illinois Quarterly* 43, no. 1 (Fall, 1980): 33-39. Discusses the common thread of "humanism" that informs the writings of most Nobel laureates, using the particular example of the French prizewinners. Also gives a good survey of the history and procedures of the prize.

"What's Wrong with the Nobel Prize?" *Books Abroad* 25, no. 2 (Spring, 1951): 114-120. Sampling of comments from a survey sent by the journal editors to three hundred authors and scholars soliciting evaluations of the prize selections in its first fifty years.

Zuckerman, Harriet. "After Winning the Prize Is When Trouble Really Starts." *The New York Times* 132 (January 2, 1983): 7. Discussion of the consequences of receiving the Nobel, particularly for the winners in science.

William Riggan

TIME LINE

YEAR	RECIPIENT	COUNTRY (language)	GENRE
1901	Sully Prudhomme (1839-1907)	France	poetry
1902	Theodor Mommsen (1817-1903)	Germany	history
1903	Bjørnstjerne Bjørnson (1832-1910)	Norway	fiction/drama
1904	José Echegaray y Eizaguirre (1832-1916)	Spain	drama
	Frédéric Mistral (1830-1914)	France (Provençal)	poetry/philology
1905	Henryk Sienkiewicz (1846-1916)	Poland	fiction
1906	Giosuè Carducci (1835-1907)	Italy	poetry/criticism
1907	Rudyard Kipling (1865-1936)	Great Britain	fiction/poetry
1908	Rudolf Christoph Eucken (1846-1926)	Germany	philosophy
1909	Selma Lagerlöf (1858-1940)	Sweden	fiction
1910	Paul Heyse (1830-1914)	Germany	fiction/poetry/drama
1911	Maurice Maeterlinck (1862-1949)	Belgium (French)	drama/poetry/ nonfiction
1912	Gerhart Hauptmann (1862-1946)	Germany	drama/fiction/ poetry/nonfiction
1913	Rabindranath Tagore (1861-1941)	India (Bengali)	poetry
1914	Reserved	—	—
1915	Romain Rolland (1866-1944)	France	fiction/drama/ nonfiction
1916	Verner von Heidenstam (1859-1940)	Sweden	poetry/fiction
1917	Karl Adolph Gjellerup (1857-1919)	Denmark	fiction/drama/poetry
	Henrik Pontoppidan (1857-1943)	Denmark	fiction
1918	Reserved	—	—
1919	Carl Spitteler (1845-1924)	Switzerland	poetry
1920	Knut Hamsun (1859-1952)	Norway	fiction/drama
1921	Anatole France (1844-1924)	France	fiction
1922	Jacinto Benavente y Martínez (1866-1954)	Spain	drama
1923	William Butler Yeats (1865-1939)	Ireland	poetry/drama
1924	Władysław Reymont (1868-1925)	Poland	fiction

YEAR	RECIPIENT	COUNTRY (language)	GENRE
1925	George Bernard Shaw (1856-1950)	Great Britain	drama
1926	Grazia Deledda (1871-1936)	Italy	fiction
1927	Henri Bergson (1859-1941)	France	philosophy
1928	Sigrid Undset (1882-1949)	Norway	fiction
1929	Thomas Mann (1875-1955)	Germany	fiction/nonfiction
1930	Sinclair Lewis (1885-1951)	United States	fiction
1931	Erik Axel Karlfeldt (1864-1931)	Sweden	poetry
1932	John Galsworthy (1867-1933)	Great Britain	fiction/drama
1933	Ivan Bunin (1870-1953)	France (Russian)	fiction
1934	Luigi Pirandello (1867-1936)	Italy	drama/fiction
1935	Reserved	—	—
1936	Eugene O'Neill (1888-1953)	United States	drama
1937	Roger Martin du Gard (1881-1958)	France	fiction
1938	Pearl S. Buck (1892-1973)	United States	fiction/biography
1939	Frans Eemil Sillanpää (1888-1964)	Finland	fiction
1940-1943	Reserved	—	—
1944	Johannes V. Jensen (1873-1950)	Denmark	fiction
1945	Gabriela Mistral (1889-1957)	Chile	poetry
1946	Hermann Hesse (1877-1962)	Switzerland (German)	fiction/poetry
1947	André Gide (1869-1951)	France	fiction
1948	T. S. Eliot (1888-1965)	Great Britain	poetry/criticism
1949	William Faulkner (1897-1962)	United States	fiction
1950	Bertrand Russell (1872-1970)	Great Britain	philosophy
1951	Pär Lagerkvist (1891-1974)	Sweden	poetry/drama/fiction
1952	François Mauriac (1885-1970)	France	fiction
1953	Winston Churchill (1874-1965)	Great Britain	nonfiction
1954	Ernest Hemingway (1899-1961)	United States	fiction
1955	Halldór Laxness (1902-)	Iceland	fiction
1956	Juan Ramón Jiménez (1881-1958)	Spain	poetry
1957	Albert Camus (1913-1960)	France	fiction/drama/nonfiction
1958	Boris Pasternak (1890-1960) (Prize declined)	Soviet Union	poetry/fiction

YEAR	RECIPIENT	COUNTRY (language)	GENRE
1959	Salvatore Quasimodo (1901-1968)	Italy	poetry
1960	Saint-John Perse (1887-1975)	France	poetry
1961	Ivo Andrić (1892-1975)	Yugoslavia (Serbo-Croatian)	fiction
1962	John Steinbeck (1902-1968)	United States	fiction
1963	George Seferis (1900-1971)	Greece	poetry
1964	Jean-Paul Sartre (1905-1980) (Prize declined)	France	fiction/drama/ nonfiction
1965	Mikhail Sholokhov (1905-1984)	Soviet Union	fiction
1966	Shmuel Yosef Agnon (1888-1970)	Israel (Yiddish/ Hebrew)	fiction
	Nelly Sachs (1891-1970)	Sweden (German)	poetry
1967	Miguel Ángel Asturias (1899-1974)	Guatemala	fiction
1968	Yasunari Kawabata (1899-1972)	Japan	fiction
1969	Samuel Beckett (1906-)	Ireland (French/ English)	drama/fiction
1970	Aleksandr Solzhenitsyn (1918-)	Soviet Union	fiction/drama/ nonfiction
1971	Pablo Neruda (1904-1973)	Chile	poetry
1972	Heinrich Böll (1917-1985)	West Germany	fiction
1973	Patrick White (1912-)	Australia	fiction
1974	Eyvind Johnson (1900-1976)	Sweden	fiction
	Harry Martinson (1904-1978)	Sweden	poetry
1975	Eugenio Montale (1896-1981)	Italy	poetry
1976	Saul Bellow (1915-)	United States	fiction
1977	Vicente Aleixandre (1898-1984)	Spain	poetry
1978	Isaac Bashevis Singer (1904-)	United States (Yiddish)	fiction
1979	Odysseus Elýtis (1911-)	Greece	poetry
1980	Czesław Miłosz (1911-)	United States (Polish)	poetry
1981	Elias Canetti (1905-)	Great Britain (German)	fiction/drama/ nonfiction
1982	Gabriel García Márquez (1928-)	Colombia	fiction

YEAR	RECIPIENT	COUNTRY (language)	GENRE
1983	William Golding (1911-)	Great Britain	fiction
1984	Jaroslav Seifert (1901-1986)	Czechoslovakia	poetry
1985	Claude Simon (1913-)	France	fiction
1986	Wole Soyinka (1934-)	Nigeria (Yoruba/ English)	drama/poetry/fiction
1987	Joseph Brodsky (1940-)	United States (English/ Russian)	poetry/nonfiction

1901

Literature
Sully Prudhomme, France

Peace
Jean Henri Dunant, Switzerland
Frédéric Passy, France

Physics
Wilhelm Röntgen, Germany

Chemistry
Jacobus Van't Hoff, Netherlands

Physiology or Medicine
Emil von Behring, Germany

SULLY PRUDHOMME
René-François-Armand Prudhomme
1901

Born: Paris, France; March 16, 1839
Died: Châtenay, France; September 7, 1907
Language: French
Principal genre: Poetry

In exquisitely crafted lyrics, Sully Prudhomme explored human conflicts between the desire for love and the inevitability of impermanence, the need for faith and the fact of doubt

The Award

Presentation

The Nobel Prize in Literature was presented to Sully Prudhomme on December 10, 1901, by Carl David af Wirsén, Permanent Secretary of the Swedish Academy. Since this was the first year that the prizes were awarded, the presenter prefaced his address with a statement as to the importance of literature. Perhaps, he reflected, the award in literature was the last to be presented because literature is the "supreme flower of civilization." As the climactic award of that first year, the 1901 prize was particularly difficult to determine. It was therefore highly significant that the Academy had selected poetry as the genre to be recognized and Sully Prudhomme as the most outstanding of many worthy poets.

The award was made to Sully Prudhomme on the basis of his art and thought. Interestingly, the Academy was more impressed by the poet's early short lyrics than by his later long, philosophical works. In the lyrics, it was believed, his flawless craftsmanship was reflected, as well as his unique spirituality. Avoiding the excesses of sentimentality, Sully Prudhomme was yet sensitive; while recognizing man's earthbound nature, Sully Prudhomme rose above mere realism by emphasizing humanity's religious and moral aspirations. Thus even Sully Prudhomme's images, while realistic, were not intended to detail external reality but instead to reveal the interior landscape.

Finally, it was considered appropriate that this poet was chosen because, although himself a student of science, he was aware of the limitations of man's knowledge. Given those limitations, Sully Prudhomme idealistically believed that in an unknowable world, man could at least know and do his duty. In awarding the first Nobel Prize in Literature to Sully Prudhomme, the Academy thus respected the idealistic intentions of Alfred Nobel.

Nobel lecture

Because of illness, Sully Prudhomme was unable to attend the Nobel Prize ceremony. No formal acceptance speech was read.

Critical reception

When the Académie Française nominated its illustrious member, Sully Prudhomme, to be first Nobel laureate, the outcome was inevitable. Although individuals and loosely organized groups had suggested other recipients, the newly organized Nobel Committee was not likely to ignore the recommendation of so prestigious a body.

The reactions of Sully Prudhomme's European contemporaries reflected their attitude toward the conservative values of the Académie Française. Certainly Sully Prudhomme was well established. For thirty-five years, he had been praised for his craftsmanship and respected for his philosophical bent. In 1881, he was elected to the Académie Française. In 1894, with the death of Charles-Marie-René Leconte de Lisle, Sully Prudhomme was considered his successor as leader of the Parnassians, then at the height of their popularity. At a time when critics had tired of what they considered Romantic sentimentality and were not yet willing to accept the new patterns of Symbolism, the Parnassian lyrics of Sully Prudhomme seemed to set the standard for poetic achievement.

Therefore the selection of Sully Prudhomme was applauded by such French publications as *La Revue des poètes*. Contemporary critics who considered him "his country's leading philosopher in verse" praised the decision of the Nobel Committee. Periodicals which espoused the Symbolist cause, such as the *Mercure de France* and *L'Occident*, attacked the decision, however, as a victory of the moralizing conservative literary faction over the defenders of poetic freedom.

In a lengthy article published immediately after the death of Sully Prudhomme in 1907, *The Times Literary Supplement* (September 13) summarized the British assessment of the French poet. "A poet for thinkers," he voiced the "thoughts and feelings" of scientists, mathematicians, and engineers as the realist Victor Hugo or the Symbolists Charles Baudelaire and Paul Verlaine could not. Clearly, Sully Prudhomme had been seen as the appropriate poet of a new age in which science hoped to improve man's lot, but in which men of science were still men, beset by doubt and despair.

The fact that the American press took almost no notice of the initial literature prize was attributed by a contemporary American critic to his countrymen's ignorance of French poetry. In an article in *The Independent* (January 25, 1902), E. E. Slosson saw Sully Prudhomme's achievement in much the same way as had *The Times Literary Supplement*, praising the poet as "the man who more than any other now living has embodied in his verse the new material gathered by science, and has best expressed the spirit of action and investigation which characterized the age." His very doubts, said Slosson, reflect the uncertainty which is so characteristic of scientific thought; similarly, his emphasis on humanitarianism as a way of life is the typical response of scientists bereft of the old certainties.

Thus Sully Prudhomme was generally seen as the acknowledged leader of that poetic movement which expressed the spirit of his age. His contemporaries could not have guessed that time would relegate him to the status of a minor poet in a movement far less significant than that of the Symbolists, who alone questioned his selection.

Biography

René-François-Armand Prudhomme was born to a middle-class family in Paris on March 16, 1839. When he was two, his father died and the future poet lived with his widowed mother and an older sister in Paris and in Châtenay, south of Paris. As a child, according to *The Times Literary Supplement*, he acquired the family's pet name for his father, "Sully."

After he was graduated at the head of his class in mathematics, Sully Prudhomme was preparing for entry into the École Polytechnique, but an attack of ophthalmia ended his hopes for a career in engineering. Two other events in his youth contributed to his lifelong melancholy. One of them involved the loss of love: The cousin whom he had loved from childhood married another man. The other loss was that of faith. After a brief period of certainty when he was in Lyons staying with devout Catholic relatives, Sully Prudhomme became a skeptic who nevertheless yearned to believe.

After a brief period as a clerk in the foundries at Le Creusot, in 1860, Sully Prudhomme turned to the legal profession and obtained a position in the office of a Paris notary. After a bequest made him financially independent, however, he left the law and devoted himself thereafter to writing. In 1865, he published *Stances et poèmes*, his first collection of poetry.

In 1870, Sully Prudhomme's life once again darkened. In January, he was stunned by the deaths of his uncle, his aunt, and his mother, all of whom lived with him. Then came the Franco-Prussian War; the hardships which he suffered in the army would leave his health shattered.

In his later years, Sully Prudhomme's poetry brought him many honors: election to the Académie Française; later, appointment as an officer of the Légion d'Honneur; and finally, the Nobel Prize. Unfortunately, his health had worsened. Increasingly troubled by paralysis and insomnia, he spent his last fifteen years in Châtenay, where he died peacefully on September 7, 1907, while sitting in the garden, with his sister by his side.

Literary Career

When Sully Prudhomme went to Paris in 1860, it was with the intention of studying law. Within two years, however, he was writing poetry, confiding to his journal that he regretted the time which his studies took from his art. One reason for his new passion was his involvement with a group of young writers who were beginning to call themselves the Parnassians, in order to indicate their association with classic order and decorum in contrast to

Romanticism, which by midcentury had become unfashionable. Sully Prudhomme probably met the leader of these young poets, Leconte de Lisle, in
1864. By that time, Sully Prudhomme had already published his first poem,
"L'Art," which had appeared in *La Revue nationale et étrangère* in 1863. According to his *Journal intime* (1922; intimate journal), he had progressed
from dissatisfaction with the mediocrity of his work to a sense of mastery of
forms and a consciousness of inspiration in subject matter.

In 1865, a friend financed the printing of Sully Prudhomme's first volume
of poetry, *Stances et poèmes* (stanzas and poems). These lyrical works were
pensive and melancholy in mood, pondering the transient sorrows and joys of
human life. Typical of them was Sully Prudhomme's most widely antholo-
gized poem, "Vase brisé" (the broken vase), which compares a vase which
seems whole but is flawed with an almost invisible crack, to a heart broken
by the unkindness of a lover. Fortunately, a Châtenay friend took *Stances et
poèmes* to the great critic and arbiter of literary taste, Charles-Augustin
Sainte-Beuve, whose favorable review ensured the success of the book and
launched the new poet on his career.

One year later, Sully Prudhomme published another lyrical volume, *Les
Épreuves* (1866; trials), which included sonnets on such topics as love, doubt,
and action. It was followed by a book of pictorial poems, *Croquis italiens*
(1866-1868; Italian notebooks) and by another volume of lyrics, *Les Solitudes*
(1869; solitudes), whose central theme was the lonely individual's desire for
love. Sully Prudhomme's alliance with the Parnassians is evidenced by the
fact that he contributed to their periodical *Le Parnasse contemporain* (the
contemporary anthology of poetry), which was made up entirely of verse
composed, whatever its subject, in the formal structures of the Parnassian
poets. The first collected volume of *Le Parnasse contemporain* was published
in 1866, the second in 1871, and the third in 1876. Works by Sully Prudhomme were included in each of these volumes. Sully Prudhomme's identification as a Parnassian is evidenced by a poem by Gabriel Marc, published
in 1870, which lists Sully Prudhomme among the seventeen younger Parnassians who were disciples of Leconte de Lisle.

As Aaron Schaffer notes, the subject matter of the Parnassians was varied,
ranging from frivolous social verse to serious philosophical poetry. According
to Schaffer, it was the insistence on careful craftsmanship and on the use of
formal structures, not the subject matter, which marked this school of poetry.
Like Leconte de Lisle, from the beginning Sully Prudhomme indicated his
philosophical concerns. Unlike his master, however, he hoped until his death
that he would discover a meaning in life which would enable him to discard
his pessimism. Sully Prudhomme also differed from the other Parnassian poets in his scientific bias. *The Times Literary Supplement* stated that "in the
mind of this poet there was buried an engineer, who had died young." His
metaphors reflected his interest. As Slosson commented in *The Independent*,

Sully Prudhomme was a "poet who sings of balloons and barometers, of submarine cables and photography, of the origin of species and specific gravity determinations."

The Franco-Prussian War had a profound influence on young poets such as Sully Prudhomme. Like the other Parnassians, he was torn between his dread of the horrors of war and his love of his country. As the war was beginning, Sully Prudhomme published his *Impressions de la guerre* (1870; impressions of war), which were pacifistic in tone; after experiencing the hardships of battle and siege and the final humiliation of defeat and occupation, however, he wrote *La France* (1870), a series of sonnets which were deeply patriotic.

Even before the war, Sully Prudhomme had sought to find the meaning of life by observing and analyzing his world. In the lyrical poems, as in "Vase brisé," he dealt with the tragedies of the human heart; in other poems, less psychological and more philosophical or even metaphysical, he questioned the existence and justice of God. Thus in the *Journal intime* entry of February 1, 1864, Sully Prudhomme commented that he could not understand God's permitting a holocaust in a Santiago church, noting that this would be a good subject for a poem. Eight years later, he published *Les Destins* (1872; destinies), a long philosophical poem which explored the implications of the Santiago catastrophe. Increasingly, Sully Prudhomme turned to such works instead of to the short lyrical poems which had made him famous. His last collection of lyrics was *Les Vaines Tendresses* (1875; vain endearments), again dealing with the hopeless need for love.

Sully Prudhomme's interest in philosophy was not new. As early as 1863, he mentioned in his journal an encounter with an old school friend. Asked about his work, the poet said that he was looking for a definition of man; when he discovered it, he continued, he would make poems about it. Indeed, there are obvious psychological, philosophical, and metaphysical implications in his lyrics. The increasing seriousness of his search for meaning is indicated by his interest in Lucretius, which led him in 1869 to do a metrical translation of the first book of *De rerum natura* (c. 60 B.C.), entitled by Sully Prudhomme *Lucrèce: De la nature des choses*.

When they were published, Sully Prudhomme's two major cycles were much admired. Both were long moral allegories dealing with the question of ideal human conduct. *La Justice* (1878; justice) suggested that a moral code could be based on scientific progress. *Le Bonheur* (1888; happiness) was Sully Prudhomme's version of the Faustus story, doubtless suggested by Johann Wolfgang von Goethe's play, which the laureate had read and admired in his youth. In *Le Bonheur*, the central character, as in the traditional story, is looking for the secret of happiness. Yet the usual order is reversed; Sully Prudhomme's Faustus begins with the senses and only then proceeds to learning. Finally, like Goethe's hero, Sully Prudhomme's Faustus finds fulfillment in service, in the task of improving the human race.

Critics disagree as to whether the Sully Prudhomme of the later years should still be called a Parnassian. The answer depends on definition. Certainly Sully Prudhomme never abandoned the precision of form and scientific accuracy of thought, a reaction against Romantic excesses, which defined the Parnassian school. On the other hand, some critics argue that the moral and didactic emphasis of his later works would separate him from the other Parnassians, who were defined as poets whose interest was in beauty, not in truth. To Schaffer, however, such a definition is too narrow. In the Parnassian group, he finds seven different genres, one of which is the philosophical; in that group, Sully Prudhomme is an important figure.

To Sully Prudhomme, as to John Keats, beauty and truth were not separable. Again the *Journal intime* is revealing. There, on July 5, 1868, Sully Prudhomme wrote excitedly that he now understood the relationship between beauty and morality. Just as the artist could create a form which was aesthetically pleasing, so a human being, responding to his moral sense, could make his own life an art form.

The list of Sully Prudhomme's prose works indicates his interest in both metaphysics and aesthetics. For example, his *Réflexions sur l'art des vers* (1892; reflections on the art of poetry) and his *Testament poétique* (1897; poetic testament) are balanced by *Que sais-je? Examen de conscience* (1895; what do I know? study of perception), which probed the limits of human knowledge, and *La Vraie Religion selon Pascal* (1905; true religion according to Pascal), a study of Blaise Pascal, the devout and profound French philosopher. Many other theoretical works were published after Sully Prudhomme's death, as well as a volume of letters (*Lettres à une amie*, 1911), the *Journal intime*, and a group of poems, *Les Épaves* (1908; flotsam). A five-volume edition of his work had appeared in 1900-1901, but a fuller seven-volume collection, *Œuvres de Sully-Prudhomme* (1908), was published posthumously.

When Sully Prudhomme turned from lyrical to philosophical poems and finally to prose, he believed that he was moving toward greater and more significant works. His public agreed, calling him the most important philosophical poet of the period, paramount because he based his worldview on the new scientific discoveries of the century. Nevertheless there were many who still preferred the early lyrics, to Sully Prudhomme's annoyance, readers who still called "Vase brisé" his finest poem. It was significant that the Swedish Academy agreed with such readers, basing their award primarily on his brief lyrical poems, while mentioning his idealism and didacticism as appropriate qualities for the first winner of the literature prize. As the century has proceeded, Sully Prudhomme's status has been reduced from that of a major poet to that of a minor Parnassian, whose "Vase brisé" appears in many anthologies, but whose long, didactic epics, the primary work of his life, are assessed as unimaginative, unpoetic, and almost unreadable. Clearly, although the Academy overrated Sully Prudhomme's rank among the poets of his time, they were correct in judging the lyrics of his youth to be his finest works.

Bibliography

Primary

POETRY: *Stances et poèmes*, 1865; *Les Épreuves*, 1866; *Croquis italiens*, 1866-1868; *Les Solitudes*, 1869; *Impressions de la guerre*, 1870; *La France*, 1870; *Les Destins*, 1872; *La Révolte des fleurs*, 1874; *Les Vaines Tendresses*, 1875; *La Justice*, 1878; *Le Bonheur*, 1888; *Les Épaves*, 1908.

NONFICTION: *Préface à la Traduction du Premier Chant de Lucrèce*, 1869; *Discours de réception à l'Académie Française*, 1882; *L'Expression dans les beaux-arts*, 1883; *Réflexions sur l'art des vers*, 1892; *Sur l'origine de la vie terrestre*, 1893; *Que sais-je? Examen de conscience*, 1895; *Testament poétique*, 1897; *L'Histoire et l'état social*, 1899; *Le Problème des causes finales*, 1899; *Le Crédit de la science*, 1902; *Sur les liens nationaux et internationaux*, 1904; *La Vraie Religion selon Pascal*, 1905; *Psychologie du libre arbitre*, 1907; *Le Lien social*, 1909; *Fragments inédits: Notes pour servir à une physiologie de l'adultère*, 1910; *Lettres à une amie*, 1911; *Journal intime*, 1922.

TRANSLATION: *Lucrèce: De la nature des choses*, 1869.

MISCELLANEOUS: *Œuvres de Sully-Prudhomme*, 1908 (7 volumes).

Secondary

Cornell, Kenneth. *The Post-Symbolist Period: French Poetic Currents, 1900-1920*. New Haven, Conn.: Yale University Press, 1958. Although the specific discussion of Sully Prudhomme's works in this study is brief, the comments about his influence on Parnassian poetic theory and the account of contemporary French reactions to his selection as Nobel laureate are valuable.

Hunt, Herbert James. *The Epic in Nineteenth-century France*. Oxford: B. Blackwell, 1941. An extended study of the epic form, as adapted by the Parnassians, in their post-Romantic return to classical themes and forms. Includes an interesting discussion of Sully Prudhomme's two epics.

Legge, James Granville. *Chanticleer: A Study of the French Muse*. New York: E. P. Dutton and Co., 1935. Reprint. Port Washington, N.Y.: Kennikat Press, 1969. The eighth chapter of this book deals with Baudelaire, the Parnassians, and the Symbolists; of the three Parnassians discussed, one is Sully Prudhomme. The analysis of three of his lyrics is included; nevertheless, the entire chapter is helpful in placing Sully Prudhomme within the context of late nineteenth century poetic movements.

Robertson, William John. *A Century of French Verse*. London: A. D. Innes and Co., 1895. The introduction to this volume discusses the importance of

Sully Prudhomme's poetic theory, and the pages of text devoted to him contain a valuable evaluation of his various works, as well as a concise, clear summary of his thought.

Schaffer, Aaron. *The Genres of Parnassian Poetry: A Study of the Parnassian Minors*. Baltimore: Johns Hopkins University Press, 1944. Probably the most thorough volume published on Parnassian poetry, this book places dozens of poets of that school within the various genres Schaffer has noted. The discussion of Sully Prudhomme as a member of the philosophical group is augmented by a large number of carefully indexed references to him throughout the book. Contains an extensive bibliography. Essential to the study of any Parnassian poet.

_____. "Parnassian Poetry on the Franco-Prussian War." *PMLA* 47 (December, 1932): 1167-1192. A good explanation of the attitudes of the Parnassians toward the Franco-Prussian War; explains Sully Prudhomme's change in attitude, as reflected in his two works inspired by the war.

Slosson, E. E. "Sully Prudhomme: A Poet of Science." *Independent* 54 (January 25, 1902): 219-222. An article by a contemporary American scholar written in response to Sully Prudhomme's winning of the Nobel Prize. The assessment of the laureate as a trailblazing "poet of science" and the comparisons to other nineteenth century poets are revealing.

Rosemary M. Canfield-Reisman

1902

Literature
Theodor Mommsen, Germany

Peace
Élie Ducommun, Switzerland
Charles Albert Gobat, Switzerland

Physics
Hendrik Antoon Lorentz, Netherlands
Pieter Zeeman, Netherlands

Chemistry
Emil Fischer, Germany

Physiology or Medicine
Sir Ronald Ross, Great Britain

THEODOR MOMMSEN
1902

Born: Garding, Schleswig; November 30, 1817
Died: Charlottenburg, Germany; November 1, 1903
Language: German
Principal genre: History

Mommsen combined scholarship in Roman law, linguistics, numismatics, and epigraphy with a vigorous writing style to bring the story of Rome alive and to create a harmony of history as both an art and a science

The Award

Presentation

On December 10, 1902, Carl David af Wirsén, Permanent Secretary of the Swedish Academy, presented the second Nobel Prize in Literature to Theodor Mommsen, whose name had been proposed by eighteen members of the Royal Prussian Academy of Sciences. Lauding Mommsen as "a veritable hero in the field of scholarship," the Academy named, as reasons for his nomination, the author's "acute judgment," "strict method," "youthful vigor," and "artistic presentation which alone can give life and concreteness to a description."

The presentation focused on defusing three questions that the Academy expected the award to Mommsen might raise: The selection of a historian rather than a belletrist, earlier criticism of Mommsen's subjective, passionate judgments in *Römische Geschichte* (1854-1856; *The History of Rome*, 1862-1866), and the advanced age of the recipient.

Noting Mommsen's Herculean scholarship in a variety of fields ranging from Roman law to epigraphy, numismatics, and archaeology, the Academy pointed out that the award was being given to honor Mommsen's mastery of the art of historical writing and especially for the artistic excellence of *The History of Rome*. The Nobel statutes, the Academy affirmed, state that literature cannot be exclusively relegated to belles lettres; it must also consider other writings distinguished by their artistic excellence. This presentation of the second Nobel Prize in Literature served notice that history might also have a place in the field of literature.

The Swedish Academy answered those critics who might have objected to Mommsen's judgments, especially to his admiration for Julius Caesar and his scorn for Caesar's opponents, by defending Mommsen's learning as it supplemented his imagination. Written with artistic skill, the brilliant character sketches and colorful descriptions make Rome come alive. Finally, speaking of Mommsen's age (eighty-five), the Academy declared him young in spirit and possessed of the fire of youth, which alone was capable of arousing enthusiasm. The Academy justified its choice vigorously, noting that Momm-

sen's impact came not only from his art but also from his unique combination
of scholarship and art.

Nobel lecture

Mommsen was not present in Stockholm to receive his Nobel Prize; the
Minister of Germany, Count von Leyden, accepted the presentation in
Mommsen's name. Nor did the eminent historian deliver what has become
the traditional Nobel lecture. Theodor Mommsen enjoyed the fame of the
award for less than a year before his death.

In place of the published lecture stands an excerpt from his great work *The
History of Rome*—a portrait of Julius Caesar, in Mommsen's words "the sole
creative genius produced by Rome." The description of Caesar, the young
noble of passion and good sense, of physical and mental vigor, illustrates the
power of Mommsen's words and images. Although vain—Mommsen suggests that he "would doubtless have surrendered some of his victories, if he
could thereby have brought back his youthful locks"—Caesar was not a slave
to his vanity: His dalliance with Cleopatra, Mommsen asserts, was only "contrived to mask a weak point in his political position."

In addition to illustrating Mommsen's skill with words and images, this
excerpt points to the historian's high moral standards—his demand that the
heroes of his narrative pursue only the highest aim: "the political, military,
intellectual, and moral regeneration of his own deeply decayed nation." It
also illustrates his skill at using comparison with more modern historical
characters to bring the actors in his drama to life. Comparing Caesar's military stamina to William of Orange and his statesmanlike leadership and
route to power with that of Oliver Cromwell, Mommsen throws the more
familiar light of modern history on the past. These techniques give *The History of Rome* an immediacy unusual in historical literature.

It was neither Mommsen's view of Caesar nor his philosophy of history
which prompted the Swedish Academy to award to him the Nobel Prize in
Literature: It was his mastery of the art of historical writing. The qualities
that Mommsen thought indispensable for the writing of history had been
expressed almost thirty years earlier in his "Rectorial Address," delivered at
the University of Berlin in 1874. History, he averred on that occasion, is nothing but the discovery and examination of evidence and the weaving of that
evidence into a narrative informed by an understanding of the people and
conditions that shaped events. Believing that historians are born, not educated, Mommsen declared that only the study of the language and the law of
a period was essential. Although the techniques of historical scholarship can
be acquired, the art of history—combining facts into a truthful and persuasive whole—is a product of no formal rule or education. Mommsen urged his
students to find their own path in the struggle against "indolence, officious-
ness, and sham learning," the enemies of scholarship.

Critical reception

No adverse criticism greeted Mommsen's selection for the Nobel Prize in Literature, nor has the award been questioned by later generations. All controversy about *The History of Rome* had been aired earlier and would not reappear until the conflict between the German Empire and the West became imminent.

While the public was delighted with the multivolume work and scholars praised its erudition, objections ranged from the charge that Mommsen took sides to accusations that his bias contained a hidden message of encouragement for contemporary Caesars. Mommsen's portrait of late Republican Rome starring Julius Caesar overturned the traditional interpretation that glamorized Caesar's opponents, especially Cicero, and his assassins. This cavalier reassessment, even based on sound evidence and analysis, annoyed the historians whose hypotheses were rejected. Some scholars objected to the substitution of human details for the impersonal dignity of traditional historical writing. Even William Warde Fowler, an admirer of Mommsen's art, suggested that the strength and vividness of his language and judgment had almost paralyzed criticism and had virtually laid a spell on subsequent historians of Rome. In a memoir published in 1909, Fowler complimented Mommsen's genius while gently chiding him for "an almost dangerous gift of historical imagination, which did indeed occasionally mislead him."

These criticisms were minor compared to the attacks of a later historian, Antoine Guilland, who in 1915 bitterly labeled Mommsen "one of the most ardent apostles of the theory that 'might is better than right'" and accused him of "bringing about the reaction against the Christian conception of human life." Guilland called Mommsen the inspiration of a new science of the psychology of races to "[explain] the superiority of the German race over all others." This extreme criticism, colored by the hostilities between Germany and France, went unanswered by the long-dead Mommsen. Mommsen had, however, responded to earlier accusations that he championed "Caesarism" by claiming that he praised Caesar's actions only because the Roman Republic was rotten, and liberty for the Roman citizens depended on a strong, if imperfect, government. In other circumstances Caesar would have been labeled a tyrant by Mommsen.

These criticisms were not made until long after the Nobel Prize ceremony in 1902. Mommsen's prodigious knowledge of law, philology, numismatics, and archaeology—as well as his voluminous publications—had blunted the negative judgments about *The History of Rome*. The only adverse comments in 1902 were aimed at the Swedish Academy. Fortunately, the Academy had foreseen these accusations and had acted to defend its choice. The award served notice that the Swedish Academy intended to consider "literature" in a broad sense when it chose recipients of the award and to consider the whole of an author's work, not simply that done during the preceding year.

Biography

Born on November 30, 1817, in Garding, Schleswig, where his father was a Protestant pastor, Theodor Mommsen lived as a German, among a German population but under a foreign government. Theodor was the eldest of three sons who were educated at home by their parents, gentle lovers of literature and respecters of learning. All three boys were reared to become distinguished classical scholars. Theodor entered the University of Kiel, where he studied law. In 1838, this meant chiefly Roman law taught by disciples of Friedrich Karl von Savigny, a founder of the historical school of jurisprudence. Having completed dissertations on the secretaries and marshals of the Roman magistrates and on the guilds and cooperative societies of Rome, Mommsen was given a research scholarship by the Danish government. This allowed him to spend three years at the Archaeological Institute in Rome collecting inscriptions related to Roman law.

Returning home in 1847, he found Schleswig and Germany in a political uproar. As a liberal, Mommsen enthusiastically joined the fight for German unity and eagerly set to work to do his part to free German national states from foreign influence. In 1848, he became the editor of the *Schleswig-Holsteinische Zeitung* for the provisional German government at Frankfurt, joining the fight for German unity. At the end of that year, however, he was glad to leave journalism for a post in civil law at the University of Leipzig. Unfortunately, he had not forsaken politics. Prosecuted (and acquitted) for seditious language and for participation in an uprising in Saxony in 1849, Mommsen was dismissed from his post at Leipzig. Reluctantly accepting a position in Zurich in 1852, he took this opportunity to seek out and copy all the Roman inscriptions in Switzerland. This exile ended two years later when he was invited to Prussia to take a position on the faculty at the University of Breslau. There he married Marie Reimer, the daughter of a bookseller, and with her he began a family that eventually included sixteen children.

Four years later, Mommsen was offered a position in the Berlin Academy, with responsibility for organizing the collection of all the Latin inscriptions in the Roman Empire from Britain to Syria in a *corpus inscriptiones latinae* (collection of Latin inscriptions). He remained in Berlin for the rest of his life as a professor of ancient history at the University of Berlin, as Permanent Secretary of the Prussian Academy of Arts and Sciences, and, finally, in 1873, as a member of the directorate of the Monumenta Germaniae Historica.

Mommsen's experience in politics had been less than satisfactory, but as an idealist and a liberal, a supporter of Otto von Bismarck and the German Empire, he entered the Prussian Parliament in 1861. Again, in 1881, he became a member of the Reichstag, championing Bismarck's *Kulturkampf* against papal controls on education and literature, but when Bismarck left the liberal camp to impose tariffs, Mommsen denounced these policies. Shaken, Bismarck prosecuted him for libel; Mommsen was acquitted. A true National Liberal, he resisted all infringements of liberty on science, literature, and art and denounced the anti-Semitic movement of the 1880's.

Disillusioned with politics but not with scholarship, Mommsen continued to work with energy and diligence to the day of his death, accumulating a bibliography of more than nine hundred titles in German, Latin, and English. He died in his sleep in Charlottenburg, just outside Berlin, on November 1, 1903.

Literary Career

As an old man with iron-gray hair worn hanging over his shoulders, a wide, mobile mouth, a thin aquiline nose, and brilliant black eyes gleaming undimmed through strong glasses, Theodor Mommsen looked like a great poet. Indeed, in his youth, he had, with his brother and the German poet Theodor Storm, collaborated on a volume called *Liederbuch dreier Freunde* (1843; songbook of three friends).

It is this poetry that informs *The History of Rome*, the centerpiece of Mommsen's literary fame. Ironically, the circumstances that caused Mommsen to write the history of Rome to the time of Caesar's death were a matter of chance. Two publishers were present in 1848 at a public lecture that Mommsen gave in Leipzig. They asked the young historian to write a Roman history for their series. He was told to tell the story, giving results, not processes, to synthesize the best scholarship into a narrative that would appeal to the general reader. He succeeded brilliantly. By selecting characteristic details that would impress themselves on the reader's mind, Mommsen wrote three volumes of the early history of Rome that were full of vivid and memorable images. Dramatic battles, picturesque descriptions, lively profiles of Gaius Marius dogged in his last days by insanity, of Pompey as a hesitant general, of Hannibal in the Alps and in battle against Scipio Africanus at Zama—these images dominate the reader's view of Roman history. Mommsen's command of language coupled with his self-confident scholarship vivify Rome for the reader.

It may also be his "scornful opinionativeness" and the immediacy of his German patriotism and political involvement that bring the past to life. In later years, the historian declined to revise *The History of Rome*, although he had changed some of his judgments. He believed that the original three volumes were an artistic whole. Later historical evidence might alter his conclusions, but the genius and passion of the work depended on that first creative act. His efforts to expand *The History of Rome* to include the end of the Roman Empire failed, because Mommsen was unable to portray the emperors with any kind of sympathy or understanding. Nor could he instill a later volume, *Die Provinzen von Caesar bis Diokletian* (1885; *The Provinces of the Roman Empire from Caesar to Diocletian*, 1886), with the picturesque humanity of the earlier works. Although the scholarship and science were as rigorous as they had always been, the artistic presentation was subdued.

Theodor Mommsen's talents were not exhausted with the publication of *The History of Rome*. Indeed, that work was not his first, nor was it typical of his scholarship. His mastery of the techniques of historical investigation, including the specialized skills demanded of historians of the ancient world, had been recognized by colleagues as early as 1847, when he returned from Italy. The inscriptions that he collected in Rome, Naples, and throughout the Italian countryside—as well as studies based on his diligent mastery of ancient Italian dialects—had all been published. Mommsen's energies were not confined to discovery and analysis; everything that he learned, he published for the benefit of fellow scholars. His stature and recognition as a scholar were based on this commitment to real knowledge. His ability to synthesize and his belief that all history, including the history of the Roman law, was charged with human life were characteristics made most evident in *The History of Rome*, but they were also evident in his more scholarly investigations.

The project of collecting all the Roman inscriptions was, when he first returned from Italy in 1847, a dream, then a distant plan, and, finally, a reality when the Berlin Academy in 1858 gave him a chair and a salary and charged him to organize the collection of all the inscriptions in the Roman Empire. This honor depended not on the success of his popular history but on his recognized ability as a scientific historian. For twenty-five years he remained in charge of this mammoth project, sending young historians out into the field in England, Spain, Germany, and the East, requiring them to see the inscriptions with their own eyes before cataloging them. Mommsen himself edited many of the forty volumes that resulted from his leadership. All of them passed before his exacting eye. While he controled the research for this project, he also obtained financial support from the Prussian government. It was this series, *Corpus Inscriptionum Latinarum* (1863-1902; collection of Latin inscriptions), edited by Mommsen, which served as the source for his work on the Roman provinces of the empire.

Three other organizational projects came to his attention during these years. In 1873 he was asked to join the directorate of the Monumenta Germaniae Historica, which had been organized in 1818 by Baron Karl von Stein, a Prussian statesman and patriot, to collect all the sources of German history from the disappearance of effective Roman rule to the invention of printing. The organization had fallen on hard times in the years immediately preceding 1870, and Mommsen's strong will was needed not only to pursue research objectives but also to moderate the directorate's tendency toward intrigue.

In 1890, he helped found an organization, a journal, and a museum devoted to the project of exploring the Limes Germanicus, or Roman boundaries from the Rhine to the Danube. Finally, in 1892, he tried, with only partial success, to use his substantial international influence to unite the academies of Germany and Austria in a project organized for writing a *thesaurus linguae latinae*, a history of every Latin word up to the sixth century. Although his dreams for international cooperation were not fulfilled at that time, his efforts helped prepare the way for the International Association of Academies, which first met in Paris in 1901, and the promise of later cooperative research endeavors.

While he was engaged in these joint history projects, he continued to produce research of his own. In 1860, he published the *Geschichte des römischen Münzwesens* (history of Roman coinage), tracing the circulation and duration of types, the rights of minting, and the problems of trade and finance. He helped found the *Zeitschrift für Numismatik* and supported another joint project, the *Corpus Nummorum*, to collect inscriptions on coins. Shortly before his death he was investigating the possibility of beginning the collection of papyrus inscriptions.

The most important books published during these later years were those that accomplished the goal that he had set for himself at the beginning of his academic career. These were the three-volume *Römisches Staatsrecht* (1871-1888; Roman public law) and the *Römisches Strafrecht* (1899; Roman criminal law). The *Römisches Staatsrecht* is the codification of the Roman constitutional law that the Romans never did. This work surveys every institution of the Roman government and administration and buttresses the descriptions with authorities and inscriptions. Mommsen concludes and presents proof that Augustus had founded not a new form of government in the principate but a new magistracy set in an old framework that rested on a balance of power between the princeps and the Senate. He pictures Rome in evolution, not revolution, as the principate became the empire. The study of Roman criminal law, his last major work, was the final building block in the edifice that he constructed to understand the public law of Rome in terms of the Roman people.

Noted as one of the foremost German historians of the nineteenth century, Mommsen's unique contribution was his ability to combine rigorous scholarship with colorful writing. This talent, in addition to his absolute devotion to the search for truth, an indomitable will, his mastery of the minutest detail, the ability to put each detail in its proper place to aid in the interpretation of the whole, and his abiding belief that all law and all history depended on their human content—all these characteristics made Mommsen not merely a great historian but a great writer and scholar as well. The judgment of the Swedish Academy in selecting him to receive the Nobel Prize in Literature has been vindicated not only by the endurance of *The History of Rome* but also by Mommsen's example as a multitalented scholar. Although many of Mommsen's more opinionated judgments have been overthrown by subsequent historical research, his ability to harmonize the art and science of history and his faith in universal rather than specialized knowledge have been vindicated by later scholars and writers.

Bibliography

Primary
FICTION: *Liederbuch dreier Freunde*, 1843 (with Theodor Storm and Tycho Mommsen).
NONFICTION: *Römische Geschichte*, 1854-1856 (3 volumes; *The History of Rome*, 1862-1866, 4 volumes); *Geschichte des römischen Münzwesens*, 1860; *Zur Geschichte und Literatur der französischen Revolution von 1791-93*, 1861; *Römische Forschungen*, 1863-1879 (2 volumes); *Die Provinzen von Caesar bis Diokletian*, 1885 (*The Provinces of the Roman Empire from Caesar to Diocletian*, 1886); *Römisches Staatsrecht*, 1871-1888 (3 volumes); *Römisches Strafrecht*, 1899; *Reden und Aufsätze*, 1905; *Führergestalten der römischen Geschichte*, 1938.
MISCELLANEOUS: *Corpus Inscriptionum Latinarum*, 1863-1902 (editor).

Secondary
Broughton, T. Robert S. Introduction to *The Provinces of the Roman Empire* and *The European Provinces*. Chicago: University of Chicago Press, 1968. Focusing on the historiographical interest of these works, the editor discusses Mommsen's critical method, his use of a universal theme with a national focus, and his integration of a concept of law as the governing principle in organizing the material. The editor points to the impact that Mommsen's study of law had on his historical research and writing.
Fowler, William Warde. "Theodor Mommsen: His Life and Work." In *Roman Essays and Interpretations*. Oxford: Clarendon Press, 1920. This lecture, originally delivered in 1909, is a memoir of the author's acquaintance with Mommsen. It is valuable for the personal information as well as for the analysis of Mommsen's work as art and science by a younger historian of the Roman Republic. Gently, the author is a witness to Mommsen's shortcomings, emphasizing his energy and his dedication to scholarship.
Gooch, George Peabody. "Mommsen and Roman Studies." In *History and Historians in the Nineteenth Century*. London: Longmans, Green and Co., 1913. Reprint. Boston: Beacon Press, 1959. Gooch presents Mommsen in the full array of his abilities, clearly emphasizing his positive aspects while presenting and belittling the criticisms of his work. It is Gooch who puts Mommsen and Leopold von Ranke together alone in the first class of nineteenth century German historians. He presents a balanced view of Mommsen as writer and editor of inscriptions and texts.
Guilland, Antoine. "Theodore Mommsen." In *Modern Germany and Her Historians*. London: Jarrold and Sons, 1915. The author lauds Mommsen's

ability to synthesize and write in a lively and expressive style. Bitterly, he charges Mommsen with creating the insidious psychology of races to glorify German racial superiority to the detriment of every other people. He further accuses Mommsen of presenting war as a machine of progress and prosperity, of defining a historical law that tolerates the right and duty of the strong to crush the weak, and of teaching Germans to value strength while ridiculing honest citizens who try to save their country's liberty.

Knowles, David. "The *Monumenta Germaniae Historica.*" In *Great Historical Enterprises*. New York: T. Nelson and Sons, 1962. Describes the undertaking of Baron von Stein to set up an institution that would collect the sources of German history from the end of the Roman Empire to the printing press, and the role that Mommsen played in that endeavor.

Stern, Fritz. "On the Training of Historians: Mommsen." In *The Varieties of History from Voltaire to the Present*. New York: World Publishing Co., 1956. Stern presents the second half of Mommsen's "Rectorial Address," delivered at the University of Berlin in 1874. Mommsen discusses his views on history as an academic subject and the proper preparation for becoming a historian.

Loretta Turner Johnson

1903

Literature
Bjørnstjerne Bjørnson, Norway

Peace
Sir William Cremer, Great Britain

Physics
Antoine-Henri Becquerel, France
Pierre Curie, France
Marie Curie, France

Chemistry
Svante Arrhenius, Sweden

Physiology or Medicine
Niels R. Finsen, Denmark

BJØRNSTJERNE BJØRNSON
1903

Born: Kvikne, Norway; December 8, 1832
Died: Paris, France; April 26, 1910
Language: Norwegian
Principal genres: Fiction and drama

Bjørnson's works, characterized by a simplicity of style yet a profundity of thought, reflect the author's unwavering faith in the positive potential of the human spirit and its ability to triumph over physical and material constraints

The Award

Presentation

On December 10, 1903, Carl David af Wirsén, Permanent Secretary of the Swedish Academy, presented the Nobel Prize in Literature to Bjørnstjerne Bjørnson. In his presentation speech, Wirsén described how Bjørnson's childhood in the Norwegian countryside and his love of Old Norse literature combined to shape Bjørnson's vital literary style. Bjørnson's novels are characterized by their poetic realism and his dramas by their highly principled treatment of contemporary issues. Wirsén praised the melody of Bjørnson's poetry and what he called the "purity" of Bjørnson's writing, which always emphasizes the positive aspects of human nature.

Wirsén also commended Bjørnson for his support of traditional values, such as sexual morality and the sanctity of the family. Even though Bjørnson's high moral demands on mankind had been called extreme by some, Wirsén noted that this "noble severity" was preferable "to the laxness that is all too prevalent in the literature of our day."

Nobel lecture

Wirsén's presentation speech scrupulously avoided any mention of the possible political ramifications of the Academy's choice of Bjørnson. The Nobel Committee intended the prize solely as a reward for Bjørnson's literary achievement, not his political activities. Given the historical circumstances, however, a political interpretation of the award was unavoidable, and Bjørnson's acceptance speech indicates that he himself perceived the award as a political act: "After the long struggle in which I have taken part to gain for Norway an equal place within the Union, a struggle which was often bitterly resented in Sweden, may I say that the decision is a credit to her name."

Bjørnson's brief allusion to the political circumstances surrounding the award is followed by a statement of his perception of the role of literature. The lecture is, in effect, a concise statement of the principles which have informed Bjørnson's authorship for the previous three decades. In Bjørnson's

view, humanity is constantly moving forward, though the route may sometimes become circuitous and the driving forces may not always be clear. The
poet possesses the ability to see ahead, and his task is to guide the course of
human progress. In fulfilling such an important role, Bjørnson stresses that
the poet must not lay aside his understanding of good and evil. The author
cannot dwell on the ugly and evil in life, if his work is to serve as a beacon to
guide mankind.

Bjørnson points admiringly to the examples of William Shakespeare, Johann Wolfgang von Goethe, Friedrich Schiller, Esaias Tegnér, Adam Oehlen-
schläger, Henrik Wergeland, Lord Byron, and Percy Bysshe Shelley. In the
case of Shakespeare, although his art contains both violence and beauty, his
works are guided by a sense of poetic justice. The other members of this ros-
ter created literature of enduring beauty and nobility, reminiscent of the literature of ancient Greece. The comedies of Molière and Ludvig Holberg
constitute the antithesis to this great art: "They are as tendentious as they are
verbose." Such comedies serve to spotlight the weaknesses of humanity. Tragedy, on the other hand, evokes the sublime and calls forth the greatest
strength in mankind.

Graciously acknowledging two fellow contenders for the Nobel Prize that
year, Bjørnson cites, as the heirs of this literary pantheon, Henrik Ibsen,
"my old friend in Norway," and Leo Tolstoy, "a grand old man in a neigh-
bouring country to the east." According to Bjørnson, both are authors whose
works have been inspired by a higher purpose. Ibsen and Tolstoy have succeeded in combining tendentiousness and art in the proper proportions.
Bjørnson then names Victor Hugo as his own literary hero, because "at the
bottom of his brilliant imagination lies the conviction that life is good."

Bjørnson's view of art as noble and good does not preclude a consideration
of evil, but he firmly believes that there is more good in life than bad, and
any picture balanced to the contrary is distorted. It is the duty of the author
to mete out poetic justice. An author who simply seeks to arouse sensations
is incompetent. The author bears a responsibility to mankind, since he leads
the procession of human progress. Bjørnson concludes with a toast to the
Swedish Academy for "promoting all that is sound and noble in literature."

Critical reception

The award of the Nobel Prize to Bjørnson was almost universally con-
strued as a reward for the moderate position that Bjørnson had adopted with
regard to the dissolution of the union between Norway and Sweden. Some
Norwegians were prepared to engage in armed conflict to expedite the dissolution, but Bjørnson, an extremely influential voice in Norway, advocated
negotiation as the only acceptable means to effect the separation of Norway
and Sweden. The Swedish Academy had already made its decision to award
Bjørnson the prize before Bjørnson made his string of speeches urging mod-

eration and negotiation upon the Norwegians, but the general public had no way of knowing this.

The reaction to Bjørnson's winning the Nobel Prize ranged from disinterest to political innuendo. Both *The New York Times* (December 11, 1903) and *The Chicago Tribune* (December 11, 1903) were more interested in the awarding of the Nobel Prize in Physics to Marie Curie and of the Nobel Peace Prize to William Cremer. Bjørnson was merely mentioned in passing and described as a "Norwegian poet and dramatist." A reporter for the *San Francisco Chronicle* (December 11, 1903), however, understood the political implications of the award. The article in that paper stressed the fact that Bjørnson had received his prize from the hands of the Swedish monarch himself, who "expressed his joy over the improved relations between Sweden and Norway." The article then made the pointed observation that "hitherto Bjornson has been devoted to the home rule cause, and in his advocacy of the democratic ideas has opposed the throne. A recent meeting with the heir apparent, however, led him to alter his views of royalty. . . ." The suggestion is that Bjørnson was flattered by Swedish royalty into abandoning his advocacy of the dissolution of the union, and the Nobel Prize was a reward for this defection. The radical factions of Norway saw the award in the same light.

It has since become traditional to view Bjørnson's Nobel Prize as a classic example of political bias on the part of the Swedish Academy. In an article from the *Saturday Review* (December 4, 1965) entitled "Is the Nobel Prize for Literature Political?" Robert J. Clements claimed that the prize was given to Bjørnson specifically to lessen political tensions with Norway. Similarly, Girolamo Ramunni claimed in *La Recherche* (October, 1983) that the prize was a reward for Bjørnson's political conversion. Both Clements and Ramunni support their assertions by comparing the literary quality of Bjørnson's writing with that of Ibsen, who was denied the prize that year. Such arguments ignore the fact that, according to the terms of Alfred Nobel's bequest, the prize in literature was not meant purely as a recognition of literary talent but as a recognition of the combination of talent and idealism in literature. Although Bjørnson's literary talent may be debated, he was indeed one of the great idealists of the nineteenth century.

Biography

Bjørnstjerne Bjørnson was born on December 8, 1832, in the small village of Kvikne in Norway. He was the eldest child of Peder Bjørnson, a farmer's son who had become a parish priest, and Elise Nordraak, an aunt of the composer Richard Nordraak. Many have noted that Bjørnson seemed to have inherited his moralistic streak from his father and his artistic bent from his mother. His childhood in the Norwegian countryside developed in Bjørnson a deep and abiding patriotism to his native land.

After attending school in the town of Molde, Bjørnson moved to Oslo in 1850 to attend secondary school, where his fellow students included Henrik Ibsen and Jonas Lie. Bjørnson did not do well in school but managed with some difficulty to pass his student exam in 1854. During this time in Oslo, Bjørnson developed a keen interest in the theater and worked as a literary and dramatic critic for various publications. Bjørnson's literary career began in 1857, with the writing of the historical play *Mellem slagene* (1857; *Between the Battles*, 1948). From 1857 to 1859, Bjørnson was a stage director at the Norske Teatret (Norwegian theater) in Bergen, and, in 1858, he took over the editorship of *Bergensposten*. That same year, he married Karoline Reimers, who was an actress at the Bergen theater. In 1860, Bjørnson made his first sojourn to the European continent and spent much time in Rome. Bjørnson returned to Norway in 1863 and eventually became the director of the Christiania Theater. During the years from 1866 to 1871 he assumed the editorship of *Norsk Folkeblad*. In 1874, Bjørnson purchased a home in Aulestad, which became his primary base of operations for the rest of his life, although he spent extended periods of time in Rome and Paris and even made one journey to the United States.

Throughout his life, Bjørnson was interested in political and social issues, and over the years he made numerous political speeches. In the 1860's, Bjørnson agitated for the establishment of a Norwegian national theater and campaigned for greater independence for Norway within the union with Sweden. He supported Denmark during the war with Prussia but later urged reconciliation and cooperation between Scandinavia and Germany. In the 1870's, Bjørnson underwent a religious crisis and broke with the church. Bjørnson spent much of his time in the 1880's fighting bohemian immorality and supporting the women's movement. In the 1890's, Bjørnson stood in the forefront of the Norwegian movement to dissolve the union with Sweden. In his later years, Bjørnson became the advocate of the politically disadvantaged. Bjørnson came to the defense of Alfred Dreyfus in the celebrated Dreyful affair, and he was active on behalf of oppressed peoples, such as the Slovaks, the Ruthenians, the Czechs, and the Finns. Bjørnson was a pacifist who sought to instigate an international peace movement.

Bjørnson was much beloved in his native country. At the time of his acceptance of the Nobel Prize in 1903, he was considered by many to be the uncrowned king of Norway. When his health began to fail, Bjørnson traveled to Paris to seek a cure. He died in Paris on April 26, 1910, while working on a poem which was to bear the title "De gode gjerninger redder verden!" (good deeds save the world).

Literary Career

Bjørnstjerne Bjørnson was reared in an age of national Romanticism, when Peter Christen Asbjørnsen and Jørgen Moe were documenting the richness of the Norwegian folktale tradition and, in Denmark, Hans Christian Andersen was transforming the folktales that he had heard as a child into works of art. In his childhood years, Bjørnson had been known as quite a storyteller himself in the small town in which he lived. He experimented with poetry as a student, but, as Bjørnson himself related, he received his true calling to become an author while on a student trip to Stockholm. The monuments to Swedish culture in the capital city kindled in the young Bjørnson a sort of nationalistic envy. Bjørnson saw it as his task to create for the Norwegians a sense of their own history and to generate a body of literature that was distinctly Norwegian. Bjørnson applied himself to the effort in the capacities of playwright, novelist, and poet.

Between the years 1856 and 1872, the young Bjørnson wrote a series of historical plays which recalled the saga age, a time of Norwegian political and cultural dominance. In doing so, Bjørnson sought to remind the Norwegians of their glorious past. Bjørnson's saga dramas are generally tragedies. The action takes place at a time of historical transition: The spirit of the Viking age is becoming inexorably tamed by the influences of Christianity and culture. The tragic hero of the saga dramas is torn apart by the conflicting claims of the Viking ethos and of Christianity upon his soul. Since he cannot control the savagery of his own nature, the hero becomes displaced in a humanitarian society. In their day, Bjørnson's historical plays enjoyed a mixed reception. Although the saga dramas possess many brilliant moments, the consensus is that Bjørnson had not yet reached his acme as a playwright.

During the same period in which Bjørnson wrote his saga dramas, he also exercised his skills as a prose writer and wrote a number of country tales. These tales consisted of depictions from modern peasant life, intended to combat negative stereotypes of the peasants on one hand and idealizations of rural life on the other. They were meant to improve the self-image of the Norwegian peasants and to encourage them to take a greater part in steering the country. One of the earliest, and perhaps the most famous, of these tales, *Synnøve solbakken* (1857; *Trust and Trial*, 1858), was generally hailed for the freshness of its style. Inspired by the prose of the sagas, Bjørnson created a vigorous prose style which was perceived as distinctly Norwegian. Like the heroes of the saga dramas, the protagonists of Bjørnson's country tales must come to terms with the darker side of their natures. Whereas the heroes of the dramas are destroyed by this dark side, the main characters of the country tales are able to overcome their baser impulses. All the country tales end happily, sending forth the message that the good in mankind can triumph over the evil.

Bjørnson's poetry during the early part of this phase was patriotic, extolling the beauty of the Norwegian countryside. Many of these poems were set to music, and one of them became the Norwegian national anthem. After Bjørnson's first trip abroad in 1860, his poetry assumed a more classic form.

The latter half of this period is generally considered the height of Bjørnson's career as a poet.

In 1873, Bjørnson went abroad for a second time, and his writing underwent a transformation during his two-year journey. Bjørnson decided that he wanted to write not for Norway alone but for all Europe. This decision resulted in two modern plays about contemporary issues: *En fallit* (1875; *The Bankrupt*, 1914) and *Redaktøren* (1875; *The Editor*, 1914). *The Bankrupt* examines a phenomenon which had become all too common in an increasingly industrialized society and which became a favorite theme of authors during the age of realism. For the latter play, Bjørnson drew upon his own experiences as a newspaper editor and depicted the conflicts involved in such a role. These two plays constituted a breakthrough in Scandinavian literature. In 1869, Henrik Ibsen had written a modern drama entitled *De unges forbund* (1869; *The League of Youth*, 1890), which presaged his later social dramas, but Bjørnson's plays were hailed by the famous Danish critic Georg Brandes as having realized what Ibsen's drama had only promised. *The Bankrupt* enjoyed considerable stage success, especially in Germany. For this reason, Bjørnson is said to have paved the way for Ibsen's subsequent success in Germany.

Bjørnson took an active part in guiding Scandinavian literature into the age of realism and social debate. His novel *Magnhild* (1877; English translation, 1883), inspired by Gustave Flaubert's *Madame Bovary* (1857; English translation, 1886), appeared at the forefront of the cascade of literary works about discontented women which would flood the 1880's. The most controversial work of Bjørnson's career was the play *En handske* (1883; *A Gauntlet*, 1886). In that play, the heroine, Svava, throws her glove in her fiancé's face when she learns that he is not as pure as she. The suggestion that men should submit to the same moral demands as women was inflammatory and generated a violent debate about sexual morality in Scandinavia which lasted a number of years. Bjørnson became a central figure in the debate, and many believed that Bjørnson's demand of chastity for both men and women before marriage was unreasonable. Despite a large amount of negative press, Bjørnson did not abandon his position, and, in 1886, he rewrote *A Gauntlet* and gave it a sharper edge. The first version had ended on a note of reconciliation; in the second version, Svava does not relent in her demand for purity in her fiancé.

Bjørnson's finest play is generally considered to be *Over ævne, første stykke* (1883; *Pastor Sang*, 1893). The title literally translates as "beyond our power," and in this play, Bjørnson showed that he was not unaware of the dangers of ideals which call for mankind to extend itself beyond its capabilities. *Pastor Sang* is largely a reaction to the writings of Søren Kierkegaard and Ibsen's play *Brand* (1866; English translation, 1891), in which claims of a strict and ideal Christianity only succeed in drawing man away from the natural goodness of ordinary human existence. Ten years later, Bjørnson wrote a sequel to this play, *Over ævne, annet stykke* (1895; *Beyond Our Power*, 1913), in which the same reservations are brought to bear on the political, rather than the religious, arena. The play deals with the struggles between labor and capital; each side presents the other with extreme and impossible demands. One character comments, "When goodness throws dynamite, what then is good, and what then is evil?" Through most of his life, Bjørnson himself was a crusader with high ideals, devoting himself to one cause after another. In his last years, he continued to crusade, but he recognized the value of negotiation and compromise. Above all, he believed that issues should be settled nonviolently.

Most of Bjørnson's work has not endured. His writing was too deeply rooted in its time and its context to be of lasting interest to the world at large. Within Norway itself, Bjørnson enjoyed enormous popularity during and between the two world wars, since his work served as a rallying point of national sentiment. Since then, however, Bjørnson's popularity has been on the decline. In 1985, the Norwegian critic øystein Rottem summarized Bjørnson's status in Norway as follows: "His prose works are hardly ever read any longer, his plays are infrequently performed; as a lyric poet, he is for many of us primarily associated with singing lessons in school in the 1950's; his function today is to serve as a source of quotations on solemn national occasions." Even so, in his time, Bjørnson was a major author on the European scene, and literary scholars studying the latter half of the nineteenth century cannot ignore him.

Bibliography

Primary
NOVELS: *Synnøve solbakken*, 1857 (*Trust and Trial*, 1858); *Arne*, 1859 (English translation, 1861); *En glad Gut*, 1860 (*A Happy Boy*, 1869); *Fiskerjenten*, 1868 (*The Fisher Maiden*, 1869); *Brudeslåtten*, 1872 (*The Bridal March*, 1882); *Kaptejn Mansana*, 1875 (*Captain Mansana*, 1882); *Magnhild*, 1877 (English translation, 1883); *Støv*, 1882 (*Dust*, 1882); *Det flager i byen og på havnen*, 1884; *På Guds veje*, 1889 (*In God's Way*, 1890); *Mors hænder*, 1892 (*Mother's Hands*, 1897); *Absalons hår*, 1894 (*Absalom's Hair*, 1898); *Mary*, 1906 (English translation, 1909).
PLAYS: *Mellem slagene*, 1857 (*Between the Battles*, 1948); *Halte Hulda*, 1858 (verse); *Kong Sverre*, 1861 (verse); *Sigurd Slembe*, 1862 (verse; English translation, 1888); *Maria Stuart i Skotland*, 1864 (*Mary, Queen of Scots*, 1912); *De nygifte*, 1865 (*The Newlyweds*, 1885); *Sigurd Jorsalfar*, 1872; *En fallit*, 1875 (*The Bankrupt*, 1914); *Redaktøren*, 1875 (*The Editor*, 1914); *Kongen*, 1877 (*The King*, 1914); *Det ny system*, 1878 (*The New System*, 1913); *Leonarda*, 1879 (English translation, 1911); *En handske*, 1883, 1886 (*A Gauntlet*, 1886); *Over ævne, første stykke*, 1883 (*Pastor Sang*, 1893);

Geografi og kjærlighed, 1885 (*Geography and Love*, 1914); *Over ævne, annet stykke*, 1895 (*Beyond Our Power*, 1913); *Paul Lange og Tora Parsberg*, 1898 (*Paul Lange and Tora Parsberg*, 1899); *Laboremus*, 1901 (English translation, 1901); *På Storhove*, 1902; *Daglannet*, 1904; *Når den ny vin blomstrer*, 1909 (*When the New Wine Blooms*, 1911); *Samlede vaerker*, 1910-1911 (12 volumes).
POETRY: *Digte og sange*, 1870 (*Poems and Songs*, 1915); *Arnljot Gelline*, 1870 (English translation, 1917).

Secondary

Beyer, Harald. "The Young Bjørnson" and "Bjørnson and the Problems of Realism." In *A History of Norwegian Literature*, translated by Einar Haugen. New York: New York University Press, 1956. These chapters provide a general overview of Bjørnson's life and work. Beyer belongs to the older generation of Bjørnson scholars, whose views about Bjørnson's achievements are influenced by nationalistic sentiments and the image of Bjørnson as the poet-chieftain of Norway. This bias is interesting in terms of the history of Bjørnson's reception and does not prevent Beyer's overview from being quite informative. The footnotes to these chapters provide valuable bibliographical information about English translations of Bjørnson's works.

Bredsdorff, Elias. "Moralists Versus Immoralists: The Great Battle in Scandinavian Literature in the 1880's." *Scandinavica* 8 (November, 1969): 91-111. Bredsdorff's article describes the debates over sexual morality which raged through Scandinavia in the 1880's and Bjørnson's part in them. Bjørnson is examined in his role as social and moral crusader.

Downs, Brian W. "Bjørnson and Tragedy." *Scandinavica* 1 (May, 1962): 17-28. Bjørnson is best known as a dramatist, and Downs's article investigates a number of Bjørnson's most famous dramas in the light of the classical tragic tradition. Downs explores the paradoxes which arise in the plays, when Bjørnson, an eternal optimist, tries to come to terms with the tragic.

Noreng, Harald. "Bjørnson Research: A Survey." *Scandinavica* 4 (May, 1965): 1-14. Most of the scholarly research on Bjørnson has been written in Norwegian, and Noreng provides a useful and concise survey of this research. This survey also serves as a study of Bjørnson's reception until 1965. The article contains some biographical information.

Rottem, Øystein. "The Multifarious Bjørnson." *Scandinavica* 24 (May, 1985): 59-64. This article discusses the spate of publications about Bjørnson in Norwegian which appeared on the occasion of the 150th anniversary of Bjørnson's birth. Of greatest interest, however, are Rottem's own incisive comments about Bjørnson. As a member of a younger generation of scholars, Rottem is not in thrall to this national hero of Norway and is able to provide a balanced view of Bjørnson.

Sehmsdorf, Henning. "The Self in Isolation: A New Reading of Bjørnson's *Arne.*" *Scandinavian Studies* 45 (1973): 310-323. Although this article examines only one of Bjørnson's tales of country life, it addresses issues which are central to Bjørnson's authorship as a whole. Sehmsdorf's sensitive reading of *Arne* (1859; English translation, 1861) exposes a dark side of the tale, which was later minimized by critics and by Bjørnson himself.

Susan Brantly

1904

Literature
José Echegaray y Eizaguirre, Spain
Frédéric Mistral, France

Peace
Institute of International Law

Physics
Lord Rayleigh, Great Britain

Chemistry
Sir William Ramsay, Great Britain

Physiology or Medicine
Ivan Pavlov, Russia

JOSÉ ECHEGARAY Y EIZAGUIRRE
1904

Born: Madrid, Spain; April 19, 1832
Died: Madrid, Spain; September 15, 1916
Language: Spanish
Principal genre: Drama

Echegaray, equally renowned for his dramatic craftsmanship and the high idealism and energy of his creations, continued and enhanced the great tradition of the Spanish national theater

The Award

Presentation

The Nobel Prize in Literature was presented to José Echegaray y Eizaguirre in December, 1904, by Carl David af Wirsén, Permanent Secretary of the Swedish Academy. Echegaray shared the 1904 prize with Frédéric Mistral, the Provençal poet and philologist, and was the first Spaniard to be awarded this honor. At the beginning of the presentation, it was reiterated that the dual nature of the award did not constitute any diminishment of its prestige or literary value. Each of the two prizes was to be considered unique and stand on its own merits. The academy also chastised those who criticized the decision to award the prize to two aging and infirm writers at the end of their careers: "The jury does not have the right to ignore a still active author of European fame, merely because he is old." In fact, youthful strength and intellectual vigor were considered key to the dramatic art of Echegaray. Although the direct literary descendant of the great dramatists of seventeenth century Spanish Golden Age theater, Echegaray's perception of the world was modern and defiantly independent. His long career as a distinguished public servant emphasized his hatred of intolerance and his rigid devotion to duty in the face of controversy. In discussing Echegaray's contributions to the Spanish stage, the Academy also lauded the dramatist's manipulation of theatrical effect wedded to a poet's gift of language.

Nobel lecture

After the acceptance of the award, it has become the custom for the Nobel laureate to respond publicly in some manner, either by a short address at the banquet or by the presentation of a special lecture. In 1904, there was no such precedent. Neither Echegaray nor Mistral attended the banquet or responded afterward in any substantive fashion to their being awarded the Nobel Prize. Up to that time, it was customary for the ambassador of the recipient country to thank the Swedish Academy and to accept the award on behalf of the laureate. The ambassador would then respond to the remarks and congratulations of the banquet speakers and add his personal contributions to the eulogies of his countryman. In 1904, however, there was no official Spanish representative present at the banquet to accept the award on Echegaray's behalf. The Minister of France to Sweden replied to the Academy on cowinner Mistral's behalf and afterward simply accepted the prize for Echegaray, without any additional comment or elaboration. The Permanent Secretary, after speaking of Echegaray's ill health, explained that it also had been impossible for the Spanish minister to attend the banquet. Wirsén gave no reasons for this absence.

Critical reception

In 1904, in the opinion of the Spanish people, Echegaray was the beloved patriarch of Spanish letters. They responded to his Nobel Prize with euphoria. This was the same public which, after the performance of Echegaray's *El gran Galeoto* (1881; *The Great Galeoto*, 1895), was so overwhelmed that a national subscription was taken up to honor the dramatist.

This aura of venerability, however, worked against Echegaray outside Spain. In fact, one of the controversies surrounding the awarding of the 1904 prize was the advanced age of the recipients. (Both Echegaray and Mistral were septuagenarians.) Many critics complained that such a presentation went directly against the spirit of the Nobel Prize itself. Alfred Nobel, they insisted, wanted his prize to go to poor, struggling writers who needed public approbation and economic support at the beginning of their careers, not to two highly respected, financially independent public figures at the end of their literary creativity. The Swedish Academy hotly disputed this claim and, in the 1904 presentation, clarified its own concept of the spirit of the Nobel Prize and emphasized that the only rigid qualification was that the works of the honoree be of "exceptional importance."

In some quarters, the dual nature of the 1904 prize was also viewed as a weakening of its importance, and as was to be expected, in France Echegaray was only briefly mentioned, while in Spain Mistral's importance was downplayed. Any public reaction in other countries was almost nonexistent. In the United States, for example, more was made of the fact that no American had ever won the Nobel Prize than of the recipients themselves. In fact, the major American papers did not even deign to announce the presentation of the award. In *The New York Times*, for example, the only oblique reference to the prize was on December 31, when it reported that Mistral was going to use his share of the prize money to build a museum.

If the 1904 prize was greeted by silence or indifference abroad, however, in Spain itself, there was literary turmoil. Echegaray may have been the darling of the Spanish people, but he was repudiated by the emerging new generation of writers, the Generation of 1898. Their outraged response was immediate and bitter. The honor and acclaim awarded to Echegaray signified to these writers a betrayal of all for which they had fought in their literary careers. In their opinion, Echegaray's drama was the epitome of all that was risible and anachronistic in Spanish life and literature. Therefore, not content merely with simple criticism and protest meetings, writers of the stature of Miguel de Unamuno y Jugo, Rubén Darío, Pío Baroja, and Antonio Machado y Ruiz formally signed a virulent manifesto against the Nobel Committee's selection.

Other critics, however, more sympathetic to Echegaray, realized that the playwright had had the misfortune to be awarded the Nobel Prize too late. His theater belonged to the period from the 1870's to the 1890's and did not and could not represent the beginning of the twentieth century, which in Spain was dominated by Jacinto Benavente y Martínez, the Nobel laureate in 1922. It was unfair, they charged, to criticize Echegaray's theater in the light of recent dramatic techniques and content. They insisted that had Echegaray won the prize even ten years earlier, there would have been no negative outcry, only praise. (It is interesting to note that Benavente himself suffered the same critical fate as Echegaray. In 1922, Benavente was acclaimed by the public but rejected by the critics and emerging dramatists of his day.)

Surprisingly, one American magazine, *The Independent* (December 15, 1904), took up Echegaray's cause and praised the award as "a recognition of the power of the drama of ideas" and pointed out that Echegaray's "moral earnestness and intensity of purpose have aroused and impressed the people as other dramatists have failed to do." The "people" versus the critics—this was the focal point around which the reaction to the 1904 prize swirled.

Biography

José Echegaray y Eizaguirre was born on April 19, 1832, in Madrid, Spain. Although proud of his Basque heritage, he was to spend the greater part of his life in the capital and be a defender of the centralized power of the federal government. Echegaray in reality had three careers. During the first forty years of his life, he was as well-known and as honored for his mathematical and scientific skills as he was to be in later years for his literary achievements. In addition, Echegaray used his analytical abilities as well as a growing interest in economics and social policy to become one of the foremost public figures of his day.

Echegaray's educational background was in mathematics and civil engineering, and, after his graduation from the School of Engineering in Madrid, he became a practicing engineer. After only a short time in the field, however, he returned to Madrid to become a professor of pure and applied mathematics at his former school. During his teaching years, his fame spread throughout Europe with the publication of such treatises as *Teorías modernas de la física unidad de las fuerzas materiales* (1867; modern theories on the physical unity of material forces) and *Problemas de geometría analítica* (1868;

problems of analytical geometry). These two works are considered classics in their field, and in 1866 Echegaray was elected to the Academy of Exact Sciences of Madrid.

Long known for his progressive economic concepts and advocacy of free trade, Echegaray was a frequent contributor to many influential publications such as *La Razón* and *El Economista*. After the Revolution of 1868 and the fall of the Borbón dynasty, he actively entered public service and for the next seven years served in several cabinet posts, such as Director General of Public Works, Minister of Commerce, Minister of Finance, and Minister of Public Instruction. He was also elected to the Cortes, where he was famous for his brilliant and flamboyant oratory. During his tenure as finance minister, he was responsible for the creation of the Bank of Spain.

In 1874, however, his political career came to an abrupt end with the restoration of the Borbón monarchy. Facing increasing official displeasure, the Echegaray family emigrated to France, where Echegaray and other exiles, notably Nicholás Salmerón, founded the Republican Progressive Party. Echegaray's stay in France was brief, however, and after returning to Madrid, for the next thirty years of his life he dedicated himself exclusively to his literary career. Only in 1904, the same year he received his Nobel Prize, did he again accept public office, becoming Director of the Treasury. In 1883, he was elected to the Spanish Royal Academy. Echegaray died in Madrid on September 15, 1916.

Literary Career

Echegaray dominated the Spanish stage for a quarter of a century. Not only was he the idol of the theatergoing public, he was also the first Spanish dramatist to cause a sensation abroad. Actors and actresses clamored for the roles in the translated adaptations of his works.

Echegaray came late to the theater. Disillusioned with politics and disinclined to continue his earlier scholarly career, he wrote his first drama at the age of forty-two, but as finance minister, he was afraid to acknowledge its authorship publicly. Therefore he signed the play *El libro talonario* (1874; the checkbook) with the anagram Jorge Hayaseca, a ruse which fooled no one. At the time of his death in 1916, he had written sixty-eight dramatic pieces, the great majority works of a tragic nature.

Echegaray is generally classified as a neo-Romantic. He considered himself to be the direct heir to the lyrical and operatic Romantic stage of José Zorrilla y Moral and Ángel de Saavedra (the Duke of Rivas) not only in content but also in style. Echegaray loved the trappings and the melodramatics of Romantic theater and continued the Spanish tradition of writing serious drama in verse. The titles of two of his early successes testify to this melodramatic flair: *En el puño de la espada* (1875; on the sword's hilt) and *En el seno de la muerte* (1879; on the bosom of death).

Nevertheless, Echegaray's drama was not a carbon copy of that of his Romantic predecessors. Although his heart might remain in the past, his innovative and progressive mind was rooted firmly in the problems of the present. Therefore, an exotic hybrid was born. Cemented on a Romantic platform, there emerged an edifice of realistic and social theater, a liberal drama of thesis. One of the first targets of Echegaray, the freethinker, was religious intolerance. In *En el pilar y en la cruz* (1878; on the pillar and on the cross), he attacked Catholic extremism; in *La muerte en los labios* (1880; death on the lips), Calvinist persecution; and in *Dos fanatismos* (1887; two fanaticisms), he flayed both the atheist and the religious bigot.

The title of his 1882 play *Conflicto entre dos deberes* (1882; conflict of duties) best illustrates the governing principle and ideology of his theater. Never abandoning his Romantic conflict and melodrama, Echegaray with mathematical precision engineered a situation in which his protagonist had to face a soul-rending moral decision. In all of his plays, this agonizing dilemma ended in defeat. Echegaray was implacable in his insistence on a tragic outcome. The sublime in drama, he believed, "lay in pain, sorrow and death." His most famous work during his lifetime, *O locura o santidad* (1877; *Folly or Saintliness*, 1895), best illustrates this dramatic philosophy. The protagonist, Don Lorenzo, discovers on the eve of his daughter's marriage to a wealthy nobleman that he himself had been adopted and thus has no claim to the wealth and prestige he now possesses. His whole life has been a lie. In fact, he is the son of a servant, and the primary condition of his adoption had been that Lorenzo not inherit the estate. Unyielding in his dedication to what he considers his moral duty, Lorenzo reveals the truth even though his actions will destroy his family. His real mother in the meantime has burned the only corroborating evidence, and when Lorenzo cannot verify the truth, his family believes him mad and has him committed to an asylum. Finally, Lorenzo himself enters into the pretense of insanity: He becomes mad because the world wants him mad. Insanity has become the only acceptable exit for him out of his moral dilemma. This work, with its harrowing message that, in the modern world, true integrity can be seen only as madness has become one of Echegaray's lasting successes.

The play that caused an unprecedented outpouring of adulation and the one which is still reproduced in modern anthologies is *The Great Galeoto*. Its style shows Echegaray's gradual progression from verse to prose; only the prologue is written in verse. Performed throughout the United States as *The World and His Wife*, *The Great Galeoto* is a symbolic work in which the protagonist is the malicious but indifferent power of slander. Teodora and Ernesto (the young playwright living in her home) do not love each other. She is faithful to her much older husband Julián, but the outside world is sure that the two young people are lovers. The accumulating power of all the insinuations finally entraps the couple and leads to the death of Julián.

Teodora and Ernesto are thrown together at the end of the play, but only because there is no one else. The outside world, rejoicing in the fact that what it believed to be true and caused to be true is now true, has now deserted them.

Echegaray's sense of fatalism was influenced by naturalism, and many of his characters must suffer the consequences of their fathers' earlier sins. For example, in both *El hijo de don Juan* (1892; *The Son of Don Juan*, 1895), with its echoes of Henrik Ibsen's *Genganere* (1881; *Ghosts*, 1885), and *Malas herencias* (1902; bad blood) a hereditary disease destroys all hope in the protagonists' lives.

Echegaray was not unaware of his critics. *Un crítico incipiente* (1891; an incipient critic) is a light satire of his own theater and its critics, and in his posthumously published autobiography *Recuerdos* (1917; remembrances), he frankly discusses the critical response to his work.

Modern criticism of Echegaray's work has not been kind, and his drama has often been relegated to historical footnote. Critics have scorned his florid style, the mechanicalness of his plots, and the deficiencies in the psychological motivations of his characters, but no one can deny him the phenomenal success that he enjoyed during his lifetime. Also, he has generally, although grudgingly, been credited for rescuing the Spanish theater from oblivion and giving it international prominence. Benavente, the man who was to reign after him, declared that "he made multitudes think and feel. . . . In half a century there is no theatrical writing that can compare with his in quantity, variety or creative force."

Bibliography

Primary
SHORT FICTION: *Cuentos*, 1912.
PLAYS: *El libro talonario*, 1874 (as Jorge Hayaseca); *La esposa del vengador*, 1874; *En el puño de la espada*, 1875; *La última noche*, 1875; *Cómo empieza y cómo acaba*, 1876; *O locura o santidad*, 1877 (*Folly or Saintliness*, 1895); *En el pilar y en la cruz*, 1878; *En el seno de la muerte*, 1879; *La muerte en los labios*, 1880; *El gran Galeoto*, 1881 (verse drama; *The Great Galeoto*, 1895; also as *The World and His Wife*); *Conflicto entre dos deberes*, 1882; *Dos fanatismos*, 1887; *El hijo de Don Juan*, 1892 (*The Son of Don Juan*, 1895); *Mariana*, 1892 (English translation, 1895); *Malas herencias*, 1902.
NONFICTION: *Teorías modernas de la física unidad de las fuerzas materiales*, 1867; *Problemas de geometría analítica*, 1868; *Un crítico incipiente*, 1891; *Algunas reflexiones generales sobre la crítica y el arte literario*, 1894; *Recuerdos*, 1917 (3 volumes).

Secondary

Brett, Lewis E., ed. *Nineteenth Century Spanish Plays.* New York: Appleton-Century-Crofts, 1935. This volume contains not only a good edition of *The Great Galeoto* but also the most objective study of Echegaray and his drama. It also includes a good bibliography and brief descriptions of some of his representative work.

Díez-Echarri, Emiliano, and José María Roca Franquesa. *Historia de la literatura española e hispanoamericana.* Madrid: Aguilar, 1960. Although incorrect in some biographical information, the study of Echegaray under the rubic "El teatro postromántico" illustrates the predominant critical response to his drama. It treats his work as historical record and divides it into strict categories, such as symbolic works and thesis plays.

Kennedy, Ruth Lee. "The Indebtedness of Echegaray to Ibsen." *The Sewanee Review* 34, no. 4 (1926): 402-415. This is one of many comparisons between Ibsen and Echegaray. It is notable that, for the first time, precise chronology has been researched, making it evident that Echegaray could not possibly have read or seen Ibsen's plays before the performances of his own works, especially *The Son of Don Juan.* Kennedy also attempts a new critical appraisal of Echegaray and considers *Folly or Saintliness* one of the masterpieces of nineteenth century European drama.

Newberry, Wilma. "Echegaray and Pirandello." *PMLA* 81 (1966): 123-129. This is an interesting attempt to reevaluate the work of Echegaray. Newberry considers him to be a precursor to modern drama. The basis for such an opinion is developed through a comparison between the central ideas of Luigi Pirandello's and Echegaray's theater.

Shaw, Bernard. "Spanish Drama and English Farce." In *Dramatic Opinions and Essays*, vol. 1. New York: Brentano's, 1906. This short work is interesting because it is the opinion of one famous dramatist about another. The article also deals with the supposed influence of Ibsen on Echegaray. Shaw claims that Ibsen's *Ghosts* and *The Son of Don Juan* spring from two entirely different moral codes and worldviews.

Valbuena Prat, Angel. *Historia de la literatura española.* 2 vols. Barcelona: Editorial Gustavo Gili, 1965. Valbuena Prat tries to "explain" the Romanticism of Echegaray by placing him in historical and literary perspective. Echegaray's work is used as a pretext to discuss Spanish Romanticism on the one hand, and on the other, the Beneventian reaction to it.

Charlene E. Suscavage

1904

Literature
José Echegaray y Eizaguirre, Spain
Frédéric Mistral, France

Peace
Institute of International Law

Physics
Lord Rayleigh, Great Britain

Chemistry
Sir William Ramsay, Great Britain

Physiology or Medicine
Ivan Pavlov, Russia

FRÉDÉRIC MISTRAL
1904

Born: Maillane, Bouches-du-Rhône, France; September 8, 1830
Died: Maillane, Bouches-du-Rhône, France; March 25, 1914
Language: Provençal
Principal genres: Poetry and philology

As the finest modern Provençal poet and the organizer of the Félibrige, Mistral was primarily responsible for the nineteenth century revival of interest in the culture, language, and literature of southern France

The Award

Presentation

The Nobel Prize in Literature was presented to Frédéric Mistral on December 10, 1904, by Carl David af Wirsén, Permanent Secretary of the Swedish Academy. In his prefatory comments, the Permanent Secretary emphasized the Academy's intention that there would be no diminution of prestige, although the two writers who shared the 1904 prize, Mistral and José Echegaray y Eizaguirre, would necessarily each receive only half the usual monetary award. The Permanent Secretary also dealt with the Academy's annual problem: Alfred Nobel had intended the prizes to go to young men who needed money to further their careers, but in making its decisions, the Academy consistently felt itself bound to recognize older, even elderly, writers who were already established and prosperous.

The presenter nevertheless pointed out that the Academy's choice of Mistral clearly fulfilled another of Alfred Nobel's stipulations: that the Nobel laureate shall have produced "outstanding work of an idealistic tendency." Mistral had devoted his life to the realization of a dream: the revival of Provençal culture, language, and literature.

All Mistral's accomplishments were centered on Provence. In his poems, the dramas were played out against the Provençal landscape, combining realistic details of daily life with his people's wealth of myth and memory. Furthermore, by writing so beautifully in contemporary Provençal and by publishing a dictionary of the language, Mistral assured its preservation. Thus the Academy recognized Mistral's achievements both as a poet and as a philologist whose life had long been dedicated to attaining recognition for the land of his nativity.

Nobel lecture

Although Mistral could not travel to Stockholm to make a formal acceptance speech, he had expressed his thanks in an earlier letter to the Academy, commenting that the monetary prize would help in his efforts to revive Provençal, while the prestige of the award would make the world aware of the grandeur of the Provençal language.

Critical reception

As early as 1901, a number of German scholars had organized a campaign to secure the Nobel Prize for Mistral. According to rumor, the award was a certainty; indeed, Mistral had already received a number of letters begging for money when the Academy announced that Sully Prudhomme was the winner. Although he was nominated again in 1902 and 1903, Mistral was again passed over, despite the rapidly increasing popularity of his narrative poems. As a lifelong crusader against the centralization of culture, as an exponent of agrarian simplicity, Mistral was becoming more and more appealing not only to specialists in Romance literature but also to the general public.

Thus when Mistral was awarded the prize in 1904, there was no surprise, except at the fact that he was sharing the award with a writer who was far less well-known. Mistral's friends scoffed publicly at the ostensible reason for a joint prize, that too many people could not read Provençal. As one critic, Richard Aldington, stated, since Mistral's poetry was translated into French, the excuse was untenable.

The articles which commented on Mistral's award were in general blandly congratulatory, noting his achievements as a writer of Provençal epics and as the leader of the Provençal renaissance. For the public, however, the real interest in Mistral's selection lay in his decision about the award money. Thus an article in *The New York Times* headed "Poet's Ethnological Museum" (December 31) announced Mistral's intention of donating his prize money to the museum of Provençal life which he had founded in 1899.

As a result of the 1904 award, travel books included that museum in their listings. In fact, the laureate was sought out by literary pilgrims, and as he had hoped, the fact that the prize had been awarded to a Provençal poet has continued to draw visitors to the countryside he loved and to demonstrate the importance of his region's traditions and literature.

Biography

Frédéric Mistral was born on September 8, 1830, in Maillane, Bouches-du-Rhône, in the region of France called Provence. His father was a well-to-do landowner who had taken as his second wife the daughter of the local mayor. Mistral was the child of that second marriage, which was evidently a happy one. During his childhood Mistral was showered with affection by his mother, who enjoyed telling him the old tales of Provence. From his father, he absorbed religious devotion, a love of ritual, and a respect for custom. The future Nobel laureate read what he wished, particularly studies of nature and the works of Jean-Jacques Rousseau, and delightedly absorbed his natural surroundings.

When he was eight, Mistral began his schooling, and at thirteen, he entered the Collège Royal d'Avignon, later to be renamed in his honor. There he fell under the influence of a college usher, Joseph Roumanille, a deeply religious young man whose interest in lyrical poetry helped turn the student's ambitions to literature. Although Mistral proceeded from Avignon to the University of Aix-en-Provence, where he took a law degree in 1851, he knew that his wealth would enable him to choose whatever pursuit he wished; later, he gave up the law for poetry, a poetry which would promote the revival of the Provençal language and Provençal traditions.

For the rest of his life, Mistral advanced his cause by writing poetry and publishing magazines in Provençal, organizing folk dances and festivals, establishing cultural centers, and, finally, opening his museum in Arles. His contacts with the outside world only confirmed his conviction that what might be lost of the southern past was far more valuable than what the northern future promised; for example, when Mistral and a Catalan poet visited Paris in 1867, they became thoroughly disgusted with the politicians of the revolution, preferring instead their own conservative folk cultures. Back in Provence, Mistral plunged into a fascinating project: the compilation of a dictionary which would preserve all the dialectal variations of the Midi. Meanwhile, Mistral's private life was just as fulfilling. When he was forty-six, he married Marie Rivière, an intelligent woman with whom he lived very happily.

In his later years, Mistral received many honors for his accomplishments, including four prizes from the French Academy, before being awarded the Nobel Prize in 1904. After he won the prize, Mistral's life continued much as before, devoted to writing and to his beloved museum. On March 25, 1914, he died at Maillane, where he had been born nearly eighty-four years before.

Literary Career

It is a truism of criticism that Mistral's subject, setting, and theme are always Provence. It may seem surprising that the champion of a region which had lost its literary prestige, as well as its political power, during the Middle Ages should be so important in the nineteenth century. Yet Mistral's efforts to reestablish the importance of Provençal culture called forth a sympathetic response in a century which had begun with Romantic agrarianism and individualism and ended in protests against the soulless anonymity of an industrial society.

Appropriately, Mistral's first literary enthusiasm was Rousseau, whose Romantic insistence on the uniqueness of the individual, combined with a love of nature, appealed to the thoughtful boy who so enjoyed his childhood in the country. At Avignon, Mistral was inspired by the classical writers,

80 Nobel Prize

particularly Homer and Vergil, who in their epics had immortalized past cultures. While there, he also fell under the benign influence of Joseph Roumanille, who was already writing poems in Provençal and who later became one of the members of Mistral's literary group which was dedicated to the revival of the culture of Provence. The devout Roumanille put his talented student to translating the Psalms, a task which Mistral did not complete until late in his life. When he was eighteen, the future Nobel laureate composed his first original poem, a work in four cantos celebrating rural life.

By the time he received his law degree in 1851, he had decided to devote his life to literature. Unpressured either by the need for money or by parental expectations, Mistral was able to craft his works at his leisure, publishing them only when he was satisfied with every line, with every word.

The passion for Provence that was shared by Roumanille, Mistral, and the other young poets of the region resulted in the publication in 1852 of *Li Prouvençalo* (the Provençal), a collection of works by Provençal writers. From this publication most critics date the beginning of a movement dedicated to preserving the Provençal heritage. That movement was not officially named until 1854, however, when seven poets from the Avignon area formed a group named for an old Provençal story in which Jesus debated seven *félibres* (doctors) of the law. Although the application of the term is unclear, the intention of the group called the Félibrige was not. Their motto, "Lou souleu me fai canta" (the sun makes me sing), implied that their sunny southern land inspired them to poetry, as once it had the troubadours. Also like their ancestors, whose culture was crushed in the Middle Ages by northern French crusaders who were hot on the scent of heresy, the new Provençals felt threatened by the Parisian establishment, with its soulless bureaucracy bent on enforcing conformity in every aspect of life. At first, the poets limited their efforts to preserving the language and literature of their own immediate area, Provence, but in time they extended their interests to the cause of southern France, the area of the *langue d'oc* as defined in Roman times.

Mistral's first major poetic effort, composed over a period of seven years, was a Homeric epic, written in a seven-line stanza; unlike Homer, however, Mistral celebrated the heroism of peasants. In the invocation, he stressed this difference, asking the blessing of the Christian God, whose Son was of humble, rural birth. *Mirèio* (1859; English translation, 1867) is the story of a wealthy farmer's daughter, a beautiful fifteen-year-old girl named Mirèio, who falls in love with Vincent, the son of a poor basketmaker. Attacked and left for dead by one of the girl's rejected suitors, Vincent miraculously recovers, only to be spurned by Mirèio's parents. At this point, Mirèio decides to flee to the famous chapel of the three Marys in order to enlist their help. Mistral follows her step-by-step across the salt marshes of the Camargue. At last Mirèio arrives at the chapel, only to collapse of sunstroke. When Vincent and her parents arrive, she is dying, and her desperate lover chooses to follow her to Paradise.

Because he was aware of the small audience for poetry written in Provençal and yet was determined to write in that language, Mistral produced two versions of each of his poems, an original in Provençal and a translation, written either by him or by one of his friends, in contemporary French. When he took *Mirèio* to Paris in order to present it to Alphonse de Lamartine, the Romantic poet to whom he had dedicated the work, Mistral chose to read the opening lines in Provençal. After listening for a few minutes, Lamartine announced that France had a great new poet. Clearly Mistral was more than the mere peasant he had styled himself in the dedication.

The fact that *Mirèio* was a critical and popular success is indicated not only by contemporary praise but also by the fact that within the year Charles Gounod had transmuted it into operatic form. As it was translated into other languages, it continued to elicit enthusiastic response. Long after Mistral's death, it continues to be judged one of his finest achievements.

Mistral's next work, *Calendau* (1867), was also the result of seven years' labor. Set at the time of the northerners' brutal crusade against the Albigensians, the narrative poem tells the story of Calendau, a fisherman who, like Vincent, loves above his station, with one minor difference: Calendau's beloved is a noble girl married to a bandit-count. Like a classical hero, Calendau performs numerous labors, including killing the evil husband, in order to win his lady at last. Although *Calendau* did not have the emotional appeal of Mistral's first long poem, it was nevertheless admired for its poetic description, in this case of coastal Provence.

In 1874, Mistral exhibited his organizational skills by arranging a highly successful festival in Avignon in honor of Petrarch. Meanwhile, he had turned his poetic endeavors to the lyric, and in 1875 he published *Lis Isclo d'or* (the golden isles), a collection of sonnets, wedding songs, and other short poems celebrating the legends of Provence, its natural beauty, and its musical language. For some years, Mistral periodically returned to these lyrical poems, publishing his final edition of them in 1889. He also became increasingly interested in writing critical essays which promoted the cause of Provençal literature in theory as his poems exhibited its possibilities in practice.

It was not until 1884 that another narrative poem by Mistral appeared. *Nerto* was again set in the turbulent medieval period, which was particularly significant to Mistral because it was the time when Provence fell to its enemies. The historical period in which *Nerto* takes place is the final weeks of the Avignon papacy. The main narrative, however, is again a Christian love story with a legendary quality. The antagonist is neither a strict father nor a possessive husband, however, but the Devil himself, to whom a girl's soul has been promised by her father. When an earthly lover, the nephew of the Pope, abducts the girl from her convent, it seems that the Devil will win, but at the end of the poem, good triumphs, the hero repents, the Devil disappears, and the purified lovers enter Paradise.

While writing lyric and narrative poems, Mistral was also collecting material for a dictionary of the dialects of the Midi, and after twenty years of labor, the new Provençal dictionary began to appear in 1876. *Lou Tresor dóu Félibrige* (the treasure of the Félibrige), as it was called, was not merely a random collection, but instead a concentrated attempt to fuse the dialects in use in southern France into a new Provençal language. Because of the publication of this work, Mistral's contributions to philology were noted along with those to the poetic art in the Nobel Prize citation.

La Rèino Jano (1890; Queen Joan) was Mistral's only attempt at verse tragedy. Again, the story is set during the Avignon papacy, when the historical Queen Joan of Naples inevitably became involved in the struggle between the two popes, was deposed, and finally was killed. The work was only moderately successful, but it was followed by Mistral's last epic, which next to *Mirèio* is considered his best work. *Lou Pouèmo dóu Rose* (1897; *The Song of the Rhône*, 1937) was written in twelve cantos of unrhymed lines. Again, the story follows travelers through Provence, but this time, the setting is a barge moving down the Rhône River. As in his earliest works, there are two lovers of unequal station: the pilot's daughter, who considers herself a child of the river god, and a prince of Orange, whose station is more obvious. Like *Mirèio* and *Nerto*, the poem ends with the deaths of the lovers, but in Mistral's final epic, it is the machine age which destroys them, for the barge is hit by the first steamboat on the Rhône and the lovers are drowned.

When he received the Nobel Prize in 1904, Mistral was applauded as a writer who had already made his reputation. In his last decade, however, Mistral produced the third of his greatest works, *Moun espelido: Memòri è raconte* (1906; *Memoirs of Mistral*, 1907). Two years before his death, Mistral published a final collection of lyrics, *Lis Oulivado* (1912; the olive-gathering). A number of short stories were published between 1926 and 1930.

There is a certain serenity about the life and work of Frédéric Mistral. When he was young, he found his certainties: the worth of the individual, the beauty of language, the power of human love, and the dominion of divine love. He also found his mission: to revive a culture which had been crushed by tyrants. Although the language he hoped to revive is so little used today that almost all of his readers must depend on the French translations of his poetry, and although his name is no longer as important as it was during his lifetime, critics continue to praise him as an artist who has captured the spirit and the scenery of Provence in poetry whose beauty is unequaled.

Bibliography

Primary

POETRY: *Mirèio*, 1859 (English translation, 1867); *Calendau*, 1867; *Lis Isclo d'or*, 1875; *La Raço Latino*, 1879; *Nerto*, 1884; *La Rèino Jano*, 1890; *Lou Pouèmo dóu Rose*, 1897 (*The Song of the Rhône*, 1937); *Lis Oulivado*, 1912.

NONFICTION: *Lou Tresor dóu Félibrige*, 1876-1886; *Moun espelido: Memori è raconte*, 1906 (*Memoirs of Mistral*, 1907); *Prose d'almanach*, 1926-1930.

Secondary

Aldington, Richard. *Introduction to Mistral*. London: Heinemann, 1956. A highly readable assessment of Mistral, reflecting critical judgments of his work forty years after his death. Emphasizes the harmonious nature of his life and work. Throughout the book, Aldington stresses the importance of the everyday details of Provençal life in Mistral's poetry.

Downer, Charles Alfred. *Frédéric Mistral: Poet and Leader in Provence*. New York: Columbia University Press, 1901. Reprint. New York: AMS Press, 1966. Based on a dissertation and originally published in 1901, Downer's work is particularly interesting because of the description of his meeting with Mistral in 1899. Includes a history of the Félibrige, a chapter on their versification practices, and other useful information. Detailed studies of Mistral's works up to the date of publication. Includes an appendix and a bibliography.

Girdlestone, C. M. *Dreamer and Striver*. London: Methuen and Co., 1937. An exposition of all Mistral's poetry, intended for the general reader. The analysis of classical and Christian influences on Mistral is especially interesting. Includes extensive discussion of Mistral as an outstanding epic poet and useful hints on the pronunciation of Provençal.

"Homer of Provence." *Current Literature* 42 (May, 1907): 526-527. An evaluation of Mistral's importance as an epic poet, this article reflects his contemporaries' understanding of his relation to the classical tradition. An important work because it suggests Mistral's success in his lifelong goal of giving Provence its own epics.

Lyle, Rob. *Mistral*. Cambridge: Bowes and Bowes, 1953. A brief but enlightening volume and a good discussion of historical background to Mistral's work. Lyle intersperses biographical details with plot summaries of works and critical comments. An appendix contains ten pages of works in original Provençal.

Rosemary M. Canfield-Reisman

1905

Literature
Henryk Sienkiewicz, Poland

Peace
Bertha von Suttner, Austria

Physics
Philipp Lenard, Germany

Chemistry
Adolf von Baeyer, Germany

Physiology or Medicine
Robert Koch, Germany

HENRYK SIENKIEWICZ
1905

Born: Wola Okrzejska, Poland; May 5, 1846
Died: Vevey, Switzerland; November 15, 1916
Language: Polish
Principal genre: The Novel

Sienkiewicz was a historical novelist whose epic style and narrative grasp uplifted both the Polish people and the world

The Award

Presentation

On December 10, 1905, Carl David af Wirsén, Permanent Secretary of the Swedish Academy, presented Henryk Sienkiewicz with the Nobel Prize in Literature. The presentation outlined Sienkiewicz's literary career, showing how it was his achievement to embody the spirit of Poland for the world. Born in 1846, Sienkiewicz achieved maturity as a writer with the publication between 1884 and 1889 of his "Trilogia" (trilogy) of historical novels. Memorable scenes and convincing characters abound in these epic adventures. The Academy noted that, although a staunch Polish patriot, the author maintained historical objectivity and depicted the negative aspects of the Poles and the noble and human aspects of their enemies whenever appropriate. Next, his two contemporary novels were briefly praised for their insight and artistry while *Quo vadis* (1896; *Quo Vadis: A Narrative of the Time of Nero*, 1896) was represented as a high-minded portrayal of the crucial struggle between paganism and Christianity whose excellent literary qualities had brought it immense international success. Finally, it was noted that Sienkiewicz returned to the setting of Polish history in 1901 with *Krzyżacy* (1900; *The Knights of the Cross*, 1900), which portrays another dramatic episode in Poland's perpetual struggle for independence.

Sienkiewicz's achievement, the Academy noted, was rooted deeply in the traditions of Polish literature, especially the epic, which reached its full development in his work. All of this earned for him the devotion of the Polish people, to which the Academy added its award of the Nobel Prize.

Nobel lecture

Sienkiewicz, like other early Nobel Prize recipients, did not deliver a formal lecture. Instead, as befitted a writer of patriotic epics, his acceptance commented briefly on the political situation of Poland in 1905. At that time, Poland was not an independent nation. During the late eighteenth century, Russia, Prussia, and Austria had divided it among themselves. Poles steadfastly refused to accept this situation as permanent, and in reaction Russia and Prussia both maintained strict and often-brutal control over the areas of Poland that they so uneasily controlled. In spite of this suppression, Sienkiewicz, who was born and lived in the Russian section, became a symbol of Polish nationalism for many people through his writings. He recognized his symbolic status and commented on it to the audience at the Swedish Academy while Imperial Russia tottered in the midst of the ultimately unsuccessful Revolution of 1905.

In his acceptance, Sienkiewicz stated that the awarding of a Nobel Prize is not simply the glorification of an individual's accomplishments; it is also a recognition of the nation and people that produced that individual. Any nation would rightly feel honored by such an achievement, but, for a captive nation such as Poland, the award had even greater significance. As Sienkiewicz eloquently put it, "It has been said that Poland is dead, exhausted, enslaved, but here is the proof of her life and triumph. Like Galileo, one is forced to think '*E pur si muove* [But it does move]' when before the eyes of the world homage has been rendered to the importance of Poland's achievement and her genius." To emphasize his point further, Sienkiewicz modestly stated that there were a number of Polish writers greater than himself and concluded by thanking the Academy as a Pole for its acknowledgement of Poland.

Critical reception

From the time the Swedish Academy made its first award, it has been criticized for its decisions on the Nobel Prize in Literature. The award to Henryk Sienkiewicz, however, was reasonably well received. Sienkiewicz was first mentioned as a candidate for the Nobel Prize in 1901 and even received two votes in the balloting. When the Academy selected Sienkiewicz in 1905, some members suggested that the prize should be shared between him and Eliza Orzeszkowa, a leading Polish realistic novelist. Since the prize had been shared the year before, however, it was decided to keep it intact, and Sienkiewicz, the more eminent writer, duly received it.

The choice of Sienkiewicz was popular in part because his work, widely available in translation, was already well-known to the international reading public; in fact, he is one of the authors with the widest contemporary name recognition to win a Nobel Prize in Literature. Furthermore, although the supporters of Leo Tolstoy were again disappointed by the Swedish Academy's decision, events conspired to mute any complaints that they might have had about passing over Tolstoy in favor of a Russian subject who was actually a symbol of Polish nationalism, for, as noted above, the announcement and awarding of the prize took place at the height of the Revolution of 1905 in Russia.

The American and English reaction to the way in which the Nobel Prizes of 1905 were awarded in general was one of mild nationalistic disgruntlement. At that point in time no Americans and only a few Englishmen had received one of the prizes. *The Outlook*, echoed by *Literary Digest*, however, defended the Swedish Academy from charges of unfairness. Furthermore, *The Independent* and *Literary Digest* both specifically found Sienkiewicz to be an inspiring patriotic novelist who was quite deserving of the prize.

At the same time, some people saw a paradox in the awarding of a Nobel Prize in Literature to Sienkiewicz, in spite of his fame and well-recognized literary talents. Alfred Nobel had established his foundation to further peace and most of Sienkiewicz's fiction deals with intense wartime situations. By the standards of the late nineteenth century, the novels of the trilogy were considered almost too bloody and graphic for female readers. *The Independent* raised this objection but ultimately dismissed it, since Sienkiewicz's purpose was to inspire patriotism and not glorify war. Patriotism, however, was the issue with which *The Cosmopolitan* began its objections to Sienkiewicz as a Nobel laureate. *The Cosmopolitan* submitted the proposition that patriotism and war went hand in hand. Awarding a Nobel Prize in Literature to a patriotic novelist therefore contradicted Alfred Nobel's intentions.

Biography

Henryk Sienkiewicz was born on May 5, 1846, at Wola Okrzejska in Russian-occupied Poland. His parents, Josef Sienkiewicz and Stefania Cieciszowska, belonged to lesser gentry families with strong military traditions. From 1866 to 1871 he attended Warsaw University, where he came into contact with then-prevalent positivist ideas. After leaving the university without graduating, he took up journalism in 1872, becoming a regular writer for the *Gazeta Polska* in 1875. He traveled extensively from 1876 to 1879 in the United States and Western Europe. Eventually returning to Warsaw, he resumed work for the *Gazeta Polska* and later became the editor of the new daily *Słowo* in 1882. Meanwhile, in 1881 he had married Maria Szetkiewicz, with whom he had two children. Unfortunately, Maria suffered from tuberculosis, which ultimately led to her death in 1885, just as Sienkiewicz's career as a novelist began to gain wide popular recognition.

During 1891 and 1892, Sienkiewicz took a break from a hectic writing schedule and made an extended visit to Egypt and central Africa. At about this time he met the young and attractive Maria Romanowska, who became infatuated with him. After some hesitation, he decided to marry her in 1894, but the marriage ended disastrously after one month. Although badly shaken, Sienkiewicz quickly recovered and began writing *Quo Vadis*, which appeared in 1896. As a result of its success, during the next five or six years he reached the height of his popularity throughout the world, a popularity which was dramatic enough to be called the "epidemia Sienkiewicziana." Poles even went so far as to organize a subscription and buy him the former family estate of Oblegorek in 1900 as a gift for his jubilee celebration. He married his third wife, the solid Maria Babska, in 1904 and this time achieved a lasting union. The next year he received the Nobel Prize, although his international popularity was already fading. World War I forced him into self-imposed exile in Switzerland, where he engaged in relief work for Polish war victims and later died of arteriosclerosis on November 15, 1916.

Literary Career

Henryk Sienkiewicz's entire life as a writer was overshadowed by his situation as a patriotic member of a defeated and politically obliterated nation while living in the zenith of European civilization. Although he did not adopt the overall optimism of that age, he also never succumbed to any debilitating pessimism that his homeland's iron captivity might have aroused. His literary career began early. *Na marne* (1872; *In Vain*, 1899) was his first published work, an immature, autobiographical novel based on student life at the university which the newspaper *Wieniec* serialized. His true training as a writer, however, came as a result of his work as a "chronicler" for the *Gazeta Polska*.

Sienkiewicz's "chronicles" were based on the type of light nonfiction writings about literary topics and current events known as *feuilletons* in French newspapers. The discipline and constant editorial scrutiny that went along with the production of these chronicles greatly improved his style between 1872 and 1875. Furthermore, the foreign travel associated with his job as a reporter widened his horizons from 1876 to 1878. His journalistic letters from the United States exercised his skills of descriptive reporting, and he continued to sharpen them as he traveled through Europe lecturing on his American adventures.

During these same years Sienkiewicz also wrote short stories and novellas. The positivism of his university days, with its practical and scientific outlook, influenced the short fiction that he wrote from 1872 to 1878. "Hania" (1876; English translation, 1897), *Szkice węglem* (1877; charcoal sketches), and "Janko muzykant" (1879; "Yanko the Musician," 1893) all deal with the social problems associated with rural and peasant life in a changing Poland. Sienkiewicz lost his attraction to positivism about 1879, when his stories started to concentrate on either relations between Poles and their conquerors, as in "Z pamietnika poznanskiego nauczyciela" (1879; "From the Memoirs of a Poznan Tutor," 1898), or the trials of Polish settlers in the United States, described by "Za chlebem" (1879; "For Daily Bread," 1898). By 1880 he had attained enough success as a writer for his fiction to be gathered into a collected edition. A few years later the now-married Sienkiewicz adopted a more settled life-style as the editor of the new daily newspaper *Słowo*.

It was during this same period that Sienkiewicz began a radically different type of fiction writing. The change first manifested itself with the appearance of "Niewola Tatarska" (1880; "Tartar Captivity," 1897). This short story constituted the writer's first use of a historical setting. Readers greatly approved of the result, although his positivist friends saw it as another manifestation of Sienkiewicz's gradual rejection of their mode of thought.

From that point onward, Sienkiewicz immersed himself in historical studies and sources dealing with Poland in the seventeenth century. The result was a masterpiece of historical fiction, his trilogy. He began writing the first part of it in 1882, and on May 2, 1883, the first installment of *Ogniem i mieczem* (1884; *With Fire and Sword: An Historical Novel of Poland and Russia*, 1890) appeared in *Słowo*. It was serialized in daily installments until March 1, 1884, a period of forty weeks. Then, following nineteenth century convention, it was published as a three-volume book. *With Fire and Sword* is set in the commonwealth of Poland at the time of the insurrection of Bohdan Chmielnicki and the Cossacks of the Ukraine during the period 1647-1651. The story centers on the adventures of Jan Skrzetuski, a young Polish nobleman, and his comrades-in-arms Longinus Podbienta, Zagloba, and Michael Wołodyjowski. Characters, whether heroes or villains, are never painted in rigid black-and-white, with the exception of Skrzetuski, who is too good to be totally convincing. That minor flaw, however, did little to deflect readers from their enthusiasm for the novel.

Sienkiewicz had made his reputation as a novelist, and he quickly reinforced it with *Potop* (1886; *The Deluge: An Historical Novel of Poland, Sweden, and Russia*, 1891), the second part of his trilogy, which began appearing in serialized form in December, 1884. It took Sienkiewicz until September, 1886, to complete this extremely long novel. *The Deluge* quickly proved popular with readers, and it was published as a six-volume book in 1886. The war between Poland and Sweden from 1655 to 1660 provided the historical background for this novel, though the personal aspect of the story concerns the difficult romance of Olenka and the originally ne'er-do-well, but ultimately heroic, Andrzej Kmicic. Kmicic is not Jan Skrzetuski. Instead, he is a more fully human character, possessing both strengths and weaknesses. In many ways he serves as a metaphor of the troubled and self-destructive Poland of the seventeenth century.

In 1887, pausing somewhat longer between books, Sienkiewicz began writing *Pan Wołodyjowski* (1887-1888; *Pan Michael: An Historical Novel of Poland, the Ukraine, and Turkey*, 1893), the final part of the trilogy. It was serialized from June, 1887, until May, 1888, after which it was quickly published as a book. This time the hero is Michael Wołodyjowski, a character who figured prominently in the first and second books of the trilogy. Although a great warrior, the short, plain Wołodyjowski spends much of his life in frustration and loneliness—until he meets and marries Basia. Yet just when Wołodyjowski and his wife find happiness, they are sent to garrison duty on the Turkish border at Kamienic. Harrowing adventures, treason, and finally the heroic death of Wołodyjowski await the couple as the Turkish-

Tartar invasion of 1672 begins. The great Polish hero John Sobieski later saves the day with a great victory over the Turks at Chocim in 1673, ending the novel ambiguously on a combined note of national salvation and personal loss.

As one of its great practitioners, Sienkiewicz believed that the historical novel was a legitimate form of writing and defended it vigorously in the essay "D powies ci historycznej" (on the historical novel) in 1889. In his opinion, it was wrong to judge the historical novel by the same standards as history, because the novel involved the use of historical imagination to a much greater degree. The novelist filled the gaps where the historian lacked information, but this imaginative approach did not mean that historical fiction could not be an accurate depiction of the past. If the novelist did his research well, then the spirit of a bygone age could be recaptured. Sienkiewicz certainly applied those standards conscientiously, since his trilogy has proved, after much criticism, to be a reasonably accurate presentation of seventeenth century Poland. Each part of the trilogy includes a great patriotic hero from Polish history: Jeremi Wisniowiecki in *With Fire and Sword; The Deluge's* defender of Czenstochwa, Prior Kordecki; and the future king John Sobieski in *Pan Michael.* Repeatedly, Poland is saved by patriotism from seemingly unstoppable foreign invasions. It was a message that did not escape the notice of late nineteenth century Poles living under foreign domination. At a difficult time in their history, Sienkiewicz gave them hope and they loved him for it.

After the trilogy, Sienkiewicz returned to contemporary settings for his next two novels: *Bez dogmatu* (1891; *Without Dogma,* 1893) and *Rodzina Połanieckich* (1895; *Children of the Soil,* 1895). It was not a popular move with the large readership that he had built as a result of his historical novels. *Without Dogma* is a psychological study of the destructive effects of aristocratic decadence which is brought on by a lack of values, or dogmas. The virtues of hard work, solid family life, and the return to the land form the focus of *Children of the Soil.* In promoting such social morality, Sienkiewicz almost seems to be returning to his former positivist outlook. In fact, such novels of social and psychological analysis were quite fashionable during the 1890's, although his two attempts did little to enhance Sienkiewicz's reputation with the reading public or most later literary scholars.

Quo Vadis is the work that truly gave Sienkiewicz an international reputation. Its appearance marked his return to the genre of the historical novel, a decision which was foreshadowed by the short story "Pojdzmy za Nim" (1892; "Let Us Follow Him," 1897). The Rome of Nero provides the setting for *Quo Vadis,* the love story of Ligia, a Christian member of a barbarian tribe, and the pagan Roman Vinicius. Once again Sienkiewicz did his historical research well and produced an authentic portrait of imperial Rome and early Christianity. The uplifting nature of the story made it his most popular work and led to its translation into many languages. Some people thought that the obscure title would injure its sales in the United States, but Sienkiewicz's existing reputation and the compelling story soon overcame any sales resistance (there were twenty-seven American editions from its publication in 1896 through 1905). *Quo Vadis* became a household phrase. The novel was quickly adapted for the stage and later was made into a film three times (in Italy, 1912 and 1924; in the United States, 1951). *Quo Vadis* remained in print into the 1980's and is indisputably Sienkiewicz's best-known work.

From ancient Rome, Sienkiewicz immediately returned to a Polish setting, this time the Middle Ages, with *The Knights of the Cross*. Its action revolves around the Poles' defeat of the cruel and aggressive Order of the Teutonic Knights at the Battle of Grunwald in 1410. There is the usual love story intermingled in the history. Patriotic themes dominate this story, since Grunwald is one of Poland's proudest victories, while the Teutonic Knights later evolved into Prussia, one of Poland's oppressors in Sienkiewicz's day. The novel's ability to inspire patriotism remains strong and was evidenced once again when the British issued a new translation of it in 1943 as they, too, faced a cruel Teutonic threat.

After 1900, Sienkiewicz's literary powers faded along with his popularity. Neither was revived significantly by the awarding of the Nobel Prize in 1905. Meanwhile, Sienkiewicz returned to the time of John Sobieski in the novel *Na polu chwaly* (1903-1905; *On the Field of Glory*, 1906). Readers were disappointed, however, since the title implied that the climax would be the legendary lifting of the siege of Vienna in 1683. Instead, the novel stopped short of that climactic event, causing people to retitle it jokingly "On to the Field of Glory." Before Sienkiewicz died in 1916, World War I had interrupted his work on a novel about the Polish legions who fought with Napoleon Bonaparte, an extremely popular historical episode among Poles.

Henryk Sienkiewicz remains an important figure in the Polish national literary tradition. In 1929 a collective edition of his works was begun by Ignacy Chrzanowski which, although never completed, went to forty-six volumes. It was not until Julian Krzyzanowski began the project anew in 1948 and completed it in 1955 that Poland finally got a definitive collected edition of Sienkiewicz's works. Simply called *Dziela* (works), it comprised sixty volumes. On the stage of world literature, however, the reputation of Sienkiewicz has faded to virtual obscurity. The genre of the historical novel, of which he was a master, is no longer at the cutting edge of contemporary fiction. Most modern readers would find his novels too long and romantic, marveling that such an author would win a Nobel Prize. This judgment is too harsh; among Poles and literary scholars he will continue to be remembered quite rightly for the artistry of his epic trilogy. His lack of a continued general appeal to readers is a clear indication of the cultural gap that the tumultuous events of the twentieth century have created between the literary tastes of the late nineteenth century and those of the present day.

Bibliography

Primary

NOVELS: *Na marne*, 1872 (*In Vain*, 1899); *Szkice węglem*, 1877; *Ogniem i mieczem*, 1884 (3 volumes; *With Fire and Sword: An Historical Novel of Poland and Russia*, 1890); *Potop*, 1886 (6 volumes; *The Deluge: An Historical Novel of Poland, Sweden, and Russia*, 1891); *Pan Wołodyjowski*, 1887-1888 (*Pan Michael: An Historical Novel of Poland, the Ukraine, and Turkey*, 1893); *Bez dogmatu*, 1891 (*Without Dogma*, 1893); *Rodzina Połanieckich*, 1895 (*Children of the Soil*, 1895); *Quo vadis*, 1896 (*Quo Vadis: A Narrative of the Time of Nero*, 1896); *Krzyżacy*, 1900 (*The Knights of the Cross*, 1900; also as *The Teutonic Knights*, 1943); *Na polu chwały*, 1903-1905 (*On the Field of Glory*, 1906); *W pustyni i w puszczy*, 1911 (*In Desert and Wilderness*, 1912).

SHORT FICTION: *Yanko the Musician and Other Stories*, 1893; *Lillian Morris and Other Stories*, 1894; *Hania*, 1897; *Let Us Follow Him and Other Stories*, 1898; *For Daily Bread and Other Stories*, 1898; *Sielanka: A Forest Picture and Other Stories*, 1898; *Life and Death and Other Stories*, 1904; *Tales*, 1931; *Western Septet: Seven Stories of the American West*, 1973.

NONFICTION: *Listy z Afryki*, 1891; *Listy z podróży do Ameryki*, 1896 (serialized 1876-1878; *Portrait of America*, 1959).

MISCELLANEOUS: *Dzieła*, 1948-1955 (60 volumes).

Secondary

Daniells, Roy. "Sienkiewicz Revisited." In *The Tradition of Polish Ideals: Essays in History and Literature*, edited by W. J. Stankiewicz. London: Orbis Books, 1981. Although without documentation, this essay persuasively argues that *The Knights of the Cross* is a significant historical novel that transcends the usual limits of that genre to inspire patriotism and commitment in its readers.

Gardner, Monica M. *The Patriotic Novelist of Poland: Henryk Sienkiewicz*. London: J. M. Dent and Sons, 1926. A chronological survey of Sienkiewicz's works. Gardner admiringly and narrowly focuses on their patriotic aspects. Although her analysis lacks depth, it still supplies important details about the early twentieth century Polish reaction to Sienkiewicz, along with useful and detailed plot summaries.

Giergielewicz, Mieczyslaw. *Henryk Sienkiewicz*. New York: Twayne Publishers, 1968. The best modern book-length survey of Sienkiewicz's life and works. Its conclusions are firmly based on a close study of his works and of the secondary literature. A biographical chapter is followed by seven chapters that critically appraise his writings in chronological order. An annotated bibliography provides excellent guidance for further reading.

_____. "Henryk Sienkiewicz's American Resonance." *Antemurale* 10 (1966): 256-354. This heavily documented and lengthy article describes the enthusiastic American reception of Sienkiewicz's works with some sidelights on the cooler English reaction. A substantial annotated bibliography lists contemporary American book reviews of Sienkiewicz's writings along with biographical and critical articles.

Krzyzanowski, Julian. *A History of Polish Literature.* Translated by Doris Ronowicz. Warsaw: PWN-Polish Scientific Publishers, 1978. First published in Polish in 1972, this survey by the editor of an edition of Sienkiewicz's works gives a brief, very positive appraisal, especially of the use of historical settings and narrative technique. In addition, the patriotic themes in Sienkiewicz's works are discussed sympathetically. Compare this with the rather negative judgment of another Polish Nobel Prize winner in Czesław Miłosz's *The History of Polish Literature* (1969, 1983).

Thompson, Ewa M. "Henryk Sienkiewicz and Alexey Konstantinovich Tolstoy: A Case of Creative Borrowing." *Polish Review* 17, no. 3 (1972): 52-66. Postulates that Sienkiewicz adopted ideas from Tolstoy's *Knyaz Serebryany* (1862; *Prince Serebrenni,* 1874) and used them in his trilogy. Sienkiewicz, however, used those ideas much more artistically. This judgment leads to a perceptive reevaluation of the trilogy as a saga about the recognition of universal human tragedy and not simply as a nationalistic epic.

Welsh, David. "Two Contemporary Novels of Henryk Sienkiewicz: A Reappraisal." *Slavic and East European Journal* 16, no. 3 (1972): 307-12. A convincing reevaluation of *Without Dogma* and *Children of the Soil* which stresses their psychological insights and places them in the context of the general European popularity of novels of analysis during the 1890's. It concludes that they have stood the test of time and probably have more appeal to modern readers than the rest of Sienkiewicz's fiction.

Ronald H. Fritze

1906

Literature
Giosuè Carducci, Italy

Peace
Theodore Roosevelt, United States

Physics
Sir J. J. Thomson, Great Britain

Chemistry
Henri Moissan, France

Physiology or Medicine
Camillo Golgi, Italy
S. Ramón y Cajal, Spain

GIOSUÈ CARDUCCI
1906

Born: Val di Castello, Italy; July 27, 1835
Died: Bologna, Italy; February 16, 1907
Language: Italian
Principal genres: Poetry and literary criticism

Carducci's poetry is distinguished by a fervid patriotism expressed in classical rhythms and characterized by restraint, dignity, and sonority

The Award

Presentation

In presenting the dying Giosuè Carducci with the Nobel Prize in Literature on November 24, 1906, Carl David af Wirsén, Permanent Secretary of the Swedish Academy, cited two major characteristics of the poet's work. Noting first the influence of Carducci's father, a physician who strongly espoused the cause of Italian political liberty, he emphasized that the young poet early became a champion of Italian unity and that his reading of the classics and the histories of Rome and of the French Revolution confirmed his revolutionary principles.

Such patriotism was the wellspring of his inspiration and the source of much of Carducci's poetry between 1850 and 1870, a period which coincided exactly with the crucial stages of Italy's struggle for independence against the Austrian empire. The presenter noted that such patriotic fervor often reflected "a ferocious assault" on Christianity, particularly the Roman Catholic church, which Carducci saw as an impediment to Italian political freedom.

A second characteristic of Carducci's poetry stemmed from his lifelong devotion to scholarship. Citing his role as a great teacher and scholar, af Wirsén observed that the political tone of the earlier period was softened into a sonorous, lyrical beauty by the poet's adaptation of classical meters to modern Italian. In his best work, notably *Odi barbare* (1877; *Barbarian Odes*, 1950), tragic tone and natural imagery combined to achieve "the pinnacle of perfection."

Finally, af Wirsén summarized his presentation by admitting that, though criticism against Carducci's work could be justified, the poet nevertheless was a supreme example of the spirit of patriotism and idealism, creating works of "rare force" and freshness of style.

Nobel lecture

Seventy-one years old and ill with pneumonia, which was to kill him only three months later, Carducci was unable to travel to Stockholm to receive his award. The Permanent Secretary of the Swedish Academy therefore spoke in Italian at the awards banquet, praising Carducci's great poetic spirit and noting the signal honor his election meant to Italy, as Carducci was the first Italian writer to win the Nobel Prize.

Critical reception

Few writers have received such unanimous recognition for a life's work as did Giosuè Carducci. In reporting on his Nobel award, *The New York Times* (November 25, 1906) spoke for the established literary community when it cited Carducci's position as the greatest of modern Italian poets. The article declared that his reputation, like that of the poet Robert Browning, would grow steadily as his work gradually became better understood. Browning's reputation, in fact, has outstripped that of Carducci, but the assessment is indicative of the popularity of the poet as well as the appropriateness of the Academy's choice. Three months later, *The New York Times* echoed its praise in its obituary of the poet (February, 1907), noting that his death was an occasion for national mourning; an estimated forty thousand persons attended his funeral in Bologna.

Reviews and popular magazines shared this favorable view. *Current Literature* (April, 1907) mourned the passing of Carducci as one of the great poets of modern times. Perhaps taking a cue from *The New York Times*, the anonymous reviewer went on to suggest that much of Carducci's work had not become well-known beyond Italy because of its "intense nationalism" and because of the individuality of the poet's diction, particularly his use of metaphor. *The Dial* of Chicago praised Carducci as the world's greatest living poet at the end of the nineteenth century.

Such enthusiasm for Carducci's work extended even to his prose. A contemporary review in *The Times* (London) called attention to the poet's "magniloquent" style of oratory and the unsurpassed sonority of his discourse. The commentator also noted Carducci's indelible influence on a generation of poets, particularly Gabriele D'Annunzio and Giovanni Pascoli.

Though the mass of critical opinion emphasized Carducci's role as a nationalistic poet—one who fought for his country's independence with the pen rather than the rifle—the bulk of examples chosen from his work focused not so much on the fervid emotion of his poems as on the lyrical, almost romantic imagery of his mature compositions. Despite the critical acclaim, however, some critics argued that the poet had not always succeeded in adapting the classic Latin rhythms and forms to modern themes, a defect not cited by the Academy, which regarded such adaptation as largely successful. By 1913, six years after Carducci's death, a full-length study of the poet's work, together with a translation of selected major poems, was published in English. This book represented the apex of Carducci's reputation. The critic and translator, G. L. Bickersteth, pointed out Carducci's literary use of the Italian past and of the classical models which helped interpret the ideal role of Italy as champion of human liberty.

Biography

Giosuè Carducci was born on July 27, 1835, in the Tuscan village of Val di Castello, of a prominent middle-class family. His father, Michele, was a physician with strong libertarian opinions, who had been imprisoned for his revolutionary activities as early as 1831. The young boy was educated largely by his parents, his father teaching him Latin and exposing him to the latest political authors. His mother read poetry to him, particularly the lyrical, romantic works of Vittorio Alfieri.

Because of the family's political activities, Carducci fled with his parents to Florence in 1848, where he received the first of his formal education in rhetoric and the humanities at the Scuole Pié. He had already begun to write poetry by the age of twelve and by eighteen had won a competitive scholarship to the University of Pisa, receiving his degree in 1856.

His family's known political affiliations prevented the young scholar from being appointed to a teaching position, and for the next few years Carducci lived in quiet poverty in Florence, making a living by tutoring and writing prefaces to reissues of Italian classics. This period must be regarded as one of the bleakest in his life. His beloved brother, Dante, committed suicide in November, 1857, plunging Carducci into a grief that deepened with the death of his father the following year. *Rime*, his first book of poetry, was published in 1857. In March, 1859, he married Elvira Menicucci.

Meanwhile, the political situation began to favor nationalists such as Carducci. In November, 1860, he was finally appointed to a teaching position as professor of literature at the prestigious University of Bologna. He held that post for almost half a century, retiring because of ill health in 1904.

He was an illustrious, brilliant, and popular teacher. Pressing on with his scholarship and overcoming personal tragedies such as the death of his three-year-old son, Dante, he continued to write poetry, criticism, and speeches which made him one of Italy's outstanding men of letters. In 1878 his fame earned for him an audience with Italy's Queen Marguerite, to whom he was to be a loyal friend for the rest of his life.

In 1890 he became a senator and was granted a pension. He died in Bologna in February, 1907.

Literary Career

The seeds of Carducci's literary career were sown in the desolate region of Maremma, where he spent the first thirteen years of his life. The tone of melancholy and quiet mystery that pervades the great odes of his mature years is the aesthetic equivalent to this sunny yet austere landscape of his boyhood, a land evocative of the past with its Etruscan burial grounds and its ruins. The value of the past, which was to become a principal idea in Carducci's work, was thus firmly implanted in the boy when he began to write poetry, as early as age twelve. Maremma itself is nostalgically evoked in a number of poems from the 1870's, such as "Traversando la Maremma Toscano" ("Crossing the Tuscan Maremma") and "Idillio maremmano" ("Maremma Idyll"), in which the speaker meditates upon the peaceful joy of his youth, now lost to life's disappointments.

This lyric quality was evident in Carducci's first book of poems, *Rime*, published in July, 1857, when the poet was barely twenty-two years old. Though far from his great poetry, the work in this first volume—later included by the poet in a volume called *Juvenilia* (1863), containing all of his work to 1860— is interesting as a clear aesthetic example of the young poet's own articulated ideas about the Romantic tradition. Only the previous year, in 1856, Carducci and several friends had established a literary club, Amici Pedanti, whose avowed purpose was the repudiation of the Romantic in literature— the immediate emotional response, the spontaneous, the uncontrolled. Instead, the young poet called for a return to a pagan simplicity, dignity, and, more aptly, a discipline. Thus Carducci became a classicist early in his literary career, and the rest of his creative life was devoted in part to poetry of classical restraint and polish.

Critics have noted Carducci's early rebelliousness, an independent spirit that kicked against not only the political establishment but the literary one as well. His career coincided with the nationalistic ferment of the nineteenth century in general and with the particular political upheaval that was to result in the formation of the modern Italian state. Carducci's sentiments were with Giuseppe Garibaldi and Italian independence; it is not surprising that, during the 1860's, the poet became a bitter critic of the Catholic church and of Pope Pius IX. Carducci viewed the Pope and the Church as reactionary, dangerous obstacles to the completion of Italian unity. The poetry of this period, collected as *Giambi* (1867; iambics; later as *Giambi ed epodi*, 1882), are satiric, acerbic attacks on the Church. Many of these he published under the pseudonym "Enotrio Romano."

The most famous work of this period—the one composition that made Carducci an international figure—was his astonishing poem "Inno a Satana" ("Hymn to Satan"). Often misunderstood in its own day, the poem was not a glorification of evil. The classicist Carducci had rather used the character of Satan as a kind of Prometheus figure, a symbol of enlightenment, of progress, the bringer of "fire" to humankind. Satan was the representative of the naturally spiritual, as opposed to the intellectually crippling institution of organized religion which the poet scorned.

The same year, 1863, saw the publication of Carducci's first great work of scholarship, an edition of the works of Poliziano. Such a project typified Carducci's genius, which allowed him to produce a literary work of scathing polemics and a critical work of objective brilliance in the same year. The subject was significant, as well, since Poliziano was both a poet and a humanist in the court of Lorenzo de' Medici, patron of the arts during one of the most glorious periods in the history of Italy and of Western civilization. Carducci no doubt felt a special kinship with Poliziano, as if Carducci's own time were destined to bear its own glories. He was convinced that a sense of the past was a vital link in the chain of man's destiny as a creature of dignity, truth, and beauty.

In *Giambi*, the acerbity of the political message which often mars much of Carducci's poetry of this period is softened by works such as "Canto dell'amore" (love song). Here the poet surveys the broad Italian landscape of mountain and plain and evokes scenes from the past: centuries of war, invasion, and domination. From this contemplation of age-old struggle, a single idea emerges: Hatred should be put aside and replaced by love for the holiness and the beauty of the world. This message from the past is nondenominational; it is pagan in the classic sense of a profound humanism which views human beings not in relationship to God but as creatures capable in their own right of goodness and beauty, even though always tinged with melancholy.

As Carducci continued to experiment with classical meters, the fire of his earlier political poetry subsided and the idea of history as a reflection of the greatness of humanity became the central theme of his best work. Published in 1877, *Barbarian Odes* combines the classical restraint and expressiveness of Latin metrical models with allusions to the medieval and modern worlds. Thematically, the odes are suffused with a sense of the past, with figures legendary and historical, and with locales rich in associations—all of which proclaim the unity of the human race and the dignity of life. The combination of pagan and modern is seen clearly in "Presso l'urna di P. B. Shelley" ("At the Urn of Percy Bysshe Shelley"). In this poem, the figures of Achilles, Roland, and even King Lear and Lady Macbeth greet the soul of Shelley, "Poet of Liberty," who has come to their faraway island for his final rest.

Included in this same volume is a poem which is proof for some critics of Carducci that his political principles shifted with time and circumstance—that his nationalistic ardor was a matter of opportunity rather than conviction. "To the Queen," addressed to the Italian Queen, Marguerite, is a paean both to the person and to the monarchy. Though the poem represents, indeed, a growing acceptance of the monarchy as the legitimate symbol of Italy's government, it also attests Carducci's lifelong personal friendship with the queen. She deeply respected the poet's achievements and his role as scholar, particularly his worldwide recognition as a leading authority on Dante. He viewed her, in turn, as a sensitive, intelligent woman, a classic stabilizing force for a nation whose republican principles were slowly being eroded by socialistic ideas.

Carducci's gradual shift from the ardent revolutionary of the 1850's and 1860's to the staunch monarchist of the 1880's to his death should not be viewed as a simplistic abandonment of the principles of liberty, for his great poems of this latter period still embrace human freedom and dignity. Rather, his conservative leanings are testimony to his intense patriotism, his recognition that a legitimate monarchy could serve both as a symbol of Italian greatness and as a protector, not destroyer, of republican ideals.

Peerless as a teacher and scholar, Carducci also ranks as one of the preeminent orators of modern times. His famous oration on the death of Giuseppe Garibaldi in June, 1882, stands as one of the hallmarks of Italian occasional prose. Composed extemporaneously, the oration bears kinship with the great poetry in its mingling of ancient and modern examples of heroism and legends; it calls upon Italy to fulfill her victorious and glorious role in the destiny of human affairs.

Giosuè Carducci has maintained an important place in the history of Italian literature. Though time has lessened the enthusiasm of critical pronouncements, it has not substantially diminished his status as a major poet whose sonority and imagery influenced a generation of Italian writers. The early assessment of Carducci as a poet whose popularity lay largely within Italy has remained valid. He is not the world figure that he was as Nobel laureate in 1906, but part of the reason for this is his patriotism, which in many poems seems quaint to a century which has seen two world wars and has become internationalized rather than nationalistic. Carducci's insistence on the past as a source of human strength and dignity for all ages remains a theme suited to the principles of the Nobel Prize.

Bibliography

Primary
POETRY: *Rime*, 1857; *Juvenilia*, 1863; *Giambi*, 1867 (later as *Giambi ed epodi*, 1882); *Levia gravia*, 1868; *Decennalia*, 1871; *Poesie*, 1871; *Nuove poesie*, 1872; *Odi barbare*, 1877 (*Barbarian Odes*, 1950); *Nuove odi barbare*, 1882 (*New Barbarian Odes*, 1950); *Ca'ira*, 1883; *Rime nuove*, 1887 ("*Rime nuove*" *of Carducci*, 1916; also as *The New Lyrics*, 1942); *Terze odi barbare*, 1889 (*Third Barbarian Odes*, 1950); *Rime e ritmi*, 1899 (*The Lyrics and Rhythms*, 1942); *A Selection of His Poems*, 1913; *A Selection from the Poems*, 1921; *The Barbarian Odes of Giosuè Carducci*, 1939, 1950 (includes *Barbarian Odes*, *New Barbarian Odes*, and *Third Barbarian Odes*).
ANTHOLOGY: *L'arpa del populo*, 1855.
MISCELLANEOUS: *Opere*, 1889-1909 (includes prose and poetry); *Opere complete*, 1940 (30 volumes; includes all of his prose and poetry).

Secondary
Bailey, J. C. *Carducci*. Oxford: Oxford University Press, 1926. Still the best biography of the poet, the book has the advantage of having access to contemporary accounts by still-living persons. Particularly interesting in its

treatment of Carducci's role as ardent nationalist.

Bickersteth, G. L. *Carducci: A Selection of His Poems*. New York: Longmans, 1913. Includes an enthusiastic, sometimes overstated appraisal of Carducci's work. This book has the virtue of being a contemporary account of the laureate's reputation; it contains a generous selection of his poems in translation.

Donadoni, Eugenio. *A History of Italian Literature*. Translated by Richard Monges. Vol. 2. New York: New York University Press, 1969. One of the most enthusiastic appraisals of the poet's work, this lengthy study groups the poems into several "stages"—landscape (external nature), introspection, nostalgia, political poetry, and history. Donadoni emphasizes that these stages are not chronological but thematic, appearing in early as well as later volumes.

Marble, Annie Russel. *The Nobel Prize Winners in Literature*. Freeport, N.Y.: Books for Libraries Press, 1969. Reprint of 1932 edition. Evaluates Carducci's contribution strictly from the point of view of the Nobel Prize Committee's criteria. Includes a good, brief biography and contemporary critical opinions.

Wilkins, Ernest Hatch. *A History of Italian Literature*. Cambridge, Mass.: Harvard University Press, 1966. A good, brief survey of Carducci's poetry. Wilkins examines the major themes and images chronologically and gives his own free translations of some of the lyrics. An example of Carducci's modern adaptation of classical forms is reproduced in the Italian, with an English prose translation.

Edward Fiorelli

1907

Literature
Rudyard Kipling, Great Britain

Peace
Ernesto Teodoro Moneta, Italy
Louis Renault, France

Physics
A. A. Michelson, United States

Chemistry
Eduard Buchner, Germany

Physiology or Medicine
Alphonse Laveran, France

RUDYARD KIPLING
1907

Born: Bombay, India; December 30, 1865
Died: London, England; January 18, 1936
Language: English
Principal genres: Fiction and poetry

An acknowledged master of vivid narrative involving real-life struggle and duty, Kipling is also beloved for his idealism and his patriotism

The Award
Presentation

The Nobel Prize in Literature was presented to Rudyard Kipling on December 10, 1907, by Carl David af Wirsén, Permanent Secretary of the Swedish Academy. The presentation summarized Kipling's career, noting the range and volume of his publications, then turned to the author's worldwide popularity with all classes: children, soldiers, common people, kings.

The Academy noted that Kipling's popularity, and hence his selection for this honor, stemmed from two related aspects of his art. As an observer of life, the presentation argued, Kipling is unsurpassed. That gift alone, however, cannot make an artist great: Kipling's true power resides in his use of observed people and places to create an idealistic vision of what he has described. His portrayals overall are not idealized but instead idealistic: a calling forth of the highest behavior of a people. His vision of the East gives England an ennobling version of its imperial experience.

The presentation goes on to observe that Kipling is not in the aesthetic tradition of John Keats or Percy Bysshe Shelley. Rather, he is the heir of Daniel Defoe, trusting to observation and the aptly turned phrase as literary tools. Nor is Kipling offered as a profoundly original thinker. He is a whole, truth-telling writer, whose works are marked by their vivid power, their genuine emotion, their sympathy which refuses to become sentimentality, their love of nature and nation, and their conviction regarding the values of duty, loyalty, and labor. The Academy concludes that, in honoring Kipling, it pays tribute to the grand tradition of English literature overall.

Nobel lecture

Two days before Kipling and his fellow honorees were to receive their Nobel Prizes, King Oscar II of Sweden died. The traditional banquet and acceptance speeches were canceled. Writing to his children, Kipling described the truncated presentation: All the awards were presented, in a nearly empty room, in less than an hour. In a day or so, he and his wife returned to England.

Few people could have been more relieved about being excused from the necessity of a lengthy public appearance and speech. All of his life, Kipling had been reluctant to receive the honors pressed upon him; receiving the Nobel Prize with a minimum amount of attention was something he considered fortunate. Overall, his experience in Sweden seems to have been dominated not by the Nobel award but by Sweden itself—its gloomy, brief December days, their gloom intensified by mourning for the dead king.

Critical reception

Upon hearing that Kipling had been awarded the 1907 Nobel Prize, A. G. Gardiner wrote in dismay that Kipling was the wrong choice at a time when "George Meredith, Thomas Hardy, and Algernon Charles Swinburne are still among us. The goldsmiths are passed by and the literary blacksmith is exalted." Gardiner was not alone in his contempt. To the Scotsman Robert Buchanan, Kipling was merely "the voice of the hooligan," a believer in cruelty and violence. Gardiner and Buchanan summarize the two types of objections to Kipling: His artistry was inferior and his political attitudes were wrong.

The British literary establishment was ready to attend closely to the Swedish Academy's choice in 1907. Before that year, no English author had been chosen for the award, and an intense lobbying effort had been mounted to pressure the Academy into honoring an Englishman. The three great authors cited by Buchanan had all been duly considered, but all were found inappropriate. For one thing, they were all elderly; receiving the award meant traveling to Sweden and giving speeches, activities these men might not have been able to perform. Too, Hardy and Swinburne did not fit the image of idealism which the Academy promoted.

Kipling's youth—he was not quite forty-two—and his idealism were what the Academy wanted. The common reader certainly concurred in the choice: Kipling's worldwide popularity was never in doubt. The literary establishment, however, made the choice one of the most controversial in the history of the Nobel Prize in Literature. Compared with the lyric strains of Swinburne or the profundities of Hardy's verse, what was the value of Kipling's *Barrack-Room Ballads and Other Verses* (1892)? Compared with Meredith's *The Ordeal of Richard Feverel* (1859), what worth could be found in *Kim* (1901)? For much of the literary establishment, men who had worked hard to see the coveted prize placed in English hands, Kipling was a pygmy among giants. *The Times* of London was typical in its response, confining itself to a scant paragraph announcing that Kipling had won the award; no coverage of the presentation itself followed. American newspapers such as the New York *World* and the *Chicago Post* charged the former Vermont resident with militarism and blind bloodlust. His complex version of imperialism was taken a priori as a stain upon him.

The predominance of India in his writing marked Kipling from the start; it was the beginning point for his admirers and also for his detractors. To his admirers, he was opening up a new world of the East and the British experience in it. To his detractors, he was celebrating the vulgarity of the common soldier whose racism, drunkenness, and varied dialect were quite unworthy of such full literary representation.

When Kipling first came on the literary scene, the novelty and vigor of his work won for him admiration in quarters where later he would be scorned. He was rich and famous before he was thirty: That sort of beginning frequently causes the critics to launch an early reappraisal. Reviews of his 1906 work *Puck of Pook's Hill* were scant and unfavorable. The *Athenaeum*, for example, noted that Kipling had "abandoned story-telling" and was interested only in "patriotic zeal." His receiving the Nobel Prize a year later, then, was noted by most critics with anger or silent disdain.

Biography

Rudyard Kipling was born on December 30, 1865, in Bombay, India, where his father was an art instructor. A sister, Trix, was born two years later. The two youngsters and their talented, indulgent parents formed an idyllic "family square," as Mrs. Kipling referred to them. When Kipling was nearly six years old, his parents sent him and his sister back to England, where they could enjoy better health and education. The children, however, were boarded with strangers who soon began to abuse the young boy. The horror of his years in what he called the "House of Desolation" remained with Kipling all of his life.

From the ages of twelve to sixteen, Kipling was a boarding student at a school which prepared young men for the military. His eyesight, however, was too weak to make the military a possible career. His delight in writing made journalism seem suitable; accordingly, his family found him a job with a provincial Indian newspaper in Lahore. By the age of eighteen he was assistant editor. His poems and stories began to appear in India, and popularity in England quickly followed.

In 1892, Kipling married an American woman, Caroline Balestier, and lived with her in Vermont for several years, as his earnings and reputation mounted. Their happiness in America was destroyed by a serious quarrel with Caroline's brother and, later, by the death of their eldest daughter, Josephine. Though Kipling was only in his thirties and some of his finest work lay ahead of him, in many ways his life began to deteriorate.

British involvement in the Boer War led Kipling to express an imperialism which made him unpopular in some circles. Cecil Rhodes and Theodore Roosevelt were his heroes, men who understood, as Kipling saw it, the "white man's burden." At the end of the Victorian era, most of the intelligentsia saw the British Empire as inevitably declining. Kipling's insistence upon its potential sealed his fate. The years of his enormous and nearly unquestioned popularity were actually quite few.

Kipling's post-Nobel years were haunted by wars, disease, and death. World War I cost him his only son, John. By all accounts an exceptionally loving father, Kipling was crippled by this blow: He had never fully recovered from the death, years earlier, of his daughter. Persistent ill health also contributed to his decline. He died on January 18, 1936, and his ashes were buried in Poets' Corner, Westminster Abbey.

Literary Career

Rudyard Kipling began his literary career as a newspaper reporter in India, working for *The Civil and Military Gazette* of Lahore. Not yet seventeen years old and already determined to become a writer, Kipling was at first disappointed at his parents' decision to find a job for him in India rather than in London, where he could have mingled with other writers. Soon, however, he realized the richness of India as a source for his writing. His work, though grueling, fed his imagination: He reported on village festivals, riots, murders, and military skirmishes. When he was not absorbing native life, Kipling observed his fellow countrymen at the Punjab Club. He also consorted with soldiers; his education at the United Services College had instilled in him a lifelong fascination with military life, and his newspaper work allowed him to cultivate an intimacy with rank-and-file soldiers which he put to good use in his tales.

Kipling's start in life as a reporter was fortuitous in many ways. It gave him unparalleled experiences of life in all levels of Indian society, and it gave him the habit of seeing writing not as a gift but as simply his work: He labored at it steadily all of his life, as though he were still meeting deadlines. Newspaper work also introduced him to the public as a writer of poetry and fiction. His poems were used as filler items, and his brief tales were, by 1886, published daily.

A brief volume of his satirical verse, *Departmental Ditties and Other Verses*, appeared in 1886. The poems reached England and were favorably reviewed by many who were interested in their mild satire on the Anglo-English establishment. As poems they have little merit, but the book did put Kipling before the English public in a position he would long occupy—as the interpreter and revealer of the English experience in India.

Kipling's first efforts in prose appeared at the same time as the poems, and the stories share the style and subject matter of the poems. His early tales, collected as *Plain Tales from the Hills* (1888), are "ditties" in prose, satires created less by plot than by the narrator's tone, one of cheeky, almost cynical worldliness. The stories allowed the Anglo-Indians to see themselves reflected in fiction for the first time, but, beyond that, the realism of these tales spoke to England, too, letting the English believe that they were in touch with this corner of their farflung empire. Though the subject matter differs, the tools of realism bind *Plain Tales from the Hills* to other realistic works of the 1880's: for example, the novels of George Gissing and Arnold Bennett.

A steady and prolific writer, Kipling had many more stories, published and unpublished, on hand. In 1888 a publisher named Moreau, who controlled railroad bookstalls distribution, published several small volumes of Kipling's stories as part of the Indian Railroad series. The success of these volumes (*Soldiers Three: A Collection of Stories, Under the Deodars, Wee Willie Winkie and Other Child Stories, The Phantom Rickshaw and Other Tales*, and *In Black and White*) allowed Kipling to consider leaving journalism, returning to England and devoting himself to writing.

He sailed for England in 1889. His journey was not a direct one. He sailed first to Burma, China, Japan, and finally the United States, where he visited friends and gathered materials for writing. His experiences and observations found their way into *From Sea to Sea: Letters of Travel* (1899), a vivid, humorous, and personal account of his various travels. It was more than six months after leaving India that he arrived in London, ready to capitalize on his early successes.

Much of the London literary establishment was prepared to lionize the young author. Although not everyone was drawn to his style, his subject matter spoke powerfully to the English. Kipling had arrived on the scene at a time when a vacuum of sorts existed in the literary world. The great writers of the Victorian Age were gone, and none of the major writers of the day— Thomas Hardy, Oscar Wilde, George Gissing, H. G. Wells, or Robert Louis Stevenson—had wholly captured the public's imagination. Kipling's writings, his youth, and his devotion to hard work made him a welcome diversion to the London literary circles.

Kipling worked steadily in London; in spite of his fame, he was far from wealthy and he needed to publish more. Some of his best work appeared in 1890. *Barrack-Room Ballads and Other Verses* proved that Kipling could grow as a poet. Many of his best-known verses appeared in this volume, including "Danny Deever," "Gunga Din," and "Mandalay." The poems show a depth and subtlety missing in *Departmental Ditties and Other Verses*.

The stories Kipling wrote during this time of pressured activity remain some of his best fiction. Brought together in the volume *The Courting of Dinah Shadd and Other Stories* (1890), these Indian tales seem to have profited from Kipling's having left India: They have more universal power, depending on the portrayal of human nature rather than on dialect or setting. All in all, Kipling was living up to his reputation. In the same year, however, he published a novel, *The Light That Failed* (1890), which does not hold up well to critical scrutiny. Set in England, this novel lacks the intensity of his Indian fiction and shows that he was not ready to conquer the novel form. Kipling was never to find unqualified success with his novels.

Kipling's personal and professional life at this time was influenced by his profound friendship with an American, Wolcott Balestier. Together they planned and wrote the novel *The Naulahka: A Story of West and East* (1892). Balestier's sudden death from typhoid fever plunged Kipling into grief. Within a few weeks, however, his family was shocked to hear that Kipling had become engaged to Balestier's sister Caroline. Their marriage, unpromising as its beginnings were, provided stability in Kipling's life and freed him from all practical concerns, which Caroline now oversaw.

After a wedding tour, the Kipling settled in Vermont. Kipling's prodigious literary output slowed for a while as he enjoyed the pleasures of the countryside and of fatherhood. He had always loved children, and having a daughter of his own inspired him to write for them. *The Jungle Book* (1894) and *The Second Jungle Book* (1895) were the results. His usual vividness marked these books, but a puckish tenderness replaced the sometimes cynical tone of his earlier work. Kipling poured genius and love into these tales; they maintain an appeal to young readers today.

Kipling's next major work, *Captains Courageous: A Story of the Grand Banks* (1897), reflected his American experiences. A novel which is sometimes viewed as a children's book, *Captains Courageous* tells of a wealthy, spoiled boy rescued from drowning by stern New England fishermen. Like *The Light That Failed*, this novel lacks convincing character development, although the action sequences are effective.

A bitter and highly publicized quarrel with his wife's family caused the Kiplings to leave their Vermont home and settle in England. This quarrel was the first of several tragic events which were to dominate the latter part of Kipling's life and age him prematurely. Though he was not much over thirty, he sounds the note of a gray-bearded bard in a poem written not long after his return to England. "Recessional" (1897) was written as a response to the orgy of self-congratulation which the nation experienced during Queen Victoria's Diamond Jubilee. Kipling suggests the unthinkable: that the days of glory could be coming to an end. The author's powers as a poet perhaps were at their highest in this well-known poem, which is sometimes read as a late-Victorian expression of angst.

In 1899, Kipling's beloved eldest child, Josephine, died. The shadow of her death was deepened by the Boer War, a conflict which embittered Kipling and intensified his belief in the military and in the "white man's burden" throughout the Empire. Out of this dual sadness came the completion of *Kim*, the most successful of his longer works. *Kim* possesses the conviction which Kipling's other novels lack. In it he was able to present fascinating characters through effective character development; Kim's search for identity and purpose rings true. Moreover, *Kim* powerfully evokes the India of Kipling's youth.

The writing of *Kim* coincided with the composition of the *Just So Stories for Little Children* (1902), tales written to amuse the Kipling children during a long sea voyage. Kipling's imagination seemed to have been given another dimension by the tragedies he had suffered. Along with these children's stories, he was working on "Wireless" (1903), a science-fiction piece which rivals any by H. G. Wells, and "They" (1904), a moving tale of the supernatural involving ghosts of dead children. These stories were followed by *Puck of Pook's Hill*, a children's book designed to teach the history of Roman involvement in Britain. The deeper lesson inculcated by the book, however, has to do with the virtues Kipling admired most: steadfastness, attentiveness to duty, and courage.

Kipling's literary productivity slowed somewhat after he received the Nobel Prize in 1907. Health difficulties, including failing eyesight, and public duties prevented him from writing at the pace he had earlier set. He devoted much of his writing time to warning the English about the rise of German imperialism. When war finally came, it brought further tragedy to Kipling: His son John was killed in action in 1915. A volume of poetry, *The Years Between* (1919), reflects Kipling's personal grief and his bitterness about the world situation, which he believed the war had failed to improve. Reviewers were generally negative about this volume, taking the line that Kipling's artistry had failed and his vision had become outmoded. Such comments further embittered Kipling.

Soon after his son's death, Kipling began a history of the military unit in which John had served. This work was completed and published in 1923 as *The Irish Guards in the Great War*. A massive, two-volume study, this book drained Kipling's waning energies and exacerbated problems with his eyesight, but its publication brought him some happiness, as it served as a kind of memorial to his lost son. Volumes of stories followed, including *Debits and Credits* (1926) and *Limits and Renewals* (1932). Readers who had admired the early Kipling's style and subject matter were puzzled over these new tales, which were ambiguous and dark, parables conceived in Kipling's own abyss of melancholy. "The Gardener," for example, shows the uselessness of a young man's death in the Great War by depicting the shallow, mercenary postwar values of the English village for which he believed he was fighting.

During the final years of his life, Kipling worked intermittently on an autobiography. When he died in 1936, the work had not been completed. A close friend, Sir Alfred Webb-Johnson, edited the manuscript and gave it the title *Something of Myself: For My Friends Known and Unknown* (1937). As Kipling's last word to the world of letters, it is rather typical: finely written, but taciturn in regard to personal matters. There is no mention, for example, of the deaths of his two children. Instead, the autobiography offers some fine descriptive passages, tales of his world travels, and some exposition of his political and social beliefs. It is not the autobiography that some wished for, but undoubtedly it is the only sort that Kipling, an intensely private man and an inveterate letter burner, could or would write.

There can be little doubt that Kipling's artistic powers decreased or were warped by events in the latter part of his life. Almost all the work for which he is remembered had been done before he won the Nobel Prize. Perhaps these relatively unproductive later years have been unfairly held against Kipling. In reevaluating his worthiness as a recipient of the Nobel Prize, readers might do well to look at all that he had accomplished by 1907, at the age of forty-one. Consideration should also be given to the notable writers who have come around to intelligent and profound appreciations of Kipling: George Orwell, T. S. Eliot, C. S. Lewis, Angus Wilson, and Harold Bloom are among the important literary figures of this century who have wrestled with a dislike for Kipling's politics but emerged with an admiration for his work, giving provocative readings to the stories and poems. Kipling continues to generate controversy, but he also continues to make readers think and feel. His place in the pantheon of Nobel Prize winners is well deserved.

Bibliography

Primary

NOVELS: *The Light That Failed*, 1890; *The Naulahka: A Story of West and East*, 1892 (with Wolcott Balestier); *Captains Courageous: A Story of the Grand Banks*, 1897; *Kim*, 1901.

SHORT FICTION: *Quartette*, 1885 (with John Lockwood Kipling, Alice Macdonald Kipling, and Alice Kipling); *Plain Tales from the Hills*, 1888; *Soldiers Three: A Collection of Stories*, 1888; *The Story of the Gadsbys: A Tale Without a Plot*, 1888; *In Black and White*, 1888; *Under the Deodars*, 1888; *The Phantom Rickshaw and Other Tales*, 1888; *Wee Willie Winkie and Other Child Stories*, 1888; *The Courting of Dinah Shadd and Other Stories*, 1890; *The City of Dreadful Night and Other Sketches*, 1890; *Mine Own People*, 1891; *Life's Handicap*, 1891; *Many Inventions*, 1893; *The Jungle Book*, 1894; *The Second Jungle Book*, 1895; *Soldier Tales*, 1896; *The Day's Work*, 1898; *Stalky & Co.*, 1899; *Just So Stories for Little Children*, 1902; *Traffics and Discoveries*, 1904; *Puck of Pook's Hill*, 1906; *Actions and Reactions*, 1909; *Rewards and Fairies*, 1910; *A Diversity of Creatures*, 1917; *Land and Sea Tales for Scouts and Guides*, 1923; *"They" and the Brushwood Boy*, 1925; *Debits and Credits*, 1926; *Thy Servant a Dog*, 1930; *Humorous Tales*, 1931; *Animal Stories*, 1932; *Limits and Renewals*, 1932; *Collected Dog Stories*, 1934.

POETRY: *Schoolboy Lyrics*, 1881; *Echoes*, 1884 (with Alice Kipling); *Departmental Ditties and Other Verses*, 1886; *Barrack-Room Ballads and Other Verses*, 1892; *The Seven Seas*, 1896; *An Almanac of Twelve Sports*, 1898; *Recessional and Other Poems*, 1899; *The Five Nations*, 1903; *Collected Verse*, 1907; *A History of England*, 1911 (with C. R. L. Fletcher); *Songs from Books*, 1912; *Sea Warfare*, 1916; *Twenty Poems*, 1918; *The Years Be-*

tween, 1919; *Rudyard Kipling's Verse: 1885-1918*, 1919; *Q. Horatii Flacci Carminum Librer Quintus*, 1920 (with Charles L. Graves, A. D. Godley, A. B. Ramsay, and R. A. Knox); *Songs for Youth*, 1924; *Sea and Sussex from Rudyard Kipling's Verse*, 1926; *Songs of the Sea*, 1927; *Rudyard Kipling's Verse: 1885-1926*, 1927; *Poems 1886-1929*, 1929; *Selected Poems*, 1931; *Rudyard Kipling's Verse: 1885-1932*, 1933; *Rudyard Kipling's Verse: Definitive Edition*, 1940.

NONFICTION: *Letters of Marque*, 1891; *A Fleet in Being: Notes of Two Trips with the Channel Squadron*, 1898; *From Sea to Sea: Letters of Travel*, 1899; *Letters to the Family*, 1908; *The New Army in Training*, 1915; *Sea Warfare*, 1916; *Letters of Travel, 1892-1913*, 1920; *The Irish Guards in the Great War*, 1923; *A Book of Words*, 1928; *Souvenirs of France*, 1933; *Something of Myself: For My Friends Known and Unknown*, 1937.

MISCELLANEOUS: *The Sussex Edition*, 1937-1939 (35 volumes).

Secondary

Birkenhead, Frederick W. F. S. *Rudyard Kipling*. New York: Random House, 1978. Written in 1948, this was to have been the authorized biography of Kipling, but Kipling's daughter disliked the book and refused permission to publish it. Lord Birkenhead updated the book for its eventual publication. It is well written and scholarly, with a careful assessment of the literature and of Kipling's place in literary history. High-quality illustrations and excellent source notes are included.

Bloom, Harold, ed. *Rudyard Kipling*. New York: Chelsea House, 1986. Part of the Modern Critical Views series, this volume is deeply interesting as a result of the excellence of the contributors, among them Randall Jarrell, Donald Davie, and Bloom himself. The essays, taken together, assert that Kipling is a greater artist than has been recognized. Especially helpful are the discussion of the usually dismissed *The Light That Failed* and Bloom's essay on Kipling's tie to Walter Pater.

Carrington, Charles. *Rudyard Kipling: His Life and Work*. London: Macmillan, 1955. Carrington was the authorized biographer of Kipling; as such, he had access to interviews, photographs, and records denied to other scholars. Although his biography is somewhat dated, it is an obvious starting point for students of Kipling.

Gilbert, Elliot L., ed. *Kipling and the Critics*. New York: New York University Press, 1965. Gilbert's brief, selective volume attempts to span Kipling criticism from the first notice in England (Andrew Lang's 1886 review) to several essays from the early 1960's. The editor's goal is to show the broad range of responses to Kipling.

Green, Roger Lancelyn, ed. *Kipling: The Critical Heritage*. New York: Barnes and Noble, 1971. This text offers sixty-one responses to Kipling, mostly book reviews. The "critical heritage" covers only Kipling's lifetime, but the well-chosen selections, many by the literary arbiters of the day, give a rich sense of the erratic nature of Kipling's popularity.

Harrison, James. *Rudyard Kipling*. Boston: Twayne Publishers, 1982. One of Twayne's English Authors series, this volume gives a brief overview of Kipling's life and work. It concludes with a most helpful chapter on Kipling and two of his contemporaries, E. M. Forster and Joseph Conrad; this comparison clarifies Kipling's achievements and failings. Includes a selected bibliography of primary and secondary sources.

Mason, Philip. *Kipling: The Glass, the Shadow, and the Fire*. New York: Harper and Row, Publishers, 1975. Mason treats Kipling as a mass of contradictions in his upbringing, tastes, and convictions. These inconsistencies, while they caused him personal grief, created his art. Mason places emphasis on Kipling's non-Indian fiction and later works, both of which are usually downplayed by critics.

Moss, Robert F. *Rudyard Kipling and the Fiction of Adolescence*. New York: St. Martin's Press, 1982. Dealing with Kipling's output from 1888 to 1901, Moss argues that Kipling's evolving treatment of adolescence shows the progress of his fictional powers overall. Moss sees this period as culminating in *Kim*, which he assesses as spiritual autobiography in the tradition of William Wordsworth's *The Prelude* (1850). In *Kim*, Moss claims, Kipling was able to reconcile himself to all aspects of his art and create a profound portrait of the adolescent's search for identity.

Shahane, Vasant A. *Rudyard Kipling: Activist and Artist*. Carbondale: Southern Illinois University Press, 1973. Shahane's study is unique in that it is the first full-length appraisal of Kipling by an Indian. The author argues that Kipling is preoccupied with the dilemma of contemplation versus action; this conflict gives shape and power to his greatest work, especially *Kim*.

Wilson, Angus. *The Strange Ride of Rudyard Kipling*. New York: Viking Press, 1977. Wilson's fine biographical-critical study suggests that Kipling's inability to look into himself was the source of some of his greatest strengths and weaknesses. Many illustrations and unusually careful notes and index add to this study's usefulness, which is enhanced by Wilson's access to Kipling's unpublished work.

Deborah Core

1908

Literature
Rudolf Christoph Eucken, Germany

Peace
Klas Pontus Arnoldson, Sweden
Fredrik Bajer, Denmark

Physics
Gabriel Lippmann, France

Chemistry
Lord Rutherford, Great Britain

Physiology or Medicine
Paul Ehrlich, Germany
Ilya Mechnikov, Russia

RUDOLF CHRISTOPH EUCKEN
1908

Born: Aurich, East Friesland; January 5, 1846
Died: Jena, Germany; September 16, 1926
Language: German
Principal genre: Philosophy

A philosopher earnestly searching for truth, Eucken had a wide range of philosophical vision, but was particularly distinguished by his development of an idealistic philosophy of life, placing his own "noological" method of scholarly investigation in contradistinction to the prevailing psychological one

The Award

Presentation

The Nobel Prize in Literature was awarded to Rudolf Christoph Eucken on November 14, 1908, and was presented to him at the ceremony held on March 27, 1909, by Harald Hjärne, Director of the Swedish Academy. The presentation emphasized, as an explanation of the rationale for choosing a philosopher rather than a writer for the award, that Alfred Nobel himself would have wished to honor the recipient since Eucken had, in an exemplary fashion, mirrored in his writing what Nobel believed a writer should strive for, namely "the ideal truth without any regard to the useful." For more than thirty years, Eucken had developed his philosophical worldview, beginning with a redefinition and reformulation of concepts of modern thought, then reassessing the concepts of the great thinkers from Plato to his own time, and finally expanding his philosophy to a broader base, including questions of the struggle for a new spiritual content of life as well as questions of contemporary religion. Eucken had always insisted that philosophical concepts naturally do change within different historical times, that philosophy remains a search for truth rather than becoming a fixed system of thought. He was opposed to utilitarianism on the one hand, since that negated a true intellectual culture, and to aestheticism on the other, since that was totally devoid of morality. The Academy stressed that his brand of philosophy operated with the forces of human evolution and was therefore a dynamic philosophy. The Academy regarded Eucken as a "*Kulturphilosoph* who fully meets the standards and needs of our age."

Nobel lecture

In his Nobel lecture, "Naturalism or Idealism?" Rudolf Eucken essentially set forth a condensed version of the tenets of his philosophy. The contrast between naturalism and idealism lay for Eucken in the question of whether the

human species is "entirely determined by nature" or can "rise above it." He
dismissed naturalism because its purpose is the "utilitarian purpose of preserving life," while idealism maintains an "emancipation of inwardness," as
he put it. Although such a formulation seems to give primacy to inwardness
and the life of the mind, what Eucken really advocated was a balance of
nature and mind, with human reason a natural and rational leading force in
the evolutionary process. Since Eucken lived in an age that placed great hope
in technology, he could be convinced, in fact, that "modern technology has
proved the superiority of man to mere nature." He could be convinced as well
that an expression of such a superiority of man was to be found within the
social movements of his time, that "the mere existence of a social movement
refutes naturalism." This belief brought Eucken to the conclusion that the
fundamental contrast between idealism and naturalism could be seen in the
latter's understanding "mind by nature" and the former's understanding
"nature by mind." For Eucken, humanity represented a new degree of reality. This new degree is characterized by intellectual activity, by means of
which, to humanity's ultimate benefit, reason will harness nature. Eucken
pointed to the "tremendous progress made in human welfare which we owe
to science." He called those new developments a decisive turn in human life,
even an "ascension to another level." In a summary statement, Eucken finally
gave literature its due, delineating its place in his philosophical scheme by
claiming: "It can raise our life to greatness . . . by the representation of eternal truths." Literature, then, would lead the way for reason, and for a
"continued belief in idealism." Thus, even though Eucken himself was not a
representative of the fraternity of belles lettres, he could claim that his aims
for the cultural realm were the same as those of the poets.

Critical reception
   Awarding the Nobel Prize in Literature to a man of philosophy rather than
to a man of letters was too unexpected not to have drawn heavy criticism,
especially from England, and also from the United States. The influential
New York biweekly *The Independent*, in its issue of December 17, 1908, took
forceful exception to the choice by the Swedish Academy. Drawing on the
Santa Claus image, the journalist writing the article first pointed out that the
men of science, of letters, and of peace all over the world had come to regard
the anniversary of the death of Alfred Nobel, December 10, with the same
feelings children have on December 25. After all, the award carried with it a
prize of the then not inconsiderable sum of $38,000, not to mention the
medal and other honors. But—the account went on—the Scandinavian committees who made the awards had been just as capricious as Santa Claus.
Apparently information had already been leaked to the press that the British
poet Algernon Charles Swinburne was up for the award in literature that
year, and the writer for *The Independent* envisioned the Stockholm academi-

cians as some college debating team trying to decide who was the greatest man, the British writer of "sensuous and sonorous verse" or the German professor of religious philosophy. There was further speculation as to the possibility that the scale was tipped by the fact that Rudyard Kipling, a countryman of Swinburne, had won the prize the previous year. Finally, the thought was entertained that Swinburne's verse might have proved too realistic, for the will of the "great dynamite maker stipulated that the prize be awarded for 'literature of an idealistic tendency.'"

The writer then launched into a belittling, dismissive description of Eucken's career: "His publisht works followed the normal order—first historical, then critical, and later constructive," he said. The writer noted in particular that while in the beginning Eucken's pen had been directed against realism and materialism, the philosopher later found the chief danger in the rise of pantheistic mysticism, "self-centered, quietistic, and barren." The connection to the United States was given its due: Noah Porter of Yale had introduced Eucken to that country, and it was he who had persuaded Professor M. Stuart Phelps to translate "The Fundamental Concepts of Modern Philosophic Thought Critically and Historically Considered."

Biography

Rudolf Christoph Eucken was born on January 5, 1846, in Aurich, the capital of East Friesland, located at its very center, halfway between Emden and Wilhelmshaven. Eucken's forefathers had been wealthy farmers who had lost all of their possessions during the great floods of 1825. Therefore Eucken's father had chosen the career of a civil servant with the German postal service. Unfortunately, he died when Eucken was only five and a half years old. Eucken's mother was the daughter of a minister, and she had a great influence on him, especially because of her literary inclinations. After a very sickly childhood, and after almost losing his eyesight during a bout with scarlet fever (making him from early childhood into a very serious boy), Eucken attended the *Gymnasium* in Aurich. Until the end of his life he spoke very appreciatively of several of his teachers there; the young man excelled particularly in mathematics, and he earned money tutoring other students.

Eucken's turn to philosophy was caused by a deep interest in religious matters. When he decided to attend the university in Göttingen, his mother gave up their house in Aurich and went with him, making a home for him there during his years of study. Eucken studied not only philosophy, a subject with which he hoped to attain an academic career, but also philology and history. After finishing his dissertation, on the language of Aristotle, at the university in Berlin in 1866, he taught at the *Gymnasium* in Husum, the hometown of novelist Theodor Storm, before being called back to Berlin after the publication of his thesis in 1868. He became a professor of philosophy in Basel, Switzerland, in 1871 and from 1874 held the chair in philosophy at the University of Jena, a position he kept until the end of his life, even though other attractive offers were presented to him. After Eucken had won the Nobel Prize, he received invitations from other countries. He was asked to lecture in England, where he appeared in London and Oxford. In 1912 he went to the United States as an exchange scholar, teaching for a semester at Harvard.

Eucken's mother had died while he was teaching in Basel. Ten years after her death, in 1882, he married Irene Passow, who also came from an academic family. They had three children, two sons and one daughter. Toward the end of his life, Eucken became interested in China, both its ancient philosophy and its current problems. He died in 1926.

Literary Career

At the age of seventy-four, Rudolf Christoph Eucken wrote his autobiography, which was published in 1921 under the title *Lebenserinnerungen: Ein Stück deutschen Lebens* (*Rudolf Eucken: His Life, Work, and Travels*, 1921). In this book, Eucken not only faithfully traces his family background and his upbringing but also discusses at some length and in some detail what in his particular case cannot be termed a "literary" career but must be termed an "academic" career. Eucken wrote neither fiction nor poetry, and the award to him of the Nobel Prize in *literature* needed an explanation, which was given in the somewhat lengthy preamble to the *laudatio* by Harald Hjärne. Some modern literary critics have claimed that any writing can be subsumed under the rubric "literature"; therefore, one would not have needed the Swedish Academy's *apologia*, for Eucken's list of publications, although non-fictional publications, is an impressively long one.

Eucken's first scholarly endeavors were centered on classical philosophy, in particular on diverse aspects of the philosophy of Aristotle. After first having written a dissertation in Latin (in 1866, at the relatively young age of twenty) about Aristotle's use of the Greek language, which was published in German in 1868 under the title *Über den Sprachgebrauch des Aristoteles: Beobachtungen über die Präpositionen* (about the use of language in Aristotle: observations about prepositions), he expanded the philological interest in this particular philosopher into other aspects of Aristotle's philosophy. In his inaugural lecture at Basel University, Eucken spoke about the significance of Aristotle for contemporary philosophy. His next book, *Die Methode der Aristotelischen Forschung in ihrem Zusammenhang mit den philosophischen Grundprinzipien des Aristoteles* (1872), examined the connection between the method of Aristotelian philosophical investigation and his basic philosophical principles.

It took Eucken six years to research and write his next book, which is understandable when one realizes that it was to encompass the development of philosophy from the Greeks to Eucken's own time. The book, published in 1878, bears the title *Geschichte und Kritik der Grundbegriffe der Gegen-*

wart (history and criticism of contemporary basic thought), and it is organized around the tracing of the history of certain philosophical concepts and their changes in etymology and usage through the centuries. Here Eucken's historical and philological training came to the fore. The reading and knowledge on which he was able to draw is of an extraordinary breadth and astuteness. He quotes those philosophers whom he discusses in their original languages; therefore, it must be assumed that he read Francis Bacon and Thomas Hobbes in English, Gottfried Wilhelm von Leibniz in French, Plato and Aristotle in Greek, Seneca, Saint Augustine, and Giordano Bruno in Latin, and Meister Eckehart in Middle High German. The etymological discussions of the terms he had chosen to elaborate are highly interesting, and as he traces and develops the received ideas, he puts forth and develops his own, in which he diverges from tradition, on the one hand, and from other contemporary philosophical developments, on the other. Eucken discusses the usage of single concepts, such as *Erfahrung* (experience), *Gesetz* (law), *Entwicklung* (development), and *Kultur* (culture), but for the most part, he yokes together two antithetical concepts, such as *subjektiv-objektiv* (subjective-objective), *Monismus-Dualismus* (monism-dualism), *mechanisch-organisch* (mechanical-organic), *Optimismus-Pessimismus* (optimism-pessimism), and, finally, *Realismus-Idealismus* (realism-idealism). Eucken sees three important stages in the development of these philosophical concepts: the philosophy of antiquity, that of the seventeenth century, and Kantian philosophy. He credits Leibniz with the most thorough clarification of the terms discussed.

As early as page 22, Eucken's discussion begins to include the junction of spirit and nature, with his emphasis that it is only a combination of the spiritual (actually he uses the term *geistig*, the connotative field of which includes both spirit and intellect) and the material that makes up the whole of the world. Human beings, according to Eucken's elaborations, are not only a part of the world; they are, to paraphrase Eucken, its co-owner, because humans possess reason. Of reason, Eucken claims: "Vernunft ist der eigentliche Weltinhalt" (Reason is the actual content of the world). That human reason can transform life from effect to cause is proof to Eucken that it is the wellspring of life. The claim of human reason as the prime mover is the basis of what Eucken calls "die noologische Methode" (the noological method), which he believes to be superior to the psychological method, which is also based on the importance of the mind but is applied in a passive and contemplative, rather than in an active, fashion. Reason, Eucken says, "sei nicht als Unterbewusstes gefasst, da es vielmehr ein Überbewusstes ist" (should not be taken as a subconscious, since it is rather a supra-conscious). This statement can be read as a rebuttal to the claim of psychology that the subconscious (psychology actually uses the term "unconscious") is of prime importance in the formation of the human ego.

Eucken finally summarizes the new contemporary idealism, which he would like to see as the new direction philosophy ought to take, while he is talking about the antithesis of reason and appearance, of an intelligible world and an empirical one:

> Aber dieser Gegensatz fällt in ein einziges Universum hinein, die Vernunft ist nichts über der Welt schwebendes [sic] und nur in sie hinein wirkendes [sic], sondern sie hat hier ihre Heimat und macht auf eben den Platz Anspruch, den die Erscheinung einnimmt. Bei solchem Zusammentreffen in einem Punkt wird der Gegensatz geradezu zu einem Widerspruch, der schlechterdings aufgehoben werden muss, und der Prozess der Aufhebung dieses Widerspruches ist recht eigentlich der Inhalt des Weltgeschehens.

> (But this antithesis falls into one single universe; reason is not something hovering above the world and something only having an effect into it, but it has its home here, and claims for its own the very spot which is taken by appearance. At such a meeting in one single point, the antithesis actually becomes an opposition which definitely needs to be resolved, and the process of the resolving of this opposition is the actual content of world events.)

This book put Eucken into the forefront of importance in Germany, not only in philosophical circles but within the general educated populace as well, as his main ideas filtered down in various shapes and guises. The book had a second edition immediately, in 1879, and came out then under the title *Geschichte der philosophischen Terminologie* (history of philosophical terminology, sketched in outline). As mentioned earlier, Eucken had been drawn to the discipline of philosophy because he had had a deep interest in religious matters beginning in early childhood. He now began to use those abstract philosophical concepts, which he had developed in his investigations, for discussions of aspects of the life of contemporary man. After he had published *Die Lebensanschauungen der grossen Denker: Eine Entwicklungsgeschichte des Lebensprobleme der Menschheit von Plato bis zur Gegenwart* (1890; *The Problem of Human Life as Viewed by the Great Thinkers from Plato to the Present Time*, 1909) and had laid the historical groundwork, Eucken began to expand his findings into quasi-prescriptions as to how to solve the problem of the general malaise of his own time. The next book was *Der Kampf um einen geistigen Lebensinhalt: Neue Grundlegung einer Weltanschauung* (1896; the battle for a new spiritual content in life: new bases for a worldview), to be followed by *Der Wahrheitsgehalt der Religion* (1901; *The Truth of Religion*, 1911). Religion—its connection to philosophical concepts and its value as a life force for human beings—remained a recurring theme in Eucken's writings, as in *Hauptprobleme der Religionsphilosophie der Gegenwart* (1907; main problems of contemporary religious philosophy) and in *Können wir noch Christen sein?* (1911; can we still be

Christians?). The growing concerns about the immediate contemporary problems of humanity even led, in 1920, to a call for the formation of an *Eucken-Bund* (Eucken alliance), because a group of followers had grown to believe that following Eucken's tenets would alleviate human suffering.

When one remembers that there had been other endeavors to fill the void so newly created by the philosophy of Friedrich Nietzsche (in the wake of Arthur Schopenhauer, discussed by Eucken as an example of philosophical pessimism)—for example, the anthroposophy of Rudolf Steiner,—it is not surprising that Eucken's idealist philosophy found such a following. It is also not surprising that Eucken now has practically been forgotten, for history has proved him wrong: The events of the twentieth century showed that humanity did not use reason for the betterment and proper use of nature. In Eucken's day, his ideas were considered to offer real hope and a positive force for the development of humankind. The many immediate translations of his works, especially into English, bear witness to the far-reaching influence Rudolf Eucken had.

Bibliography

Primary

NONFICTION: *De Aristotelis dicendi ratione, Pars Prima: Observationes de particuliarum usa*, 1866; *Über den Sprachgebrauch des Aristoteles: Beobachtungen über die Präpositionen*, 1868; *Die Methode der Aristotelischen Forschung in ihrem Zusammenhang mit den philosophischen Grundprinzipien des Aristoteles*, 1872; *Über die Bedeutung der Aristotelischen Philosophie für die Gegenwart*, 1872; *Geschichte und Kritik der Grundbegriffe der Gegenwart*, 1878; *Geschichte der philosophischen Terminologie*, 1879; *Über Bilder und Gleichnisse in der Philosophie*, 1880; *Prolegomena zu Forschungen über die Einheit des Geisteslebens in Bewusstsein und Tat der Menschheit*, 1885; *Beiträge zur Geschichte der neuern Philosophie*, 1886; *Die Philosophie des Thomas von Aquino und die Kultur der Neuzeit*, 1886; *Die Einheit des Geisteslebens in Bewusstsein und Tat der Menschheit*, 1888; *Die Lebensanschauungen der grossen Denker: Eine Entwicklungsgeschichte des Lebensprobleme der Menschheit von Plato bis zur Gegenwart*, 1890 (*The Problem of Human Life as Viewed by the Great Thinkers from Plato to the Present Time*, 1909); *Der Kampf um einen geistigen Lebensinhalt: Neue Grundlegung einer Weltanschauung*, 1896; *Der Wahrheitsgehalt der Religion*, 1901 (*The Truth of Religion*, 1911); *Gesammelte Aufsätze zur Philosophie und Lebensanschauung*, 1903; *Grundlinien einer neuen Lebensanschauung*, 1907 (*Life's Basis and Life's Ideal: The Fundamentals of a New Philosophy of Life*, 1912); *Hauptprobleme der Religionsphilosophie der Gegenwart*, 1907; *Der Sinn und Wert des Lebens*, 1908 (*The Meaning and Value of Life*, 1909); *Einführung in eine Philosophie des Geisteslebens*, 1908 (*The Life and the Spirit: An*

Introduction to Philosophy, 1909); *Können wir noch Christen sein?*, 1911;
Erkennen und Leben, 1912 (*Knowledge and Life*, 1913); *Zur Sammlung
der Geister*, 1913; *Die weltgeschichtliche Bedeutung des deutschen Geistes*,
1914; *Die Träger des deutschen Idealismus*, 1915; *Die geistesgeschichtliche
Bedeutung der Bibel*, 1917; *Die geistigen Forderungen der Gegenwart*, 1918;
Mensch und Welt: Eine Philosophie des Lebens, 1918; *Was bleibt unser
Halt? Ein Wort an ernste Seelen*, 1919; *Die deutsche Freiheit*, 1919; *Der
Sozialismus und seine Lebensgestaltung*, 1920; *Unsere Forderung an das
Leben*, 1920; *Lebenserinnerungen: Ein Stück deutschen Lebens*, 1921 (*Rudolf Eucken: His Life, Work, and Travels*, 1921); *Das Lebensproblem in
China und in Europa*, 1921 (with C. Chang).

Secondary
Boldt, Ernst. *Rudolf Steiner und das Epigonentum.* Müchen: Rösl und Cie,
    1923. The second chapter in this book deals with the relationship between
    Steiner and Eucken. According to Boldt, Eucken believed himself capable
    of founding a social activism based on what Boldt calls "abstract meta-
    physics" and "nebulous mysticism." Eucken sees in Steiner a "mythic dan-
    ger," and he says so, whereas Boldt, as a true disciple, believes the "reality-
    directed spiritualism" of Steiner to be the direction of philosophy's future.
Booth, Meyrick. *Rudolf Eucken: His Philosophy and Influence.* London: T.
    Fisher Unwin, 1913. For two years Booth studied with Eucken at the Uni-
    versity of Jena. He believed that Eucken's philosophy, rather than remain
    an academic specialty, should become a power in the lives of the people;
    therefore Booth avoided all technical terminology in his explicatory work.
    Booth discusses what Eucken saw as the central problems of his time, from
    the neglected soul of modern man to state socialism, and focuses on
    Eucken's rejection of utilitarianism and on his influence on education.
Gibson, W. R. Boyce. *Rudolf Eucken's Philosophy of Life.* London: Adam
    and Charles Black, 1906. Gibson's book was widely read, not only in En-
    gland (Gibson was a lecturer in philosophy at the University of London)
    but in the United States as well. Even though Gibson had some criticism to
    level at Eucken—in chapter 12 he speaks of Eucken's "irrationality,"
    meaning that some of his concepts need further clarification—he is basic-
    ally a follower of Eucken.
Haskamp, Reinhold J. *Spekulativer und Phänomenologischer Personalismus.*
    Munich: Karl Alber, 1966. Haskamp's study discusses the influences of
    Johann Gottlieb Fichte and Rudolf Eucken on Max Scheler's philosophy of
    the human being, of "personalism." Haskamp points out in particular the
    irrational elements of the noological method.
Herman, Emily. *Eucken and Bergson: Their Significance for Christian
    Thought.* Boston: Pilgrim Press, 1913. The author focuses on the convic-
    tion that the works of Eucken and Henri Bergson are pregnant with the-

ological implications and that they contain powerfully formative elements of future Christian thought.

Jones, Abel John. *Rudolf Eucken: A Philosophy of Life*. London: T. C. and E. C. Jack, 1912. The aim of this rather short book is to give the reader a brief and clear account of Eucken's philosophical ideas, to inspire the reader to examine the works of Eucken. Jones considers Eucken a "great ethical teacher and an optimistic prophet" but criticizes the absence of the material world in Eucken's philosophical system, and the absence of any real attention to the psychological implication of his theories.

Kennedy, Francis. "The Struggle for a Spiritual Content of Life." In *Princeton Contributions to Philosophy*, edited by Alexander T. Ormond. Princeton, N.J.: Princeton University Press, 1899. Kennedy calls the work of Rudolf Eucken "a remarkable contribution to the metaphysics of our time."

Liselotte M. Davis

1909

Literature
Selma Lagerlöf, Sweden

Peace
Baron d'Estournelles de Constant, France
Auguste Beernaert, Belgium

Physics
Guglielmo Marconi, Italy
Karl Braun, Germany

Chemistry
Wilhelm Ostwald, Germany

Physiology or Medicine
Emil Kocher, Switzerland

SELMA LAGERLÖF
1909

Born: Mårbacka, Värmland, Sweden; November 20, 1858
Died: Mårbacka, Värmland, Sweden; March 16, 1940
Language: Swedish
Principal genre: Fiction

Lagerlöf mastered and transcended the conventions of realism, incorporating in her fiction not only the accurate depiction of nature and of country life but also the imaginative reality of her native Värmland represented by folktales and legends

The Award
Presentation

The Nobel Prize in Literature was presented to Selma Lagerlöf on December 10, 1909, by Claes Annerstedt, President of the Swedish Academy. In his presentation address, Annerstedt pointed out that although Lagerlöf had won recognition throughout the world, her genius was uniquely Swedish. Her inspiration came from her knowledge of peasant life and of the folktales and legends which were so important a part of that life; the natural settings that she described so vividly were typical of her native Värmland; the cadences of her tales reflected the simple storytelling style of simple people.

Lagerlöf's universal appeal, however, was the result of more than her highly original use of native stories and settings. In her understanding of human nature, she transcended country and class. Furthermore, that understanding was a generous one. Always seeking the best in human nature, Lagerlöf wrote of the power of love, of the human capacity for self-sacrifice, and of the human need for the eternal.

Nobel lecture

Selma Lagerlöf's Nobel lecture is perhaps the most unusual, as well as the most charming, ever delivered. Beginning as an account of her train journey to Stockholm, it soon becomes an imagined conversation with her dead father in Paradise, a Paradise not unlike Mårbacka, with a porch and a flower-filled garden. Obviously, Lagerlöf wishes to tell her father about the Nobel Prize, but she chooses to approach the subject indirectly.

The problem which she has brought to her father, Lagerlöf tells him, is that she does not know how to pay her debts. Gracefully, then, she transforms the conversation into a modest expression of gratitude toward those who were responsible for the novelist's success, all of those who stimulated her imagination, beginning with her father and the rest of her family but also including the old men and women who told her folktales and the vagabonds who wandered through her youth, even the very creatures of nature. She mentions all the writers who have influenced her, particularly the great Norwegians and Russians, and then concentrates on the recent writers of her own country, who created the language and the intellectual climate that made her own work possible. She is indebted to her readers, from the king to the schoolchildren, even to a critic whose praise brought her new readers all over the world, as well as to those friends who encouraged her.

At this point, Lagerlöf must tell her father of the final debt, and thus she confides that she has won the Nobel Prize. His eyes filled with tears, he hears the final question: How can she pay the debt of gratitude to the Academy? The old man is too happy to worry about it. Returning to this world, Lagerlöf then says helplessly that she has received no answer as to how to pay her debt, and she proposes a toast to the Academy.

It is said that the guests at the Nobel Prize presentation, always a solemn and dignified occasion, were at first surprised to hear a story instead of the serious lecture that they had expected. Then, as they fell under Lagerlöf's spell, they realized that, as in her fiction, she was expressing profound feelings and ideas in the form of an imagined incident. Soon the audience was smiling, charmed by her whimsical manner and impressed by her sincere modesty. In her Nobel lecture, Selma Lagerlöf had once again been simply herself.

Critical reception

In 1904, Lagerlöf was awarded a Gold Medal by the Swedish Academy. That year, with both the critical approbation and the general popularity of her works steadily increasing, she was first nominated for the Nobel Prize in Literature. Year after year thereafter, her name was placed in nomination. In 1908, after the success of *Nils Holgerssons underbara resa genom Sverige* (1906-1907, 2 volumes; *The Wonderful Adventures of Nils*, 1907, and *The Further Adventures of Nils*, 1911), it seemed likely that Sweden's great novelist would at last be the recipient of the Nobel Prize. The children's books which she had just published, however, written at the request of progressive Swedish teachers, had infuriated conservative pedagogues, who actively opposed her. Some members of the Academy also argued that she had insulted them by joining the objection to Leo Tolstoy's being ignored when the 1901 prize was awarded.

When Lagerlöf was rejected in 1908, the furor that ensued, both in Sweden and throughout the world, threatened the prestige and even the continued existence of the Swedish Academy. In 1909, therefore, seven members of the Academy joined in insisting that Lagerlöf was long overdue for the award. Although opponents, including the Permanent Secretary, Carl David af Wirsén, continued their machinations, Lagerlöf's supporters won, and she received the prize. When the Permanent Secretary refused to present the prize to her, the President of the Swedish Academy took his place.

Because of her worldwide popularity and the general feeling that this recognition was long overdue, the critical reception of the award was favorable. The objections of the Swedish pedagogues had represented a minority viewpoint. Lagerlöf's large reading public was delighted. In the United States, where she had only recently become well-known, with the publication of a translation of *Kristuslegender* (1904; *Christ Legends*, 1908), the response was similar. Typical was the comment of *The New York Times* (December 11, 1909) that "it would be pretty hard for any one to say who better deserves the prize." The *American Review of Reviews* (February, 1910) pointed out that Lagerlöf "is known and loved throughout the whole Western world."

From the beginning, the Nobel Prize in Literature had been considered in the context of Alfred Nobel's goals. Therefore, the Academy hesitated to award the prize to writers, however popular or talented, who seemed devoid of idealism. This qualification tended to rule out the more pessimistic realists or naturalists who dominated Lagerlöf's period. As a writer for *The New York Times* commented, "Literature of an idealistic tendency is very rare nowadays the world over," indicating that Lagerlöf was an outstanding writer who met the standard of idealism.

The *American Review of Reviews* also found it important to discuss her at length in relation to other literary trends of her time. Like the writers of the Romantic period, it was stated, Lagerlöf could understand the human heart, while like the naturalists, she was a meticulous observer who could reproduce accurately the events of daily life. Praising her unusual combination of clear observation and superb imagination, the periodical summarized her unique achievement by calling her a "seldom surpassed teller of fairy tales of that rare kind that may be read with equal pleasure by children and grownups."

Thus, after years of opposition, Selma Lagerlöf had become the first woman to win the Nobel Prize. Despite the pettiness of a few of her own countrymen, the world, which had come to love her, applauded the Academy's choice.

Biography

Selma Ottiliana Lovisa Lagerlöf was born on November 20, 1858, at Mårbacka in Värmland, Sweden. Her father was a member of a landed family that had lived in Värmland since the seventeenth century; her mother, the daughter of a prosperous ironmonger. At Mårbacka lived Selma's parents, her four brothers and sisters, an aunt, and a grandmother, in addition to the governess, servants, and farmhands.

When Lagerlöf was three, she became partially paralyzed and was unable to walk for some months. The next year, when her parents took her to the seaside, she became convinced that the bird of paradise which she was to see on an acquaintance's ship would be able to cure her, and as soon as she saw it, she walked. She continued to be lame throughout her life, however, despite two attempts at therapy in Stockholm.

Meanwhile, Lagerlöf's father, troubled by ill health and financial burdens, began to drink, accelerating the decline of the family fortunes. Although she had determined from childhood to be a writer and was known in Värmland for her occasional poems, there was no money for her further education. Fortunately, at a wedding in 1880, Lagerlöf met Eva Fryxell, a feminist, who encouraged her to borrow money in order to prepare for a teaching career at a teachers' college for women in Stockholm. Completing her studies in 1885, she took a teaching position in a girls' school in Landskrona. Her father had died that year, and three years later, Mårbacka was auctioned off, leaving the young teacher without a home and with the obligation of paying for her studies.

After the publication of her first novel and a collection of short stories, Lagerlöf was recognized as a promising young writer. In 1895, she received a Royal Traveling Scholarship, took leave from her teaching position, and visited Switzerland, Germany, Belgium, and Italy. On her return, she moved to Falun in Dalecarlia, northeast of Värmland, and set about supporting herself totally by writing.

In later years, Lagerlöf traveled with friends to the Near East, to Finland, and to Russia, but she always considered her home to be the rich agricultural area of Sweden where she had been reared. As her career flourished, she was at last able to buy back the house at Mårbacka, where she returned in 1908. After she won the Nobel Prize in 1909, she spent her prize money buying the land around the house. During the rest of her life, she lived on her farm, supervising the farm work and continuing to write. Lagerlöf died at Mårbacka on March 16, 1940.

Literary Career

In her third autobiographical volume (*Dagbok, Mårbacka III*, 1932; *The Diary of Selma Lagerlöf*, 1936), Lagerlöf describes the genesis of her writing career. As a child, she was introduced to the world of imagination both by her father, who encouraged her to immerse herself in literature, and by her grandmother and the old peasants at Mårbacka, who told her the ancient folktales and legends of Värmland. It is not surprising that she began to imagine poems and novels before she ever began to write them. By the time she was seven, Lagerlöf had determined to be a writer. When she went to Stockholm in her early teens, she enjoyed telling stories to her cousins; a few years later, she was writing puppet plays and occasional verse. It was one of these occasional poems, read at a wedding, that caught the attention of the feminist Fryxell, who convinced Lagerlöf to prepare for enrollment in a teachers' college whose standards were very near to those of a university. At college, Lagerlöf attended lectures and studied in the daytime and wrote poetry at night—at one time, she says, a spate of sonnets. She pinpoints the moment, however, when her material seized her. One late autumn day in 1881, when she was twenty-two, she was walking down the street with a packet of books under her arm, on the way from a lecture to her rooms. Suddenly, with a shock that stopped her in her tracks, she realized that her memories of Värmland were demanding to be written down, particularly the saga of the Värmland cavaliers.

During the rest of her college career and the following five years of teaching, Lagerlöf worked on the story that had demanded to be told. She cast it first in verse, then in dramatic form, and finally in narrative prose. With prose, she had problems. The realistic, analytical prose style then in vogue was not suitable for a whimsical, fanciful tale based on a half-legendary character. Influenced by Homer and by Thomas Carlyle, however, she determined at last to create her own style, and once she had arrived at it, the work went rapidly.

Gösta Berlings saga (1891; *The Story of Gösta Berling*, 1898; better known as *Gösta Berling's Saga*) was a group of interrelated stories loosely woven together. The central conflict involves the battle for control of Ekeby Manor between a group of individualistic, fun-loving vagabonds, led by a defrocked pastor, Gösta Berling, and aided by the devil, and a dedicated, hardworking mistress of the manor. At the end of the story, the cavaliers must leave because they have not been proper stewards of the land.

In 1890, Lagerlöf submitted five chapters of the novel, which had a certain unity, to a novella competition being conducted by a Swedish women's magazine. When it was announced that she had won the first prize, her friend Baroness Sophie Lejonhufvud Adlersparre, who was especially interested in women writers, arranged for a year's leave of absence from her teaching duties, during which time Lagerlöf was to complete her novel.

When it was published in 1891, the readers of *Gösta Berling's Saga* found it a marvelous story. Many critics, however, seeing in the style, the tone, and the material a resurgence of supposedly defunct Romanticism, were less enthusiastic and even hostile. It was the influential and judicious Danish critic Georg Brandes who in 1893 recognized Lagerlöf's genius and ensured the success of her work. By 1895, a second edition was in print.

After the publication of a short-story collection in 1894, Lagerlöf and her friend Sophie Elkan, who were traveling in Italy, happened on an account of a counterfeit statue of Christ that had been venerated by the devout. From this story came Lagerlöf's next novel, *Antikrists mirakler* (1897; *The Miracles of Antichrist*, 1899). Set in Sicily, the novel contains realistic depictions of peasant life, combined with fanciful folktales, which are similar to the Värmland material in *Gösta Berling's Saga*. It is obvious that in this work

Lagerlöf is comparing the ethical implications of socialism with those of Christianity.

Lagerlöf's next major work was the two-volume novel comprising *Jerusalem I: I Dalarne* (1901; *Jerusalem*, 1915) and *Jerusalem II: I det heliga landet* (1902; *The Holy City: Jerusalem II*, 1918). The work was based on an occurrence in Dalecarlia in 1896, shortly before Lagerlöf settled there. Led by a former resident who had joined a group of mystics in America, half a parish of Dalecarlian peasants became convinced that the end of the world was imminent, sold their property, and followed God's supposed summons to Jerusalem. There, shunned by other Christians, who considered them insane or heretical, and unable to adapt to a climate and way of life so unfamiliar, many of them sickened and died. Fascinated by the story, Lagerlöf visited the survivors in the Holy Land and returned to Sweden to write a fictionalized account of the episode, dramatizing the conflict between the peasants' ties to the land which they had farmed for generations and the demands of God that they abandon the world and follow Him.

In 1904 came two more much-praised volumes: *Christ Legends*, a collection of Eastern stories about Christ—its publication in the United States finally made Lagerlöf a popular success in that country—and *Herr Arnes penningar* (1904; *The Treasure*, 1925), a novella that is generally considered to be her finest work in that form. The novella is set on the coast of Sweden, rather than in inland Värmland. Based on a sixteenth century account of a massacre by Scots which left only one witness, a young girl, Lagerlöf's version becomes a story of horror, revenge, and doomed love. Her central character, the witness, falls in love with a charming, gallant Scot, who promises her the luxurious life of a lady if only she will elope with him. Warned by the ghost of her murdered foster sister, who has returned to seek justice, the protagonist at last realizes that her Scot and his two friends are indeed the murderers. When she reveals her knowledge, the man she loved and trusted seizes her as a shield to ensure his escape. Driving a spear into her own body, she dies. At this point, nature takes a hand, keeping the harbor frozen until the murderers are removed from their ships. They are apprehended and punished, and the young girl who suffered for love and died for justice becomes a legendary martyr.

The next major work by Lagerlöf, which appeared in English as *The Wonderful Adventures of Nils* and *The Further Adventures of Nils*, constituted her only venture into children's literature. This work was commissioned by the Swedish National Teachers Society, which wanted an appealing book from which schoolchildren between the ages of nine and eleven could learn about Swedish history and geography. Lagerlöf decided to write a single, unified story, rather than a series of tales, and, inspired by Rudyard Kipling's *The Jungle Book* (1894), she planned to incorporate animal characters into the story of a human boy. The result was the tale of Nils Holgersson, a lazy, disobedient little boy, who was punished by being changed into a small nonhuman creature and banished from human society. Among the animals, he mends his ways, avoids the snares of the villain, a fox, and aids two children who are searching for their father. In the course of a journey on the back of a wild goose, he travels to Lapland and back to the south of Sweden, thus gaining an aerial view of his country. At the end of the story, he is good enough to be changed back into a human being.

Although some conservative pedagogues found grounds to criticize this story, teachers, parents, and children found it delightful. Translated into forty languages, it became Lagerlöf's best-known work.

In the ten years from 1904 to 1914, Lagerlöf's growing literary reputation was indicated by the honors awarded her: the Gold Medal of the Swedish Academy in 1904, an honorary doctorate from Uppsala University in 1907, the Nobel Prize in Literature in 1909. In 1914, she was elected the first woman member of the Swedish Academy.

Meanwhile, she entered upon two highly productive decades. She published a collection of short stories, *En saga om en saga och andra sagor* (1909; *The Girl from the Marshcroft*, 1910), followed by four novels, two of which have stood the test of time. *Liljecronas hem* (1911; *Liliecrona's Home*, 1914), which was modeled on her grandmother's life, tells the story of a young girl tormented by an evil stepmother who is actually a troll in disguise. Finally the girl is liberated by a young violinist, and the stepmother, exposed, disappears. *Kejsaren av Portugallien* (1914; *The Emperor of Portugallia*, 1916) is a poignant tale which Lagerlöf said could be called a Swedish *King Lear*, the story of a father abandoned by the daughter who has always been his reason for living, driven to madness and finally to suicide by her heartlessness. After his death, the daughter repents and once more becomes the physically and spiritually beautiful creature whom he loved so dearly.

During the 1920's, Lagerlöf wrote the trilogy that she entitled *Löwensköldska ringen* (1925-1928; *The Ring of the Löwenskölds: A Trilogy*, 1928), a family history which covers a period from 1700 to 1830. The story begins with a grave robbery, the theft of a ring from the finger of a dead general, and soon proceeds to the murder of the peasants who are unjustly accused of the robbery. The curse of the ring and the curse of the injustice predispose the following generations to tragedy. Lagerlöf also traces the character weaknesses which result in misery: for example, the spitefulness of the spoiled young curate who decides to propose to the first girl he encounters and then, as his peasant bride adapts herself nobly to her new life, continues on his self-righteous road to damnation. The final volume of this trilogy was the last novel that Lagerlöf wrote.

In the 1920's, Lagerlöf also published the first two volumes of what might be called her autobiography, *Mårbacka* (1922; English translation, 1924) and *Ett barns memoarner* (1930; *Memories of My Childhood*, 1934). These two books were actually more about Mårbacka than about Lagerlöf herself. In the third book, *The Diary of Selma Lagerlöf*, however, the writer, then in her seventies, so effectively placed herself in the mind of the teenage Selma that some critics could not believe that the book was not a real journal.

As the Nazi regime came to power, Lagerlöf sacrificed much of her German reading public because of her firm opposition to oppression and anti-Semitism. In 1933, she gave the royalties from one of her works to a fund for exiled intellectuals. At the time of her death, she was writing a biography for her lifelong friend Elkan. The completed chapters, which focus on Elkan's early years as a young Jewish girl, appeared in a posthumous collection.

After a period of declining health, Lagerlöf died on March 16, 1940, at her beloved Mårbacka. Her accomplishments had been important to her country and to literature. By drawing upon the folktales and legends of her people, she had preserved much of her country's past. By insisting upon developing her own style to suit that subject matter, she had helped to release later novelists from the bonds of realism and naturalism. Behind her she left memorable novels, short stories, and autobiographical volumes. Years after her death, her first book was still one of the most popular novels in Sweden, and the work which began as a children's geography book was still read throughout the world. Although some critics argue that she fell short in depth of characterization and in the full realization of passionate love, no one denies that as a spellbinding, convincing storyteller she is the finest of the Scandinavian novelists and one of the best the world has produced.

Bibliography

Primary
LONG FICTION: *Gösta Berlings saga*, 1891 (*The Story of Gösta Berling*, 1898; better known as *Gösta Berling's Saga*, 1918); *Antikrists mirakler*, 1897 (*The Miracles of Antichrist*, 1899); *Jerusalem I: I Dalarne*, 1901 (*Jerusalem*, 1915); *Jerusalem II: I det heliga landet*, 1902 (*The Holy City: Jerusalem II*, 1918); *Herr Arnes penningar*, 1904 (*The Treasure*, 1925); *Liljecronas hem*, 1911 (*Liliecrona's Home*, 1914); *Körkarlen*, 1912; *Kejsaren av Portugallien*, 1914 (*The Emperor of Portugallia*, 1916); *Bannlyst*, 1918 (*The Outcast*, 1922); *Löwensköldska ringen*, 1925-1928 (*The Ring of the Löwenskölds: A Trilogy*, 1928), includes *Löwenskölda ringen*, 1925 (*The General's Ring*, 1928), *Charlotte Löwensköld*, 1925 (English translation, 1928), and *Anna Svärd*, 1928 (English translation, 1928); *Höst*, 1933 (*Harvest*, 1935).
SHORT FICTION: *Osynliga länkar*, 1894 (*Invisible Links*, 1899); *Drottningar i Kungahälla*, 1899 (*From a Swedish Homestead*, 1901; also in *The Queens of Kungahälla and Other Sketches*, 1917); *Kristuslegender*, 1904 (*Christ Legends*, 1908); *En saga om en saga och andra sagor*, 1909 (*The Girl from the Marshcroft*, 1910); *Troll och människor*, 1915, 1921 (2 volumes).
NONFICTION: *Zachris Topelius*, 1920; *Mårbacka*, 1922 (English translation,

1924); *Ett barns memoarner*, 1930 (*Memories of My Childhood*, 1934); *Dagbok, Mårbacka III*, 1932 (*The Diary of Selma Lagerlöf*, 1936). CHILDREN'S LITERATURE: *Nils Holgerssons underbara resa genom Sverige*, 1906-1907 (2 volumes; *The Wonderful Adventures of Nils*, 1907, and *The Further Adventures of Nils*, 1911).

Secondary
Björkman, Edwin. "Selma Lagerlöf: A Writer of Modern Fairy Tales." *American Review of Reviews* 41 (February, 1910): 247-250. A perceptive article on Selma Lagerlöf's achievement published shortly after she received the Nobel Prize. Surveys her work to date and, in a final section, lists the translations available to Americans. Most of the author's judgments are still solid.

Danielson, Larry W. "The Uses of Demonic Folk Tradition in Selma Lagerlöf's *Gösta Berling's Saga*." *Western Folklore* 34 (July 3, 1975): 187-199. After some introductory explanation of Lagerlöf's childhood acquisition of folktales and legends, Danielson concentrates on the exploration of the satanic character Sintram in *Gösta Berling's Saga*. An extremely interesting and valuable article about a figure who has been neglected in studies of Lagerlöf's works.

Edström, Vivi. *Selma Lagerlöf*. Translated by Barbara Lide. Boston: Twayne Publishers, 1984. This study in the Twayne's World Authors series is invaluable for the study of Lagerlöf. In addition to a biographical chapter, it has extensive analyses of the major works, along with a chapter on short fiction and a final commentary on the author's significance. Useful comments on her relationship to the feminist movement. Has drawing of Lagerlöf as frontispiece. Includes an extensive bibliography.

Gustafson, Alrik. *Six Scandinavian Novelists*. Minneapolis: University of Minnesota Press, 1940. The introduction places Lagerlöf within the context of modern Scandinavian literature. Gustafson's fifty-page section on Lagerlöf, "Saga and Legend of a Province," uses *Gösta Berling's Saga* as the focus in a study of Lagerlöf's work. Very helpful.

Lagerlöf, Selma. *The Diary of Selma Lagerlöf*. Translated by Velma Swanston Howard. New York: Doubleday, Doran, and Co., 1936. Reprint. Millwood, N.Y.: Kraus Reprint Co., 1975. Illustrated with charming sketches and with a portrait of young Selma. This volume, written when Lagerlöf was more than seventy, recaptures the spirit of the teenage Selma, discovering Stockholm, love, herself, and her vocation as a writer. An essential source.

Radzin, Hilda. "Idealism, Imagination, and Spiritual Perception in the Literary Work of Selma Lagerlöf." *Folio: Papers on Foreign Language and Literature* 11 (1978): 129-135. Concentrating on the supernatural and the spiritual, this study views Lagerlöf's work from a Christian perspective.

Radzin argues that all Lagerlöf's imaginative work is subordinated to her essentially religious viewpoint. A study which is interesting, though the ideas are insufficiently developed.

Rosemary M. Canfield-Reisman

1910

Literature
Paul Heyse, Germany

Peace
International Peace Bureau

Physics
J. van der Waals, Netherlands

Chemistry
Otto Wallach, Germany

Physiology or Medicine
Albrecht Kossel, Germany

PAUL HEYSE
1910

Born: Berlin, Germany; March 15, 1830
Died: Munich, Germany; April 2, 1914
Language: German
Principal genres: Fiction, poetry, and drama

Heyse, who reached a wide audience with his idealistic works in many literary genres, was a master of the novella form

The Award

Presentation

The Nobel Prize in Literature was presented to Paul Heyse on December 10, 1910, by Carl David af Wirsén, Permanent Secretary of the Swedish Academy. The presentation emphasized that although many famous writers from a number of countries had been proposed for the prize that year, the jury wished to express its admiration, first and foremost, for the German writer who had become an institution in letters long before the more than sixty prominent Austrian and German professors of literature, art history, and philosophy proposed him, early in 1910, for the award.

Referring to Heyse's literary accomplishments, the presentation noted that his psychological novellas had given joy to a vast reading public for more than fifty years. It was with this genre that he achieved his most noteworthy and sustained success. His first famous novella, *L'Arrabbiata* (1855; English translation, 1857), was written in 1853. Many others followed in its wake. Heyse also developed a remarkable theory of the novella, and that theory contributed further to the promotion of the literary genre with which his name will forever be associated.

The presentation mentioned that it was remarkable, too, that Heyse not only had touched the hearts of countless readers through the medium of the novella, but also had gained considerable attention with his novels, his verse, and his plays. His numerous brilliant translations of some of the finest gems of Italian literature had also found a large admiring public and made him almost as popular in Italy as in Germany.

Nobel lecture

Heyse could not attend the ceremonies in Stockholm because of his advanced age and infirmity, so he gave no lecture. The German ambassador to Sweden, Count von Pückler, replied on his behalf. The ambassador expressed his delight that another German was selected for the award only two years after the German philosopher Rudolf Christoph Eucken had received the prize. The count congratulated the jury for recognizing that German fiction had enriched world literature as much as German philosophy had.

Critical reception

The reactions to the announcement that the Nobel Prize had been conferred on Heyse ranged from unconditional reverence to outright cynicism. Heading the list of the elated were the luminaries of the German academic establishment. They had been the main driving force in securing this award. Rarely had the energies constituting the glory of the humanities at so many German universities been marshaled to the extent that they were in 1910, when the petition on Heyse's behalf was signed by one illustrious professor after another. Practically the entire academic intelligentsia in Germany and Austria had rallied in support of this nomination. It was the conviction of these sages, according to the document on which they placed their signatures, that Heyse deserved the prize because he was the most venerable living German author. During sixty years of uninterrupted literary activity, the statement added, Heyse had passionately promoted the cause of belles lettres and stoutly affirmed—often single-handedly—literature's right to appeal to the public's idealistic yearnings.

If the academic community in Germany could take obvious delight in the fact that its nominee had carried away the laurel wreath, the avant-garde of German literature could only snicker, and understandably so, for by 1910 the great Heyse had the misfortune to outlive the huge popular success that he had once enjoyed in the nineteenth century. Nowhere was the cynicism of the avant-garde expressed more curtly than on the pages of *Der Sturm* (November 17, 1910), the leading literary forum of the younger generation. Sarcastically commenting on those antiquarians and patriots who were reveling because Heyse had been chosen for the award, an editorial remarked: "May God continue to grant them joy in their innocent narrowmindedness and bless their decadent impersonator of the classics."

Opinion in Germany about the wisdom of the Swedish Academy's choice was, therefore, sharply divided, and this division was noticed as much outside the country as within it. The French press, always eager at that time to play up dissension among the Germans, quickly called attention to the controversy. A review in *Le Correspondant* (November 25, 1910) gloatingly pointed to the contradictory reactions elicited in Germany by the news about its new Nobel laureate. The French reviewer, to be sure, had an ulterior motive: He sought to inquire into the justification for the Swedish jury's selection of Heyse, hoping to prove that the prize should have been awarded to a more deserving French author. This reaction was quite in line with the thinking of the time, for it was well-known that up to that point a new Franco-German war had been fought every year over the awarding of the prize. Curiously, however, the Frenchman's inquiry came to a conclusion that was just the opposite of what might have been expected: Heyse's stylistic splendor and the charm of his stories gave him every right to take his seat alongside the other great writers who had been honored by the Swedish Academy.

Predictably, the Italian press was jubilant that Heyse had been given the award. Heyse had always loved Italy; with his fictional paintings of the Italian countryside he had gladdened the hearts of Italian readers as much as he had won friends for Italy in his native Germany. Newspapers in Rome, Florence, Pisa, Turin (and doubtless many other Italian cities) commented, therefore, that the jury in Sweden could not have made a better choice. Six months later the periodical *Der Sturm* (June 1, 1911) mocked at this rejoicing for Heyse on the part of the Italian press, saying that the colorful description of Italian life in much of Heyse's fiction had inordinately prejudiced Italian opinion in Heyse's favor.

The American reaction to the conferring of the prize on Heyse was more sober. *The Independent* of New York (December 15, 1910) believed the decision to be "safe and sane." In order to substantiate this belief, the editorial mentioned that Heyse's most famous novel, *Kinder der Welt* (1873; *Children of the World*, 1882), had long been popular in English-speaking lands. In the early 1890's, the article continued, Professor William Lyon Phelps had prescribed it for his Yale University students of fiction, and "the course proved so popular that it had to be nipped in the bud." In New York *The Outlook* (December 3, 1910) also seemed to understand why the prize had gone to Heyse: "For many years the two men in Munich in whom visitors from all parts of the world were most interested were [Franz von] Lenbach, the painter . . . , and Paul Heyse, the poet, dramatist, and novelist." Heyse's "long list of volumes in verse and prose" was cited in further justification of the award. Heyse had furthermore composed works to which the reading public could not remain indifferent. His two long novels *Children of the World* and *Im Paradiese* (1875; *In Paradise*, 1878), for example, had been greeted "with storms of applause and of criticism."

Biography

Paul Heyse was born on March 15, 1830, in Berlin. His father and grandfather were distinguished grammarians, while his mother came from a prominent family of bankers. Early in life he had been shocked by the events of the 1848 revolutions, to which he had been an eyewitness in Berlin. While the pall of despair was still hanging over the city, he took up the study of classical and Romance languages and literatures at the universities of Bonn and Berlin. He earned his doctorate in 1852. A postdoctoral fellowship gave him the opportunity to study Old French manuscripts in Italy, primarily at the Vatican Library, but the trip was perhaps more notable for instilling in him an abiding love for Italian life and letters.

Returning to the Prussian capital the following year, he married the daughter of the art historian Franz Kugler and renewed his earlier affiliation with the Berlin writers' club Der Tunnel über der Spree (the tunnel over the Spree). His first attempts at fiction were brought almost immediately to the attention of the art-loving king of Bavaria, Maximilian. The monarch was so impressed that in 1854 he invited the young Prussian to take up residence in Munich with a comfortable pension and no duties, save that of attending the symposia which the royal patron organized at the palace one evening each week for the critical discussion of literature, art, and music.

When not in attendance at the royal court, Heyse wrote for his ever-widening circle of readers. Much time was also spent on extensive travel. After the death of his first wife in 1862, he married a seventeen-year-old beauty from Bavarian society and, together with her, regularly entertained in their fashionable Munich home many of the best minds of the city. With only few changes, Heyse continued this life-style until he died in Munich on April 2, 1914.

Literary Career

As with a number of other important German men of letters in the nineteenth century, the start of Heyse's literary career can ultimately be traced to his shattering experience in the 1848 revolutions in Germany. Strangely enough, though, little mention has been made in Heyse scholarship of how seminal this experience proved to be for his development as a writer. Heyse had just turned eighteen and was, therefore, at a most impressionable age, when he became the eyewitness to a bloody rebellion that suddenly erupted on the streets of his native Berlin. The citizens had demanded universal suffrage and an end to the absolutist rule by the monarch. Fearful that his throne might topple, Frederick William IV quickly announced his readiness to make concessions. Yet, for some unexplained reason, shots rang out from among the rebels. Royalist troops responded with a volley of gunfire. Immediately, revolution was in full swing; the entire city was permeated with the vapor of cannons and the reek of blood. The young Heyse was shocked and profoundly moved by what he saw. "I have never been so agitated in my life," he wrote on March 20, 1848. "I can understand the anger. I have seen the corpses lying in front of the City Hall, young and seemingly robust bodies, soiled with blood, a hole in the chest or the skull. . . ."

The shock that Heyse suffered as a result of this tragic experience impelled him to flee the turmoil of the city and seek solace in the more politically stable Catholic Rhineland, where he then escaped even further from the horrors of the present by immersing himself (at the peaceful University of Bonn) in the aureole worlds of ancient literature and medieval French love poetry. That refreshment which Heyse found in the light and color of beautiful art from the past triggered in him the wish to become a literary artist. From that point onward the itch to recapture the beauty and enchantment that he found in classical and Romance literatures never left him.

Still, for all of his literary inclinations, Heyse might not have become an enormously successful writer of fiction had he not been, since 1849, a member of Der Tunnel über der Spree. In his affiliation with this group he reaped the benefit of a singularly valuable literary apprenticeship. Nowhere in the world at the time could the excellence of the literary schooling of Der Tunnel über der Spree be matched, except perhaps in the congregation of remarkable literati gathered around Hans Christian Andersen in Copenhagen. In both cases the membership was an association of highly civilized men. Each group met regularly in order to apply its collective intelligence to the practical criticism of literature. To a company of congenial men thoroughly conversant in good literature Heyse was thus able to present his first attempts at writing fiction; he could observe them taking pleasure in his successes or shaking their heads in dismay over his blunders. As a result, he learned to orchestrate words, manipulate plots, switch details, regulate the overall balance, and avoid irrelevant sallies, all the while adding credibility to what he said. Best of all, he learned to time the delivery of the punch line—in other words, to enlist even the most discriminating of audiences in his favor.

Heyse combined this exemplary schooling in literary technique with his burning desire to revive the sense of beauty and enchantment that he discovered in the art of the past. He worked hard, and it did not take him long to be recognized as the most conspicuous oracle of a new craft of fiction in Germany.

The work which propelled him into the forefront of German literary life was *L'Arrabbiata*. This extraordinarily successful story invoked the literary model which had been successfully implemented by the fourteenth century Italian author Giovanni Boccaccio: the novella possessing a strongly marked silhouette, telling about a situation rather than a development. This type of novella contains only a few characters, so well drawn that they fairly live and breathe before the reader's eyes, and a plot turning on a single critical event or master passion which stirs the imagination and concentrates the interest. As with Boccaccio, the setting for Heyse's novella is Italy, the land of art and beauty; as with Boccaccio too, a cleverly constructed tale of love and seduction serves as the keynote for much of the novella's appeal.

The instantaneous, indeed almost hypnotic, success of Heyse's imitation of Boccaccio's literary model and sensuously delightful theme encouraged the young author to take further flights into the world of artistic imagination. More than one hundred additional novellas from his facile pen would continue to captivate a huge reading public seeking, as did the author himself, aesthetic refreshment and escape from the political as well as the social misery of post-1848 Germany. Yet all Heyse's novellas written subsequent to *L'Arrabbiata* remain essentially variations on the pattern that he established with that work. Thus, when Heyse's obituaries were finally written, it became clear that this early novella had given him the popularity that he retained to the end.

The success with which he imitated the art, grace, and charm of a

Boccaccian novella led Heyse to develop a critical theory of the genre which then became as famous as the novellas themselves. This theory also took its inspiration from Boccaccio. In one of the novellas of that author a noble knight sacrifices all of his possessions to gain his lady's love. He has nothing left but a precious falcon. When the lady comes to his ruined castle, he kills his last treasure to make a meal for her. This final proof of his devotion wins her heart and she then accepts his marriage proposal. From this work Heyse developed his "falcon" theory of the novella. It is of the essence of the novella, he declared, that its plot should stand in sharp relief, such that if the matter of it were told in five lines it would make a memorable impression on the reader.

As if the revival of Boccaccio's practice of novella writing and the accompanying theory of the novella with which Heyse tried to induce other creative artists to follow his example did not provide him with sufficient release from the cruder realities of contemporary civilization, Heyse sought to promote the pleasure and comfort of the novella further by compiling multivolume anthologies of known and unknown models of the genre. In search of these novellas he tirelessly scoured Europe. Twenty-four volumes of collected novellas, with the title *Deutscher Novellenschatz* (treasury of German novellas), were published between 1871 and 1876. Another anthology, fourteen volumes of foreign novellas, *Novellenschatz des Auslandes* (treasury of foreign novellas), began to appear in 1872. A further collection of German novellas, the twenty-four-volume *Neuer deutscher Novellenschatz* (new treasury of German novellas) was placed before a vast reading public in 1884-1887. With all these volumes readers in every corner of German-speaking Europe were invited to join Heyse in the world of well-constructed artifice.

The esteem in which Heyse was held as practitioner and promoter of the genre of the novella touched his vanity to such an extent that when, in the late nineteenth century, the novel gradually began to supersede the novella as the dominant form of fiction in Germany, he wished to win the favor of the reading public with that genre too. The applause that he received for his novels, however, never matched the acclaim with which his contributions to the novella had met.

Like his novellas, these longer forms of fiction constituted conscious attempts to find refuge in an imagined higher world apart from an oppressive political situation. By the time Heyse started to write novels, after 1870, he had been living in Munich, the capital of Catholic Bavaria, for many years and had become thoroughly acquainted with the inflexible clericalism that informed so much of Bavarian political life. Officially, there was no place in either city or state for attitudes that did not conform to the moral code proclaimed by the Catholic church. With his novels, Heyse now attempted to offer the Bavarian public a fictional release from the constricting web of values sanctioned and sustained by a firmly entrenched Catholic hierarchy. In these novels Heyse openly preaches the doctrine of free love. In the sphere of domestic relations there is a constant playing with fire. Impulse rather than reason presides over human behavior, especially between the sexes. All restricting conventions are made to look outdated.

In essence, then, these novels constituted scurrilous attacks on the mores of Catholic society. The two novels which showed the greatest impatience with the established order of things were *Children of the World* and *In Paradise*. These works aroused strong responses, both favorable and adverse, for no one at the time could remain neutral to these impassioned pleas for a revolt against the prevailing ethics of behavior.

When the Swedish Academy justified the Nobel award to Heyse, it mentioned that he was "the most important lyrical poet of contemporary Germany." No one today would agree with this statement. Indeed, there were a number of poets in Kaiser Wilhelm's Germany who were superior to Heyse, the most notable of whom was Stefan George. It must be remembered, however, that these more accomplished lyrical voices were much newer to the literary scene and hence not nearly as widely known at the time. Heyse had begun to write poetry before the greater contemporaries of his old age were born. Many of his poems found their way into the numerous elegantly bound anthologies of verse which adorned ladies' drawing rooms in the 1870's and 1880's. Fashionable ladies loved to read these verses because the birdlike melodies and beautiful images of sunny Italy offered a welcome relief from a world that seemed to have become sad and ugly as a result of revolution, Otto von Bismarck's three wars, and the industrialization of mid-nineteenth century Germany. As curious as the Nobel Committee's statement seems today, there can be no doubt that Heyse's poetry brought joy to countless readers throughout his lifetime.

Both in quantity and in quality Heyse's poetry played a subsidiary role to his prose. Much the same can be said about his plays. Although Heyse wrote several dozen plays, they do not command anywhere near the amount of space in the volumes of his collected works as the combination of his novellas and novels. In general, too, it can be said that as a dramatist Heyse never acquired much of a reputation with the German public. His plays were, to be sure, often performed on the prestigious stages of Germany soon after they were written, but rarely did they hold the stage for long. The stringent plots which the public admired in Heyse's novellas proved fatal for the development of the action which theater audiences wanted to see. If a few of his plays did, however, attain some moderate success, it was not because they were especially good plays but because they succeeded in turning back the clock and in sending the viewers' minds wandering through intriguing picture galleries of an idealized yesteryear.

The passing of time has not been kind to Heyse. His plays are no longer a part of the German stage repertoire; for theater audiences in the twentieth century the shadowy appeal that Heyse's plays once enjoyed has completely vanished. His long, tendentious novels have also lost their urgency; for readers liberated from the dictates of an oppressive clericalism, veiled attacks on Catholic ethics no longer seem relevant. His lyrics have disappeared from anthologies of German poetry; the once-popular oleographs of the Mediterranean could hardly interest today's readers, who can easily acquire a first-hand knowledge of Italy if they wish. Only a few of his best novellas continue to be reprinted and find readers who, like the first president of the Federal Republic of Germany, Theodor Heuss, admire their grace and charm.

Heyse was too much of a preacher of overt escapism, too much of a slavish imitator of Italian poetics, and too much of a verbal trickster to be an outstanding artist. His importance is not in the intrinsic merit of his artistry but in the leadership that he took in promoting the exaltation of art as the supreme form of human endeavor.

Bibliography

Primary

LONG FICTION: *Die Brüder*, 1852; *Urica*, 1852; *Novellen: 1 Sammlung*, 1855; *Die Blinden*, 1855 (*Blind*, 1867); *L'Arrabbiata*, 1855 (English translation, 1857); *Die Braut von Cypern*, 1856; *Thekla*, 1858; *Das Mädchen von Treppi*, 1858 (*The Maiden of Treppi*, 1874); *Neue Novellen: 2 Sammlung*, 1858; *Andrea Delfin*, 1859 (English translation, 1864); *Vier neue Novellen: 3 Sammlung*, 1859; *Anfang und Ende*, 1859 (*Beginning and End*, 1870); *Neue Novellen: 4 Sammlung*, 1862; *Im Grafenschloss*, 1862 (*Count Ernest's Home*, 1867); *Rafael*, 1862; *Der Weinhüter von Meran*, 1864; *Gesammelte Novellen in Versen*, 1864; *Meraner Novellen: 5 Sammlung*, 1864; *Fünf neue Novellen: 6 Sammlung*, 1866; *Die kleine Mama*, 1866 (*Walter's Little Mother*, 1867); *Novellen und Terzinen: 7 Sammlung*, 1867; *Auferstanden*, 1867 (*Doomed*, 1870); *Beatrice*, 1867 (English translation, 1870); *Die Stickerin von Treviso*, 1868 (*The Embroideress of Treviso*, 1874); *Moralische Novellen: 8 Sammlung*, 1869; *Am toten See*, 1869 (*A Fortnight at the Dead Lake*, 1870); *Lottka*, 1869 (English translation, 1874); *Der verlorene Sohn*, 1869 (*The Lost Son*, 1874); *Gesammelte Novellen in Versen*, 1870; *Das schöne Käthchen*, 1871 (*The Fair Kate*, 1874); *Geoffroy und Garcinde*, 1871 (English translation, 1874); *Barbarossa*, 1871 (English translation, 1874); *Ein neues Novellenbuch: 9 Sammlung*, 1871; *Ein Abenteuer*, 1872; *Kinder der Welt*, 1873 (*Children of the World*, 1882); *Neue Novellen: 10 Sammlung*, 1875; *Im Paradiese*, 1875 (*In Paradise*, 1878); *Neue moralische Novellen: 11 Sammlung*, 1878; *Zwei Gefangene*, 1878; *Das Ding an sich und andere Novellen: 12 Sammlung*, 1879; *Die Madonna im Ölwald*, 1879; *Die Eselin*, 1880 (*The Donkey*, 1888); *Frau von F. und römische Novellen: 13 Sammlung*, 1881; *Das Glück von Rothenburg*, 1881 (*The Spell of Rothenburg*, 1914); *Troubadour-Novellen: 14 Sammlung*, 1882; *Der Traumgott*,

1882; *Unversgessbare Worte*, 1882 (*Words Never to Be Forgotten*, 1888); *Unvergessbare Worte und andere Novellen: 15 Sammlung*, 1883; *Buch der Freundschaft: 16 Sammlung*, 1883; *Nino und Maso*, 1883 (*Nino and Maso*, 1914); *Siechentrost*, 1883; *Buch der Freundschaft, Neue Folge: 17 Sammlung*, 1884; *Auf Tod und Leben: 18 Sammlung*, 1886; *Der Roman der Stiftsdame*, 1887 (*The Romance of the Canoness: A Life History*, 1887); *Villa Falconieri und andere Novellen: 19 Sammlung*, 1888; *Liebeszauber*, 1889; *Merlin*, 1892; *Marienkind*, 1892; *Aus den Vorbergen*, 1893; *In der Geisterstunde und andere Spukgeschichten*, 1894; *Melusine und andere Novellen*, 1895; *Über allen Gipfeln*, 1895; *Einer von Hunderten, Hochzeit auf Capri*, 1896; *Abenteuer eines Blaustrümpfchens*, 1896 (*Adventures of a Little Blue-Stocking*, 1896); *Das Rätsel des Lebens und andere Charakterbilder*, 1897; *Männertreu, Der Sohn seines Vaters*, 1897; *Medea, Er soll dein Herr sein*, 1898; *Die Macht der Stunde, Vroni*, 1899 (*The Power of the Hour*, 1904); *Fräulein Johanne*, 1900; *Auf der Alm*, 1900; *Der Schutzengel*, 1900; *Tantalus, Mutter und Kind*, 1901; *Ninon und andere Novellen*, 1902; *Novellen vom Gardasee*, 1902; *Moralische Unmöglichkeiten und andere Novellen*, 1903; *Crone Stäudlin*, 1905; *Victoria Regia und andere Novellen*, 1906; *Gegen den Strom*, 1907; *Menschen und Schicksale*, 1908; *Herzensbande*, 1908; *Helldunkles Leben*, 1909; *Die Geburt der Venus*, 1909; *Seelsorger*, 1909; *Das Ewigmenschliche, Ein Familienhaus*, 1910; *Plaudereien eines alten Freundespaares*, 1912; *Letzte Novellen*, 1914.

SHORT FICTION: *Der Jungbrunnen*, 1850; *Neue Märchen*, 1899.

PLAYS: *Francesca von Rimini*, 1850; *Hermen*, 1854; *Meleager*, 1854; *Die Pfälzer in Irland*, 1854; *Die Sabinerinnen*, 1859; *Die Grafen von der Esche*, 1861; *Ludwig der Bayer*, 1862; *Elisabeth Charlotte*, 1864; *Maria Moroni*, 1865; *Hadrian*, 1865; *Hans Lange*, 1866 (English translation, 1885); *Die glücklichen Bettler*, 1867; *Kolberg*, 1868; *Der Rotmantel*, 1868; *Die Göttin der Vernuft*, 1870; *Adam und Eva*, 1870; *Die Franzosenbraut*, 1871; *Der Friede*, 1871; *Ehre um Ehre*, 1875; *Graf Königsmarck*, 1877; *Elfride*, 1877; *Unter den Gründlingen*, 1879; *Die Weiber von Schorndorff*, 1881; *Alkibiades*, 1882; *Das Recht des Stärkeren*, 1883; *Don Juans Ende*, 1883; *Drei einaktige Trauerspiele und ein Lustpiel*, 1884; *Getrennte Welten*, 1886; *Die Hochzeit auf dem Aventin*, 1886; *Die Weisheit Salomos*, 1887; *Gott schütze mich vor meinen Freunden*, 1888; *Prinzessin Sascha*, 1888; *Weltuntergang*, 1889, *Kleine Dramen: Erste Folge*, 1889; *Kleine Dramen: Zweite Folge*, 1889; *Ein überflüssiger Mensch*, 1890; *Die schlimmen Brüder*, 1891; *Weihnachtsgeschichten*, 1891; *Wahrheit*, 1892; *Ein unbeschriebenes Blatt*, 1893; *Jungfer Justine*, 1893; *Wolfram von Eschenbach*, 1894; *Rolands Schildknappen: Oder, Die Komödie vom Glück*, 1896; *Vanina Vanini*, 1896; *Die Fornarina*, 1896; *Drei neue Einakter*, 1897; *Der Bucklige von Schiras*, 1898; *Maria von Magdala*, 1899 (*Mary of Magdala*, 1900); *Das verschleierte Bild zu Sais*, 1901; *Der Heilige*, 1902 (*The Saint*, 1902);

Mythen und Mysterien, 1904; *Die törichten Jungfrauen*, 1905; *Ein Kanadier*, 1905; *Sechs kleine Dramen*, 1905; *König Saul*, 1909; *Mutter und Tochter*, 1909; *Die Geister des Rheins*, 1910.

POETRY: *Frühlingsanfang 1848*, 1848; *Fünfzehn neue deutsche Lieder zu alten Singweisen: Den deutschen Männern Ernst Moritz Arndt und Ludwig Uhland gewidmet*, 1848; *Gedichte*, 1872; *Gedichte*, 1885; *Das Goethehaus in Weimar*, 1896; *Verratenes Glück, Emerenz*, 1896; *Neue Gedichte und Jugendlieder*, 1897; *Ein Wintertagebuch*, 1903; *Waldmonologe aus Kreuth*, 1908; *Gedichte*, 1914; *Ausgewählte Gedichte*, 1919.

NONFICTION: *Studia romanensia: Particula I*, 1852; *Romanische Inedita auf italiänischen Bibliotheken gesammelt*, 1856; *Vincenzo Monti*, 1858; *Ein Münchener Dichterbuch*, 1862; *Meine Erstlingswerke*, 1894.

TRANSLATIONS: *Spanisches Liederbuch*, 1852; *José Caveda: Geschichte der Baukunst in Spanien*, 1858; *Italienisches Liederbuch*, 1860; *William Shakespeare: Antonius und Kleopatra*, 1867; *William Shakespeare: Timon von Athen*, 1868; *Giacomo Leopardi: Werke*, 1878; *Italienische Dichter*, 1889-1905 (5 volumes); *Italienische Volksmärchen*, 1914; *Drei italienische Lustspiele aus der Zeit der Renaissance*, 1914.

ANTHOLOGIES: *Deutscher Novellenschatz*, 1871-1876 (24 volumes); *Novellenschatz des Auslandes*, 1872-1873 (14 volumes); *Neuer deutscher Novellenschatz*, 1884-1887 (24 volumes).

Secondary

Bennett, Edwin Keppel. *A History of the German Novelle*. Edited by H. M. Waidson. 2d ed. Cambridge, England: Cambridge University Press, 1961, 1974. This study has become an indispensable handbook in the English-speaking world for those wishing to learn about the theory and practice of the novella. The sections on Heyse are informative but not particularly sympathetic to him.

Brandes, Georg. *Creative Spirits of the Nineteenth Century*. Translated by Rasmus B. Anderson. New York: Thomas Y. Crowell, 1923. This volume contains, in English translation, the classic account of Heyse's contribution to world literature, written by an eminent Danish critic who knew the poet personally. The perceptive insights gathered here have remained untarnished by the passage of time.

Lewis, George Henry. "Realism in Art: Recent German Fiction." *Westminster Review* 14 (1858): 488-518. This essay by a noted English critic is obviously dated. Yet, despite its Victorian limitations, the brilliant commentary on Heyse's craft of fiction sustains and sparks interest at every turn.

Lo Cicero, Donald. *Novellentheorie*. The Hague: Mouton and Co., 1970. Written in English, this volume includes a chapter on Heyse's theory of the novella and explores the theory in conjunction with analyses of other important theories of the novella in nineteenth century Germany.

Mitchell, Robert McBurney. *Heyse and His Predecessors in the Theory of the Novelle*. Frankfurt: Joseph Baer and Co., 1915. An American doctoral dissertation. A tedious historical description, but patient readers can learn much from its extensive treatment of the subject.

Negus, Kenneth George. "Paul Heyse's *Novellentheorie*: A Revaluation." *The Germanic Review* 40 (May, 1965): 173-191. An unusually close scrutiny of Heyse's theory of the novella. Certainly the most rewarding study of its kind. Distinguished, moreover, by the critical acumen of its author.

Paulin, Roger. *The Brief Compass: The Nineteenth-century German Novelle*. Oxford: Clarendon Press, 1985. Another examination of Heyse's theory of the novella can be found in a chapter of this book. Refreshing because, unlike other inquiries, it addresses itself to the theory's pan-European context.

Prawer, S. S. *German Lyric Poetry: A Critical Analysis of Selected Poems from Klopstock to Rilke*. London: Routledge and Kegan Paul, 1952. An interpretation of "Treueste Liebe" in this volume constitutes the best study available on any of Heyse's lyrics. Although the author can find nothing charitable to say about Heyse, the argument is, nevertheless, persuasive.

Clifford Albrecht Bernd

1911

Literature
Maurice Maeterlinck, Belgium

Peace
Tobias Asser, Netherlands
Alfred Fried, Austria

Physics
Wilhelm Wien, Germany

Chemistry
Marie Curie, France

Physiology or Medicine
Alvar Gullstrand, Sweden

MAURICE MAETERLINCK
1911

Born: Ghent, Belgium; August 29, 1862
Died: Nice, France; May 6, 1949
Language: French
Principal genres: Drama, poetry, and nonfiction

A poet, dramatist, and essayist, Maeterlinck first achieved fame as a Symbolist playwright but later developed a more realistic style as he continued to examine human emotions and the metaphysical questions of the meaning of life and the inevitability of death

The Award
Presentation
The award ceremony for the Nobel Prize in Literature in 1911 took place on December 10, with Maurice Maeterlinck *in absentia*. The presentation address by Carl David af Wirsén, Permanent Secretary of the Swedish Academy, praised Maeterlinck for his great originality, idealism, and spirituality—qualities which touched the inner depths of each of his readers. A sketch of Maeterlinck's life and artistic development recognized his early poems as the true beginning of his career and noted that his first venture into the drama was an astounding success: delightful, vigorous, and important. Nine other plays and five essays received specific mention because they exhibited the typical characteristics of the honoree's style and thought. In the dramas, the setting was usually a remote area that could not be assigned to a specific time and place, where characters frequently moved slowly and helplessly against invisible opposing powers—though in some plays more optimism prevailed. In his best plays Maeterlinck was a Symbolist in his poetry and an agnostic—though never a materialist—in his thought. His message was that the spiritual life must be found in areas beyond where the limitations of man's reason may take him. The plays would have been improved if their author had been more of a Deist, but the Academy recognized that Maeterlinck thought sincerely and profoundly in his search for truth. The Permanent Secretary also observed that in the essays a note of hope for mankind appeared and that profound reflective moments abounded. The conclusion praised Maeterlinck's vision, the nobility and charm of his conception of human life, and stated that his ideas were expressed in language which was inspired and capable of inspiring the hearts of others.

Nobel lecture
Maeterlinck, complaining of influenza, did not go to Stockholm for the ceremony and did not prepare an acceptance speech. Even without a debili-

tating illness, the ceremony would have been difficult for him because of his shyness and lack of confidence in speaking before large gatherings. Present to accept the award on Maeterlinck's behalf was Charles Wauters, Belgium's minister to Sweden.

Critical reception

New York newspapers reacted warmly to the announcement that Maeterlinck had won the Nobel Prize. *The New York Times* called him the major writer of the age, having universal appeal. According to the article, Maeterlinck wrote with perfection of style, a love for the beautiful, and a deep feeling for the magical elements in nature and man; virtually every line was a valuable contribution to the thought of a troubled age. *The New York Times* also referred to a comment in *The Evening Post* on November 9, in which Maeterlinck received praise as the most important literary figure in Europe at the time.

Several articles on Maeterlinck appeared in *The Atlantic Monthly* and *The Nation* during the weeks following the news of his award. In the December 7, 1911, issue of *The Nation*, a writer signing his name only as "S. D." was extremely critical, asserting that the literature prize, according to Alfred Nobel's will, had to go to an idealist and that the Nobel Committee went almost two decades into the past to find one. This sarcasm ignored several successful works written by Maeterlinck since 1902, including a highly praised play in 1909. Other statements were more to the point: Although Maeterlinck wrote in French, he had never won any significant portion of the French reading public; his works, in thought and feeling, were Belgian, and his name was evidently of more significance in Great Britain, America, and (it would seem) Sweden than in France; his reading public consisted only of the young, who lacked knowledge of literary tradition. Concerning Maeterlinck's essays on animals, the writer asserted that they were filled with humanlike insects, and of Maeterlinck's reputation as mystic and seer, the derisive comment was that he gave the world the latest news flashes from the land of Death.

In France and Belgium, many believed Maeterlinck to be undeserving of the prize. In fact, when Paul-Henri Spaak had initially proposed Maeterlinck for the honor, he had listed him with Émile Verhaeren as a joint entry, and both names went to the Belgian minister for sciences and arts, Baron Descamp-David, who then took them to the Nobel Committee. After Maeterlinck alone had been selected, resentment flared among many Frenchmen and Belgians who thought Maeterlinck egotistical, self-centered, materialistic, and concerned primarily with ensuring his own physical comfort.

Writing in the Brussels periodical *Le Thyrse* in January of 1912, Joseph Henri Rosny, one of the Goncourt Academy's founding members and, like Maeterlinck, a Belgian who chose to reside in France, expressed the opinions of others when he criticized the honoring of Maeterlinck and listed those whom he would have preferred to see crowned: Georges Eekhoud, Camille Lemonnier, or Émile Verhaeren.

From other sources, praises showered on the first Belgian laureate. In France, both the novelist Paul Hervieu and Raymond Poincaré, who would be the French prime minister after January, 1912, suggested that Maeterlinck should stand for election to the immensely prestigious French Academy. From Belgium, the Ghent bar sent its congratulations to one who had left its membership more than two decades earlier. In Brussels, a huge festival honored Maeterlinck. Nevertheless, two of his oldest friends, the writers Charles Van Lerberghe and Grégoire Le Roy, were not pleased. Le Roy, who had not been invited to the festival, expressed particularly bitter resentment in an article entitled "Le Poète prodigue," published in *Le Masque*, in which he complained that Maeterlinck had won through cleverness rather than talent (Le Roy did not sign the article). At the Brussels gala, Albert I and Queen Elisabeth honored Maeterlinck by presenting him with the insignia of the Order of Leopold.

Biography

Maurice-Polydore-Marie-Bernard Maeterlinck was born on August 29, 1862, in Ghent, Belgium, of an old Flemish Catholic family of comfortable means. After attending a Jesuit school for seven years, he entered Ghent University in 1881, receiving a law degree in 1885. Later that year, in Paris, he met several French Symbolists who gave impetus to his literary interests. Returning to Ghent, he began his law practice but wrote extensively in his spare time. By 1889, he had published several individual poems, a volume of verse, his first play, and a major translation. The favorable reception of the play in 1889, including an extremely flattering review published in Paris by Octave Mirbeau, encouraged Maeterlinck to abandon the law and devote himself to literature. His first plays to be performed were staged successfully in Paris in 1891.

In 1895, Maeterlinck met the actress Georgette Leblanc, who remained with him as his companion until 1918; she relieved him of much of the despair that had marked his life and work in the previous decade and influenced major changes in the style and characterization of the plays that he wrote in the years preceding the award of the Nobel Prize in 1911.

During World War II, Maeterlinck made speeches and wrote articles in support of the Allies. In 1919, he married Renée Dahon, an actress whom he had met in 1911. They lived in southern France until World War II drove them to seek refuge in the United States. After the war, they returned to Nice, where the laureate succumbed to a heart attack on May 6, 1949. Because of his agnostic beliefs, Maeterlinck had requested that his funeral not include any religious rites; after a municipal ceremony in Nice on May 10, 1949, his remains were cremated.

Literary Career

Maeterlinck's literary career began in 1883. The Belgian magazine *La Jeune Belgique* published his first poem, "Les Joncs" ("The Rushes"), in its November 1 issue. The poem shows young Maeterlinck as a follower of the Parnassians and their message of art for art's sake.

In 1885, while in Paris ostensibly to study law, he met several leading figures among the Symbolists, including Villiers de L'Isle-Adam, whose ideas influenced Maeterlinck greatly. On a second visit to Paris, in 1886, Maeterlinck published a short story, "Le Massacre des Innocents" ("The Massacre of the Innocents"), which transposes the biblical story to medieval Flanders, converting Herod's soldiers to Spanish troops and the Hebrew babies to Flemish village children. The story expresses Maeterlinck's doubts about the goodness of a deity who permits human atrocities to occur. Villiers objected to the realism of the story, advising Maeterlinck to concentrate on the Symbolists' values of mood, music, and imagery.

The story appeared in a new magazine, *La Pléiade*, which also published six of Maeterlinck's poems during the next month. Twelve more poems appeared in 1887 in *La Parnasse de la Jeune Belgique*. In 1888, a second short story, "Onirologie," manifested his continuing interest in the occult, a Symbolist obsession: An American youth, who is totally unaware of his origins, dreams of a strange village; years later, on a trip to Europe, he sees a village which corresponds exactly to the one in his dreams. The story shows Maeterlinck's indebtedness to Edgar Allan Poe and Nathaniel Hawthorne.

The year 1889 marked a major turning point for Maeterlinck. Early in the year he produced at his own expense a volume of verse, *Serres chaudes, poèmes* (*Hot Houses*, 1915); the title refers both to the hothouses of flower-loving Ghent and to the suffocating ennui of the poet's own unhappy existence. In October, Maeterlinck finished translating a work recommended to him by Villiers, *Die Chierheit der gheesteliker Brulocht* (1350; *The Adornment of Spiritual Marriage*), written by the medieval Flemish mystic Jan van Ruysbroeck; at the time he was translating the Flemish into French for his *L'Ornement des noces spirituelles* (1891), Maeterlinck still suffered from torpor and disillusionment, but he evidently believed in the possibility of direct mystical communication with God. The study of Ruysbroeck led to studies of Plato, Plotinus, Jakob Boehme, Samuel Taylor Coleridge, and Ralph Waldo Emerson.

Maeterlinck's first play, *La Princesse Maleine* (*The Princess Maleine*, 1890), also appeared in 1889, as a serial in *La Société nouvelle*, a Brussels journal; later, Maeterlinck published it himself in a single volume. The setting and major characters are typical of his early work. Princess Maleine's betrothal to Prince Hjalmar is broken when a misunderstanding develops between their families; in love with Hjalmar, she runs away to search for his castle. In disguise, she learns that he is about to marry Princess Uglyane, daughter of Jutland's vicious Queen Anne. A chance meeting with Hjalmar in the garden prompts her to reveal her true identity to him. The prince then tells Queen Anne that he wishes to be released from his vow to Uglyane, and Anne later strangles Maleine. Grief-stricken, Hjalmar kills Anne, then commits suicide. The play, as is true of several others by Maeterlinck, contains elements of the fairy tale and abounds with symbols: sun, moon, forest, water, castle, tower. *The Princess Maleine* also seems to have established Maeterlinck's reputation as a mystic. It certainly established his reputation as a great playwright. Maeterlinck sent a copy to Stéphane Mallarmé, who passed it along to Mirbeau. Mirbeau wrote an extremely flattering review of it in *Le Figaro*, calling it an extraordinarily pure and original masterpiece and comparing Maeterlinck favorably with William Shakespeare.

Maeterlinck then began writing his "death dramas," which earned for him the title "poet of terror." In *L'Intruse* (1890; *The Intruder*, 1891), the first of Maeterlinck's plays to be staged (1891), a family of six waits in one room for the recovery of the mother from childbirth. The family expects another relative to visit, but Death (the intruder) is the one who will actually come. His approach is marked with increasing dramatic tension: One of the daughters wonders why the nightingales have suddenly stopped singing; then she notices that the swans have all moved to the far side of the lake. Outside, they hear the sound of a scythe being sharpened—by a field hand, they say. Finally, a door opens and shuts downstairs, and footsteps are heard on the stairs. Death has arrived.

Later in 1891, Maeterlinck staged *Les Aveugles* (1890; *The Blind*, 1891) at Paul Fort's Théâtre d'Art in Paris. In this terrifying play, twelve blind people, one with an infant in her arms (thirteen is a number symbolizing Death), are taken by an elderly priest for a walk in a forest. The weary priest sits down to rest and, unknown to the others, dies. The blind soon become nervous and impatient; when they discover the priest dead, they become fearful. Suddenly, they hear footsteps approaching—once again Death has the physical qualities given to it in the stories of French and Belgian peasantry. One of the blind begs the approaching stranger to have mercy on them. Then all is silence—until it is shattered by the wail of the newborn child, which symbolizes the agony of all who are born to die.

The death dramas continued with the publication of *Les Sept Princesses* (1890; *The Seven Princesses*, 1909), in which a prince awakens six princesses from their long, deathlike sleep; the one he cannot awaken is the one he loves. Although much of the play reflects the despair dominating Maeterlinck at the time, the ending, as light replaces darkness on the stage, indicates the hope and trust in the creative literary power which carried the poet forward to his next play.

Pelléas et Mélisande (1892; *Pelléas and Mélisande*, 1894), staged in Paris at the Bouffes-Parisiens, is the story of adulterous lovers. Pelléas falls in love with Mélisande, the wife of his half brother, Golaud. The jealous husband then kills him and wounds her. Yet Mélisande lives to give birth to a child, so renewal will occur. This child represents something very different from the wailing infants of earlier works, whose screams indicated hopelessness and death. Critical reaction was mixed: Some Parisian critics disliked the play intensely, but the Symbolists, including Mallarmé, asserted that the play would revolutionize the drama of Europe. *Pelléas and Mélisande* increased Maeterlinck's fame greatly, particularly after 1902, when Claude Debussy wrote his opera, *Pelléas et Mélisande*, based on Maeterlinck's play.

In the next stage of his career, Maeterlinck composed plays for marionettes: *Alladine et Palomides* (*Alladine and Palomides*, 1896), *Intérieur* (*Interior*, 1896), and *La Mort de Tintagiles* (*The Death of Tintagiles*, 1899), all published in 1894. Maeterlinck saw an important analogy between the puppets and man—the one controlled by the puppeteer, the other controlled by occult forces. Maeterlinck, having read some of the writings of Arthur Schopenhauer, agreed with the German that man had almost no control over his own will.

The first of the puppet plays is another tragedy of adulterous young lovers and is a slight piece. *Interior*, another play about death, is especially interesting for its staging and its emphasis on the mimetic. Inside a house, in which a family can be seen through large windows, life goes on as usual, while outside in the garden, several others wonder how to tell those inside about the drowning of one of the family's children. As the scene develops, the actions of the puppets inside the house begin to reflect the doubt and anxiety of those conversing in the garden. In *The Death of Tintagiles*, the title character, a boy, dies because of the hatred of a cruel queen, from whom his sisters cannot save him. Nevertheless, the effort of the sisters to preserve him is a positive element lacking in earlier plays about death and represents a major change in the playwright's attitudes: Characters fight against their fate and do not passively succumb.

In 1894, Maeterlinck, always interested in English drama, finished his translation of John Ford's *'Tis Pity She's a Whore* (1633), having been drawn to it perhaps by Ford's study of illicit love and the fierce revenges resulting from it. Maeterlinck also translated two works by Novalis around this time. All three translations received critical approval.

Early in 1895 Maeterlinck met Georgette Leblanc, an attractive actress and singer. They fell in love, and their relationship changed Maeterlinck's life and work. The new happiness he found with Georgette relieved him of his personal despair; her strength and intelligence led him to create several plays with strong female characters, most to be played by Georgette. *Aglavaine et Sélysette* (1896; *Aglavaine and Selysette*, 1897) was written to please Georgette, but she did not like the role of Aglavaine, the widowed sister-in-law of Selysette. Aglavaine visits Selysette and her husband, Méléandre; almost immediately, she begins to win Méléandre's love away from his wife, who eventually leaps from one of the castle towers to her death, leaving the others to a lifetime of remorse. Although the play would receive lengthier discussion and higher praise than any other in the Nobel Prize presentation address fifteen years later, Maeterlinck was aware of some of its deficiencies: prolixity, repetitiveness, and a lack of effective imagery. He used several key symbols rather heavily in this play (the tower, the strange green bird flying around it, and Aglavaine herself), but the work marks the end of his Symbolist drama and the beginning of new directions for his career.

Maeterlinck did not compose another play for six years, instead writing extensively in other forms during this period. *Douze Chansons* (*XII Songs*, 1912), a collection of peasant songs, appeared in 1896. In that year he also issued his first major prose essay, *Le Trésor des humbles* (*The Treasure of the Humble*, 1897), an attempt to understand the nature of the human soul. A famous essay, *La Sagesse et la destinée* (1898; *Wisdom and Destiny*, 1898), marks Maeterlinck's abandonment of the negativism of Schopenhauer and movement toward the Stoicism of Marcus Aurelius and others. *La Vie des abeilles* (1901; *The Life of the Bee*, 1901) was the first of Maeterlinck's essays on plants and animals. The work makes no pretense of being a true scientific study; Maeterlinck merely wanted to draw parallels between bees and men: In particular, he defended the role of the sage in human society, who, as is the case with some bees, seems to be doing little or nothing but in reality is carrying out a function necessary to the survival and development of his kind.

Maeterlinck returned to drama with *Ariane et Barbe-Bleue* (1901; *Ardiane and Barbe Bleue*, 1901), a feminist work. The drama concentrates on the seventh wife of Barbe Bleue (Bluebeard), Ardiane, strong willed and intelligent. Having been told by Bluebeard not to unlock a certain door, she disobeys and finds her husband's six previous wives imprisoned. Her attitude toward the locked door reflects Maeterlinck's belief that in doing only what is permitted, mankind learns nothing new; only by proceeding to unlock the secret, the hidden, the occult does humanity's knowledge progress. Ardiane survives and leaves her husband; the other women remain. Ardiane was played by Georgette, and the work was a major success.

Sœur Béatrice (1901; *Sister Beatrice*, 1901) and *Monna Vanna* (1902; English translation, 1903) gave Georgette two more important roles. In the former, she played a nun who leaves the convent to pursue earthly love; the statue of the Virgin Mary, before whom Beatrice has prayed for guidance just before leaving, comes to life and takes Beatrice's place for twenty-five years. Beatrice returns, begs forgiveness, and dies; the Virgin then returns to the pedestal. The play, based on a thirteenth century miracle drama, reconciles divine and earthly love. When the Virgin takes Beatrice's identity, the spiritual and the material can no longer be opposing forces; they work harmoniously together.

In contrast, *Monna Vanna* presents a flesh-and-blood heroine, a political figure. Monna Vanna, to save her besieged city, agrees to the enemy commander's demands that she give herself to him. He, recognizing her honor and idealism, declines to take advantage of her. Later, when he is captured by her husband, she, now believing him to be honorable, plans to help him escape. This thesis play indicates a further move away from Maeterlinck's early Symbolist tendencies; it reflects his new belief that the poet should deal with truth itself rather than with the symbols of it.

In 1903, Maeterlinck's interest in Shakespeare was shown by *Joyzelle* (English translation, 1906), based on *The Tempest* (1611). In *Joyzelle*, Merlin dies because he represses his love for Joyzelle, allowing her to go to the young man whom she truly loves and who loves her. The play was not a success, and neither were his next few plays. Maeterlinck returned to the essay form, showing his continuing interest in both nature and metaphysics in *Le Double Jardin* (1904; *The Double Garden*, 1904) and *L'Intelligence des fleurs* (1907; *The Intelligence of Flowers*, 1907).

One of Maeterlinck's greatest successes was achieved, late in 1908, when *L'Oiseau bleu* (*The Blue Bird*, 1909) was staged in Moscow with Konstantin Stanislavsky directing his fairy tale of two children's search for the Blue Bird. Audiences were enthralled with the highly symbolic dramatization of mankind's search for happiness. Although William Butler Yeats would later term the play unsuccessful, *The Blue Bird* raised Maeterlinck to immense heights of popularity in both Europe and America. The winning of the Nobel Prize in 1911 added even further to his worldwide acclaim.

Maeterlinck lived almost thirty-eight years longer, but the greatest works of his career were already completed. He wrote another fifteen plays—as many as he had previously composed. Of these, the most interesting are perhaps *Le Bourgmestre de Stilmonde* (1919; *The Burgomaster of Stilemonde*, 1918), a wartime propaganda play, and *Les Fiançailles* (1922; *The Betrothal*, 1918), a sequel to *The Blue Bird*. He also continued to publish essays containing metaphysical speculations. *La Mort* (1911; *Death*, 1911) was so unacceptable to the Catholic church that the work was placed on the Index in 1913. *Le Grand Secret* (1921; *The Great Secret*, 1922) and several other essays in the following two decades illustrated his continuing obsession with metaphysics. In 1948, Maeterlinck wrote his memoirs, *Bulles bleues* (blue bubbles), which showed him to be full of happy reminiscences in the year before his death.

Bibliography

Primary

PLAYS: *La Princesse Maleine*, 1889 (*The Princess Maleine*, 1890); *L'Intruse*, 1890 (*The Intruder*, 1891); *Les Aveugles*, 1890 (*The Blind*, 1891); *Les Sept Princesses*, 1890 (*The Seven Princesses*, 1909); *Pelléas et Mélisande*, 1892

(*Pelléas and Mélisande*, 1894); *Alladine et Palomides*, 1894 (*Alladine and Palomides*, 1896); *Intérieur*, 1894 (*Interior*, 1896); *La Mort de Tintagiles*, 1894 (music by Jean Nouguès; *The Death of Tintagiles*, 1899); *Aglavaine et Sélysette*, 1896 (*Aglavaine and Selysette*, 1897); *Ariane et Barbe-Bleue*, 1901 (*Ardiane and Barbe Bleue*, 1901); *Sœur Béatrice*, 1901 (*Sister Beatrice*, 1901); *Monna Vanna*, 1902 (English translation, 1903); *Joyzelle*, 1903 (English translation, 1906); *L'Oiseau bleu*, 1908 (*The Blue Bird*, 1909); *Le Bourgmestre de Stilmonde*, 1919 (*The Burgomaster of Stilemonde*, 1918); *Les Fiançailles*, 1922 (*The Betrothal*, 1918); *La Princesse Isabelle*, 1935; *L'Abbé Sétubal*, 1940; *Le Jugement dernier*, 1959.

POETRY: *Serres chaudes, poèmes*, 1889 (*Hot Houses*, 1915); *Douze Chansons*, 1896 (*XII Songs*, 1912); *Poésies complètes*, 1965.

NONFICTION: *Le Trésor des humbles*, 1896 (*The Treasure of the Humble*, 1897); *La Sagesse et la destinée*, 1898 (*Wisdom and Destiny*, 1898); *La Vie des abeilles*, 1901 (*The Life of the Bee*, 1901); *Le Double Jardin*, 1904 (*The Double Garden*, 1904); *L'Intelligence des fleurs*, 1907 (*The Intelligence of Flowers*, 1907); *La Mort*, 1911 (*Death*, 1911); *Le Grand Secret*, 1921 (*The Great Secret*, 1922); *Bulles bleues*, 1948.

TRANSLATIONS: *L'Ornement des noces spirituelles*, 1891 (of Jan van Ruysbroeck's *Die Chierheit der gheesteliker Brulocht*); *Annabella*, 1895 (of John Ford's *'Tis Pity She's a Whore*); *"Les Disciples à Saïs," et "Les Fragments"* de *Novalis*, 1895 (of Novalis' *Die Lehrlinge zu Sais* and *Fragmente und Studien*).

Secondary

Bailly, Auguste. *Maeterlinck*. Translated by Fred Rothwell. London: Rider and Co., 1931. This analysis of Maeterlinck's philosophy is of value. Bailly argues that *Wisdom and Destiny*, though admirable, is of less merit than Maeterlinck's later speculative works. No index, no bibliography.

Halls, W. D. *Maurice Maeterlinck: A Study of His Life and Thought*. Oxford: Clarendon Press, 1960. This extremely valuable critical biography discusses Maeterlinck's major works and the development of his thought in connection with his readings, his loves and friendships, and his involvement in legal problems and practical theater matters. It is excellent for information about his family and friends, his literary sources, and his personal strengths and weaknesses. Notes, photographs, and extensive index and bibliography.

Knapp, Bettina. *Maurice Maeterlinck*. Boston: Twayne Publishers, 1975. Excellent analyses of Maeterlinck's plays, including the key symbols and the occult background lying behind them, are among the more valuable elements of this study. A lengthy summary of Maeterlinck's philosophy completes the volume. Notes, bibliographies, and index.

Leblanc, Georgette. *Souvenirs: My Life with Maeterlinck*. Translated by

Janet Flanner. New York: E. P. Dutton and Co., 1932. One of several books about her life with Maeterlinck by the singer-actress who was his companion for more than twenty years and who performed the leading roles in several of his plays. Offers detailed information about their relationship. Numerous illustrations.

Mahoney, Patrick. *Maurice Maeterlinck: Mystic and Dramatist.* Washington, D.C.: Institute for the Study of Man, 1979. The latter of two books on Maeterlinck by an American who knew him well between 1941 and 1947 (when the Maeterlincks resided in the United States) provides interesting glimpses into the dramatist's everyday life as well as information about the music and staging of the plays. In spite of its title, the volume is of little use on the subject of Maeterlinck's mysticism. One illustration.

Taylor, Una. *Maurice Maeterlinck: A Critical Study.* New York: Dodd, Mead and Co., 1915. The strength of this study is its excellent criticism of the individual plays. Of considerable interest is the analysis of the treatment of death in the early plays and its background in the beliefs of the peasantry. Useful discussions of the early lyrics also appear. Bibliography of primary works only.

Thomas, Edward. *Maurice Maeterlinck.* New York: Dodd, Mead and Co., 1911. This study contains highly appreciative discussions of Maeterlinck's early work. Thomas does not consider Maeterlinck a mystic, even though he writes about mysticism. Eight illustrations and an extensive index. Some bibliography in the prefatory section.

Howard L. Ford

1912

Literature
Gerhart Hauptmann, Germany

Peace
Elihu Root, United States

Physics
Nils Gustaf Dalén, Sweden

Chemistry
Victor Grignard, France
Paul Sabatier, France

Physiology or Medicine
Alexis Carrel, France

GERHART HAUPTMANN
1912

Born: Obersalzbrunn, Silesia, Germany; November 15, 1862
Died: Agnetendorf, Silesia, Germany; June 6, 1946
Language: German
Principal genres: Drama, fiction, poetry, and nonfiction

A practitioner of all literary genres, Hauptmann was a pioneer in naturalist drama, whose grainy fidelity to working-class conditions revolutionized German literature

The Award

Presentation

The Nobel Prize in Literature was presented to Gerhart Hauptmann on December 10, 1912, by King Gustaf V Adolf of Sweden. Hans Hildebrand, Acting Secretary of the Swedish Academy, delivered the presentation address. Hauptmann's nomination as the prize's recipient had been made on October 16, 1912.

The presentation address opened by drawing attention to the recipient's historical significance and by underlining the originality and modernity of his contribution to the drama. Hauptmann's fidelity to the working-class inhabitants of his native Silesia and to their problematical morality was also stressed, and the social implications of his dramatic vision were explicated: "The realism in Hauptmann's plays leads necessarily to brighter dreams of new and better conditions and to the wish for their fulfillment."

In addition, reference was made to the work of Hauptmann's postnaturalist phase, when his work for the stage and in fiction expressed a mystical component to his thought, with particular reference to the novel *Der Narr in Christo Emanuel Quint* (1910; *The Fool in Christ: Emanuel Quint*, 1911). In this novel, as in his work generally, "Hauptmann's particular virtue is his penetrating and critical insight into the human soul. . . . The plays reveal his great art by their powerful concentration which holds the reader or spectator from beginning to end. Whatever subject he treats, even when he deals with life's seamy side, his is always a noble personality. That nobility and his refined art give his works their wonderful power."

In conclusion, the presentation address characterized Hauptmann as a possessor of "the divine gift of intuition," which enabled him to probe beneath the surface of the familiar, while at the same time providing veracious depictions of the everyday world. Hauptmann's intuitive gifts were most abundantly expressed by the range and vitality of his *dramatis personae*. Moreover, these gifts were intimately connected to an admirable capacity for thought. The combination of due thought and keenly sympathetic insight "will gradually lead the true artist to the precious conviction, 'I have finally reached the truth.'" Hauptmann had "attained the highest rank of art," which the award of the Nobel Prize ratified, "primarily in recognition of his fruitful, varied, and outstanding production in the realm of dramatic art."

Nobel lecture

Hauptmann's Nobel lecture was brief and anticlimactic. Rather than use the occasion to address a world audience, as many more recent recipients have chosen to do, Hauptmann barely remained within the bounds of courtesy and protocol with his remarks. The decision to speak only in generalized, and rather platitudinous, terms seems all the more worthy of note in view of the publication in *The New York Times* of December 8, 1912 (two days before the Nobel Prize ceremony), of a translation of a combative article by Hauptmann entitled "Tolerance," which first appeared in the *Berliner Tageblatt*. This article will strike the reader as bearing a close resemblance to Nobel Prize acceptance speeches made since the 1960's.

Nevertheless, despite its essentially formulaic and uncontroversial nature, Hauptmann's acceptance speech does connect the prize with some of his own concerns. In language somewhat reminiscent of that of his plays, he associates the prize and his acceptance of it with "the memory of those men whose self-denying and lyncean task on this earth consists in attending to the cultivation of the mind's soil, so that the weeds may be rooted out and the good shoots be nurtured." Moreover, Hauptmann salutes, in terms that generally echo those of the article on tolerance, the Nobel Foundation's dedication to world peace, invoking at the same time "that great, ultimate, and purely ideal Nobel Prize which humanity will bestow upon itself when brute violence is banished from the intercourse of nations, as it has been banished from that of individuals in civilized societies."

Critical reception

Gerhart Hauptmann was not a popular choice for the 1912 Nobel Prize in Literature. This reaction has much to do with the nature of the literary material with which he made his name. The increasing tendency toward realism in literature, together with the typically proletarian scenarios on which the new literary movement drew, created cultural and political shock waves throughout Europe and the United States from the 1880's onward. To have this school of literary thought canonized in the person of Hauptmann displeased some, who pointed to the supposedly more deserving cases of Anatole France and Gabriele D'Annunzio.

Not all the criticism was based on literary criteria. The new laureate, it was noted, was a citizen of the newly powerful German Empire, as were a putatively disproportionate number of Nobel laureates before him. As a result, diplomatic rumblings were to be heard from imperial capitals hostile to German pretensions, namely London and Paris. One typical expression of this nonliterary dimension of Hauptmann's award was made in the influential *Pall Mall Gazette*, where it was hinted that other nations' disappointment over the neglect of their favorite literary sons might be compensated for by the fact that "Herr Hauptmann represents a school of dramatic art with which the Kaiser can scarcely be in sympathy."

The brief announcement of Hauptmann's success in *The Times* of London was characterized by a certain aloofness; the announcement merely noted that the author was "overwhelmed with congratulations" in Berlin, implying that this was not the case in London. A more comprehensive expression of the general air of hostility was given in *The New York Times*. An editorial that appeared on the day of the award ceremony stated: "It would be hard to convince any unprejudiced student of literature that [Hauptmann] is a great writer. . . . He has done nothing in the service of the Ideal that will last through the ages." (This last sentence echoes the language of the Nobel Prize citation, which states that the award is made for "the most excellent work of an idealistic tendency.") Despite the paucity of its actual news coverage of the award and the award ceremony, *The New York Times* did not fail to mention the financial details of Hauptmann's success ($40,000 in prize money).

It is clear from these accounts and reactions, however, that there was no awareness that Hauptmann received the prize on the third time that he was considered. His name was first put forward ten years previously and was strongly advocated again in 1906. Had Hauptmann been a success earlier, the outcry would undoubtedly have been much more vociferous. On the other hand, the ill-judged and unsympathetic reception that Hauptmann's Nobel laureateship received reveals more than that particular author's reputation. It also illuminates how poorly prepared the custodians of public opinion seem to have been for the onslaught of modernism, which the naturalism espoused by Hauptmann, among many others, presaged. The Swedish Academy was more in touch with at least one manifestation of the temper of the times than were more powerful cultural barometers in London and New York.

Biography

Gerhart Hauptmann was born on November 15, 1862, in Obersalzbrunn in Silesia, Germany, a part of the country where his family had long been established. (His father owned the hotel in the town.) Hauptmann's literary credentials were shared with his older brother Carl, a poet. A slow learner, Hauptmann was initially given the opportunity to become a farmer. This he rejected, preferring instead to attend classes in sculpture at Breslau Academy of Art. After two years there, he transferred for a semester to the University of Jena. In 1883, Hauptmann went to Rome to follow his desire to sculpt. By 1884, he was back in Germany, taking classes in graphic art at the Dresden Academy. Further attempts to educate himself led Hauptmann to study history for a year in Berlin, where he also took acting lessons. His life finally shed its meandering and unproductive character in 1885, when he married the wealthy Marie Thienemann and settled near Berlin, where he began to write.

Beginning not unsuccessfully as a writer of both prose and verse, Hauptmann quickly found his true métier in the theater. His naturalistic play *Vor Sonnenaufgang* (1889; *Before Dawn*, 1909) established his reputation at once. Despite continuing success, however, his marriage began to fail, leading to his divorce in 1904 and his remarriage, to Margarete Marschalk, in the same year. Extensive travel in Italy and Greece, both before and after World War I, broadened the range of his literary concerns, producing a combination of verbosity and loftiness which is at the core of the novelist Thomas Mann's caricature of him, as Mynheer Peeperkorn, in Mann's novel *Der Zauberberg* (1924; *The Magic Mountain*, 1927).

Despite undiminished productivity and increased intellectuality, Hauptmann's career fell into something of an artistic decline after his receipt of the Nobel Prize, and he allowed himself to become a sort of national monument. The effect of this lack of self-awareness led to his name being used to support the Nazis: Hauptmann remained in Germany throughout the Nazi period. Hauptmann died at the age of eighty-three in his home at Agnetendorf, Silesia. (The house was in the hands of Polish and Russian troops at the time.) He is buried on the island of Hiddensee in the Baltic Sea.

Literary Career

In a certain sense, the career of Gerhart Hauptmann is a striking example of what may be achieved by the perfect coincidence of a man and his time. Not only did Hauptmann identify his literary talents with the most challenging and modern artistic idiom of the day, naturalism, but he also chose a medium for that idiom—the theater—which was undergoing one of the more decisive changes in its history. The revaluation of mid-century realism which, inspired by the work of Émile Zola, the naturalists undertook, found forceful expression in a new sense of experimentation in the theater. The result was twofold. On the one hand, a new and different type of theater came into being, such as the Théâtre Libre of André Antoine in Paris and the Independent Theatre of J. T. Grein in London. In addition, a new generation of playwrights, George Bernard Shaw and Anton Chekhov among them, created work that irreversibly altered future audiences' awareness of the social significance and cultural relevance of the theater.

Hauptmann's initial success crystallizes the coincidence of novelty and change. Chronologically, he was subject to the influence of Henrik Ibsen, which swept the European theater at the end of the nineteenth century. Culturally, his path-breaking work *Before Dawn* was first produced in Berlin's Freie Bühne, a small, independent, radical theater. Both the play and the production are widely held to be of decisive importance in the development of the theater in Germany, to the extent that it is difficult to overestimate their impact.

Hauptmann's overnight success resulted in his nomination as *"Hauptmann* [captain] of the wild band of the naturalists" by local critics. For a time, Hauptmann did his best to live up to this characterization, with plays such as *Der Biberpelz* (1893; *The Beaver Coat*, 1912), *Fuhrmann Henschel* (1898; *Drayman Henschel*, 1913), *Rose Bernd* (1903; English translation, 1913), and, above all, the work that is considered to be his dramatic masterpiece, *Die Weber* (1892; *The Weavers*, 1899). These works and numerous others— Hauptmann was prolific—consolidated his position as one of Europe's leading dramatists.

There are a number of reasons that *The Weavers*, which was first produced at the Freie Bühne in 1893, may be considered Hauptmann's greatest work for the theater, some of which have less to do with the play's formal and aesthetic merits than with the controversial nature of its subject. *The Weavers* deals with social conditions created by the impact of mechanized means of production on traditional weaving practices in the author's native Silesia. Thus, together with the grim naturalistic approach, the material itself is politically explosive and reveals Hauptmann as a trenchant critic of capitalism. The combination of politically disturbing subject matter and artistically challenging treatment caused the play to be banned by the Berlin authorities. Despite its notoriety, however, *The Weavers* is a superb piece of theatrical orchestration, offering the opportunity of consummate ensemble playing and written with a rare mixture of sympathy and objectivity. In this play it is possible to glimpse the artistic and thematic origins of two of the giants of twentieth century theater, Sean O'Casey and Bertolt Brecht.

While much has been made of Hauptmann's identification with and promotion of naturalism, it is inaccurate to consider him as nothing but an exponent of that artistic approach. His earliest known writing was in verse, and he never forsook for very long his commitment to what he perceived to be the poetic dimension of his authorial gifts. Thus, it is important to note that while Hauptmann's output in the years between the production of *Before Dawn* and his acceptance of the Nobel Prize consisted largely of plays written in the naturalistic mode, he also produced other kinds of drama. The most important of the other genres are historical drama and works written in the poetic vein. None of his historical plays merits attention here. Of the poetic plays, however, mention must be made of *Hanneles Himmelfahrt* (1893; *The Assumption of Hannele*, 1894), first produced by Antoine at his Théâtre Libre. Subtitled "A Dream Poem," it has more in common with the symbolic drama of Maurice Maeterlinck than with the work Hauptmann had been doing up to that point. Indeed, considering the development of Hauptmann's career after 1912, it could well be argued that this play provides a more accurate view of his artistic temperament than do the naturalistic plays.

The achievement of *The Assumption of Hannele* at a comparatively early period in Hauptmann's career bears out André Gide's observation about him: "He knew how to renew himself constantly." Undoubtedly Gide meant the remark to be complimentary. It is not clear, however, that the course of Hauptmann's career after his receipt of the Nobel Prize, in which his dramatic talents were turned almost exclusively to poetic and symbolic drama, added very much to his stature as a luminary of European literature. There is an inescapable irony in the fact that, beginning at the moment of public apotheosis that the Nobel Prize represents, Hauptmann's career lost its bearings, lost its sense of a public and of a time. Hauptmann's own admission late in life that he had "always kept to the outskirts of history" explains the ambit of his later works. Unwittingly, no doubt, the statement also suggests the rarefied and remote character of much of these works. The broadening of concerns found in the later works—most successfully perhaps in *Und "Pippa tanzt!* (1906; *And Pippa Dances!*, 1907)—tempted him to compare his talents with those of William Shakespeare, Johann Wolfgang von Goethe, and the Greek tragedians. His pursuit of the artistic range and depth with which those names are synonymous led to pastiches such as *Hamlet in Wittenberg* (1935) and the work which occupied his last years, *Die Atriden-Tetralogie* (1949), which includes *Iphigenie in Delphi* (1941), *Iphigenie in Aulis* (1943), *Agamemnons Tod* (1946; Agamemnon's death), and *Elektra* (1947).

Another aspect of that fertility to which André Gide's comment refers is Hauptmann's willingness to work in all literary forms, from the verse epic to the novella. His success in the latter genre is in inverse proportion to that which he achieved through artistic sallies into saga. From the beginning of his career, however, Hauptmann was producing work in prose that also has a permanent place in his country's literature, though perhaps a less prominent one than his plays occupy. His novella *Bahnwärter Thiel* (1888; *Flagman Thiel*, 1933) created a strong impression when it appeared (Hauptmann later adapted it for the stage), as did his atmospherically powerful *Der Ketzer von Soana* (1918; *The Heretic of Soana*, 1923).

In addition, Hauptmann wrote full-length novels and, again, was doing so when his career as a naturalistic playwright was far advanced. His first novel is his most successful and may have been the proximate stimulus for the Nobel Committee's decision, particularly in view of the favorable references to it in the presentation address. The novel, *The Fool in Christ*, tells the story of how a naïve believer in the power of Jesus Christ's example was repudiated and condemned, ultimately leading to delusion and insanity. This long, ambitious novel commanded widespread attention as a result of the controversial nature of its theme. It is, however, a work that is finally unable to articulate the message that it continually seems on the brink of making. Hauptmann's other well-known novel, *Atlantis* (1912; English translation, 1912), more closely resembles a potboiler: Its story line combines disaster at sea (in the year of the ill-fated *Titanic*'s sailing) with loosely conceived love plots.

Despite the artistic success of his prose fiction, it seems unlikely that Hauptmann would have commanded the same public and the same degree of international attention with it as he did with his plays. This conclusion becomes even more tenable when one takes into account the elaborate verse works that Hauptmann published in the late 1920's into the 1930's. Of these, only *Till Eulenspiegel* (1927) is worthy of mention, on the basis that it gives the interested reader another version of a familiar German tale. Ultimately, the abundance and the variety of Hauptmann's oeuvre lead to the irresistible conclusion that in it a dissipation of the author's talents is perceived, rather than a consolidation of them. One of the means of assessing Hauptmann's final standing in the ranks of other Nobel laureates is to consider how many of the very greatest devoted themselves to one, or at most two, literary forms. Hauptmann, on the other hand, seemed to suffer from an exaggerated sense of his own creative vitality. Although Thomas Mann's statement that Hauptmann "combined all the essential features of every known style" is meant in a kindly way, it also points to a fundamental weakness in Hauptmann's artistic development.

In this regard, it is instructive to compare the career and the aesthetic-philosophical commitments of Hauptmann's work with those of the other major German writer of his generation, Nobel laureate Thomas Mann. Mann's early work shows an overly facile engagement with the ethereal, which can result from ideologically disengaged, or unironically idealistic, art. One reason, at least, for Mann's Nobel Prize honor was his obvious maturation as an artist, which yielded an increasing awareness of cultural and social and national questions that pressed upon him. The intellectual complexity and artistic sophistication with which Mann enacted the interplay between these two spheres are in marked contrast to the largely generalized, culturally detached, and imaginatively vapid character of too much of Hauptmann's work after 1912.

Hauptmann's exclusion from the front rank of Nobel laureates still puts him in excellent literary company, bearing in mind that the Nobel Prize was, in Hauptmann's day, the sole preserve of European authors. He is certainly not the least significant author to have received the prize. In any case, while the overall quality of his output is questionable, his work from the beginning of his career until 1912 resulted in some remarkable texts for the theater. Moreover, nothing can diminish the significance of the revolution in European theater in which he participated and which he helped to characterize, or the momentous impact on German literature effected by his plays.

At their best, Hauptmann's plays speak in brutal, direct tones and show decisive action on matters that previously were concealed or that were re-

jected as being inadequate for literary treatment. The fact that Hauptmann
would not deny either the nature of his material or his sense of how it demanded to be communicated argues for the artistic integrity of his major
work. It is because of that integrity—the refusal to compromise either art or
the life on which it draws—that Hauptmann merits attention and merits also
his place among those who, by their literary efforts, have shaped the consciousness of the age. To these efforts, Thomas Mann has paid a fitting
tribute:

> He did not speak in his own guise, but let life itself talk with the tongues of
> changing, active human beings. He was neither a man of letters nor a rhetori-
> cian, neither an analyst nor a formal dialectitian; his dialect was that of life it-
> self; it was human drama.

Bibliography

Primary

NOVELS: *Der Narr in Christo Emanuel Quint*, 1910 (*The Fool in Christ:
Emanuel Quint*, 1911); *Atlantis*, 1912 (English translation, 1912); *Die Insel
der grossen Mutter*, 1924 (*The Island of the Great Mother*, 1925).

SHORT FICTION: *Fasching*, 1887; *Bahnwärter Thiel*, 1888 (*Flagman Thiel*,
1933); *Der Apostel*, 1890; *Lohengrin*, 1913; *Parsival*, 1914 (English translation, 1915); *Der Ketzer von Soana*, 1918 (*The Heretic of Soana*, 1923);
Phantom, 1922 (English translation, 1922); *Der Schuss im Park*, 1941; *Das
Märchen*, 1941; *Mignon*, 1947.

PLAYS: *Vor Sonnenaufgang*, 1889 (*Before Dawn*, 1909); *Das Friedensfest*,
1890 (*The Reconciliation*, 1910); *Einsame Menschen*, 1891 (*Lonely Lives*,
1898); *Die Weber*, 1892 (*The Weavers*, 1899); *Kollege Crampton*, 1892
(*Colleague Crampton*, 1929); *Der Biberpelz*, 1893 (*The Beaver Coat*, 1912);
Hanneles Himmelfahrt, 1893 (*The Assumption of Hannele: A Dream
Poem*, 1894); *Florian Geyer*, 1896 (English translation, 1929); *Die
versunkene Glocke*, 1896 (*The Sunken Bell*, 1898); *Fuhrmann Henschel*,
1898 (*Drayman Henschel*, 1913); *Schluck und Jau*, 1900 (*Schluck and Jau*,
1929); *Michael Kramer*, 1900 (English translation, 1911); *Der rote Hahn*,
1901 (*The Conflagration*, 1929); *Der arme Heinrich*, 1902 (*Henry of Auë*,
1929); *Rose Bernd*, 1903 (English translation, 1913); *Elga*, 1905 (wr. 1896;
English translation, 1906); *Und Pippa tanzt!*, 1906 (*And Pippa Dances!*,
1907); *Die Jungfern vom Bischofsberg*, 1907 (*The Maidens of the Mount*,
1929); *Kaiser Karls Geisl*, 1908 (*Charlemagne's Hostage*, 1915); *Griselda*,
1909 (English translation, 1929); *Die Ratten*, 1911 (*The Rats*, 1929); *Gabriel Schillings Flucht*, 1912 (wr. 1905-1906; *Gabriel Schilling's Flight*,
1929); *The Dramatic Works of Gerhart Hauptmann*, 1912-1929 (9 volumes); *Festspiel in deutschen Reimen*, 1913 (*Commemoration Masque*,
1929); *Der Bogen des Odysseus*, 1914 (*The Bow of Odysseus*, 1917);

Winterballade, 1917 (*Winter Ballad*, 1929); *Der weisse Heiland*, 1920 (*The White Savior*, 1924); *Indipohdi*, 1920 (English translation, 1925); *Peter Brauer*, 1921 (wr. 1910); *Veland*, 1925 (English translation, 1929); *Dorothea Angermann*, 1926; *Spuk: Oder, Die schwarze Maske und Hexenritt*, 1929; *Vor Sonnenuntergang*, 1932 (*Before Sunrise*, 1948); *Die goldene Harfe*, 1933; *Hamlet in Wittenberg*, 1935; *Ulrich von Lichtenstein*, 1939; *Die Tochter der Kathedrale*, 1939; *Iphigenie in Delphi*, 1941; *Magnus Garbe*, 1942 (wr. 1914-1915); *Iphigenie in Aulis*, 1943; *Die Finsternisse*, 1947 (wr. 1937); *Agamemnons Tod*, 1946; *Elektra*, 1947; *Die Atriden-Tetralogie*, 1949 (includes *Iphigenie in Delphi, Iphigenie in Aulis, Agamemnons Tod*, and *Elektra*); *Herbert Engelmann*, 1952 (wr. 1924).

POETRY: *Anna*, 1921; *Die blaue Blume*, 1927; *Till Eulenspiegel*, 1927; *Der grosse Traum*, 1942; *Neue Gedichte*, 1946.

NONFICTION: *Griechischer Frühling*, 1908; *Um Volk und Geist*, 1932.

Secondary

Garten, Hugh F. *Gerhart Hauptmann*. New Haven, Conn.: Yale University Press, 1954. The leading English-speaking authority on Hauptmann presents here a succinct, thoughtful overview of his subject's life and thought. For student and general reader alike. Contains an index and bibliography.

Klenze, Camillo von. *From Goethe to Hauptmann: Studies in a Changing Culture*. New York: Viking Press, 1926. Reprint. New York: Biblo and Tannen, 1966. Despite being somewhat dated, this work continues to be a valuable guide to the German cultural context from which Hauptmann emerged, an understanding of which is crucial to an appreciation of his drama's originality. In addition to an index, there are valuable notes and bibliographies.

Shaw, Leroy R. *Witness of Deceit: Gerhart Hauptmann as Critic of Society*. Berkeley: University of California Press, 1958. This scholarly study covers the subject's career up to 1896, the year in which the author detects a decisive shift of emphasis in Hauptmann's work from specifically social to more generally metaphysical concerns. Hauptmann is depicted as an enemy of *Kulturlüge*, or social lie, a view that is developed in the light of the writings of Max Nordau, a contemporary German ideologue. In addition to an index and an extensive bibliography, this brief study contains a chronology of Hauptmann's life and work up to 1896.

Sinden, Margaret. *Gerhart Hauptmann: The Prose Plays*. Toronto: University of Toronto Press, 1957. Reprint. New York: Russell and Russell, 1975. This substantial book concentrates on Hauptmann's pre-Nobel career and deals in detail with the plays that have ensured for him his lasting reputation. A clear case is argued for the superiority of the early plays; in every way this book is the most satisfying scholarly study of the important aspects of Hauptmann the dramatist.

Weisert, John Jacob. *The Dream in Gerhart Hauptmann*. New York: King's Crown Press, 1949. A scholarly mapping of dream phenomena and dream interpretation in Hauptmann's work. This brief work concentrates on the lesser-known and less-accessible poetic dramas, particularly the output of Hauptmann's post-Nobel years.

George O'Brien

1913

Literature
Rabindranath Tagore, India

Peace
Henri Lafontaine, Belgium

Physics
H. Kamerlingh Onnes, Netherlands

Chemistry
Alfred Werner, Switzerland

Physiology or Medicine
Charles Richet, France

RABINDRANATH TAGORE
1913

Born: Calcutta, India; May 7, 1861
Died: Calcutta, India; August 7, 1941
Language: Bengali
Principal genre: Poetry

A mystical poet who merged faith and thought, Tagore was distinguished by his universal quality, by the spiritual quality of his verse, and by his efforts to reconcile Eastern and Western thought

The Award

Presentation

The Nobel Prize in Literature was awarded to Rabindranath Tagore on November 13, 1913, by Harald Hjärne, Chairman of the Nobel Committee of the Swedish Academy. The presentation stressed the "idealistic tendency" of Tagore's verse, which the poet had himself translated from his native Bengali into English, thereby making it accessible to the "entire Western world." Tagore's "profundity of thought" and his "warmth of feeling" were praised by the Academy, which regarded his work not as "erotic" but as "universally human in character."

The presentation stressed the religious quality of Tagore's work, which was regarded from a Christian perspective and tied to the "rejuvenating force" of the Christian mission in India. For example, the Brahmo Samaj religious community to which Tagore and his father belonged was discussed in terms of interpreting Hindu traditions in the light of the "spirit and import" of Christianity. Even Tagore's background was "Westernized." While noting his travels in India and his "contemplative hermit life" on the Padma River, the Academy also called attention to the European mores Tagore acquired in England, where he studied briefly in his youth.

As a mystical poet, Tagore served as an instructive "intermediary" who posited a culture at odds with the materialistic "cult of work" in the West. Yet Tagore's mysticism was seen not as stereotypically Eastern in its rejection of personality but as Western in its active search to discover the "living Father of the whole creation." Since this search, which the Academy associated with *bhakti* (a monotheistic strain in Hinduism), also has Christian ties, Tagore's efforts to draw people together effectively bound East and West at a time when strife threatened.

Nobel lecture

Tagore, who had returned to India after his tour of the United States and England, a tour that brought him to the attention of Western literary critics and perhaps aided in his selection, received word of the Nobel Prize while he was at Santiniketan. There was no Nobel lecture, only a telegram of acceptance: "I beg to convey to the Swedish Academy my grateful appreciation of the breadth of understanding which has brought the distant near, and has made a stranger a brother." The reconciliation of opposites and the emphasis on universal brotherhood, themes the Swedish Academy had found in his poetry, were also present in the telegram.

Critical reception

The Indian response to the award was nationalistic; in fact, the announcement of the award in the newspaper *Empire* noted that Tagore was the first Asiatic to receive the award and that, with the award, Bengali was finally recognized as a literary language. Tagore's Indian critics, those who had suggested that he dabbled in too many literary forms and those who had faulted his Bengali, were temporarily silenced and organized a public reception for him at Santiniketan. Unfortunately, Tagore uncharacteristically insulted the crowd, which contained many of his former detractors. While his behavior was attacked by many of his critics, Bipin Chandra Pal, writing in the *Hindu Review*, defended Tagore's rebuke to his audience. On the whole, Tagore's recognition seemed to indicate an acceptance of his ideal of a new world civilization based on the best qualities of East and West.

In the Western world too, Tagore's award was regarded not only as due recognition of literary merit but also as a symbol of the West's overdue recognition of a vital non-Western language; it became impossible to ignore neglected Asian humanity and its potential contributions to world culture. Jean Guehenon, a French critic, declared that Tagore's award proved the narrowness of Western civilization and made Westerners aware of the "relativity of our European concepts." The English reaction was more imperialistic; the Birmingham *Post* praised "Indian-English" poetry and incongruously coupled Tagore with Rudyard Kipling, since the two were the only "English" authors to have received the award. In a similar vein, the *Irish Citizen* linked Tagore with William Butler Yeats because of the mystical element in their poetry and saw Tagore's nomination as a vindication of Irish literature. For Western Christians, who regarded Tagore's poems as reflecting the influence of Christianity in Hinduism, the award heralded the advent of a new Christianized India.

In the United States, the press, except for *The New York Times*, paid little attention to the award. The first mention of the award (November 14, 1913) remarked on Tagore's race in distinctly American terms: It was the "first time that this prize has been given to anybody but a white person." This article, which also praised the Tagore family, was followed the next day by a notice in "Topics of the Times." American reaction was described as a mixture of surprise and resentment that Occidental writers were passed over in favor of a "Hindu bard" with "a name hard to pronounce." The writer added that Tagore, "if not exactly one of us, is, as an Aryan, a distant relation of all white folk" and observed that Tagore had a Western education and did translate his poems into "good sound English" before submitting them to the public. While acknowledging the spiritual quality of Tagore's verse, the writer concluded that spirituality alone did not make literary greatness and regarded the award as evidence of a lack of great contemporary writers.

The New York Times of November 23, 1913, was more favorable to Tagore, though the writer noted Tagore's relative anonymity and implied that the prize might have more appropriately been given to Alfred Noyes, the English poet. Rather than discuss Tagore's poetry, the reviewer praised his "versatility" as singer, composer, editor, philosopher, spiritual leader, and estate administrator and then reprinted, without comment, some of the poems. There were also the almost obligatory comparisons to Western mystics such as Yeats and Thomas à Kempis. Such comparisons were developed in *The New York Times* of November 30: The reviewer attributed Tagore's success to the awakening interest in things Oriental and to the "Western drift to mysticism" as manifested in contemporary European writers and in the Celtic revival. Even this favorable response had less to do with the poetry than with the man, intellectual currents, and political ideas. Perhaps because there was so little of Tagore's poetry in English—and that little only recently available—there was a lack of literary criticism. Even at this stage of his career Tagore the poet was subordinate to Tagore the man, the institution, the symbol of the Third World.

Biography

Rabindranath Tagore was born on May 7, 1861, in Calcutta, India, the descendant of a wealthy, aristocratic family prominent in the cultural life of Bengal. His parents were Debendranath Tagore, a businessman and religious leader, and Sarada, née Devi. The artistic and literary interests of his extended family and their close associates made an early convert of Tagore, who wrote his first work while in his early teens.

An inveterate reader but an undisciplined student, Tagore was sent to study English literature at University College in London when he was seventeen. After a year and a half he returned to India, where he resumed his literary career, writing devotional songs, musicals, prose dramas, and literary criticism, as well as editing journals. After becoming active in politics—he led public protests against the Bengal Partition Order—he left India for the United States and England, where he gained the attention of Western literary critics. After he returned to India in 1913, he received the Nobel Prize in Literature and was knighted in 1915.

After receiving the Nobel Prize, he became an international figure whose time was consumed by traveling and lecture tours, which he undertook primarily to raise money for the Visva-Bharati University he had established in 1918 at Santiniketan. While he continued to write throughout his life, he dedicated himself increasingly to educational reform, to philosophical and religious concerns, and—at the age of seventy—to painting. When he died in 1941, he had become a Renaissance man of letters and an international institution.

Literary Career

Few writers have been as fortunate in their upbringing as Tagore, who was born into a cultured and artistic family that not only encouraged his literary pursuits but also had the financial resources to enable him to devote his life to literature. His childhood served almost as an apprenticeship for his life's work, for he benefited from an impressive education, the company of renowned artists, and a father who instilled in his son a passion for synthesis in religion, a commitment to the Bengali language, and an appreciation for the rural Bengal landscape.

It is hardly surprising that Tagore wrote his first poem when he was eight and that he continued to write voluminously throughout his life. Before he left for England in 1878, he had already published stories, essays, and plays, some of which were performed at the Tagore home. In 1880 he abandoned the study of law at University College in London and returned to India, but he brought back with him an appreciation of English literature and Western music, which influenced his musical drama. By the time he was twenty-five, he was an established lyric poet whose use of repetition and refrain distinguished him from his contemporaries.

His work was primarily influenced by the Vaishnava lyrics, but he was also influenced by Percy Bysshe Shelley, whose "Hymn to Intellectual Beauty" he particularly admired. The work written beyond 1886 contains much experimentation, but changes in Tagore's life, his marriage in 1883 and the death of his older brother Jyotirendranath's wife (she and Tagore had been close), brought his youthful period to a close. In fact, in *Jivansmriti* (1912; *My Reminiscences*, 1917) Tagore stated that 1886 marked the end of a literary phase: "So having escorted them to the door of the inner sanctuary I take leave of my readers."

Edward John Thompson labels the years 1887 to 1897 as the "Shileida and Sādhanā Period" because during this period Tagore lived at Shileida managing the family estate in Bengal and editing the periodical *Sādhanā*. While he administered the estate on the Padma River, he also observed the Bengali peasants and the seasons, and corresponding moods, of the year. The acquisition of his subject matter and his imagery made these years, by his own admission, his most productive ones. That productivity was exhibited in *Sādhanā*, which he filled with stories and articles about economics and politics and which occupied much of his time during this period.

Tagore's most notable poetry of the period was *Sonār tari* (1893; *The Golden Boat*, 1932), which reflects his belief in the *jibandelbatā* (life deity), the complex interplay between a life deity and the poet: The deity is realized through the poet's work. The plays of the period are devoted to political issues, which attracted his attention. In 1897 he attended the Bengal Provincial Conference, which he attempted to have conducted in Bengali, rather than English. Despite his admiration for English literature, he knew that language and politics are related and saw nationalism, including the use of Bengali, as a means of national self-expression. (He was more successful in 1908, when his presidential address at this conference broke the English-language tradition.)

At the turn of the century, Indian history was characterized by political unrest as nationalist sentiment increased, while the Boer War suggested that Great Britain might not be invincible. As is always the case with Tagore, life and literature were one, and his political activity resulted in a lessening of his poetic productivity, though he wrote some dramas set in India's past. His poetry of this period is epitomized by *Naivedya* (1901; offerings), which contains patriotic lyrics and religious poems. His editorial work continued: He became editor of *Bhārati* in 1898 and of *Bāngadarshar* in 1901, the year he moved his family to Santiniketan, where he used the family estate to establish an experimental school. The school became his lifelong commitment, and money from his extensive lecture tours, as well as the Nobel Prize funds, went to financing it. The school also served as a retreat for Tagore, who found poetic inspiration and subject matter in the arid upland plain, the other Bengal, as opposed to the river at Shileida. The Abode of Peace, as his father had named the estate, served Tagore well at a time when he experienced personal tragedy: In 1902, his wife died; in 1904, his second daughter; and in 1905, his father.

In 1905, Tagore was stirred to action by the Bengal Partition Order, which was designed to weaken Indian nationalism, and he wrote prose and patriotic songs, which he himself sang, in support of the nationalist movement. Though he was regarded as a subversive nationalist by the British, his nationalism was more cultural than political; he wanted to establish Indian culture and to reconstruct Bengali village life. When he became disenchanted with the nationalistic movement, which had neglected social reform and which had become increasingly violent, he abruptly retired to Santiniketan, where he resumed writing poetry and, in particular, symbolic dramas which stressed republicanism and criticized monarchy.

It was his poetry, however, that afforded Tagore the opportunity to become an international writer, rather than a Bengali poet. In 1910 Tagore published *Gitānjali*, a collection of poems rich in details from the world of nature. William Rothenstein, a young painter who had organized the India Society in London, toured India in 1911 and visited Tagore. It was the start of a long relationship rich in correspondence, and it was at Rothenstein's urging that Tagore translated *Gitānjali* into English and visited the United States and England in 1912. That year, through Rothenstein's efforts, the India Society published a private edition of Tagore's translated poems as *Song Offerings*.

Tagore became a literary sensation, largely because of the efforts of William Butler Yeats, a fellow mystic who introduced Tagore's poetry to influential critics and writers—among them Ernest Rhys, who published one of the first English critical books on Tagore. Tagore's reputation spread to the United States, where he visited and lectured in 1913 and where his poems had been published in the prestigious literary journal *Poetry*. These foreign visits accomplished what Tagore and his supporters had hoped: He was awarded the Nobel Prize in Literature in 1913.

Other honors followed, among them the doctor of letters degree from the University of Calcutta and knighthood from the British in 1915. Despite the lecture tours and the obligatory public ceremonies—he was already becoming an institution—Tagore published his greatest book of lyrics, *Balākā (A Flight of Swans*, 1955, 1962), in 1916, when he was at the crest of his international popularity, as a result of the numerous editions of *Song Offerings*. Since the swans in *Balākā* symbolize the passage of the soul through this world to eternity, the book added to his reputation as a mystical poet. In 1918, Tagore founded the Visva-Bharati University at Santiniketan with money he had received from the Nobel Prize, his lectures, and writing. This high point of his career was followed, however, by political problems in India, where British repressive measures culminated in the Amritsar Massacre in 1919. In protest, Tagore resigned his knighthood.

From 1919 until his death in 1941, Tagore continued to publish poetry, even though he acknowledged that his poetic talent was fading. In fact, Sisirkumar Ghose, who has written a book on Tagore's "later poems," finds that the later works have a greater number of weak poems and calls the poetry unequal and uneven; on the other hand, Ghose claims that some of the poems are among Tagore's best. At any rate, Tagore's last years marked a turn to internationalism as he traveled widely, lecturing in England, the United States, China, Argentina, Italy, Japan, the Soviet Union, and Southeast Asia. These years, despite many successes, were punctuated by problems with his health, with public relations (Benito Mussolini had used a visit by Tagore for propaganda purposes), and with declining interest in a world at odds with his philosophy. Tagore's energy and versatility did not flag. At the age of seventy he began painting and soon exhibited his paintings internationally, and in 1930 he delivered the Hibbert Lectures at Oxford University (the lectures were published as *The Religion of Man* in 1931). In recognition of his achievements, he was awarded the University Chair of Bengali in 1932, and in 1940 he received the doctor of letters degree from Oxford.

Tagore's honors, significant as they are, scarcely do justice to his accomplishments as a writer and as a citizen of the world, and therein lies the problem in assessing him. His life (with its religious, educational, and political achievements) is his literature, and Tagore critics are hard-pressed to assess his literary work by itself, for the force of Tagore's life pervades it. He was a poet and a symbol—of Western recognition of Third World literature, of a synthesis of Hinduism and Christianity—when he was awarded the Nobel Prize, which ultimately enshrined him as an institution. Though a nationalist in his advocacy of Bengali and of social reform, he was untainted by the narrow aims of contemporary nationalism, which does not advocate a world of synthesis but retreats into parochialism and xenophobia. (Ironically, his songs have become the national anthems of India and Bangladesh.) Consequently, his political views were faulted by Indians and Eastern leaders, and the criticism sometimes extended to his poetry. In fact, of the Nobel Prize winners, he is among the best-known recipients, while his poetry is perhaps among the least known, because of the language barrier and the public's preoccupation with his role in transforming Indian culture from the nineteenth to the twentieth century.

Bibliography

Primary

NOVELS: *Bau-Thakuranir Hat*, 1883; *Chokher bāli*, 1902 (*Binodini*, 1959); *Gorā*, 1910 (English translation, 1924); *Chaturanga*, 1916 (English translation, 1963); *Ghare bāire*, 1916 (*Home and the World*, 1919); *Jogajog*, 1929; *Shesher kabita*, 1929; *Dui bon*, 1933 (*Two Sisters*, 1945).

SHORT FICTION: *Hungry Stones and Other Stories*, 1916; *Mashi and Other Stories*, 1918; *The Runaway and Other Stories*, 1959.

PLAYS: *Prakritir Pratishodh*, 1884 (verse; *Sanyasi: Or, The Ascetic*, 1917); *Rājā o Rāni*, 1889 (verse; *The King and the Queen*, 1918); *Visarjan*, 1890 (verse, based on his novel *Rajarshi*; *Sacrifice*, 1917); *Chitrāngadā*, 1892 (verse; *Chitra*, 1913); *Prayaschitta*, 1909 (based on his novel *Bau-Thakuranir Hat*); *Rājā*, 1910 (*The King of the Dark Chamber*, 1914); *Dākghar*, 1912 (*The Post Office*, 1914); *Phālguni*, 1916 (*The Cycle of Spring*, 1917); *Arupratan*, 1920 (revision of *Rājā*); *Muktadhārā*, 1922 (English translation, 1950); *Raktakarabi*, 1924 (*Red Oleanders*, 1925); *Chirakumār Sabhā*, 1926; *Natir Pujā*, 1926 (*Worship of the Dancing Girl*, 1950); *Sesh Rakshā*, 1928; *Paritrān*, 1929 (revision of *Prayaschitta*); *Tapati*, 1929 (revision of *Rājā o Rāni*); *Chandālikā*, 1933 (English translation, 1938); *Bānsari*, 1933; *Nritya-natya Chitrangādā*, 1936 (revision of *Chitrangādā*); *Nritya-natya Chandālikā*, 1938 (revision of *Chandālikā*).

POETRY: *Saisab sangit*, 1881; *Sandhya sangit*, 1882; *Prabhat sangit*, 1883; *Chabi o gan*, 1884; *Kari o komal*, 1887; *Mānashi*, 1890; *Sonār tari*, 1893 (*The Golden Boat*, 1932); *Chitra*, 1895; *Chaitāli*, 1896; *Kanika*, 1899; *Kal-*

pana, 1900; *Katha o kahini*, 1900; *Kshanikā*, 1900; *Naivedya*, 1901; *Sisu*,
1903 (*The Crescent Moon*, 1913); *Smaran*, 1903; *Utsarga*, 1904; *Kheya*,
1905; *Gitānjali*, 1910 (*Song Offerings*, 1912); *The Gardener*, 1913; *Gitali*,
1914; *Balākā*, 1916 (*A Flight of Swans*, 1955, 1962); *Fruit-Gathering*, 1916;
Gan, 1916; *Stray Birds*, 1917; *Love's Gift, and Crossing*, 1918; *Palataka*,
1918 (*The Fugitive*, 1921); *Lipika*, 1922; *Poems*, 1922; *Sisu bholanath*,
1922; *The Curse at Farewell*, 1924; *Prabahini*, 1925; *Purabi*, 1925; *Fifteen
Poems*, 1928; *Fireflies*, 1928; *Mahuya*, 1929; *Sheaves: Poems and Songs*,
1929; *Banabani*, 1931; *Parisesh*, 1932; *Punascha*, 1932; *Vicitrita*, 1933;
Bithika, 1935; *Ses saptak*, 1935; *Patraput*, 1936, 1938 (English transla-
tion, 1969); *Syamali*, 1936 (English translation, 1955); *Khapchada*, 1937;
Prantik, 1938; *Senjuti*, 1938; *Navajatak*, 1940; *Rogsajya*, 1940; *Sanai*, 1940;
Arogya, 1941; *Janmadine*, 1941; *Poems*, 1942; *Sesh lekha*, 1942; *The Her-
ald of Spring*, 1957; *Wings of Death: The Last Poems*, 1960; *Devouring
Love*, 1961; *A Bunch of Poems*, 1966; *One Hundred and One*, 1967; *Last
Poems*, 1973; *Later Poems*, 1974.
NONFICTION: *Jivansmriti*, 1912 (*My Reminiscences*, 1917); *Personality*, 1917;
Nationalism, 1919; *Creative Unity*, 1922; *The Religion of Man*, 1931; *To-
wards Universal Man*, 1961.
MISCELLANEOUS: *Collected Poems and Plays*, 1936; *A Tagore Reader*, 1961.

Secondary
Bose, Abinash Chandra. *Three Mystic Poets: A Study of W. B. Yeats, Æ, and
Rabindranath Tagore*. Kolhapur, India: School and College Bookstall,
1945. Reprint. Kolhapur, India: Norwood Editions, 1976. Bose defines
mysticism, applies his definition to Tagore's poetry, explores the Indian
sources of mysticism, quotes copiously from the poems, and praises his
subject's versatility; yet there are few critical comments about the poetry
itself. For Bose, Tagore is among the greatest poets of modern times, but
the critic does not provide the necessary evidence to convince his readers.
Ghose, Sisirkumar. *The Later Poems of Tagore*. Westport, Conn.: Greenwood Press, 1961. The book, which concerns only those poems written
during Tagore's last ten years, explores the Dionysian—the terrible, evil,
enigmatic, fatal—aspects of the poems, which he finds permeated by conflict and contradictions. His book forces readers to reevaluate the Western
image of Tagore. Ghose includes a bibliography of general and critical
studies, which is particularly rich in Indian criticism.
Ghosh, J. C. *Bengali Literature*. London: Curzon Press, 1976. Originally
published by the Clarendon Press in 1948, Ghosh's summary of Bengali literature culminates in a chapter on Tagore, whom he faults for sentimentality and affectation, particularly in Tagore's English poems and translations.
Part of Ghosh's hostility stems from his perception that Tagore was
"Westernized," though he does approve of Tagore's international national-

ism. There is a short bibliography.

Hay, Stephen N. *Asian Ideas of East and West: Tagore and His Critics in Japan, China, and India.* Cambridge, Mass.: Harvard University Press, 1970. A study of the intellectual leaders of India, Pakistan, China, and Japan, the book focuses on how Tagore stimulated Eastern leaders. Chapters 1 and 4 are devoted to Tagore in relation to his family, nation, and culture. Hay relies on Tagore's letters and poetry, where he finds Tagore's thoughts expressed.

Kripalani, Krishna. *Rabindranath Tagore: A Biography.* New York: Grove Press, 1962. Regarded as the best English biography of Tagore, the book was written by a scholar who knew the Tagore family well. Kripalani focuses on Tagore as poet and as "*kavi,* seer, an intermediary between the human and the divine." The book contains several photographs and a chronological bibliography of the works Tagore published in English.

Lago, Mary M. *Rabindranath Tagore.* Boston: G. K. Hall and Co., 1976. Organized generically, with the focus on the poetry and short fiction, rather than chronologically, Lago explores Tagore's traditions and considers the years 1912 to 1913 as pivotal in marking his transition from poet to institution. The book contains a helpful chronology of events in Tagore's life as well as a "selective bibliography" of critical books and articles.

Mukherji, Probhat Kumar. *Life of Tagore.* Translated by Sisirkumar Ghosh. Thompson, Conn.: Inter Culture Associates, 1975. A condensed edition of the author's four-volume biography, the book focuses on Tagore's political life; though the author claims not to interpret his subject's "creative life," it is almost impossible to separate life from literature, particularly in Tagore's case. The book is rich in its examination of modern Indian history.

Rhys, Ernest. *Rabindranath Tagore: A Biographical Study.* New York: Macmillan, 1915. Despite its title, Rhys provides scant details about Tagore's life while he devotes chapters—with quotations, summaries, and paraphrases of the work—to other Indian poets and to Tagore's short stories, plays, and poems. Rhys sees in Tagore the "intermediary" to bring Indian wisdom "home" to the West and to bring about, despite world strife, a universal community of men. Illustrations but no index.

Singh, Ajai. *Rabindranath Tagore: His Imagery and Ideas.* Ghazibad, India: Vimal Prakashan, 1984. Singh's book, which is the first discussion in English of Tagore's imagery, is not based on English translations but on the poems in Bengali. Singh examines the imagery related to love, beauty, life, and the eternal and concludes that Tagore's poetry deals with religious, rather than poetic, ideas. There is an extensive bibliography.

Thompson, Edward John. *Rabindranath Tagore: His Life and Work.* London: Oxford University Press, 1921. An early chronological treatment that views Tagore's literature and life as interdependent, the book was the first to base its conclusions on the study of the original Bengali, which Thompson translated into English. Thompson, who knew Tagore personally, provides firsthand anecdotes as well as perceptive critical insights.

——————. *Rabindranath Tagore: Poet and Dramatist*. Westport, Conn.: Greenwood Press, 1975. Originally published by Oxford University Press in 1926 and updated in 1948. Thompson's book was the first thorough study of Tagore's poetry and drama and successfully weaves necessary biographical material into the literary narrative. The book is especially valuable for its analysis of Tagore's often-neglected dramas and for its appendices, which detail Tagore's knowledge of English poetry and compare his English and Bengali books.

                                                          Thomas L. Erskine

1915

Literature
Romain Rolland, France

Peace
no award

Physics
Sir William Bragg, Great Britain
Sir Lawrence Bragg, Great Britain

Chemistry
Richard Willstätter, Germany

Physiology or Medicine
no award

ROMAIN ROLLAND
1915

Born: Clamecy, France; January 29, 1866
Died: Vézelay, France; December 30, 1944
Language: French
Principal genres: Biography, drama, and the novel

An idealistic writer, Rolland believed that all art should convey moral truth, encourage faith in humanity, and evoke sympathy for artists and the poor (his "great Defeateds")

The Award

Presentation

Nobel awards and ceremonies created great difficulties for the Swedish Academy during World War I, and the Nobel Prize awarded to Romain Rolland was no exception. In 1914, twenty-four candidates had been proposed, and by that summer, the Nobel Committee had reached agreement to recommend the Swiss writer Carl Spitteler for the literature prize. In August, however, war broke out and this change in circumstances caused the Academy to forgo the distribution of prizes in 1914. The members reasoned that the purpose of the prize was to aid humanitarian causes, not to aggravate national rivalries, and to give the prize to a Frenchman or to a German could be misinterpreted as favoring one nation over another. In the spirit of Alfred Nobel, then, the Nobel Committee postponed the award to avoid exacerbating the situation.

The Academy's action resulted in divided opinions. Some Swedes believed that the Academy had failed to live up to its duties: It was cowardly to cave in to the war spirit. The homeland of Carolus Linnaeus and Jöns Jakob Berzelius should have, in the name of peace and order, awarded the prizes as usual. Others agreed with the Academy's action. It was better for little Sweden to remain in the background and not to become entangled, even indirectly, in the hostilities.

Against this background, it is easy to see why the candidacy of Rolland became attractive. Rolland's humane purposes corresponded with Alfred Nobel's ideals. The author's books served to inspire those who believed in pacifistic internationalism. The Swedes also knew that Rolland was suffering for his idealistic stand. In addition, they were becoming familiar with his works, for a series of translations had recently appeared in Sweden.

In 1915, Henrik Schück, a literary historian, formally proposed Rolland for the Nobel Prize in Literature. This nomination, however, met with objections. Several members of the Committee, though they admired Rolland's idealism, believed that these ideals were expressed in highly imperfect works of art. Although opinions were divided in the Committee, with a majority of the numbers supporting the Spanish author, Benito Pérez Galdós, Rolland enjoyed greater favor in the Academy itself. Nevertheless, because of this disagreement and the belief that the Swedish Academy must preserve strict neutrality, the 1915 prize was reserved for a later date.

Discussions about the prizes resumed in 1916. By this time many members were convinced that the awards should no longer be withheld, and on November 9, the Committee decided on the simultaneous awarding of the prizes for 1915 and 1916. A Swedish writer, Verner von Heidenstam, was given the 1916 literature prize, and the 1915 prize was given to Romain Rolland. His diploma briefly described the Committee's rationale: "As a tribute to the lofty idealism of his literary production and to the sympathy and love of truth with which he has described different types of human beings." Rolland's posthumously published diary, *Journal des années de guerre, 1914-1919* (1952; journal of the war years), gives his reaction to the news of the award, communicated to him by telegraph in Geneva. Surprisingly, his first impulse was to renounce the prize, since he thought that it might lessen his liberty and cause him further persecution. Further consideration led him to accept it, and he celebrated his decision with a small group of friends.

Nobel lecture

Because of the war, Rolland was not invited to Stockholm and no celebrations were held. He received the prize money in Switzerland, and he distributed it, by means of the International Red Cross and other welfare organizations, to relieve war suffering. Although Rolland gave no Nobel lecture, one gathers what his reaction to the award would have been through his response to the congratulations of a group of Allied soldiers interned in Switzerland: "It is not on me, but on our country that this distinction has been conferred; and it is for this reason that I accept it, and I feel happy to think that it can contribute towards spreading the ideas which have made France loved throughout the world."

In his letter of thanks to the Swedish Academy, he expressed his gratitude for its appreciative recognition of thirty years of his work. The award made him feel proud to be a Frenchman, and he offered the prize in homage to his country, for he believed that he owed France both his high idealism and his indestructible faith in humanity. His letter continued:

> I am merely a too-weak interpreter and faithful servant of the spirit of reason, of tolerance, and of pity, which is the heritage of Montaigne, of Voltaire, and of the French philosophers of the eighteenth century. May you be thanked for the new strength which your respected suffrage brings, in this hour of bloodshed, to the hopes which we place in the wisdom of the future and in a reconciled Europe, in spite of the tragedies of the present.

In the years after the award, Rolland maintained good relations with the Academy, and in a further gesture of gratitude, he gave them the manuscript of *Jean-Christophe* (1904-1912; *John-Christopher*, 1910-1913, better known as *Jean-Christophe*), his most famous work.

Critical reception

An announcement of the Nobel Prizes appeared on the first page of *The New York Times* for November 6, 1915; in this brief notice, Rolland was named as the literature prizewinner. According to the Nobel Foundation, the 1915 prize was reserved, and it was not formally given to Rolland until 1916. Because of the premature announcement, reaction to Rolland's prize began in 1915, and just as a division of opinion existed in Sweden over the award, so too this division characterized the reaction in the rest of the world. Rolland's efforts before and during the early years of World War I to unite the intellectuals of Europe against the war had made him very unpopular with most literary critics both in Germany and in the Allied countries. On the other hand, these same views caused him to be admired as an idealist in the neutral countries. In Sweden, for example, before the spread of Rolland's works, many Swedish critics had turned against French culture, which was depicted as a world of decadent and undisciplined individualists. France's literature was superficial, and her art was symbolized by Henri de Toulouse-Lautrec's portraits of the Parisian demimonde. Rolland's works revealed the distortions in this depiction. His writing spoke for a France full of intense moral feelings and integrity of spirit.

In the Allied countries, literary critics tended to question Rolland's stature both as a writer and as a man. For example, Mary Duclaux, commenting on various French writers from across the Channel in Great Britain, criticized Rolland's confusing literary style and his self-imposed exile from his country during the war. She recognized that in this exile he occupied his hands and his heart with works of mercy but stated that his mind gave no support to his fellow Frenchmen, doubtless because the attractions of Germany were too strong. The Nobel award did not moderate Duclaux's critique. Indeed, she found that Rolland's attitude continued to be one of self-defense.

Across the ocean in the United States, reactions to Rolland's award were similar. For example, Pierre de Bacourt of Columbia University assailed Rolland as nonrepresentative of French intellectual opinion. In a letter to *The New York Times*, Bacourt stated that, despite the Nobel Foundation's approval of Rolland's pacifist sentiments, his interpretation of the war was incorrect: France never wanted the war; it was forced upon her by Germany. Since Rolland was not representative of the best of French culture (that is, those who fought against German barbarism), the sanctification of his work by the Nobel Prize was clearly inappropriate.

On the other hand, Albert Einstein and other internationalists in Europe and the United States approved of Rolland's laureateship. Both Einstein and Rolland agreed that intellectual and political leaders should try to heal the misunderstandings between the French and German peoples peacefully. Einstein, however, thought that the blame for the war was unequivocally rooted in the corrupt, militaristic Prussian spirit, while Rolland was more willing to apportion blame for the war among all the belligerents.

The negative view of Rolland intensified during the 1920's and 1930's, as he became more sympathetic to Communism. Even those who admired his idealism recognized that his literary talents were not of sufficiently high caliber to give exact and refined expression to his noble sentiments. Since his death, his books have had fewer and fewer readers, and it has become difficult for modern critics to think of his work as being the equal of the writings of such French Nobel laureates as Anatole France, Henri Bergson, André Gide, François Mauriac, Albert Camus, and Jean-Paul Sartre.

Biography

Romain Rolland was born into a provincial Catholic family at Clamecy, a little town in the center of France, on January 29, 1866. His father was a notary and his mother was the daughter of one. His mother, a pious woman and a lover of music, had the most influence on the child. He was bright but sickly, and in his early years he developed a love of great heroes through his reading of works by William Shakespeare. To guarantee an excellent education for Rolland, his mother moved the family at great cost to Paris, where he entered the Lycée Louis-le-Grand. He then attended the École Normale Supérieure, where he specialized in history with Gabriel Monod and where he obtained his bachelor's degree in 1889. While at the École Normale, he lost his religious faith and discovered the writings of Baruch Spinoza and Leo Tolstoy. Depressed by the shallow materialism of Parisian culture, he wrote to Tolstoy, whose kind reply had a deep effect on him.

After his Paris education, Rolland spent two years in Rome at the École Française d'Archéologie et d'Histoire. His most important learning, however, occurred because of his friendship with Malwida von Meysenbug, a German of Huguenot descent. Then in her seventies, Meysenbug was the author of *Memoiren einer Idealistin* (1875; memoirs of an idealist); she was also a socialist whose circle of friends had included Alexander Herzen, Giuseppe Mazzini, Richard Wagner, and Friedrich Nietzsche. Her discussions with Rolland about these men awakened his sympathy for the struggles of genius.

In October, 1892, upon his return to Paris, he married Clotilde Bréal, the daughter of a famous philologist. The couple left for Rome, where Rolland researched and wrote his doctoral thesis, a history of early European opera. He presented his thesis brilliantly and was appointed to teach the history of art at the École Normale Supérieure in 1895, a position he held for the next five years. Unfortunately, his marriage was troubled during this period, and in 1901 he went through a painful divorce. Rolland found solace in a disciplined academic life (he taught the history of music at the Sorbonne from 1900 to 1912) and in his writings. He retired from teaching in 1912.

To improve his health, for many years Rolland had spent his summer holidays in Switzerland. He was there in the summer of 1914 when World War I broke out, an event that marked an important division in his life: His writings, friendships, and influence were all cut in two. To his compatriots, he seemed to be a coward who had deserted France during the time of her greatest need. Despite these attacks, however, he remained in Switzerland, doing work consistent with his international sympathies.

Rolland returned to Paris in 1919 to be with his mother, who was seriously ill. After her death, he returned to Villeneuve in Switzerland and lived there, with his sister and father, from 1922 to 1938. During this period, he became interested in socialism and eastern religions. In 1929, he met Veuve Marie Koudachev, a woman who gave him much help in the remaining years of his life. He married her in 1934.

In 1937, Rolland left Switzerland for Vézelay, a town not far from his native village of Clamecy. There he continued to write. During the Occupation, he was placed under house arrest because of his anti-Nazi activities. He died at home on December 30, 1944, a month before his seventy-ninth birthday.

Literary Career

Rolland's literary career evolved from the contradictions in his own personality. From his father he absorbed the Gallic spirit—critical and free; from his mother he absorbed an artistic sensibility—musical and mystical. This psychological genealogy accounts for the odd epithets with which Rolland has often been described: a religious socialist, an anticlerical mystic, a revolutionary idealist, a nondogmatic Christian. He also insisted on international cooperation in a century of great nationalistic competition. Rolland loved France but refused to admit that a national state could be a rational and necessary entity. Thus there seemed to exist in him a series of dichotomies, and he consciously used these in his works of fiction and nonfiction.

As a young man, Rolland developed a strong sense of social responsibility, believing that art has a duty to society. Eager to participate in the intellectual life of his time, he sought to bring the virtues of faith, hope, love, and courage to his society. This belief explains why he wrote first for the stage—to rekindle the heroism and faith of his nation. He found little help in classic or romantic French drama, and so he proposed the creation of a new form built on the traditions of French history. A good example is his play *Les Loups* (1898; *The Wolves*, 1937), inspired by the Dreyfus affair. This play was later incorporated into a partially completed cycle of ten Revolutionary dramas, of which the best known are *Danton* (1900; English translation, 1918) and *Le*

Quatorze Juillet (1902; *The Fourteenth of July*, 1918). The love of cycles and spacious forms that may be seen in his plays would also characterize his other works.

Frustrated by the exigencies of the stage, Rolland turned to the study of famous men. He wrote a successful lyrical life of Ludwig van Beethoven in 1903 and followed it with equally successful studies of Michelangelo (1905) and Tolstoy (1911). These monuments to his heroes were not critical biographies but were instead poetic attempts to capture the spirit of these great men. They were also contemplative meditations on the creative spirit, and Rolland saw them as meaning more than their subjects' lives. While painting Beethoven's portrait, that is to say, Rolland was also trying to paint the portrait of the twentieth century and its dreams.

Rolland's interest in biography is reflected in his massive and most famous novel, *Jean-Christophe*. This cyclical novel inaugurated those great saga novels of the twentieth century that sought to capture the experience of an entire life. *Jean-Christophe* traced the evolution of a German musician through his many artistic struggles. Critics have discerned elements of the lives of Beethoven, Wolfgang Amadeus Mozart, and Wagner in the protagonist, but Rolland intended it as the study of a hero who is a true child of Europe, unconfined by any frontier.

Rolland denied that this work is a novel, and its rambling construction and style certainly reveal his weak grasp of form. For Rolland, however, the life of a man cannot be shut into the narrow confines of literary form. *Jean-Christophe* is about the struggle of a musical genius with himself, his art, and his society. Rolland created a character filled with contradictions and inconsistencies, an intensely sincere artist with a great enthusiasm for life who is misunderstood by a hostile society. Edmund Gosse ranked *Jean-Christophe* as the noblest work of fiction in the twentieth century.

Modern critics, on the other hand, have been much harsher with this most famous of Rolland's works. For some, it is too episodic and diffuse. For others, it lacks a sense of style: There are quantum leaps of tone, and the language oscillates between the Dionysian and the Apollonian. Rolland was subjected to these criticisms even while he was alive, and he defended *Jean-Christophe* as being as episodic and accidental as life itself. For him the meaning of his work was the continuity of life, a spark spreading from soul to soul.

The publication of *Jean-Christophe* firmly established Rolland's reputation in the literary world of the early twentieth century. Interestingly, he foresaw in this novel the development of a war that would be the ruin of Europe, and soon after the work was completed such a war broke out. He wrote a series of articles against World War I, and he published a pamphlet, *Au-dessus de la mêlée* (1915; *Above the Battle*, 1916), appealing to intellectuals in the warring countries to agitate for peace. This work unleashed the fury of the literary establishment upon him. French critics saw him as merely a high-minded scold; this little volume made Rolland the most unpopular writer in France and created a breach between him and young Frenchmen that was probably never healed.

Rolland continued to write in exile in Switzerland during the war. He completed two novels and a play in the style of Aristophanes, but these had little influence. His Rabelaisian novel *Colas Breugnon: Bonhomme vit encore!* (1919; *Colas Breugnon*, 1919) was actually written before 1914 but not published until later. The more hostile critics believed that it marked the end of Rolland's career; the more sympathetic thought that it was the caprice of an out-of-touch author.

Rolland's pacifism and socialism influenced his writings in the 1920's and 1930's. In 1923, he helped establish the international review *Europe*, an influential journal of the Left. His later work manifested a highly individual mixture of Marxism and Oriental mysticism. These themes can be seen in his cyclical novel *L'Âme enchantée* (1922-1933; *The Soul Enchanted*, 1925-1934), in which he exposed the cruelty of political sectarianism. The novel abounds in political agents, Bolsheviks, revolutionaries, and counterrevolutionaries. The main character, though, is a female counterpart of Jean-Christophe, and the main story portrays the evolution of this young woman and her son from intransigent individualism to a more communal ideal.

In the 1930's, Rolland foresaw a new war, and he wrote against the impending crisis in a number of articles, collected in two volumes, *Quinze ans de combat, 1919-1934* (1935; *I Will Not Rest*, 1936) and *Par la révolution, la paix* (1935). When the war came, he continued to write. His most important work during that period was his study of Charles Péguy, who had become his friend during the Dreyfus affair and who had been killed in World War I. A few day before Christmas, 1944, Rolland visited his Paris publisher to arrange for the publication of this book, which he never saw in print.

Since his death, Rolland's reputation has declined both in France and throughout the world. France never wholeheartedly took to the laureate because of his sentimental attitude toward art and because of his lack of classic control in his writings. His faded reputation is also the result of a change in cultural climate: The late twentieth century is a more cynical age that finds Rolland's brand of idealism pretentious. François Mauriac lamented the neglect of *Jean-Christophe*, though he too had to admit that it was full of badly drawn portraits and counterfeit tragedy.

Rolland was involved in the major social, political, and religious events of his age. He truly believed that art must portray genuine emotions and convey an ennobling morality, that it must combat the entropy of the mind and heart. He consistently pleaded for the freedom and dignity of the human spirit, and he championed the oppressed. His writings may have been deeply flawed, but one can still admire the nobility of his ideals.

Bibliography
Primary

NOVELS: *Jean-Christophe*, 1904-1912 (*John-Christopher*, 1910-1913, better known as *Jean-Christophe*, 1913; includes *L'Aube, Le Matin, L'Adolescent, La Révolte, La Foire sur la place, Antoinette, Dans la maison, Les Amies, Le Buisson ardent,* and *La Nouvelle Journée; Colas Breugnon: Bonhomme vit encore!*, 1919 (*Colas Breugnon,* 1919); *Clérambault: Histoire d'une conscience libre pendant la guerre,* 1920 (*Clerambault: The Story of an Independent Spirit During the War,* 1921; initially serialized as *L'Un contre tous,* 1917, incomplete version); *Pierre et Luce,* 1920 (*Pierre and Luce,* 1922); *L'Âme enchantée,* 1922-1933 (*The Soul Enchanted,* 1925-1934).

PLAYS: *Saint Louis,* 1897; *Aërt,* 1898; *Les Loups,* 1898 (*The Wolves,* 1937); *Le Triomphe de la raison,* 1899; *Danton,* 1900 (English translation, 1918); *Le Quatorze Juillet,* 1902 (*The Fourteenth of July,* 1918); *Le Temps viendra,* 1903; *Théâtre de la révolution,* 1909 (includes *Les Loups, Danton,* and *Le Quatorze Juillet*); *Les Tragédies de la foi,* 1913 (includes *Saint Louis, Aërt,* and *Le Triomphe de la raison*); *Liluli,* 1919 (English translation, 1920); *Le Jeu de l'amour et de la mort,* 1925 (*The Game of Love and Death,* 1926); *Pâques fleuries,* 1926 (*Palm Sunday,* 1928); *Les Léonides,* 1928; *Robespierre,* 1939.

NONFICTION: *François Millet,* 1902 (published only in English); *Beethoven,* 1903 (English translation, 1907); *Le Théâtre du peuple: Essai d'esthétique d'un théâtre nouveau,* 1903 (*The People's Theater,* 1918); *Michel-Ange,* 1905; *La Vie de Michel-Ange,* 1906 (*The Life of Michelangelo,* 1912); *Haendel,* 1910 (*Handel,* 1916); *Vie de Tolstoï,* 1911 (*Tolstoy,* 1911); *Au-dessus de la mêlée,* 1915 (*Above the Battle,* 1916); *Les Précurseurs,* 1919; *Mahatma Gandhi,* 1924 (*Mahatma Gandhi: The Man Who Became One with the Universal Being,* 1924); *Goethe et Beethoven,* 1927 (*Goethe and Beethoven,* 1931); *Beethoven: Les Grandes Époques créatrices,* 1928-1945 (*Beethoven the Creator,* 1929, partial translation); *Essai sur la mystique et l'action de l'Inde vivante,* 1929-1930 (Prophets of the New India, 1930); includes *La Vie de Ramakrishna* (*Ramakrishna*) and *La Vie de Vivekananda et l'Évangile universel (Vivekananda); Empédocle d'Agrigente, suivi de l'éclair de Spinoza,* 1931; *Quinze ans de combat, 1919-1934,* 1935 (*I Will Not Rest,* 1936); *Par la révolution, la paix,* 1935; *Compagnons de route, essais littéraires,* 1936; *Le Voyage intérieur,* 1942 (*The Journey Within,* 1947); *Péguy,* 1944 (2 volumes); *L'Inde: Journal 1915-1943,* 1949; *Journal des années de guerre, 1914-1919,* 1952; *L'Esprit libre,* 1953 (includes *Au-dessus de la mêlée* and *Les Précurseurs*); *Mémoires et fragments du journal,* 1956.

MISCELLANEOUS: *Cahiers Romain Rolland,* 1948-

Secondary

Brombert, Victor. *The Intellectual Hero: Studies in the French Novel, 1880-1955.* Philadelphia: J. B. Lippincott Co., 1961. This book is not a survey of twentieth century French literature, but an attempt to analyze some key works, Rolland's among them, around a central theme: the emergence of a new type of hero. Since one of Rolland's basic creations is the intellectual hero, this work illuminates some of his writings while casting light on some modern literary trends.

Duclaux, Mary. *Twentieth Century French Writers: Reviews and Reminiscences.* London: W. Collins Sons and Co., 1919. Reprint. Freeport, N.Y.: Books for Libraries Press, 1966. This book contains a chapter on Rolland that gives a good insight into the critical response to his work during and just after World War I. Duclaux also has an incisive critique of *Jean-Christophe* in this chapter.

Starr, William Thomas. *A Critical Bibliography of the Published Writings of Romain Rolland.* Evanston, Ill.: Northwestern University Press, 1950. This book by a prominent Rolland scholar contains the most extensive bibliography in English of Rolland's published works.

_____. *One Against All: A Biography.* The Hague: Mouton, 1971. This biography seeks to rescue Rolland's reputation from its decline in the period since his death. Starr also analyzes Rolland's place in the history of the twentieth century European novel.

_____. *Romain Rolland and a World at War.* Evanston, Ill.: Northwestern University Press, 1956. The author, who has done extensive research on myth and symbolism in the works of Rolland, analyzes Rolland's pacifism. Contains a good discussion of Rolland's personality.

Zweig, Stefan. *Romain Rolland: The Man and His Work.* Translated by Eden Paul and Cedar Paul. New York: T. Selzer, 1921. Reprint. New York: Haskell, 1970. This biography was soundly criticized on its appearance for its extravagant adulation of its subject, but it does have its defenders. Zweig was himself well-known as a dramatist, novelist, and poet, and if one does not require a critical biography, this book, in which the events of Rolland's life are mentioned only in passing, gives a passionate appreciation of his intellectual achievement.

Robert J. Paradowski

1916

Literature
Verner von Heidenstam, Sweden

Peace
no award

Physics
no award

Chemistry
no award

Physiology or Medicine
no award

VERNER VON HEIDENSTAM
1916

Born: Olshammar, Sweden; July 6, 1859
Died: Övralid, Sweden; May 20, 1940
Language: Swedish
Principal genres: Poetry and the novel

A last representative of nineteenth century Swedish aristocracy, Heidenstam was deeply interested in his nation's past, and much of his prose stems from that fascination; in his verse, he was a spokesman of Swedish idealism, combining a concern for humanity with an inherently conservative cast of mind

The Award
Presentation

The Nobel Prize in Literature was given to Verner von Heidenstam on November 9, 1916; the presentation speech was made by Sven Söderman, critic, translator, and member of the Swedish Academy's Nobel Foundation. The presentation was largely an account of Heidenstam's creative career. Söderman emphasized the importance that Heidenstam had always attached to the power of the imagination, even though his topics changed from hedonism and aestheticism to patriotism and a sense of duty. Söderman did not stint his praise, calling Heidenstam one of the masters of Swedish literature, the creator of a new epoch in Swedish letters with his first collection of poems, the author of numerous great prose epics, and the forger of a cult of humanity; according to Söderman, Heidenstam was sustained in all these accomplishments by a constantly fresh inspiration.

Söderman's encomiastic miniature biography of Heidenstam provided the background to the inscription of the Nobel Award; the prize was given "in recognition of [Heidenstam's] importance as the champion of a new epoch in our literature." In idealized terms, Söderman then presented a sketch of Heidenstam's personality. He hinted at experiences which were simultaneously "noble" and "unhappy" and observed that Heidenstam—the perfect aristocrat—had a "proud and tolerant virility" and was a "manly poet." Heidenstam's concept of life, as Söderman described it, was that of a knight without fear and without reproach who, as he aged, attained and expressed a serene sense of the value of loneliness, of love, and of creative humility. Concluding, Söderman turned Heidenstam into a sublime figure by quoting the latter's verses about the winning of wisdom: "Oh human being, you will only become wise,/ when you reach the top of the heights, cool with evening,/ where the earth can be surveyed."

Nobel lecture
Although well-known as a public speaker, Heidenstam did not make an
address at the Nobel ceremonies. The reason for this is unclear; Heidenstam
may have been in poor health at the time.

Critical reception
   The New York Times, which customarily reported the election of Nobel
Prize winners, did not mention Heidenstam's award. *The Times* of London
(November 10, 1916) had a brief combined notice, with the headline "Nobel
Prize to Romain Rolland." The text simply said that the prize for 1915 had
gone to Rolland and for 1916 to "the Swedish poet Verner von Heidenstam."
The only immediate American reaction to the event was an essay by Charles
Wharton Stork in *The Nation* (November 30, 1916). While Stork described
Heidenstam's career, attempting to place him in Swedish literature of the
day, he was not markedly generous toward the poetry and evidently preferred the "splendid vigor" and "wider appeal" of Erik Axel Karlfeldt. No
bones were made about the difficulties of Heidenstam's lyric language; attention was called to his compression and abruptness and the fact that he usually
"contradicts the reader's expectations." In order to give some idea of Heidenstam's verse, Stork compared him in "sensitiveness" to Francis Thompson, in
his "lavish use of color" to Dante Gabriel Rossetti, and—on points un-
specified—to Hugo von Hofmannsthal, yet Stork said that Heidenstam had
much more trouble in developing his thought consistently than any of the
three poets just named. Finally, Stork asked why, "with his many palpable
defects," Heidenstam had won such a high place in Swedish letters. He
answered his own query by noting Heidenstam's "sincerity" and "freshness,"
best demonstrated in his patriotic lyrics.
   In *Bookman* (February 1, 1917), Stork wrote another essay about the
Nobel Prize winner. He was more enthusiastic, but plainly preferred
Heidenstam's narratives to his oeuvre in verse. Wondering why the prize was
awarded to Heidenstam, Stork guessed that it was given because he had
come to represent to the Swedish people "their new nationalism"—he was
Sweden's "recognized spokesman." The essay ended with a judgment similar
to the opinion that Stork had expressed in *The Nation*: When Heidenstam is
"personal and introspective" in his lyrics, he becomes "extremely difficult";
when he is patriotic, he is clear and direct. Two other articles appeared in
American periodicals in the wake of the prize: Svea Bernhard, writing in *Poetry* (April, 1917), told first about the happiness that the choice had caused in
Sweden and then reported on Heidenstam's prose, saying little about the
lyrics. In the *American-Scandinavian Review* (May/June, 1917), in an essay
translated and abbreviated from a Swedish original, the literary scholar
Ruben Gustafsson Berg gave a general picture of Heidenstam's work, using
the biographical mode; at the outset, he admitted that Heidenstam was

extremely hard to characterize. Like Stork and Bernhard, Berg stressed Heidenstam's patriotism (one factor in the work that was readily definable), remarking that he "bravely stood for pride, courage, joy in labor, and love of country."

Two translations of Heidenstam's works, both by the indefatigable Stork, may be regarded as products of the interest engendered in the United States by the Nobel Prize. In 1919, the Yale University Press published *Sweden's Laureate: Selected Poems of Verner von Heidenstam*, and a year later, the American-Scandinavian Foundation brought out Stork's rendering of Heidenstam's novel *Karolinerna* (1897-1898; *A King and His Campaigners*, 1902) as *The Charles Men*: It comprised volumes 15 and 16 in the foundation's series, *Scandinavian Classics*.

Biography

Verner von Heidenstam was the son of a chief engineer in the lighthouse service, Lieutenant-Colonel Nils Gustaf von Heidenstam; his mother, equally blue-blooded, was the former Magdalena Charlotta Rütterskjöld. Born and reared on the family estate at Olshammar, young Heidenstam spent much of the year in Stockholm with his parents, attending an elegant boys' school. His poor health led to his withdrawal in 1876. His father sent him on a trip to the Near East and Greece, during which he decided to become a painter, a plan which took him to Rome in 1879. The next year Heidenstam married the first of his three wives (all the marriages would end in divorce). In Paris to continue his art studies, he turned to literary plans, and in Switzerland he met August Strindberg, who temporarily sparked his interest in political and social radicalism.

In 1887 Heidenstam returned to Sweden and, shortly thereafter, published his first books. Rebelling against the naturalism of the 1880's, he quickly became a central literary figure and participated in the reorganization of a major newspaper, *Svenska Dagbladet*. Upon the dissolution of his second marriage, in 1903, he left Stockholm for a country house at Naddö; in these years he strove to be recognized as Sweden's great national poet and was celebrated as such on his fiftieth birthday. Yet his reputation was diminished by the long "feud" with Strindberg, in which Heidenstam took a sternly conservative position. Elected to the Swedish Academy in 1912, he reached the culmination of his literary career with *Nya dikter* (1915; new poems); thereafter he wrote little.

Accompanied by his Danish friend Kate Bang, he resided in Denmark during the immediate postwar years. In 1925, after undertaking restless journeys to Italy, Switzerland, and the Riviera, he settled at Övralid, the mansion that he built near Lake Vätter in the vicinity of his childhood home. He was unable to complete several new literary plans, and his attractive autobiography, or family chronicle, *När kastanjerna blommade* (1941; when the chestnuts were blooming), remains a fragment. In his last years he suffered from arteriosclerosis and perhaps should not be held accountable for statements showing some sympathy with Adolf Hitler's Germany. He was buried at Övralid, where the Övralid Foundation maintains his home and gives an annual prize to authors and scholars.

Literary Career

Heidenstam's relatively late appearance on the Swedish literary scene, with the travel sketches of *Från Col di Tenda till Blocksberg* (1888; from Col di Tenda to Blocksberg) and the poems of *Vallfart och vandringsår* (1888; pilgrimage and wander years), did not mean that he had suddenly decided to be a writer. Although he destroyed most of his early production, evidence exists that he modeled his first lyrics on those of the great Swedish-language poets of Finland's national awakening, Zacharias Topelius (to whom he sent two manuscripts, receiving a favorable opinion in return) and Johan Ludvig Runeberg, whose stern simplicity and love of country he admired. The conversational tone of Strindberg's verse is also re-created in some parts of *Vallfart och vandringsår*. Yet at his debut Heidenstam was already very much his own man, using the Oriental coloring with which he had become so familiar in his travels and composing grandiose and sometimes melodramatic word paintings—with violent action, historical scenery, and beautiful girls—that have reminded critics of the art of Eugène Delacroix and the Austrian Hans Makart.

As in all Heidenstam's collections to come, the themes and styles are many. For example, he repeatedly praises hedonism but also returns to Runeberg's proud and lonely stoicism. His wide-ranging imagination changed the face of Swedish letters with a single blow: The gray, earnest tone of the 1880's became passé, and Heidenstam's example—bolstered by his defense of the imagination's sovereignty in the tract *Renässans* (1889; renaissance) and in the satirical, polemical *Pepitas bröllop* (1890; Pepita's wedding), which was written with his friend Oskar Levertin—opened the door for the neo-Romantic style of the 1890's and the accomplishments of Gustaf Fröding, Selma Lagerlöf, Erik Axel Karlfeldt, and other representatives of that brilliant literary decade.

Heidenstam's sense of independence led him to the Oriental novel *Endymion* (1889), which celebrates what he saw as the heritage of a "happiness in life itself" that Arab culture had received from Greece. The book also deals with Arab nationalism, a distinctly unusual theme in the Scandinavian literatures of the time and one more sign that Heidenstam was determined to go his own way. *Endymion* was followed by the lengthy novel of ideas (and, in a way, self-portrait) *Hans Alienus* (1892), in which Heidenstam takes his aesthete-hero from the papal Rome of the 1880's to the realms of the past (including the pleasure gardens of Sardanapalus at Nineveh) and back to

Sweden in a dizzying phantasmagoria: Narrative styles change rapidly and prose and poetry are intermingled. The book puzzled and sometimes irritated public and critics; yet in it a shift could be detected from a cult of pleasure to a cult of beauty, sought and admired no matter what the cost. In England, less ponderously, Oscar Wilde made similar proposals; in Germany, Friedrich Nietzsche had repeatedly preached the right of the superior individual, different from others (as Hans Alienus was), to form life—and worship beauty—on his own terms.

Heidenstam's next lyric book, *Dikter* (1895; poems) shows a poet who has become devoted to his homeland and to the sheer experience of having a home. One of the masterpieces of Swedish lyricism is the poem based on the fate of Gunnar of Hlidarend in *Njál's Saga* (c. 1280; English translation, 1861): "For me there is no path from my home's door." The same spirit is to be found in "Home," with its longing for the woods of Heidenstam's childhood, as well as in the not wholly successful opening suite, "The Forest of Tiveden," named after a forest near Olshammar. (Heidenstam cannot restrain his overly fecund inventiveness, and puts a Pan-like creature, rather comically named "Söndag," meaning "Sunday" into the midst of the gnarled and windswept Swedish woods.)

It is impossible to summarize the various attitudes present in the book. There is, for example, the bitter railing against traditional symbols of noble striving in "The Stars" and then the clear-cut idealism of "We Thankless Ones." There is the praise of war in "The Nine-Year Peace" and the praise of a quiet summer day in "The Morning." There is the revolutionary "Barricade Song" and the reverence for an ancient family's traditions in "By the Chest with the Family Relics." In addition, readers witness the erotic dead end of "Childhood Friends" and the cozy love scene of "By the Fire," the unadorned ruthlessness of "Malatesta's Morning Song" and the visionary world of "Jairus' Daughter," about the girl whom Jesus brings back from the dead (Mark 5, Luke 8). In Heidenstam's reworking of the biblical story, the girl does not want to return, preferring to cling to the infinite realms of paradise, where, in a distinctly non-Christian fashion, she has undergone transformation upon transformation: "I become the storm on the sea, I become the star on the mountains."

The patriotic Heidenstam appeared in all of his glory in *Karolinerna*, a set of historical novellas (sometimes more like prose poems) centered on the figure of Charles XII of Sweden—his initial military successes, his defeat at Poltava by Peter the Great, his internment in Turkey, his return to Sweden, and his mysterious death. Like Strindberg, Heidenstam was fascinated and dismayed by the "warrior king" who demonstrated such disregard for the lives of his men and, ultimately, the fate of his nation. Heidenstam was aware of the magnetism that Charles could exert, by means of which the monarch abused the spirit of sacrifice of his soldiers, the real heroes and victims in the book. All the same, Heidenstam was fascinated by the spectacle of destruction. Unlike Strindberg, he revels in the splendid failure of a king and of a nation that undertook a task beyond their power. It may be added that, more subtly than *Hans Alienus, Karolinerna* is something of an autobiographical book. With his feverish and sometimes destructive imagination, Charles may be a critical portrait of Heidenstam himself.

The same devotion to the greatness of the Swedish nation informed the third of Heidenstam's books of poetry, *Ett folk* (1902; a people); its concluding poem, "The Invocation and the Promise," was published in 1899. There Heidenstam, as in "The Nine-Year Peace," declared that a national tragedy was necessary for a people's renewal. Since the peaceful Sweden of the century's turn seemed an unlikely candidate for disaster, Heidenstam looked almost enviously at Finland, just then resisting the Russification policies of Nicholas II. Certainly this is the attitude of a "Greeting to Finland from the Year 1900," which he did not include in *Ett folk* (he saved it for his last collection), wishing instead that *Ett folk* be a wholly Swedish monument—and it was. *Ett folk* contained what would become the Swedish national anthem ("Sweden"), an appeal for national community among all classes ("Citizens' Song"), and the bombastic "Soldiers' Song," which concludes: "We will become a people that's heard/ The day it roars in anger."

Heidenstam returned to his exploration of the past with *Heliga Birgittas pilgrimsfärd* (1901; Saint Birgitta's pilgrimage). The saint, it has been remarked, is in fact not only a central figure from Sweden's late Middle Ages but also one more representative of Heidenstam's cult of the exceptional person, placed in the service of a higher calling. The historical work was essentially concluded with *Folke Filbyter* (1905; English translation, 1925) and *Bjälboarvet* (1907; *The Bjälbo Inheritance*, 1925), the two parts of *Folkungaträdet* (1905-1907; *The Tree of the Folkungs*, 1925). The first part has been called the greatest Swedish historical novel, because of its portrait of the ugly, grasping, and cruel Folke who nevertheless, in his search for his grandson, shows a measure of humanity. The sequel is about a later generation of the great Folkung clan and has as its main characters the hostile brothers, King Valdemar, the last of Heidenstam's hedonists, and Magnus, pious, orderly, and tormented, the leader of a successful revolt against the ruler. A coda to Heidenstam's historical writing was a reader for schools, *Svenskarna och deras hövdingar* (1908-1910; *The Swedes and Their Chieftains*, 1925).

His energies in the next years were absorbed by his ever more violent attacks on Strindberg—"the full-blooded barbarian in our cultural life"—in *Proletärfilosofiens upplösning och fall* (1911; the dissolution of proletarian philosophy), in which he also assaulted the leaders of the Swedish workers' movement. Following a public display of sympathy for Strindberg's liberal social standpoint and the dramatist's death, Heidenstam returned to poetry, compiling the book which, his disciple and biographer Fredrik Böök claimed, perfectly met Alfred Nobel's requirement that the prize should go to "the past year's most distinguished work in an idealistic direction." The verse forms and the language of *Nya dikter* are much simpler than before, except in some poems from the turn of the century, previously uncollected. The book is full of efforts to utter final truths, as in "At the End of the Way": "All is transfigured there, and all is redeemed." Present-day readers may be less moved by these expressions of wisdom (to some, they are reminiscent of the works of Johann Wolfgang von Goethe) than by the lyrics betraying the anxieties of a premature old age. In "The First Night in the Churchyard," the dead man, trapped in the grave, filled with a "terror without pity," speaks of what the poet in "Sleeping Farms" had wanted to ignore: "Night . . . hide from us our coming days."

Heidenstam was a defeated man. His heroic Sweden of the past would never return, and he saw too few signs of spiritual greatness in contemporary Sweden; his hopes of becoming a genuine poet of the people, like Norway's Bjørnstjerne Bjørnson, had not been realized. Indeed, certain circles had mocked him for having entertained such dreams: He was too idiosyncratic and too self-absorbed to play the part that he had chosen for himself in the nation's life.

Surely, Heidenstam is one of the most interesting figures in Swedish literature at the turn of the century; yet, placed alongside the works of his sometime mentor and then his foe, Strindberg, his own products may seem, despite their rhetorical flourish, their high colors, and their passion for detail, icy and abstract. Nevertheless, some of Heidenstam's poems will remain in the Swedish canon, as will his historical narratives, even though the latter may find a relatively small audience.

Bibliography

Primary

NOVELS: *Endymion*, 1889; *Hans Alienus*, 1892; *Karolinerna*, 1897-1898 (*A King and His Campaigners*, 1902; better known as *The Charles Men*, 1920); *Heliga Birgittas pilgrimsfärd*, 1901; *Folkungaträdet*, 1905-1907 (2 volumes; *The Tree of the Folkungs*, 1925).

SHORT FICTION: *Sankt Göran och draken*, 1900; *Skogen susar*, 1904.

POETRY: *Vallfart och vandringsår*, 1888; *Dikter*, 1895; *Ett folk*, 1902; *Nya dikter*, 1915; *Sweden's Laureate: Selected Poems of Verner von Heidenstam*, 1919; *Sista dikter*, 1942; *Fragment och aforismer*, 1959.

NONFICTION: *Från Col di Tenda till Blocksberg*, 1888; *Renässans*, 1889; *Pepitas bröllop*, 1890 (with Oskar Levertin); *Modern Barbarism*, 1894; *Klassicitet och germanism*, 1898; *Tankar och tekningar*, 1899; *Svenskarna och deras hövdingar*, 1908-1910 (*The Swedes and Their Chieftains*, 1925); *Dagar och händelser*, 1909; *Proletärfilosofiens upplösning och fall*, 1911;

Vad vilja vi?, 1914; *När kastanjerna blommade*, 1941; *Tankar och utkast*, 1941.
MISCELLANEOUS: *Samlade skrifter*, 1909-1949 (23 volumes).

Secondary

Berg, Ruben Gustafsson. "Verner von Heidenstam." *American-Scandinavian Review* 5 (1917): 160-169. Berg offers a brief life-and-works account of Heidenstam's career, introducing many of the intellectual and thematic strands in his production. Since Berg's essay was originally prepared for a Swedish public, some of his allusions will not be clear to the uninitiated.

Borland, Harold. *Nietzsche's Influence on Swedish Literature, with Special Reference to Strindberg, Ola Hansson, Heidenstam, and Fröding*. Gothenburg: Göteborgs Kungliga Vetenskaps- och Vitterhets-Samhälle, 1955. Borland explores Heidenstam's reactions to Nietzsche in Heidenstam's letters and articles, and he traces the appearance of Nietzschean ideas in Heidenstam's works before he had read Nietzsche. A clear Nietzschean impulse is found in the novel *Hans Alienus*; in Heidenstam's later works, affinities with Nietzsche are evident, but Heidenstam's own artistic independence was such that he never fell into the "Nietzschean excesses of which . . . Strindberg [was] blatantly guilty."

Gustafson, Alrik. *A History of Swedish Literature*. Minneapolis: University of Minnesota Press, 1961. The summary of Heidenstam's literary career is deftly executed and, in a small space, provides a clear picture of Heidenstam's strengths and shortcomings. The author's attitude toward Heidenstam is much more critical here than in his earlier study of the laureate's narratives.

—————. "Nationalism Reinterpreted: Verner von Heidenstam." In *Six Scandinavian Novelists*. Princeton, N.J.: Princeton University Press, 1940. Gustafson's treatment of Heidenstam's narrative prose is preceded by biographical anecdote; the interpretations themselves contain long quotations (in English translation) and plot summaries but do little probing beneath the surface.

Schoolfield, George C. "Charles XII Rides in Worpswede." *Modern Language Quarterly* (September, 1955): 258-267. An attempt to prove that Rainer Maria Rilke's poem "Karl der Zwölfte von Schweden reitet in der Ukraine" (Charles XII of Sweden rides in the Ukraine) in *Das Buch der Bilder* (1902, 1906; the book of pictures), was inspired in part by Rilke's reading of the first part of the German translation of Heidenstam's *Karolinerna*.

—————. "Rilke and Heidenstam: Public Praise and Hidden Trails." In *Studies in German Literature of the Nineteenth and Twentieth Centuries: Festschrift for F. C. Coenen*, edited by Siegfried Mews. Chapel Hill: University of North Carolina Press, 1970. The essay offers further and binding proof of Rilke's admiration for Heidenstam's novel and adduces some evidence of Rilke's having received an impression of Heidenstam's lyrics through an impromptu German translation by a Swedish friend.

George C. Schoolfield

1917

Literature
Karl Adolph Gjellerup, Denmark
Henrik Pontoppidan, Denmark

Peace
International Red Cross Committee

Physics
Charles Barkla, Great Britain

Chemistry
no award

Physiology or Medicine
no award

KARL ADOLPH GJELLERUP
1917

Born: Roholte, near Præstø, Denmark; June 2, 1857
Died: Klotzsche, Germany; October 11, 1919
Languages: Danish and German
Principal genres: Fiction, drama, and poetry

A scholar of Buddhist mysticism as well as a visionary poet, whose works often neglect artistic form, Gjellerup combined an intellectual search for truth with a continuous desire for beauty expressed through intuition and fantasy

The Award

Presentation

Karl Adolph Gjellerup shared the Nobel Prize in Literature with Danish writer Henrik Pontoppidan. The Nobel Prize was awarded to him on November 8, 1917, "for his varied and rich poetry, which is inspired by lofty ideals." No award ceremony was held and neither a presentation nor a Nobel lecture was given. In his "Biographical-Critical Essay," Sven Söderman, Swedish critic and member of the Swedish Academy's Nobel Institute, divides Gjellerup's career into three periods. As a young student of theology, he became attracted by the radicalism of the critic Georg Brandes. He published a series of derivative works, which were strongly influenced by Charles Darwin and evolutionism, fiercely rejecting Christianity. During a trip abroad, however, Gjellerup became estranged from the theories of naturalism and returned to the world of antiquity and German classicism for which he had a greater affinity. He was also introduced to the ideas of Richard Wagner. As a result, Gjellerup matured as a writer. His drama *Brynhild* (1884) and his novel *Minna* (1889; English translation, 1913), in particular, have been called masterpieces of both form and content, the latter being ranked among the finest in Scandinavian belles lettres.

During this second period, Gjellerup set himself apart from Brandes and the school of naturalism in works characterized by "idealism and moral elevation." Söderman emphasizes that Gjellerup's works hereafter are permeated with high moral ideas, which have not always found satisfactory artistic expression.

The third period of Gjellerup's career is considered the most significant. Gjellerup's enthusiasm for Wagner's operas led him to the study of Eastern philosophy and culture, of Buddhism and Hinduism, and his writings after 1900 treat these subjects "so poetically and idealistically" that they form the climax of his oeuvre. In these works, Gjellerup describes with acuity and poetic intuition the essence of the Buddhist worldview with its concepts of self-denial, Nirvana, and universal destruction, raising philosophical theory to the level of great art.

The essay concludes by characterizing Gjellerup as the "classic poet of Buddhism," failing to mention Gjellerup's last novels, which signal a dissociation from Eastern philosophy and a gradual return to Christianity.

Nobel lecture

In lieu of a lecture, Gjellerup submitted a two-page autobiography, which places the major stages of his artistic development in chronological order and lists his works with a few, mostly biographical or bibliographical, comments. Describing his early years in the home of his uncle, a Lutheran minister, Gjellerup stresses the country life which "made an indelible impression" on his mind, leaving its mark on most of his prose works. After a brief mention of his studies at the University of Copenhagen, Gjellerup in some detail explains how after his literary debut in 1878 he came under the influence of Charles Darwin and how his interests for some time took a distinct scientific direction. Gjellerup dwells on this period of his life and—even though his later writings took a totally different direction—characterizes his works from the early 1880's, inspired by Darwinism and English naturalism, as noteworthy.

Gjellerup briefly describes his travel abroad in 1883-1884, where he took lessons in painting during a three-month stay in Rome. He notes that he subsequently came to terms with the naturalist school of Brandes and then lists his works from the following years. Highlights of this period are his marriage in 1887, the awarding of a lifelong annual grant from the government in 1889, and the successful publication of the drama *Wuthorn* (1893).

A move to Dresden in 1892 clearly had an important impact on Gjellerup's career. From that time, he also wrote his works in German, a language which he considered his true medium. He concludes his autobiography with a discussion of his debut novel *En Idealist* (1878; an idealist). According to Gjellerup, its title symbolizes the author himself, guided as he has been by German Idealism, the models of which were Immanuel Kant and Arthur Schopenhauer. It constitutes the leitmotif for his authorship and the "rightful habitat" for the author himself.

Critical reception

The award of 1917 was one of the rare instances in which the Nobel Prize in Literature was divided between two authors. After Henrik Pontoppidan had succeeded the recently deceased Jakob Knudsen as the conominee together with Gjellerup, one group within the Nobel Committee favored Pontoppidan as the sole recipient of the prize, while another group favored Gjellerup. Gjellerup's candidacy was strongly supported by the leading Danish literary historian, Vilhelm Andersen, who emphasized Gjellerup's idealistic efforts in a period influenced by opposite trends. The Danish press was equally divided in its reaction to the award.

The contemporary foreign press was preoccupied with the events of World War I and paid little attention to the announcement and presentation of the award. *The New York Times* (November 10, 1917) briefly characterizes Gjellerup as a strongly religious writer and compares him with Leo Tolstoy. His career is described as being marked by a continuous philosophical quest which has finally led to Buddhist mysticism.

The much more extensive treatment of the award in *The Times Literary Supplement* (December 20, 1917) begins by suggesting that since Norway and Sweden had each received a Nobel Prize in Literature (Bjørnstjerne Bjørnson and Selma Lagerlöf), the Nobel Committee must have decided that it was Denmark's turn. The article states that Gjellerup and Pontoppidan are the two most popular Danish novelists from the pre-twentieth century period, drawing some parallels between them, but noting one crucial difference: Whereas Pontoppidan has kept himself unaffected by all contemporary influence, Gjellerup "is a chameleon who takes his colour from whatever intellectual object he rests upon." The anonymous critic of *The Times Literary Supplement*, who is well-informed about Gjellerup's early years in particular, gives a detailed biographical account stressing Gjellerup's study of English literature, in particular the writings of Percy Bysshe Shelley and Algernon Charles Swinburne, who became models for his unsuccessful early poetry. With regard to his later career, which is seen as more closely related to Germany than to Denmark, it is noted that even though Gjellerup has improved as a lyrical poet, it is his prose, of which the two novels *Minna* and *Møllen* (1896; the mill) are highly recommended, that has the greatest literary merit.

Nevertheless, the critic strongly disagrees with the Nobel Committee's selection of Gjellerup "with all respect for [his] industry and capacity." He can in no way be compared with previous recipients such as Anatole France, Gabriele D'Annunzio, or Thomas Hardy, and without mentioning any names it is suggested that several other Danish writers would have been worthier candidates. Finally, the Swedish Nobel Committee is accused of having been led by pro-German political sentiments in choosing a "Danish writer who is profoundly absorbed by the spirit of Germany." Criticism for the Nobel Committee's choice of Gjellerup has continued to the present.

Biography

Karl Adolph Gjellerup was born on June 2, 1857, in Roholte, near Præstø, south of Copenhagen. He was descended, both on his father's and mother's sides, from well-established families of scholars and Lutheran clergymen. His father, Carl Adolph Gjellerup, died when he was only three years old, and Gjellerup grew up in the Copenhagen home of the minister and writer

Johannes Fibiger, the cousin of his mother, Anna Johanne Elisabeth, née Fibiger.

In 1874, the same year that Gjellerup was graduated from Haderslev Grammar School, his foster father moved to the Zealand countryside, where Gjellerup spent his summers. The country vicarage became a source of inspiration which resurfaces in most of his works with a Danish setting. After studying theology at the University of Copenhagen, Gjellerup earned his Bachelor of Divinity degree in 1878, the year of his literary debut. In 1881, he received the Gold Medal of the University of Copenhagen for a thesis on Darwin's evolutionary theories.

After a trip abroad to Germany, Italy, Switzerland, Greece, and Russia in 1883-1884, Gjellerup stayed for six months in Copenhagen and then moved to Dresden, where he lived from 1885 to 1887. On October 24, 1887, he married the German-born Eugenia Anna Caroline, née Heusinger, and settled in the Copenhagen suburb of Hellerup. In 1889, Gjellerup received a lifelong annual pension from the Danish government. In 1892, he moved back to his wife's native town of Dresden. From this period on, Gjellerup wrote his works in Danish as well as in German. He died on October 11, 1919, in Klotzsche, Germany.

Literary Career

Gjellerup's authorship falls into three phases. The first, from 1878 to 1882, is dominated by his infatuation with classical culture and is marked by his study of the radical German biblical criticism of David Friedrich Strauss and Ludwig Feuerbach. Even before he received his degree, he turned fiercely against the Christian environment of his youth. At the same time, he was a voracious reader of such German writers as Friedrich Schiller and Heinrich Heine. The first made him forever a disciple of German Idealism; the latter provided him with *Weltschmerz* and innumerable quotes for his first immature, sloppily written novels. Both *En Idealist*, published under the pseudonym "Epigonos," and *Det unge Danmark* (1879; young Denmark) are autobiographical settlements with Christianity and Danish Romantic tradition in their portrayals of the main character's wavering between orthodoxy and atheism.

A similar contrast forms the main motif in the novella *Antigonos* (1880), which uses second century Greece and Asia Minor as the background for a fierce theological debate about the authenticity of the New Testament. Gjellerup's strong beliefs are even more openly expressed in his first poetry collection, *Rødtjørn* (1881; hawthorne), dedicated to Brandes. Brandes' radical views of religion and society, as well as Gjellerup's own preoccupation with Charles Darwin's and Herbert Spencer's evolutionary theories, now turned him into a militant atheist. In 1881, he won the Gold Medal of the University of Copenhagen with a thesis on evolutionism and determinism

Arvelighed og Moral (1881; heredity and morals) and thereafter wrote the poem *Aander og Tider* (1882; spirits and times), "a requiem on Darwin." Both poetry volumes are strongly influenced by the ingenious verses in classical style of Shelley and Swinburne, which Gjellerup, following the advice of Brandes, had eagerly studied. This entire development is sketched in Gjellerup's next novel, *Germanernes Lærling* (1882; the Teutons' apprentice), a *Bildungsroman* which, in the first half, is marred by superficial satire and reminiscences from the author's extensive secondary reading. In common with the novel's second half is a lacking capability for realistic description. An increasingly strong commitment to German culture and an ethical point of view in juxtaposition to modern French frivolity express the author's true allegiance, at the same time adding a genuine artistic quality to the work.

During his educational journey of 1882-1883, Gjellerup had begun two new novellas, *Romulus* (1883), influenced by Russian naturalism, in particular Ivan Turgenev, and *G-Dur* (1883; G major), heralding the second phase of his authorship. Both are subdued, introverted love stories devoid of any polemics, the latter set in the South Zealand region of Gjellerup's childhood. His travelogues, *En klassisk Maaned* (1884; a classical month) and *Vandreaaret* (1885; wander year), mark his final, very personal rejection of Brandes and naturalism. From this time on, Gjellerup, after having returned to the German Idealism of his youthful readings, developed considerably as an artist. A plan to write a tragedy, already planned during his student years, now matured. *Brynhild* became his most significant work for the stage. It takes its form mainly from the Greek tragedy, its material from old Norse mythology, the German *Niebelungenlied*, and Wagner's and Schopenhauer's philosophy of renunciation and Nirvana. Inspired by his future wife's divorce proceedings, after thirteen years of marriage with the musician Fritz Bendix, it focuses, in a language of great poetic beauty, on the conflict between the individual and the norms of society, in which the individual, by living up to his ideals, nevertheless must succumb.

Increasingly influenced by Friedrich Nietzsche's theories of the superman, Gjellerup's next dramas, *Hagbard og Signe* (1888; Hagbard and Signe), based on a Danish folk ballad, and the Schiller-inspired contemporary tragedies *Herman Vandel* (1891) and *Wuthorn* (1893), are all based on this conflict. The individual's rights are passionately defended against pragmatic and compromise-seeking modern society. Yet the language in these works has become so stilted and the character delineation so abstract that they have been drained of dramatic life and poetic sentiment. The earlier Turgenev-inspired melancholy mood is convincingly struck again, but on a larger scale, in the novel *Minna*, set in Saxony. The title character, the embodiment of German culture, is a woman objecting to the contemporary ideas of women's liberation and sexual promiscuity. She does not thrive in the brilliantly depicted artistic circles of Copenhagen, in which she is forced to live and from which she is unable to liberate herself. The first-person narrator of the novel must therefore renounce her, and Gjellerup resumes the theme of renunciation which later became so predominant in his writings. It resurfaces in another masterpiece, *Møllen*. This novel is a strange mixture of Émile Zola's symbolic concept of naturalism, through its description of the mill as an almost living organism, and a Dostoevskian analysis of a crime of passion. The crime is committed by the miller, a complex character, who by nature is a religious seeker attempting to transgress his own self.

This novel leads into Gjellerup's third phase, beginning around 1900, which is permeated with the pessimism of Wagner and Schopenhauer and, initially, with Buddhist mysticism. The legendary play *Offerildene* (1903; sacrificial fires), based on the Indian *Upanishads* (c. tenth century B.C.), was successfully performed in Dresden and Copenhagen. It contains passages of exquisite, almost spiritual, beauty, which can also be found in Gjellerup's Buddha-drama *Den Fuldendtes Hustru* (1907; the wife of the perfect one). The novels *Pilgrimen Kamanita* (1906; *The Pilgrim Kamanita*, 1911) and *Verdensvandrerne* (1910; the world wanderers) are also influenced by Eastern philosophy. The first describes the various stages of a soul's journey toward Nirvana, accompanied by his beloved, in a setting totally devoid of nature and human beings. The second is a well-structured epic set in contemporary India, bursting with colorful and precisely drawn scenery. Gjellerup never visited India; every detail is taken from secondary literature.

Gjellerup's last, rather insignificant books indicate a return to the Christianity of his childhood, while retaining the motifs of self-denial and withdrawal from the world. *Rudolph Stens Landpraksis* (1913; the country practice of Rudolph Sten) is set in the Danish provinces and contains material that is autobiographical. It offers a characterization of the Christian God not as the creator but as the redeemer of mankind from the impure existence of the world. *Guds Venner* (1916; God's friends), on the other hand, is based on themes from medieval mysticism in its portrayal of the religious person's liberation from the things of the world. *Den gyldne Gren* (1917; the golden bough), set in the time of the early church, marks his final confession of faith in the Gospel.

The weakness of Gjellerup's writings is that they deal with worldviews as theories rather than with their embodiment in concrete experiences. His works are didactic, burdened with religio-philosophical learning. Nevertheless, they are continuously striving for aesthetic beauty and ethical purity, which makes Gjellerup's present oblivion undeserved.

Bibliography

Primary
LONG FICTION: *En Idealist*, 1878; *Det unge Danmark*, 1879; *Antigonos*, 1880;

Germanernes Lærling, 1882; *Romulus*, 1883; *G-Dur*, 1883; *En arkadisk Legende*, 1887; *Minna*, 1889 (English translation, 1913); *Pastor Mors*, 1894; *Møllen*, 1896; *Konvolutten*, 1897; *Ved Grændsen*, 1897; *Tankelæserinden*, 1901; *Pilgrimen Kamanita*, 1906 (*The Pilgrim Kamanita*, 1911); *Verdensvandrerne*, 1910; *Rudolph Stens Landpraksis*, 1913; *Guds Venner*, 1916; *Den gyldne Gren*, 1917; *Madonna della laguna*, 1920.

SHORT FICTION: *Ti Kroner og andre Fortællinger*, 1893; *Villaen ved Havet, Judas*, 1910.

PLAYS: *Brynhild*, 1884; *Saint-Just*, 1886; *Thamyris*, 1887; *Hagbard og Signe*, 1888; *Bryllupsgaven*, 1888; *Herman Vandel*, 1891; *Wuthorn*, 1893; *Kong Hjarne Skjald*, 1893; *En Million*, 1894; *Hans Excellence*, 1895; *Gift og Modgift*, 1898; *Offerildene*, 1903; *Elskovsprøven*, 1906; *Den Fuldendtes Hustru*, 1907.

POETRY: *Rødtjørn*, 1881; *Aander og Tider*, 1882; *Min Kjærligheds Bog*, 1889; *Fra Vaar til Høst*, 1895; *Fabler*, 1898; *Das heiligste Tier*, 1919.

NONFICTION: *Arvelighed og Moral*, 1881; *En klassisk Maaned*, 1884; *Vandreaaret*, 1885; *Richard Wagner i hans Hovedværk "Nibelungens Ring,"* 1890; *Mit formentlige Høiforræderi mod det danske Folk*, 1897.

TRANSLATION: *Den ældre Eddas Gudesange*, 1895.

Secondary

Bang, Herman Joachim. "Karl Gjellerup." In *Realisme og Realister*. 2d ed. Copenhagen: Gyldendal, 1966. Bang, a contemporary of Gjellerup, points to the heavy dependence on Heinrich Heine in his first two novels. He criticizes the stereotyped character delineation but, at the same time, stresses Gjellerup's excellent use of dialogue. Bang finally suggests that Gjellerup at one point might turn to the writing of plays.

Gjellerup, Karl. *Karl Gjellerup, der Dichter und Denker: Sein Leben in Selbstzeugnissen und Briefen*. 2 vols. Leipzig: Quelle and Meyer, 1921-1922. The author's memoirs, partly based on letters, which deal with Gjellerup's biography rather than with his writings. The volume is prefaced by a totally uncritical essay by P. A. Rosenberg.

Paul, Fritz. "Gjellerup und die Aufwertung des Jugendstils." *Danske Studier* 66 (1971): 81-90. Paul suggests a reevaluation of Gjellerup, particularly in the light of the general revalorization of the Art Nouveau epoch. He focuses on the Buddhist-inspired works from Gjellerup's last period and convincingly demonstrates how closely related these works are to Art Nouveau. When discussed within this framework, Gjellerup's at times quite esoteric and embellished language and imagery, which are more distinctly present in the German than in the Danish versions of his works, take on a quality which has so far been ignored.

Zberea, Nicolae. "K. Gjellerup: A Master of Expression of Indian Thought." *The Indo-Asian Culture* 19, no. 1 (1970): 30-33. The essay focuses on

Gjellerup's late, Buddhist-inspired works, in particular his novel *Pilgrimen Kamanita*, which is hailed as "a masterpiece of beauty and originality." A parallel is drawn to Johann Wolfgang von Goethe's *Faust* and, in addition, Zberea briefly discusses Schopenhauer's influence on Gjellerup in general.

Sven H. Rossel

1917

Literature
Karl Adolph Gjellerup, Denmark
Henrik Pontoppidan, Denmark

Peace
International Red Cross Committee

Physics
Charles Barkla, Great Britain

Chemistry
no award

Physiology or Medicine
no award

HENRIK PONTOPPIDAN
1917

Born: Fredericia, Denmark; July 24, 1857
Died: Charlottenlund, Denmark; August 21, 1943
Language: Danish
Principal genre: Fiction

A realist author with in-depth knowledge of all social and geographical areas of contemporary Danish life, Pontoppidan strove to unveil false sentimentality and superficiality, employing an objective epic description that contained a strong lyrical and romantic vein

The Award

Presentation

Henrik Pontoppidan shared the Nobel Prize in Literature with another Danish writer, Karl Adolph Gjellerup. The Nobel Prize was awarded to him on November 8, 1917, "for his authentic descriptions of present-day life in Denmark." No award ceremony was held and neither a presentation nor a Nobel lecture was given. Sven Söderman, Swedish critic and member of the Swedish Academy's Nobel Institute, begins his "Biographical-Critical Essay" by placing Pontoppidan among the generation of the writers of the so-called Modern Breakthrough in the 1870's, ranking him "first among contemporary Danish novelists."

A brief biographical sketch mentions Pontoppidan's family background of Lutheran clergy, his studies at the Polytechnical Institute and initial career as a teacher. The author's lifelong fight against pretentiousness, escapism, and moral cowardice is stressed throughout the succeeding presentation of his works. The early works, in particular, are strongly satirical, attacking the Danish educational system as well as the political corruption of all parties. On a more psychological level, Pontoppidan exercises his irony on the hypocrisy of snobbish city life and civilized man's trendy and superficial worship of nature. He advocates a life developed in complete freedom without societal constraints. Söderman stresses that Pontoppidan's "revolutionary" message is never expressed directly. Rather, he lets his characters speak for themselves. He employs a seemingly objective narrative technique, a device which conceals the fact that Pontoppidan is actually a lyricist nourished on what he himself has labeled "the stale milk of romanticism."

The essay focuses on Pontoppidan's two major epic cycles from the turn of the century, the masterpieces of his entire oeuvre. These works constitute monumental cross sections of Danish social and spiritual life in the countryside, the provinces, and in Copenhagen. They feature protagonists caught in a battle between illusion and reality in which, because of their inability to adapt their dreams to everyday life, they succumb. One, an idealistic min-

ister, dies from a mental disease; the other, a materialistic engineer, falls victim "to that Christian romanticism which he has in his blood." Pontoppidan's
third novel cycle portrays another failing character, a politician who is unable
to find any genial soil for his radical ideas. The work's strength lies in its vivid
character delineation as well as its social descriptions of Danish society, but it
fails to reach the artistic level of the two preceding major cycles.

Only a few of Pontoppidan's other works are examined, and there are no
in-depth discussions of his language and style, even though he is labeled as
"the classicist of the new Danish realism." Pontoppidan's writings display
brilliant insights into all levels and aspects of Danish society which are only
secondary to their essential object: "man and his destiny." His distinctly in-
dividualized character portraits, endowed with an intense inner life, are not
created in isolation but are seen in interaction with constantly changing emotional and psychological situations. All details are put together to create a
carefully composed entirety that displays Pontoppidan both as "an incom-
parable artist" and "an epic author of great range."

Nobel lecture

In lieu of a Nobel lecture, Pontoppidan submitted a one-page autobiography with only minimal information of value. It contains a few biographical
statements covering the period up to his debut and a scant listing of selected
works.

Pontoppidan stresses his family background of Lutheran clergy, his experience of the Prussian and Austrian invasion of his native Jutland when he was
six years old, and his move to Copenhagen in 1873, where he began to study
at the Polytechnical Institute. After mentioning a summer trip to Switzerland, "which was rich in experiences," Pontoppidan states that his writing
developed from a description of nature and folk life into character analysis.

This change in subject corresponds to a change in genre. Whereas Pontoppidan's early works consisted of short prose pieces, "smaller tales," of
which he mentions *Fra Hytterne: Nye Landsbybilleder* (1887; from the huts),
he soon turned to the more spacious novel form, which he describes as a primary genre of the nineteenth century. Pontoppidan sees his three major
novel cycles as a coherent trilogy. His purpose has been to give a continuous
picture of all aspects of contemporary Danish life, seen indirectly through
the minds and fates of the characters. Apart from this more sociologically
and historically oriented part of his authorship, Pontoppidan lists the titles of
a number of smaller works, which reflect a more personal, imaginative, and
poetic approach. He concludes with the laconic statement that his collected
works "comprise approximately forty volumes."

Critical reception

The award of 1917 was one of the rare instances in which the Nobel Prize in Literature was divided between two authors. Danish writer Jacob Knudsen had initially been suggested as the recipient, together with Gjellerup. Knudsen died in 1917, however, and as Gjellerup was regarded as not sufficiently deserving to be the sole recipient, Pontoppidan was nominated as the replacement for Knudsen. Hereafter, the Nobel Committee divided into two camps, one favoring Gjellerup as the recipient of the entire prize, the other favoring Pontoppidan. The Danish press was equally divided in its reaction to the award; the consensus is now that the Nobel Committee erred in placing Gjellerup on the same level as the much more prolific Pontoppidan.

The contemporary foreign press was preoccupied with World War I and hardly paid any attention to the award. *The New York Times* (November 10, 1917) briefly characterizes Pontoppidan as an excellent stylist and a keen observer of Danish life but points to a difference of opinion among critics about his rank as an author.

The much more extensive treatment in *The Times Literary Supplement* (December 20, 1917) starts out by suggesting that having awarded Nobel Prizes to authors from Norway and Sweden (Bjørnstjerne Bjørnson and Selma Lagerlöf), the Nobel Committee must have decided that it is Denmark's turn. According to rumors, however, Pontoppidan initially should have refused to share the prize with anybody. The article draws certain parallels between Gjellerup and Pontoppidan but also notes one important difference: While Gjellerup adapts his approach and style to the object he is treating at the moment, Pontoppidan has remained unaffected by all contemporary trends. Clearly, the critic's sympathy is with the latter, whom he characterizes as "the leading living novelist of Denmark."

By far the largest part of the article is taken up with the discussion of Gjellerup. With hardly any biographical information at all, the brief characterization of Pontoppidan's oeuvre opens by mistakenly labeling his debut volume as "melancholy little tales about Jutland." The climax of the succeeding works, which are of increasing quality, is the eight-volume *Lykke-Per* (1898-1904; lucky Per), a masterpiece the quality of which is primarily seen in its depiction of country and city life of nineteenth century Denmark. In general, Pontoppidan's development away from the role of satirist and social critic toward that of an objective observer of the human scene is noted with enthusiasm by the critic, who praises him for his ability at creating a local *Comédie humaine* in the tradition of Honoré de Balzac. Indeed, Pontoppidan should be ranked "just below the great names of European fiction."

Biography

Henrik Pontoppidan was born on July 24, 1857, in the Jutland town of Fredericia. His parents were Dines Pontoppidan and Birgitte Christine Marie, née Oxenbøll. In 1865, his father, a highly respected Lutheran clergyman, was transferred to Randers, where Pontoppidan grew up. He was graduated from high school in 1873 and moved to Copenhagen, where in 1877, having interrupted his studies to travel to the Swiss Alps in 1876, he successfully completed the first part of his course in engineering at the Polytechnical Institute. Two years later, he gave up his studies to pursue his career as a writer.

Until 1882, Pontoppidan served as a science teacher at two folk high schools in Northern Zealand run by his brother Morten. In 1881, he made his literary debut and married Mette Marie Hansen. During these years, Pontoppidan traveled extensively in Denmark and abroad. From 1887 to 1889, he worked as a journalist for the radical newspaper *Politiken* and during the next two years for *Kjøbenhavns Børstidende*. In 1892, Pontoppidan divorced his first wife and married Antoinette Caroline Elise, née Kofoed. After trips to Germany and Italy, Pontoppidan settled in the Northern Zealand town of Fredensborg. After 1910 he lived permanently in Copenhagen. He received an honorary doctorate from the University of Lund in 1929 and became an honorary citizen of Randers in 1933. Henrik Pontoppidan died on August 21, 1943, in Charlottenlund, Denmark.

Literary Career

A major theme in Pontoppidan's authorship is already introduced in the story "Kirkeskuden" (the ship model), which concludes his debut work, *Stækkede Vinger* (1881; clipped wings): the impact on man of his heredity and environment and his futile rebellion against these forces. The rebellion is usually aimed at the milieu of the childhood vicarage, combined with a satirical description of the prevalent stupidity and materialism among the population of the countryside. "Kirkeskuden" is thus a naturalist parable based on Darwinist determinism, similar to the better-known classic, "Ørneflugt" ("Eagle's Flight"). The moral of this sketch is that one cannot expect to live the life of an eagle if one has grown up in a farmyard surrounded by domestic fowl.

The satirical element becomes stronger in Pontoppidan's succeeding works—broad, realistic descriptions of the life among peasants and impoverished crofters. The novel *Sandinge Menighed: En Fortælling* (1883; Sandinge parish) contains his first attacks on the personally experienced folk high school milieu, its hypocrisy, pseudoreligiosity, and self-aggrandizement. Yet Pontoppidan's sarcasm is simultaneously aimed at the flaws to be found in all segments of Danish society. The underlying general disillusionment becomes more pronounced in the collections of brief sketches, *Landsbybilleder* (1883; village sketches) and *Fra Hytterne*. Both are unsparing rejections of the romantic concept of rural idyll, exposing the injustice of poverty, the power of money, as well as the corruption of the clergy. Pontoppidan introduces another recurrent theme, the contrast between a conventional marriage of convenience and romantic love guided solely by passion.

A political dimension is added in Pontoppidan's collection *Skyer: Skildringer fra Provisoriernes Dage* (1890; clouds). His attacks, however, are aimed both at the right and the left wings in Danish politics, an example of his so-called double viewpoint. During this period, Pontoppidan's factual, realistic style, totally devoid of any sentimentality when describing the misery of the rural proletariat, was replaced by a freer, more imaginative narration, sometimes interspersed with romanticized descriptions of nature and an added symbolic dimension. Thus, the title character of the novella *Isbjørnen: Et Portræt* (1887; the polar bear), an eccentric, maverick clergyman, battling his more conservative colleagues, represents the individual's clash with the conformity of bourgeois society. The title character himself is a cheerfully executed, colorful, and humorous portrait of almost Rabelaisian dimensions.

In a number of novellas from this period, this shift in style is accompanied by a diminishing of the narrowly focused social and political critique. Instead, a wider concept of man's destiny is introduced, which transgresses determinism and other related concepts of naturalism. Thus *Ung Elskov: Idyl* (1885; young love), surprisingly demonstrates the catastrophic consequences of unrestricted passion in clear, conservative opposition to naturalism's advocacy of the rights of free love. *Mimoser: Et Familieliv* (1886; *The Apothecary's Daughters*, 1890) is written as a contribution to the fierce discussion on sexual morals that took place in Scandinavia in the 1880's, involving, among others, Bjørnstjerne Bjørnson and August Strindberg. It is a seemingly objective account of conventional marriage versus unrestricted passion. Only in the concluding chapter does it seem that Pontoppidan favors the latter possibility. This is also the case in *Spøgelser: En Historie* (1888; ghosts), which, in contrast to the two preceding works, is a light love story with a happy ending. Pontoppidan here introduces yet another major theme: the tension between the rural and the urban, nature and culture, which is continued in *Natur: To smaa Romaner* (1890; nature). The satire here, particularly aimed at a Copenhagener's unsuccessful back-to-nature attempts, becomes fully developed in Pontoppidan's first novel cycle and is later resumed in the poetic novel *Højsang: Skildring fra Alfarvej*; (1896; hymn), rewritten in dramatic form as *De vilde Fugle: Et Skuespil* (1902; the wild birds). A further departure from Pontoppidan's initial naturalistic approach toward the neoromantic and symbolist trend in the Danish literature of the 1890's can be seen in *Krøniker* (1890; chronicles), a collection of parables and fairy tales with an ironic twist, partly based on Danish folk legends.

In Pontoppidan's first novel cycle, the trilogy *Det forjættede Lande: Et Tidsbillede* (1898; the promised land), which includes *Muld: Et Tidsbillede* (1891; *Emmanuel: Or, Children of the Soil*, 1892), *Det forjættede Land: Et Tidsbillede* (1892; *The Promised Land*, 1896), and *Dommens Dag: Et Tidsbillede* (1895), the sociological examination of Danish society from his early naturalistic phase becomes fully developed. The satirical treatment of the folk high school from *Sandinge Menighed* is enlarged and forms the partial background to the destiny of the minister Emanuel Hansted, an echo of Jean-Jacques Rousseau's and Leo Tolstoy's anticultural messages. Rootless and homeless in his bourgeois milieu, Hansted seeks refuge among the Zealand peasantry, whose loyalty and love he attempts to win by walking behind a plow and marrying a peasant girl. Yet he fights in vain against the prejudices and primitive materialism which permeate the rural milieu, and "the promised land" remains unattainable. Completely isolated from his new environment and lacking the stamina to come to grips with this reality, Hansted deserts his wife and his parish and roams about as a preacher of repentance, gradually identifying himself with Christ, until he dies in a mental institution. Once again, Pontoppidan's double viewpoint manifests itself. The protagonist is not condemned for his failure to grasp reality. Pontoppidan's view of him vacillates between that of a martyr and a daydreamer, between empathy and mockery. Hansted's idealism is shattered when he loses faith in his congregation, in humanity in general, as well as in his original mission. He possesses, nevertheless, in his ruin, an honesty and consistency which compels respect, even admiration.

During the next years, Pontoppidan published a number of small but significant novels which stylistically signal his development toward epic concentration, stylistic lucidity, and linguistic simplicity. Thematically, they reach back to the short novels from the late 1880's in their analyses of the tension between realism and poetic imagination, naturalism and romanticism. They have in common a discussion of the rights of passion. They also seek the subjective expression, are first-person narratives, and pursue a poetic atmosphere. The artist's novel *Nattevagt* (1894; night watch) symbolically depicts a clash of two opposite life philosophies, illustrated in the battle between the radical naturalism of the preceding decades and the poetic-religious renaissance of the 1890's. The sterile theorizing of both trends has a fatal effect on human development, artistic creativity, and the ability to love. This message is repeated, many years later, in *Hans Kvast og Melusine* (1907; Merry Andrew and Melusina). The almost metaphysical sense of infinity which this novel's major character, Dr. Martens, expresses is already sketched in *Den gamle Adam: Skildring fra Alfarvej* (1894; the old Adam) and *Højsang*. These works also portray people who strive beyond themselves but in return must pay a tragic price.

The motif of the eagle's flight is resumed in Pontoppidan's magnum opus, his second novel cycle in eight volumes, *Lykke-Per*. Like the previous cycle, it contains autobiographical material. Per, the son of a Jutland clergyman, feels just as homeless in the authoritarian and puritanical milieu of his childhood as in the extravagant financial and intellectual circles into which, as a young engineering student, he is introduced upon his arrival in Copenhagen. He nurtures grandiose plans of changing Denmark into a modern industrial nation, plans which are rejected by experts as unrealizable. On the surface highly ambitious, Per is nevertheless a daydreamer who repeatedly fails to carry out his great plans. Halfheartedness becomes the distinctive feature in the relationship with Per's Jewish fiancée, Jakobe, the finest character of Pontoppidan's entire oeuvre. Like Emanuel Hansted, Per betrays love and, like Hansted, he symbolizes the entire Danish nation: reflective as well as passionate and lyrically gifted, but weak when action is required. All the same, Per is not described without sympathy. Although he has rebelled against his religious upbringing, he has inwardly remained a seeker for God and become more and more involved in philosophical speculations. The cycle concludes with his own realization that he has always been striving for solitude and self-denial. By fleeing to a lonely area in Northern Denmark, he severs all links to that external reality which he had failed to incorporate into his own persona. Influenced by Buddhist philosophy, medieval mysticism, and the Pietism of his childhood, he is finally able to realize the inner reality of his religious self and find true happiness.

As a prelude to his third novel cycle, Pontoppidan wrote a number of shorter novels which once again discuss the establishment of marriage versus the reign of uninhibited passion. In *Det ideale Hjem* (1900; the ideal home), Pontoppidan seems to favor the latter possibility, whereas *Borgmester Hoeck og hans Hustru: Et Dobbeltportræt* (1905; Mayor Hoeck and his wife), in spite of its portrayal of a misalliance, accepts marriage as a norm. The novel's atmosphere of gloom and fear, a result of the couple's estrangement, foreshadows the tragic outcome of the work—the death of the wife. Whereas earlier treatment of the topic focused on the social context, Pontoppidan now concentrates on the psychological implications of human isolation and loneliness and their impact on the characters. With *Det store Spøgelse* (1907; the great apparition), he wrote a study not only of people who have become alienated from their fellow man, but who are also suffering from a fear of the hidden secrets of their own soul and of the unknown forces in nature. This fear takes on a more existential dimension in *Den kongelige Gæst* (1908; *The Royal Guest*, published in the 1977 *The Royal Guest and Other Classical Danish Narratives*). This fear is caused by unexpected, irrational forces that foreshadow catastrophe and destruction and that lurk behind man's worship of joy and his pleasure of the moment.

An essentially universal angst permeates the five-volume novel *De Dødes Rige* (1912-1916; the realm of the dead). Almost in the form of a religious, didactic prose poem, this work sums up Pontoppidan's increasingly pronounced pessimistic outlook. Life is an evil dream experienced by the three principal characters. They succumb because of their inability to give and receive love. Their disillusionment is total. "Now I am dying, and yet I have never lived," exclaims the woman Jytte. Afraid of committing herself totally, her feelings of love are crippled and can only be expressed as jealousy.

Pontoppidan's previous disappointment with the Danish political system resurfaces in the portrait of the old politician Enslev, who is being dumped by the party he himself has brought to success. The cycle constitutes an overall settlement with contemporary, liberal society and concludes in an almost Old Testament-like Doomsday vision. In its consistent fatalism and expression of the nothingness of life, *De Dødes Rige* is unique in European literature.

Pontoppidan's last novel, *Mands Himmerig* (1927; man's heaven), is yet another satirical treatment of contemporary Denmark and her spirit of compromise in the years immediately preceding World War I. In this work, however, Pontoppidan's ironic double viewpoint is totally absent. He sides completely with his main character, an influential journalist, who demands involvement and commitment from the apathetic population. The journalist's appeal, however, is in vain. In his tragic fight, he destroys not only his career but also the happiness of himself and that of the woman he loves. Thus, Pontoppidan's last novel characteristically turns into yet another story of defeat.

It is difficult to put a label on Henrik Pontoppidan's oeuvre. Even though the tendency of his early works is clearly naturalistic, focusing on social injustice and political repression, his later works, as they incorporate certain neoromantic and aristocratic views of the 1890's, reach beyond any specific literary school. Pontoppidan offers an impressively thorough analysis of the spiritual, social, and political developments in Denmark over a period of half a century as well as of the mechanisms behind them. A similar insight and care for detail in his character delineation makes him a master of the psychological portrait. By having the ideals and fantasies of his characters confronted by reality, Pontoppidan manages to reveal the subtle, psychological patterns of their personalities.

Throughout his life, Pontoppidan consistently reworked and shortened his prose to achieve greater lucidity and more precise descriptions and dialogue. Yet even though he seemingly attempts objectivity, Pontoppidan is a traditionalist as a narrator: omniscient and sometimes projecting himself into the narrative. A strong moral indignation determines the actual point of departure of Pontoppidan's authorship: a striving for truth and consistency, and a proclamation of the intrinsic quality of the individual seen in a spiritual perspective.

Bibliography

Primary

LONG FICTION: *Sandinge Menighed: En Fortælling*, 1883; *Ung Elskov: Idyl*, 1885; *Mimoser: Et Familieliv*, 1886 (*The Apothecary's Daughters*, 1890); *Spøgelser: En Historie*, 1888; *Natur: To smaa Romaner*, 1890; *Muld: Et Tidsbillede*, 1891 (*Emmanuel: Or, Children of the Soil*, 1892); *Det forjæt-*

tede Land: Et Tidsbillede, 1892 (*The Promised Land*, 1896); *Minder*, 1893; *Nattevagt*, 1894; *Den gamle Adam: Skildring fra Alfarvej*, 1894; *Dommens Dag: Et Tidsbillede*, 1895; *Højsang: Skildring fra Alfarvej*, 1896; *Lykke-Per*, 1898-1904 (8 volumes); *Lille Rødhætte: Et Portræt*, 1900; *Det ideale Hjem*, 1900; *Borgmester Hoeck og hans Hustru: Et Dobbeltportræt*, 1905; *Det store Spøgelse*, 1907; *Hans Kvast og Melusine*, 1907; *Den kongelige Gæst*, 1908 (*The Royal Guest*, 1977); *De Dødes Rige*, 1912-1916 (5 volumes); *Et Kærlighedseventyr*, 1918; *Mands Himmerig*, 1927.

SHORT FICTION: *Stækkede Vinger*, 1881; *Landsbybilleder*, 1883; *Fra Hytterne: Nye Landsbybilleder*, 1887; *Isbjørnen: Et Portræt*, 1887; *Skyer: Skildringer fra Provisoriernes Dage*, 1890; *Krøniker*, 1890; *Kirkeskuden: En Fortælling*, 1897.

PLAYS: *De vilde Fugle: Et Skuespil*, 1902; *Asgaardsrejen: Et Skuespil*, 1906; *Thora van Deken*, 1922 (with Hjalmar Bergstrøm).

NONFICTION: *Reisebilder aus Dänemark*, 1890; *Kirken og dens Mænd: Et Foredrag*, 1914; *En Vinterrejse: Nogle Dagbogsblade*, 1920; *Drengeaar*, 1933; *Hamskifte*, 1936; *Arv og Gæld*, 1938; *Familjeliv*, 1940.

Secondary

Ekman, Ernst. "Henrik Pontoppidan as a Critic of Modern Danish Society." *Scandinavian Studies* 29 (1957): 170-183. A detailed treatment of the social criticism in *Lykke-Per* and *De Dødes Rige* in particular.

Jolivet, Alfred. *Les Romans de Henrik Pontoppidan*. Paris: Bibliothèque Nordique, 1960. A review of Pontoppidan's major works, interpreting them as historical documents and stressing the author's demand for justice in society and integrity of personality.

Jones, W. Glyn. "Henrik Pontoppidan: The Church and Christianity After 1900." *Scandinavian Studies* 30 (1958): 191-197. A study of Pontoppidan's religious views, centered on *De Dødes Rige*.

Mitchell, Phillip Marshall. *Henrik Pontoppidan*. Boston: Twayne Publishers, 1979. This volume is an excellent introduction to the writings of Pontoppidan. It places the author in the Danish literary tradition and offers precise analyses, not only of Pontoppidan's three major cycles but also of his often-overlooked novellas and short stories. The volume contains a selected bibliography of primary and secondary sources.

Sven H. Rossel

1919

Literature
Carl Spitteler, Switzerland

Peace
Woodrow Wilson, United States

Physics
Johannes Stark, Germany

Chemistry
no award

Physiology or Medicine
Jules Bordet, Belgium

CARL SPITTELER
1919

Born: Liestal, Switzerland; April 24, 1845
Died: Lucerne, Switzerland; December 29, 1924
Language: German
Principal genre: Poetry

An independent master of the epic form, devoted to the creation of idealistic verse of rare beauty and harmony, Spitteler willingly isolated himself from the distractions, artistic conventions, and material rewards afforded by contemporary society

The Award

Presentation

On December 10, 1920, the Nobel Prize in Literature for 1919 was presented to Carl Spitteler in particular appreciation of his epic *Olympischer Frühling* (1900-1905, four volumes; Olympic spring) by the Chairman of the Nobel Committee of the Swedish Academy, Harald Hjärne. The presentation recognized that the artistic merits of a work "so out of step with [its] times" had long been obscured but that the critical controversy it still inspired was sure testimony of its rich significance. The Academy stressed that Spitteler's unswerving dedication to his poetic muse led him to select knowingly a form and content which would challenge and even repel his readers as they negotiated the dramatic pathways of action, dialogue, and soliloquy carved into this original, mythological edifice.

The mythology, despite a nominal resemblance to classical Homerian tales, was acknowledged to be the idiosyncratic product of Spitteler's creative genius. It is an ideal landscape of the imagination, free of the impediments of imitation or allegory, against which he evokes the turmoils and disappointments of his "supermen," representatives of an embattled humanity, locked in a struggle of free will against necessity. That the aesthetic preoccupations of the literary environment incline his colleagues to reject "this seemingly fantastic mixture of dream and reality with its willful abuse of mythological names" can, according to the Academy, be of little concern to such an artist.

Hjärne emphasized that no summary could portray the vivid power and integrity of this vast and often-humorous work, which transports the reader from the transcended ecstasies of Olympus to earthly realms of "impotent despair." The Olympian heroes themselves are subject to both the powers of fate and the mechanistic forces of a soulless nature, which, when abused by self-interest, lead to certain destruction. The presentation concluded by admiring the "independent culture" of this uniquely creative poet.

Nobel lecture

Spitteler, who was seventy-five years old at the time of the award, was unable to attend the presentation as a result of a prolonged illness, characterized mainly by severe pulmonary difficulties and circulatory disturbances. The prize was accepted for him by Count Wrangel, the Swiss Minister of Foreign Affairs. The Academy expressed its concern for Spitteler's failing health, along with hopes that he would be able to continue his remarkable work.

Critical reception

The immediate journalistic reaction to the award's going to an internationally unknown and aged Swiss author was characterized by genuine astonishment and marred by querulous objections. One exception was the British critic J. G. Robertson, whose article in *The Contemporary Review* (1921) stressed that "few of the selections made by the literary advisors of the Nobel Fund are open to less cavil than this." That Spitteler was not a "recognised notability" stemmed, he believed, from the author's determined and laudable refusal to abandon his remarkable "spiritual independence." Spitteler, "perhaps the loneliest poet in Europe," is assigned an almost messianic role in the future of German poetry, a master of the poetic form whose works remained enigmatic "by virtue of a depth and obscurity which made him inaccessible to those that would read as they run." Robertson "rejoiced" to see the potential savior of German poetry fittingly and finally rewarded for works which embodied the noblest poetic and spiritual aspirations of the epoch.

In general, however, the Swedish and the British press expressed an almost schizophrenic dissatisfaction with the "fact" that the laureate was both "known" and "unknown." While acknowledging that Spitteler was "hailed in France as embodying the Helleno-Latin intelligence and . . . known as the Swiss Flaubert," *The Times* of London (November 13) titled its response "Nobel Prize Surprise" and expressed concern that such a prestigious award had been given to a poet about whom "very little is known . . . outside a small and immediate circle of admirers." Stockholm's *Dagens Nyheter* (day's news) predicted that "the choice will make people open their eyes with amazement abroad." The dismayed Swedish press believed that the award was contrary to Alfred Nobel's original intentions, stating that "it might have been less surprising if Carl Spitteler had been a young, unknown genius struggling with adverse circumstances and lacking the moral and material support which Nobel meant that his prizes should afford." It was suggested that, as a "creative force," this pecuniarily stable, seventy-five-year-old poet was "only deserving of a literary pension," although the Swedish journalist was quick to add that he intended "no disparagement of [Spitteler's] literary work, which, for those that know it, may be valuable."

Stockholm's Tidning (Stockholm's journal) pointed a somewhat more accurate journalistic finger at the heart of the controversy which surrounded the Academy's choice:

> So it has not been an Englishman who has been found to be most worthy of the Nobel Prize. It will be a bitter disappointment to interested circles that a seventy-five-year-old Swiss poet of no international importance has been preferred to the grand old man of English literature, Thomas Hardy.

The *Social Demokraten* was of the same opinion, as was the *Dagen Nyheter*, which prophesied considerable public surprise that the Academy did not recognize the appropriateness of honoring an English poet, stating that "the single prize awarded to Mr. Rudyard Kipling is scarcely adequate acknowledgement of the position of English writers."

That Spitteler was almost completely unknown to the American press is evident in the article "Nobel Prize Winner Beloved by Swiss," which appeared in *The New York Times* (November 14), a masterpiece of stereotypical generalities and misinformation in which Spitteler, who had been ill for many months and who had been too sick to attend the award ceremonies in December, was described as "still vigorous for his age," as he cheerfully carried home his market vegetables and indulged in his favorite hobby of "planting different kinds of trees, especially conifers." In fact, Spitteler's correspondence reveals that the very act of writing exhausted him. The observation that "at a distance, Spitteler might pass for a Scotchman" is offered in place of any attempt at a literary evaluation. Spitteler was depicted as a long-venerated national and literary hero, but, while at the time of the award he had indeed achieved general recognition as Switzerland's greatest poet, his abilities were generally recognized only after the publication of *Olympischer Frühling*, that is, when he was already in his sixties, and much of his celebrity resulted from his one act of political activism: a speech to his countrymen during the war.

Indeed, both *The Times* and *The New York Times* referred directly to this speech, "Our Swiss Standpoint," given in Zurich, in December, 1914. The indirect implication was that the speech provided a possible political motivation for the award. Calling for national unity, Spitteler had articulated the radical difference between cultural and political attachment, proclaiming Switzerland's independence from Germany and Germany's improper acts of wartime aggression. German publications too, for whom Spitteler was but a minimally familiar and by no means generally popular literary figure, also suspected this same political basis to the award, interpreting it as the Academy's obeisance to the Entente. Most remarkable is the lack of substantive German literary articles assessing Spitteler's literary contribution to the German canon in the light of this great international honor.

One informed and sensitive assessment of Spitteler's literary merits was published in the British press. On November 25, 1920, *The Times Literary Supplement* published a letter by Paul Lang in the "Correspondence" section, ostensibly offered by the Zurich academician because the decision of the Academy caused some comment; the letter stated that "a few points of information on the winner may be welcomed by British readers." Lang assigned the highest praise to *Olympischer Frühling*, referring to the "perfect harmony in the disposition of the plot" and the "steady flow of interesting characters." He concluded by noting that "outsiders can hardly realize what Spitteler's famous speech of December, 1914, meant for Switzerland. It broke the spell of incertitude and hesitation and freed the nation's conscience," demonstrating that "poets are still bearers of light in the hour of darkness and leaders of men."

Biography

Carl Georg Friedrich Spitteler was born on April 24, 1845, in the small town of Liestal, Switzerland, in the canton of Basel. In July of 1848 the family moved to Bern, where Spitteler's father took an appointment as treasurer of the Swiss Confederacy and began the study of the law. Nine years later, when the family returned to Liestal, Spitteler took a room with his aunt in Basel so that he could attend the humanistic *Gymnasium*, where he developed a passionate fondness for drawing and music. In 1860 he returned to Liestal and began traveling daily by train to Basel to attend an *Obergymnasium*, the Pädagogium, where he was influenced by Wilhelm Wackernagel and Jakob Burkhardt, but Spitteler proved to be neither a distinguished nor a cooperative student. In May, 1863, he was awarded the *Abitur*, having passed the qualifying exams for university, and, to please his father, entered the law faculty at the University of Basel. After suffering what appears to have been a complete breakdown, he undertook theological studies at the universities of Zurich, Heidelberg, and Basel. Spitteler initially failed his final examination, but he was finally accepted and granted a modest pastorship, from which he resigned almost immediately in order to accept a position as a private tutor in St. Petersburg. His sojourn to Russia and Finland allowed him to work on his first prose epic. The time abroad lasted until 1879, when Spitteler returned to Switzerland to accept a brief teaching position at a school in Bern.

In 1881 Spitteler published *Prometheus und Epimetheus* (1881; *Prometheus and Epimetheus*, 1931) at his own expense, under the pseudonym Carl Felix Tandem. The work was almost completely ignored, and a disappointed Spitteler was forced to support himself by teaching. He continued to write and publish, however, marrying Marietje op den Hooff in 1883. Within two years he began a new journalistic career for the *Grenzpost* and later became editor of the *Neue Zuricher Zeitung*.

In July, 1892, the death of a relative left him financially independent, and he retired to Lucerne to devote himself to his writing, publishing novels, po-

etry, and aesthetic essays, which brought him the beginnings of critical recognition. After the publication of *Olympischer Frühling*, Spitteler was honored with national acclaim. In December, 1914, he united his country with
his famous speech. Even as his health declined, Spitteler continued to live
and write quietly in Lucerne until his death at midnight on December 29,
1924, his life virtually unchanged by the award of the Nobel Prize.

Literary Career

In the autumn of 1862, Carl Spitteler made a decision that was to change
his whole life. At the age of twenty-two he embraced his mission as an epic
poet and joyfully committed himself to the lifelong pursuit of his poetic
ideals. He had spent several school years struggling to complete a drama
fragment, "Saul," but now his attention was captured by the "importunate
shade" Prometheus, a figure which was to fascinate him until his death and
which first appeared to him "in soul-shattering visions." During his years in
Russia and Finland, Spitteler struggled to fashion these overwhelming but
elusive apparitions into the language of poetic reality, and finally, in 1881, the
prose epic *Prometheus and Epimetheus* was published. To Spitteler's intense
disappointment, however, it caused barely a ripple on the literary waters of
the time.

"A profound allegory of exalted idealism," *Prometheus and Epimetheus*,
written in a rhythmical, almost biblical, prose, is a cosmological re-creation
of the Prometheus myth. The brothers Prometheus and Epimetheus have
withdrawn from the mundane morality of the community, yet, in response to
the temptations of the Angel of God, Epimetheus is persuaded to betray the
inspiration of his Soul for the conventions of Conscience and, as a result, is
granted wealth, royalty, and happiness. Prometheus, however, follows his
beloved Soul into exile and misery with his Lion, faithful in hate, and his
Dog, faithful in love. Eventually, Prometheus must rescue his brother and his
kingdom from an evil beyond the ken of traditional morality, and the epic
ends with the reconciliation of the brothers.

Replete with passages of extraordinary beauty, the first part of the epic
was highly praised by the great Swiss writer Gottfried Keller, who recognized
it as the "product of a creative imagination of the highest order," but the
work, in which Spitteler had invested such hope, failed to reach a wider critical audience. In form, the prose epic resembles Friedrich Nietzsche's *Also
sprach Zarathustra* (1883-1892, four parts; *Thus Spake Zarathustra*, 1896),
and in later years, Spitteler was, despite the obvious chronological impossi-
bility, falsely accused of having drawn on the more famous author's work.

Threatened by a bitter depression and forced to continue with the monoto-
nous burdens of teaching, Spitteler plunged his bruised poetic ego into the
Extramundana (1883), a speedily written collection of poetic tales, in large
part, "cosmic myths": the complicated "Der verlorene Sohn" (the prodigal

son) and "Der Prophet und die Sibylle" (the prophet and the sibyl). All are written in a clumsily insistent trochaic measure, divided into a tripartite structure of theme, myth, and antitheme. Even the few critics who had looked favorably on Spitteler's first work rejected the *Extramundana* as an embarrassing poetic "derailing," and Spitteler himself admitted that the execution of his original conception had been hasty and superficial.

Spitteler's life changed radically when, after fourteen years as a tutor and a teacher, he turned to journalism, for it afforded him the opportunity both to earn a living by his writing and to improve his position in the literary world. His editorial tasks left him scarcely more time to devote to his muse than had his teaching position at La Neuveville. It was in his journalistic capacity that the young German writer Ferdinand Avenarius invited him, in September, 1887, to contribute to the newly founded cultural journal the *Kunstwart*, and, despite protests over Spitteler's first contribution, Avenarius continued to support him, asking for six further contributions that year.

Spitteler remained faithful to the *Kunstwart* for more than a quarter century, developing his unmistakable essay style of elegant, sharp brevity. It became clear to him in his later years that the beginning of his affiliation with this journal marked the turning point in his literary career. This period also marked the beginnings of an important, though brief, literary relationship: his correspondence with Nietzsche, who had been impressed with the clarity of Spitteler's essays on dramaturgy and musical instruments and who had secured for him the invitation to join the *Kunstwart*. Nietzsche regarded Spitteler as "the finest aesthetic writer of the day" and had written to Avenarius, describing the Swiss journalist's essays as "marked by an extraordinarily thoughtful and keen sense for the history and criticism of art and culture" and added that they were "instinct with a delightful humour."

Although Spitteler continued to attempt the dramatic form, his most successful work of this period was a delightful childhood idyll, appearing first in serial form in the 1890's, titled *Die Mädchenfeinde* (1907; *Two Little Misogynists*, 1922): the story of two ten-year-old cadets, Gerold and Hansli, as they leave for school after their summer vacation and their sweetly painful friendship with their cousin Gesima. The purity of the childhood vision is not disturbed by the darker periphery of adult problems which frame the story, and the summer's rapture is broken only by the foolish anguish of the suicidal student, perhaps a voice from Spitteler's own past.

Spitteler's next venture into the narrative form was technically more challenging. In September, 1896, he began work on sketches for an autobiographically based story, telling of a son's struggles against his tyrant father. Written partly as the idealist poet's challenging reply to what for him had become the problem of realism, the novella *Conrad der Leutnant* (1898; Conrad the lieutenant) belongs more to the naturalist movement. The work has been described as "a tragic story of village life, told with intense rapidity of action and an almost cruel naturalism." In his prefatory remarks, Spitteler described the work as a *Darstellung*, a depiction or a prose form whose style afforded the most intimate reading experience possible. This he would achieve by the traditions of classical French drama: unity of character, perspective, and time—the daily conditions of reality. Nevertheless, the reader is struck by the artificiality of the text, despite the use of dialect and the indisputable consistency of the intricate web of motives and motivation. The drama of the text is clearly apparent, but the characters degenerate into broadly drawn and rather unconvincing types. For Spitteler, who was comfortable with the broad, sweeping rhythms of epic poetry, the writing of prose was always painstaking and unbearably slow, and he complained frequently about the snail's pace at which he labored.

As soon as *Conrad der Leutnant* was finished, Spitteler began work on a collection of his past essays, but he soon regretted this decision, for he found that the difficulties of such a personal editorship outweighed those involved in the creation of a new work. Despite the pithy clarity of the essays involved, in later years, Spitteler distanced himself from *Lachende Wahrheiten* (1898; *Laughing Truths*, 1927), never counting it among his important works. Of particular interest here are such essays as "The Forbidden Epic," in which he refutes the notion that "the primitive days of the nations, the youth of mankind, and a naïve outlook on the universe form the only tolerable atmosphere for the epic," and "Criterion of the Epical Gift," in which he describes the fundamental requirements of the epic poet. Neither characterization nor psychology can be his main business, for it is "the supreme law of epical art to transform spiritual states into objective appearances," whereas its triumph is to invent "such materialisations as render it possible, in the briefest and most intelligible manner, to work back to the spiritual postulates on which they rest."

Meanwhile, Spitteler was struggling with a personal and artistic decision to return to the seductive rigors of the epic form, and in October, 1887, he wrote of an almost irresistible decision to begin work on what was to become *Olympischer Frühling*—more than twelve hundred lines of verse, a twelve-year undertaking. Using only the nomenclature of classical mythology, Spitteler molds the characters, histories, and natural geography of the Greek gods in idiosyncratic, Swiss fashion. Written in paired Alexandrines, the work demonstrates many of the epic theories of style and characterization which Spitteler published in *Laughing Truths*.

The first book depicts the fall of Kronos and the old gods and the release of the new gods from Erebos at the decree of Ananke, omnipotent Necessity and Ruler of the Universe. Arriving at Olympus, in the second book, the new gods compete for the hand of Hera, ruler of this divine domain. Queen of the Amazons and tainted with mortality, she must give herself to the winner of three contests: dream interpretation, song, and chariot racing. Although Apollo is the real victor, Ananke awards Hera to the sly, deceitful Zeus, whose unscrupulousness makes him fit for political office. With Hera's collusion, he assumes power, and together they murder the army of the Amazons.

In the third book, a time of spring and peaceful festivity reigns. Zeus and Apollo settle their differences, creating a pact of power and beauty, and Hera and her consort then abandon reality for each other's arms. The world bathes in the warm springtime blossoming of artistic harmony as the gods are free to follow their hearts' desires, and the poet sings of their exploits in a series of mini-epics, loosely connected technical masterpieces.

The fourth book concludes with the escapades of Aphrodite and the intervention of Ananke, who shatters the rich palette of the high festival. Zeus is awakened to his sovereign responsibilities and Hera to the grim specter of her own inevitable death. In an almost Nietzschean conclusion, Herakles, an incarnation of the new humanity, is sent earthward as a model. The fantastical cosmos is constructed on pillars of Schopenhauerian pessimism, concluding with the defiant renunciation of happiness and fulfillment. Nevertheless, the work inspired the critics of the day. Spitteler demonstrated that there was indeed a "higher realism," one that demanded "a higher form." His longtime friend Joseph Viktor Widmann wrote, "We need the great epic because beside the good, we must have the best: a thousand novels cannot take its place. There must be houses to live in, to be sure, but there must also be Cologne Cathedral."

Shortly after finishing *Olympischer Frühling*, Spitteler published his third volume of poetry, *Glockenlieder* (1906; bell songs), which is also included in *Selected Poems* (1928). Although Spitteler was never at his best as a lyric poet, he "here reached the full maturity of his power as a lyricist, and he displays a complete mastery of the various metrical patterns he uses." The work is marked by a pervasive sense of humor and by what may be an overreliance on personification.

The enthusiastic reception received by *Olympischer Frühling* and the reissuing of his first work under his own name, gave Spitteler the courage, in 1905, to shape the agonies involved in the creation of *Prometheus and Epimetheus* into literary form. The autobiographical novel *Imago* (1906), is remarkable for its psychological insights and its portrayal of severe emotional turbulence. Spitteler himself commented, "*Imago* is the explanation of *Prometheus and Epimetheus*. *Imago* relates what really happened, *Prometheus* shows what a poet made of it."

Imago is the novelistic retelling of the crisis involved in the stressful final stages of Spitteler's first epic, caused by his unhappy love for Ellen Brodbeck. He had previously rejected the possibility of marrying her "because he believed that personal happiness was incompatible with his vocation as a poet and the obligation to attain greatness." The main character of the novel,

Viktor, returns to his hometown in Switzerland determined to avenge his wounded ego and confront the woman, Theuda, who "betrayed him and the world of the imagination in which he is most truly at home." Still desperately in love with her, he resolves his inner conflicts by transferring his affections to an idealized image he holds of her, "Imago," while she herself becomes the perfidious "Pseuda," false not only to him but also to the purity of her idealized image. Sigmund Freud was one of this interesting novel's most distinguished admirers, entitling his journal on the applications of psychoanalysis to the humanities simply "Imago."

In 1911 Spitteler began a verse reworking of the Prometheus material, and in 1914 he published the charmingly lyrical autobiographical volume *Meine frühesten Erlebnisse* (1914; my earliest experiences), which had begun appearing in serial form in the *Süddeutsche Monatshefte* in December, 1913. The following year the now-famous author was honored by celebrations in Zurich and Lucerne for his seventieth birthday. The University of Lausanne awarded him an honorary doctorate, and he was elected a member of the Swiss Writers' Guild. Forty-eight years after committing himself to the cruel vagaries of a poetic muse, Spitteler was finally recognized as an epic genius in his own country, although he lamented that his speech "Our Swiss Standpoint" had won for him, in a few minutes, more fame than a whole lifetime of dedicated literary productivity. From 1912 onward, Swiss academicians began suggesting Spitteler's name to the Swedish Academy, and finally, mainly through the intervention of Romain Rolland, Spitteler was awarded the Nobel Prize in Literature for 1919. He made the last few changes to *Prometheus der Dulder* (1924; Prometheus the patient sufferer) and committed it to print. His last work, on which he had labored for more than thirteen years, appeared a few weeks before he died.

After Spitteler's death Rolland wrote:

> He is the greatest of you all. . . . Permit a stranger. . . to honour, now that he has joined the dead, Our Homer, the greatest German poet since Goethe, the only master of the epic since Milton died three centuries ago. But a more solitary figure amid the art of his day than either the one or the other of these.

Carl Spitteler is still a solitary figure, for he and his work have faded into obscurity. His art is as much out of step with today's world as it was with his own, and his inability to excel at forms other than the epic has sealed his inconspicuous fate. In recognizing the value of his work, however, the Swedish Academy rewarded his tireless idealism and the determined independence of his literary goals.

Bibliography

Primary

FICTION: *Conrad der Leutnant*, 1898; *Imago*, 1906; *Die Mädchenfeinde*, 1907

(*Two Little Misogynists*, 1922).
POETRY: *Prometheus und Epimetheus*, 1881 (as Carl Felix Tandem; *Prometheus and Epimetheus*, 1931); *Extramundana*, 1883; *Olympischer Frühling*, 1900-1905 (4 volumes); *Glockenlieder*, 1906; *Meine frühesten Erlebnisse*, 1914; *Prometheus der Dulder*, 1924; *Selected Poems*, 1928.
NONFICTION: *Lachende Wahrheiten*, 1898 (*Laughing Truths*, 1927).

Secondary

Boesche, Albert William. "The Life and Works of Carl Spitteler." In *The German Classics: Masterpieces of German Literature*, edited by Kuno Francke. New York: German Publication Society, 1914. A short, general appraisal of Spitteler's works up to *Olympischer Frühling*. High-quality reproductions of the Swiss artist Böcklin's famous paintings throughout the text alert the reader to the similarities between the two artists' works. Excellent summaries are provided of the complex action of *Prometheus and Epimetheus* and, in particular, *Olympischer Frühling*. A very positive assessment with genuine literary insight. Includes some extended passages of translation following the text, but no bibliography.

Boyd, Ernest. "Carl Spitteler." In *Studies from Ten Literatures*. New York: Charles Scribner's Sons, 1925. A very useful, general summary of Spitteler's oeuvre. A short article, it does, however, provide much useful information on such texts as *Conrad der Leutnant*'s relation to naturalism, including an excellent translation of Spitteler's prefatory note to the work. Clear summaries of the major works with apposite evaluations.

Günther, Werner. "Carl Spitteler." In *Swiss Men of Letters: Twelve Essays*, edited by Alex Natan. London: Oswald Wolff, 1970. Translated from a longer article in German, this is one of the very few modern assessments of Spitteler and is about eighteen pages long. Günther asserts that the controversy that surrounded the Nobel award was, and is still, justified. An interesting but very negatively biased interpretation without sufficient textual documentation for such sweeping general criticism. Includes notes and a bibliography.

McHaffie, Margaret. "Prometheus and Viktor: Carl Spitteler's *Imago*." *German Life and Letters* 31 (1977): 67-77. An excellent ten-page literary article on two important texts. McHaffie makes insightful connections and notes relationships, rather than simply summarizing the texts. A firm and extensive knowledge of Spitteler's works is obvious. Reference to materials from Spitteler's estate which are not widely available. Excellent use of German quotations. Includes notes, but no bibliography.

Robertson, J. G. "Carl Spitteler." *The Contemporary Review* 119 (January-June, 1921): 72-78. A short article of seven pages that is one of the few contemporary reactions to Spitteler's award in the British press. A positive and sensitive interpretation of his works, in particular *Prometheus and*

Epimetheus and *Olympischer Frühling*, which are well summarized. A good resource article by an author very familiar with Spitteler's life and works. Includes no bibliography.

Ingrid Walsoe-Engel

1920

Literature
Knut Hamsun, Norway

Peace
León Bourgeois, France

Physics
Charles Guillaume, Switzerland

Chemistry
Walther Nernst, Germany

Physiology or Medicine
August Krogh, Denmark

KNUT HAMSUN
Knut Pedersen
1920

Born: Lom, Gudbrandsdal, Norway; August 4, 1859
Died: Nøholm, Grimstad, Norway; February 19, 1952
Language: Norwegian
Principal genres: Fiction and drama

Hamsun's Growth of the Soil *was recognized for its portrayal of the essential struggles of life, as seen in the lives of those who clear, plow, and plant the fallow lands of Norway; Hamsun was commended for his realism and for the richness of his prose*

The Award
Presentation

On December 10, 1920, Harald Hjärne, Chairman of the Nobel Committee of the Swedish Academy, presented the Nobel Prize in Literature to Knut Hamsun, in recognition of Hamsun's novel *Markens grøde* (1917; *Growth of the Soil*, 1920). citing Hamsun's stark realism and his evocation of humankind's long and difficult struggle to overcome the powerful and hostile forces of nature, Hjärne called *Growth of the Soil* a classic work of literature in which a significant statement about the human condition is taken directly from life and preserved for posterity.

Growth of the Soil is, above all, a universal work of literature, one that portrays not only the Norwegian or Scandinavian experience but also the human experience in general. Its characters struggle against the forces of nature to eke out a living, to endure the trials and struggles of surviving in a world that is clearly inhospitable to their existence. The characters are common people, but in their endurance they establish a kind of nobility, elevating their actions to the level of spiritual achievement. That achievement cuts across barriers of culture and language to appeal to readers worldwide.

The novel's appeal, however, exists almost in spite of Hamsun's rather clear indictment of civilization. The main character, a type of ideal laborer, devotes his life to clearing the land, but in order to be a simple farmer, he must overcome not only the obstacles of a stubborn and recalcitrant natural world but also the considerable obstacles put in his way by civilized men. In portraying that struggle against civilization itself, Hamsun envisions a new culture, one that arises from physical labor, one that has its roots in ancient times, when values—and problems—were simpler and more personal.

Hamsun's people, his characters, though fictional creations, reflect their Norwegian heritage; they are hard, often-cold people who seem to spring from the hard, cold Norwegian soil that they struggle to cultivate. They, like the crops that they raise, are fruits of the earth, farmers that are also products of their labors. These characters run the gamut from unimaginative and taciturn survivors who endure their hardships through strength of will and sinew to troubled, bewildered wanderers who, ultimately, cannot cope with the contradictory messages that they receive from the land and from civilized society. Thus, Hamsun's people are real, good and bad, just as the products of their newly cleared land are also good and bad, fruit and weed. The struggle, the process, not the product of the labor, defines the individual's success or failure in life, and that process is clearly under the control of the individual, while the product is at the mercy of natural and societal forces far beyond the individual's control. It is in this understanding of the basic nature of life that the novel expresses its idealism and earned for its author the epithet Nobel laureate.

Nobel lecture

In his brief acceptance speech, Hamsun declined the opportunity to make a substantive oration. Instead, he expressed the feeling that he had been swept off his feet by the award, carried away by the honor that the Swedish Academy had done him and his native Norway. At the same time, Hamsun expressed his thanks to the Swedish poets of the last generation whose lyrics had had such a positive influence on his own writing. Concluding with the statement that the only thing he lacked for complete contentment was youth, Hamsun proposed a toast to the young people of Sweden and of the world, to "all that is young in life."

While this brief personal message charmed the audience at the ceremony, it provides little help in understanding Hamsun's approach to literature. It does, however, demonstrate the man's characteristic public reticence—he tried to avoid the presentation entirely and only agreed to the inevitable when friends promised to protect him from the press. It also reveals the extent to which growing old bothered him. His despair over the fading of youth is reflected in his closing remarks, and that despair, eventually working itself out in a kind of regretful resignation, also represents a major theme in his fiction.

Critical reception

The reaction to Knut Hamsun's selection for the Nobel award was positive, although to understand how the prize figured in his career it is necessary to divide that reaction into two parts: that from the English-speaking world and that from the non-English-speaking world. In Europe, for example—except in England, where few of his books had appeared—Hamsun was already recognized as the preeminent Scandinavian writer since August Strindberg. He was already very widely respected, not only for his novels, which by 1920 had been translated into twenty-three languages, but also for his poetry and his plays. In England and the United States, however, only a few of Hamsun's works had appeared—five in England and only two in the United States. For English-speaking readers, then, the award had the effect of broadening Hamsun's appeal and educating publishers and readers alike to the value of his work.

European audiences, though small, had long appreciated Hamsun's relentless realism. Viewing him as an honest writer, readers and critics paid him increasing homage, from the publication of *Sult* (1890; *Hunger*, 1899) through the appearance of *Segelfoss by* (1915; *Segelfoss Town*, 1925). As Hamsun's vision emerged, he was valued more and more as a writer for the age. In *Hunger* and the other early novels, Hamsun's characters are outcasts, loners who suffered from the capriciousness of the society around them. Up one minute and down the next, loved one day and despised the next, there is something Kafkaesque—if that can be said of writings that appeared before Kafka's—about these people, who are not so much despisers of civilization as they are despised by it.

Increasingly, during the early twentieth century, Hamsun's vision enlarged and matured, and he became, for a world headed into its first world war, a voice that evoked the past. He told them of agrarian values, of a past in which happiness and success depended on the labor of one's hands rather than the variety of one's social calendar or the strength of one's political connections. Hamsun was the voice of reaction for Europe, an almost prophetic voice telling Europeans that their so-called civilization could only result in barbarism on a huge scale, while their only hope lay in the past, in a kind of positivist primitivism that would allow them to coexist peacefully. His was a message of self-sufficiency, and he warned of the dangers of allowing one's life to be dictated by others, by a society that would inevitably betray people who obeyed its dictates to the letter.

That message is at its strongest in *Growth of the Soil*, the prizewinning novel, and that novel was judged worthy primarily because, unlike the earlier novels, it contains an unmistakable strain of idealism. The earlier novels have the same basic vision as *Growth of the Soil*, but they are more negative, more in the character of warnings to their readers. The earlier novels offer objections to the status quo, but no strong, clear vision that the world could ever be different from the sordid and unappealing place it was. *Growth of the Soil*, however, offers a way out. In that novel, Hamsun uses the idea of cultivation both literally and metaphorically, dealing with the way persevering effort can slowly improve the land—clearing it, planting, it, tending it, so that eventually it bears more fruit than weeds, more good (metaphorically speaking) than evil. Life, Hamsun suggests, works the same way. Constant, close labor is required by individuals, not societies, to increase the level of good in the world. Hamsun consistently regards state action as inherently suspect (hence his long hatred of socialism) and individual effort as good.

There can be no real surprise that such a vision, appearing as it did in the middle of World War I, appealed to Europe and to the world.

The reaction in England and the United States, where Hamsun had not been well-known, was nevertheless positive, and the effect was to stimulate interest in Hamsun's work in both countries. In the United States, for example, only two of Hamsun's books had appeared by 1920: *Hunger* and *Ny jord* (1893; *Shallow Soil*, 1914), and the latter had been out of print since 1916. By the middle of 1921, though, *Shallow Soil* was back in print, *Growth of the Soil* had appeared, and three other novels were due within the year, primarily American editions of novels already in print in England, where by 1920 five of Hamsun's novels had been translated. Overall, the American reaction was certainly positive. *The New York Times* remarked that Hamsun was the greatest living Scandinavian writer, and a later critic, writing in *The New York Times Book Review*, hailed the prize for its justness. In England, meanwhile, *Growth of the Soil* had already been hailed as a masterpiece, and *The Times* of London expressed its favor for Hamsun's selection. As a result of the prize, then, Hamsun's reputation spread throughout the English-speaking world, and his stature in the rest of Europe was enhanced to the point that he was widely regarded, throughout the 1920's, as the world's greatest living writer.

Biography

Knut Hamsun was born Knut Pedersen on August 4, 1859, in Lom, near the center of Norway. He was the fourth of Peder and Tora Pedersen's six children. When Knut was four years old, the family moved to Hamarøy, in the far north of Norway, to live with an uncle, a stern tailor and merchant, Hans Olsen. There the family leased the farm Hamsund from Olsen, who took nine-year-old Knut into his household to work. The bleakness of the arctic landscape—Hamarøy is one hundred miles north of the Arctic Circle—was reinforced by the harshness of life in Olsen's household. Knut worked in the field as a shepherd and in the house as a scribe. He was given little food, beaten frequently, and forced to listen to his uncle's sermons. As a result, Knut fled Hamarøy at the age of fourteen, returning to Lom to work for a distant relative.

Thus began a period of wandering. By 1874 Knut was back in Hamarøy working for a powerful merchant of the district. The next year, when the merchant went bankrupt, Knut became a peddler. That began a succession of occupations and changes of residence: cobbler's apprentice and then dock worker in Bodø; schoolteacher and bailiff's assistant in Vesterålen; highway construction worker and sometime journalist in Kristiania; lecturer, private secretary, farm worker, streetcar conductor, and teacher on two trips to the United States (1882-1884 and 1886-1888). In 1885 he adopted the name "Hamsun" and his return to Scandinavia in 1888 marked the real beginning of his literary career. Though he had published two novels in the 1870's, the 1890 publication of *Hunger* brought him his first success, and *Mysterier* (1892; *Mysteries*, 1927) and *Pan* (1894; English translation, 1920) further solidified his position as a promising young novelist.

In 1898 Hamsun married Bergljot Bech, who bore him a daughter, Victoria, before the marriage ended in divorce in 1906. Three years later, Hamsun married Marie Andersen, an actress with the Swedish National Theater who was twenty-three years younger than he. In 1911, the Hamsuns settled at Hamarøy, a farming enterprise that ultimately failed because of the tension between Hamsun's occupations as farmer and writer. They moved south in 1918, establishing their household at Nørholm in southern Norway, where they would live, for the most part, until Hamsun's death in 1952. Marie bore four children, two sons and two daughters, and at Hamsun's urging she became a poet and a writer of popular children's stories.

Hamsun's stature as Nobel laureate and preeminent man of letters, together with his reactionary political leanings and his extreme anglophobia, led him to support the Nazi regime during World War II. Normally a very private man, he traveled widely in Norway and in the rest of Nazi-controlled Europe to promote the cause of Adolf Hitler's Third Reich. As a result of these activities he was arrested after the war, interned in an old age home, diagnosed as having "permanently impaired mental faculties" (an effort on the government's part to avoid the necessity of a criminal trial), and finally stripped of all of his money by confiscatory fines. A memoir of this period, *På gjengrodde stier* (1949; *On Overgrown Paths*, 1967), is his last published work. He died February 19, 1952, at Nørholm, a pauper whose wife wrote, a few hours before he died, "At this point Hamsun is being played and read in the world. They call him the greatest of living writers, and we do not have the money to get him buried. And he is lying in rags on his death bed now."

Literary Career

Knut Hamsun has been, perhaps more than anything else, the voice of the far north. As noted above, he was reared more than one hundred miles north of the Arctic Circle, among some of the most beautiful scenery on earth and some of the harshest living conditions, and his books are filled with the spirit of that place. Fully one-third of his novels are actually set in the far north, but the impact that that setting had on Hamsun's consciousness goes deeper than a sense of place. His characters are lone, self-contained, stoic, enduring people who generally find the world a cold, forbidding place which can be improved only slowly and at great cost to the individual. This is the world in which Hamsun was reared, and it is this part of him, more than any other, that finds its way into his fiction.

The decade from 1888 to 1898 contains the most important years of Hamsun's career, even though he produced his most significant fiction twenty years later. From 1888, however, when he returned from his second visit to the United States, until 1898, when he traveled to Russia, he reached maturity as a novelist and gained an audience in his native Scandinavia. He began with *Hunger*, an autobiographical novel based on his own stay in Kristiania in 1885-1886 and written in the vein of American realism, after the manner of Mark Twain and William Dean Howells. The novel is the first-person account of a frustrated writer's attempt to survive in a world in which only he cares if he lives or dies. Both a rebel and an outcast, the narrator establishes a major theme in Hamsun's work, that of the outsider trying to survive, physically or mentally, in a hostile world. Hamsun's narrator in *Hunger*, like his later characters, is neither good nor bad, but complex, unpredictable, real.

Hamsun's other novels of this first decade follow through on the successes of *Hunger*. *Mysteries*, based on Hamsun's exeriences in Lillesand in 1890, tells of a figure similar to the narrator in *Hunger*, except that instead of surviving his ordeal, this "hero" fails, ultimately committing suicide. *Mysteries* therefore partakes of a darker vision than *Hunger* does, as the only way the protagonist can remain true to his own peculiar vision is to take his own life. Hamsun followed with *Pan*, perhaps his best early novel and certainly the most interesting from the standpoint of situation. *Pan* is ostensibly the diary of Thomas Glahn, a hunter who provokes his own murder after being disappointed in love. A dreamer amid a dream landscape—*Pan* is the first of Hamsun's major novels to be set in the north of Norway—Glahn is destroyed by the scheming of Ferdinand Mack, a hugely successful merchant who represents what Hamsun increasingly saw as a pragmatic, corrupt society. This developing vision works in a more complex fashion in *Victoria* (1898; English translation, 1929), a sentimental love story that at first seems quite out of place in Hamsun's ever more heavily naturalistic canon. Yet the lovers in this sweet story never manage to unite. Johannes, a poet with a lower-class background, and Victoria, a beauty from an aristocratic family, love each other, but they never manage to be available at the same time. Thus, *Victoria* unites with Hamsun's earlier work because of Johannes' position as an outsider in a world that has no room in it for his happiness.

The period from *Victoria* to *Growth of the Soil* was one of great turmoil and frantic activity for Hamsun. His outcast hero evolved into a wanderer who retires from society and seeks peace in the deep forest, thus softening but not really compromising the sense of isolation in Hamsun's fiction. This softening occurred despite great stress in Hamsun's life. He produced thirteen novels in the twelve years between 1898 and 1910, a period in which he also married, became a father, divorced his wife, and remarried. Perhaps his own struggle for contentment is reflected in his work, in which he seems to be searching for new ideas and for new methods of representation.

The Benoni trilogy—*Sværmere* (1904; *Dreamers*, 1921), *Benoni* (1908;

English translation, 1925), and *Rosa* (1908; English translation, 1926)—shows these new directions. There is more humor here, harking back to Hamsun's approach in *Hunger*, yet there is more sentimentality, following the direction set in *Victoria*. The three novels tell the story of the upstart Benoni, who rises to prominence through trade. He is, therefore, an outsider who finds a way to come inside, and *Rosa* carries him to a happy ending, as he marries the patrician Rosa and finds permanent acceptance in society. The happiness, however, is artificial, the result of Benoni's acquisitions—Rosa among them—not of his development as a human being. Hamsun's further dissatisfaction with that kind of narrow success finds expression in the wanderer trilogy, where the main character is Knut Pedersen—Hamsun's real name. *Under høststjernen* (1906; *Under the Autumn Star*), *En vandrer spiller med sordin* (1909; *A Wanderer Plays on Muted Strings*)—both translated in 1922 in a volume titled *Wanderers*—and *Den siste glæde* (1912; *Look Back on Happiness*, 1940) follow Pedersen—another first-person narrator—as he travels from village to village, job to job, woman to woman, looking for youth or renewal. Pedersen is fleeing the industrial society of the cities in search of the older, agrarian, even feudal, society of the country.

Both the attack on industrialism and the call for a return to the land broadens in the novels leading up to *Growth of the Soil*. *Born av tiden* (1913; *Children of the Age*, 1924) and its sequel, *Segelfoss Town*, are social novels reminiscent of the 1880's, social and economic histories of a district in the north of Norway. Hamsun here takes on society's ills more directly, while focusing less on his central characters. Instead, he develops the major theme of change as opposed to conservation, and, unhappily but realistically, change wins. These novels set the stage for Hamsun's most important work and for his detailed look at life in the city—a place he sees as destructive at best.

Growth of the Soil, the novel that would win for Hamsun the Nobel Prize, addresses the so-called advantages of the city: the high level of education, the excellence of medical care, the opportunities offered by the professions. Hamsun undercuts these advantages, though, by developing the metaphor of the city as prison, by demonstrating that the city dwellers are in fact trapped by their advantages, and by setting the prison-city in opposition to the freedom of the country. Close on the heels of *Growth of the Soil* came *Konerne ved vandposten* (1920; *The Women at the Pump*, 1928), a novel in which the central metaphor is the city as anthill. Again, there is a good side and a bad side to the situation. On the good side, everyone is occupied, set firmly and securely in a role in society. Yet that very structure means that society is too segmented, and each person has too narrow a view. These people, like ants, crawl all over one another, for they cannot see further than their own needs, their own situations. Thus, in their actions they are short-sighted and destructive. The cycle closes with *Siste kapitel* (1923; *Chapter the Last*, 1929), in which the city is viewed as a sanatorium, filled with the criminal and the insane. Throughout these three long novels Hamsun increasingly deplores the values of city dwellers and their urban, industrial society while celebrating the rural life, the old ways of a society in which the individual's effort tends to improve the medium of life—the soil—for subsequent generations.

Another difficult period followed these three major novels, and this time Hamsun's response was a failure to write. Depressed over Germany's defeat in World War I, over the failure of the Weimar Republic, and over his own marital difficulties, Hamsun ultimately tried psychoanalysis, which seemed to have broken the hold of his depression and allowed him to write again, beginning with the August trilogy. *Landstrykere* (1927; *Vagabonds*, 1930; also as *Wayfarers*, 1981), *August* (1930; English translation, 1931), and *Men livet lever* (1933; *The Road Leads On*, 1934) tell of the relationship between Edevart Andersen and August, friends and business partners who are the vagabonds of the title of volume 1. Hamsun uses these two opposites to explore the theme of displacement. Edevart is a farmer, a child of the soil who is uprooted, twice led to emigrate to the United States, while August is a sailor who comes into the town of Polden and decides to stay, though he finds at best an uneasy home there. Hamsun is more sympathetic, less the misanthrope, in his portraits, though his vision is still essentially reactionary. These two men experience all the virtues of modern society. At one time or another they have money, status, and respected professions, but none of these does them any good. They are clearly better off attached to the land, but society will not let Edevart rest in Polden, nor will it allow August to settle there comfortably. Both men are lured away from the land, to their detriment.

The August trilogy and *Ringen sluttet* (1936; *The Ring Is Closed*, 1937) stand as testimony that even in his seventies a writer can maintain and expand upon his most youthful visions. Hamsun's career offers a massive exploration of the role of the individual in society, and the timing of the Nobel Prize maximized his influence. In 1920, only three of his novels had appeared in English, but by 1940 all of them, major and minor, had been translated, and Hamsun was universally recognized as a major figure in world literature. Indeed, his stature was so great that even his support for the Nazis in the years before and during World War II could not shake his reputation. His autobiography, *On Overgrown Paths*, was seen as a vindication for the ninety-year-old author, who had had to defend himself against charges of collaboration and impaired mental faculties. Since then, all the major novels have been retranslated in more scholarly editions, and Hamsun's literary importance has been unquestioned.

Bibliography

Primary
NOVELS: *Den gådefulde*, 1877; *Bjørger*, 1878; *Sult*, 1890 (*Hunger*, 1899); *Mys-*

terier, 1892 (*Mysteries*, 1927); *Ny jord*, 1893 (*Shallow Soil*, 1914); *Redaktør Lynge*, 1893; *Pan*, 1894 (English translation, 1920); *Victoria*, 1898 (English translation, 1929); *Sværmere*,. 1904 (*Dreamers*, 1921); *Under høststjernen*, 1906 (*Under the Autumn Star*, 1922); *Benoni*, 1908 (English translation, 1925); *Rosa*, 1908 (English translation, 1926); *En vandrer spiller med sordin*, 1909 (*A Wanderer Plays on Muted Strings*, 1922); *Den siste glæde*, 1912 (*Look Back on Happiness*, 1940); *Børn av tiden*, 1913 (*Children of the Age*, 1924); *Segelfoss by*, 1915 (*Segelfoss Town*, 1925); *Markens grøde*, 1917 (*Growth of the Soil*, 1920); *Konerne ved vandposten*, 1920 (*The Women at the Pump*, 1928); *Wanderers*, 1922 (includes *Under the Autumn Star* and *A Wanderer Plays on Muted Strings*); *Siste kapitel*, 1923 (*Chapter the Last*, 1929); *Landstrykere*, 1927 (*Vagabonds*, 1930; also as *Wayfarers*, 1981); *August*, 1930 (English translation, 1931); *Men livet lever*, 1933 (*The Road Leads On*, 1934); *Ringen sluttet*, 1936 (*The Ring Is Closed*, 1937).

SHORT FICTION: *Siesta*, 1897; *Kratskog*, 1903; *Stridende liv*, 1905.

PLAYS: *Ved rigest port*, 1895; *Livets spil*, 1896; *Aftenrøde*, 1898; *Munken Vendt*, 1902; *Dronning Tamara*, 1903; *Livet ivold*, 1910 (*In the Grip of Life*, 1924).

POETRY: *Det vilde kor*, 1904.

NONFICTION: *Fra det moderne Amerikas aandsliv*, 1889 (*The Spiritual Life of Modern America*, 1969); *I æventyrland*, 1903; *På gjengrodde stier*, 1949 (*On Overgrown Paths*, 1967).

Secondary

Ferguson, Robert. *Enigma: The Life of Knut Hamsun*. New York: Farrar, Straus and Giroux, 1987. Among the few sources in English, Ferguson's biography looms large as the most useful in any study of Hamsun's life and works. Ferguson treats the works in the context of Hamsun's life and includes an excellent selected bibliography of books and articles on Hamsun.

Gustafson, Alrik. "Man of the Soil." In *Six Scandinavian Novelists*. Princeton, N.J.: Princeton University Press, 1940. A useful, though un-critical, brief introduction to Hamsun's works, oriented primarily to the general reader and intended to promote exposure to Hamsun and five other Scandinavian novelists.

Larsen, Hanna Astrup. *Knut Hamsun*. New York: Alfred A. Knopf, 1922. A fairly wide-ranging, superficial treatment of Hamsun's works, Larsen's book does contain a useful early look at Hamsun's female characters. Larsen presents a basic introduction of Hamsun to the American reader unfamiliar with his pre-Nobel Prize works.

Lowenthal, Leo. "Knut Hamsun." In *Literature and the Image of Man*. Boston: Beacon Press, 1957. Lowenthal deals with the social interaction among Hamsun's characters, ultimately examining the larger issue of

Hamsun's concept of society.

McFarlane, James W. "The Whisper of the Blood: A Study of Knut Hamsun's Early Novels." *PMLA* 71 (1956): 563-594. Focusing on Hamsun's major works during the 1890's, McFarlane provides an important, even seminal, article on the growth of Hamsun's critical reputation in the United States.

Næss, Harald. *Knut Hamsun*. Boston: Twayne Publishers, 1984. Næss provides an excellent, comprehensive introduction to Hamsun's life and works. The book contains a short biographical treatment and four chapters focusing on the major periods in Hamsun's career. Also valuable is the selected bibliography, which is amplified by commentary on the usefulness of the major critical studies.

Simpson, Allen. *Knut Hamsun's "Landstrykere."* Oslo: Gyldendal, 1973. Simpson's detailed study of Hamsun's 1927 novel contains an enlightening exploration of Hamsun's technique and a discussion of the degree to which a writer should be held responsible for the opinions expressed by his characters.

Wiehr, Joseph. "Knut Hamsun: His Personality and His Outlook upon Life." *Smith College Studies in Modern Languages* 3 (1921-1922): 1-129. Wiehr, like Larsen, wrote principally for those who were unfamiliar with Hamsun's works and yet had had their curiosity aroused by the Nobel award. This monograph-length study is useful primarily as a general introduction to Hamsun's works through *Growth of the Soil*.

William Condon

1921

Literature
Anatole France, France

Peace
Karl Branting, Sweden
Christian Lous Lange, Norway

Physics
Albert Einstein, Switzerland

Chemistry
Frederick Soddy, Great Britain

Physiology or Medicine
no award

ANATOLE FRANCE
Jacques-Anatole-François Thibault
1921

Born: Paris, France; April 16, 1844
Died: La Béchellerie, near Tours, France; October 12, 1924
Language: French
Principal genre: Fiction

Widely admired for both his wit and his wisdom, France combined mockery of human pretension and compassion for human suffering, couched in a deceptively simple style of the most elegant classical purity

The Award

Presentation

To a Europe still suffering the aftereffects of a terrible war, the Swedish Academy seemed anxious, in the fall of 1921, to announce an award of the Nobel Prize in Literature that could in some way respond to the public longing for peace and could be based on achievements that materially benefited mankind, as was traditionally the case for the Nobel Peace Prize and for the various prizes in science. The choice of Anatole France, long eminent in the world of letters and at the same time well-known as spokesman for humanitarian and pacifist causes, seemed to fill the need of the moment exactly, though the Academy was aware that the choice would also be controversial, because of France's less-popular socialist and anticlerical views. Accordingly, the public announcement of the award to France, on November 10, 1921, pointedly emphasized France's sympathy for the oppressed and his hatred of war and violence as those qualities which had especially commended his work to the Academy's attention. Indeed, the presentation ceremony itself, which took place on December 10, 1921, began with a welcoming speech which specifically noted the symbolic importance of the fact that the two laureates sharing the stage that day were a German chemist and a French man of letters. The actual presentation of the literature prize, made by the Permanent Secretary of the Swedish Academy, Erik Axel Karlfeldt, also stressed Anatole France's strong advocacy of international peace and cooperation. Karlfeldt—himself a distinguished poet who would be posthumously honored with a literature prize a decade later, in 1931—did not fail to evoke France's specific literary claims to eminence, noting the quality and variety of his literary activity; his committed humanist outlook which revered the great books of the past; and his famous limpid style, which made even his learned writings accessible to so many. Nevertheless, Karlfeldt's presentation left no doubt that for him, the laureate's greatest value for the contemporary world was that, in those painful postwar years, amid efforts by both the French and the Germans to build new walls between the two nations, Anatole France had been a resounding voice in favor of free intellectual interchange, reminding people that they needed one another.

Nobel lecture

France's prepared acceptance speech was hardly the usual Nobel lecture, except in its initial expressions of gratitude to the members of the Swedish Academy for having chosen him for this honor. He did not choose to use the occasion for a statement of his own literary principles, or even for a lofty pronouncement on the proper role of literature in human affairs. Instead, he fell readily into the spirit of the times and spoke passionately about the prospects for peace in postwar Europe. Even the conventional expressions of gratitude to the Academy with which he began moved him toward the subject of peace, for he compared his own prize to that of his immediate predecessor as a French recipient of the Prize in Literature, his friend Romain Rolland, recalling that the Academy had awarded Rolland the 1915 prize in explicit recognition of his long commitment to Franco-German intellectual ties, thus making the prize a pointedly public symbol for peace only a year after the outbreak of hostilities. France expressed his pleasure at being in that same lineage of recipients, adding that the decisions of the Swedish Academy had always possessed an international value in which he rejoiced, because it reinforced his own belief in the beneficial influence exerted by international intellectual and artistic exchange.

France then proceeded to discuss the state of political affairs in Europe in the wake of the Treaty of Versailles and received his loudest applause when he observed that the warring parties had signed a "peace" treaty which would not end the most destructive war in human history but would continue it, adding that Europe was doomed unless reason soon reentered its councils. Those were bold and provocative words for a Frenchman to utter in 1921, and he was severely criticized for them by many of his compatriots. They have also proved to be the only memorable ideas offered in France's otherwise quite unremarkable acceptance speech, emphasizing for posterity as they do that the laureate defiantly embraced the Swedish Academy's decision to award him the Nobel Prize more as a political statement demanded by the times than as an assessment of the literary and aesthetic worth of his writings.

Critical reception

The enthusiastic applause of the audience attending the award ceremony in Stockholm, contrasted with the sometimes bitter denunciations of France made by France's enemies at home, can suggest the full range of attitudes with which news of his award and his acceptance speech were received. It was a painfully mixed reception. France had many fervent international admirers who delighted in his graceful but bittersweet literary creations and who approved of what he stood for politically as an advocate of a peaceful and united postwar Europe. Those supporters applauded the action of the Academy. Typical of the friendly reactions was an article by Herbert S. Gorman which appeared in *The New York Times* on November 20, 1921, only ten days after the announcement of the award; it called the award "peculiarly appropriate" because France was "the one giant of letters who confronts a perplexed world." Gorman added that, in his own judgment, France's books were among the wisest and wittiest of modern times.

France was warmly supported as worthy of the award not only by certain friendly critics in the French press, such as Léon Blum and Benjamin Crémieux, but also by such political enemies as Paul Bourget and Charles Maurras, who put aside their disagreements, for this occasion, and praised his literary art. Outside his native land, favorable assessments were also offered by George Bernard Shaw, Theodore Dreiser, and even Albert Einstein, whom the laureate visited in Germany on his way home from Stockholm. The support of his large public was again manifested on the occasion of the official celebration (in Paris) of his eightieth birthday in the spring of 1924, for which many of the best-known literary figures wrote warm tributes. The most dramatic evidence of the esteem in which he was held was the state funeral decreed by the French government in October of 1924—only the second such state funeral ever held in France for a literary figure, the other having been for Victor Hugo in 1885.

Opposition to the award, mainly for nonliterary reasons, was most prominently manifested by the Catholic church, which, early in 1922, belatedly placed all France's writings on the Index of proscribed books. The Church's action was echoed by politically conservative critics who expressed distaste for his leftist politics and for what they perceived as his antipatriotic and antireligious attitudes. Yet the opposition on specifically literary grounds was much more vehement, reflecting an opinion that had begun to form as early as the turn of the century, when certain ambitious younger writers took pleasure in pointing out that their celebrated compatriot actually had feet of clay. They suggested that all of his ideas were borrowed from others, that his style was facile rather than graceful, that his imagination was too limited, and that his work lacked power and conviction. By the time of the award, France was being denigrated by a considerable phalanx of literary figures of genuine prominence: André Gide, Paul Valéry, the Surrealists, and writers of the Catholic Revival such as François Mauriac and Georges Bernanos. Gide, for example, complained that France's works "had no penumbra," a subtly malicious way of accusing him of superficiality. The Surrealist group, led by André Breton, distributed a pamphlet on the day of the laureate's state funeral, boldly asserting that he had been dead for many years, insofar as art and ideas were concerned; the pamphlet was entitled "A Cadaver." As for

Valéry, who had been France's friend and who was elected soon after the funeral to fill France's seat in the Académie Française, he composed the
obligatory speech in praise of his predecessor in a manner so ambiguous that
it was generally regarded as a polite subversion of France's official status as a
great writer. Bernanos expressed the view of Catholic writers when he satirized France by means of a savage caricature included in a novel published in
1926. Internationally, there was no shortage of voices among the younger
generation of writers willing to denounce the laureate as a false "great man,"
unworthy of the Nobel accolade. Among others, Miguel de Unamuno y Jugo
and José Ortega y Gasset in Spain, and Edmund Wilson and H.L. Mencken
in the United States, publicly noted their reservations about France's greatness in the 1920's.

The truth is that, for a decade prior to the Nobel award, France's reputation had been slowly but surely undergoing a considerable revision, especially
among the new literary generation. His supporters were mainly those of his
own generation, who remembered him as he had been in his glory days
nearly thirty years earlier, when he had published his finest works of fiction
and had played a heroic role on the pro-Dreyfus side of the Dreyfus affair.
France had published little of note since 1912, however, and had moreover
exhibited dismayingly erratic political judgment during and immediately after
World War I. Accordingly, when the award was announced in 1921, it was
really not possible for most of his younger colleagues to regard him as anything more than an irrelevant relic of the past. While the criticisms of France
made by that younger generation in the 1920's were certainly unjust and self-
serving, they soon attained the status of accredited opinion, as France's contemporary defenders died off. It was an irony, which France himself would
have relished, that, by the 1930's, the decision of the Swedish Academy to
award a Nobel Prize to him—a decision which had seemed so compellingly
logical in 1921—had become quite incomprehensible to the general public,
both in his own country and abroad.

Biography

Born in 1844, the only son of a well-known Paris book dealer, Anatole
France seemed destined from birth for the world of letters. Indeed, he never
held or wanted to hold any position outside the world of books. He acquired
as much of his education in his father's bookstore as in the schools of Paris,
since he spent long hours talking with the intellectuals who frequented the
shop, which specialized in historical studies. When he became a writer in the
late 1860's, he recalled that his father was always called "France" (short for
François) by his friends; France selected a pen name for himself by using his
given names Anatole and François, with the second name truncated according to what had become family custom.

Because of a naturally timid nature, the young France declined to enter his father's business (he did not want to have to work with the public) and began instead to develop his ambition to be a writer, while earning a living as a free-lance researcher and journalist. In his thirties, he obtained a civil service post, working in the Senate Library; contracted an unfortunate marriage; and began to publish his own writings. Establishing an independent literary career for himself, however, proved to be a long and arduous task. France was well past his fortieth birthday before he attained enough visibility to be known to the public and to earn a living from book sales. By that time, he was also one of the best-known book critics in Paris and was able to publish a collection of selected articles of book criticism he had written for *Le Temps*, a leading newspaper of the time. In 1890, the critical and financial success of his novel *Thaïs* (English translation, 1891) enabled him at last to give up his civil service and journalism positions.

For the next two decades, he enjoyed the most productive period of his career, composing his finest novels and short stories and becoming active in public affairs; he was especially drawn, by his outraged sense of justice, into the emotionally charged issue of the Dreyfus case and into leftist politics. France lacked the temperament, however, for public controversy and debate; during the early years of the twentieth century he began to withdraw quietly into his private world again and to participate in public affairs only through the written word. The outbreak of war in 1914 left the seventy-year-old author deeply disillusioned and pessimistic. He wrote little, aside from auto-biographical pieces, and struggled to reconcile his pacifist beliefs with his concern for the welfare of his beloved country, which was caught up in a war of which he could not approve. The last decade of his life brought him many honors, including the Nobel Prize, yet he felt increasingly weary and un-inspired as a writer and was widely perceived to be no longer relevant to the literary scene. He was given an impressive state burial in Paris in 1924, but the achievements which justified it seemed by then already to belong to a distant past.

Literary Career

Although he published a brief historical essay—at his own expense—in his teens, and a book-length literary study in his twenties, France's career as a creative writer took an unusually long time to develop. He was over thirty when he published his first original, imaginative works: a collection of short poems and a verse drama, both deservedly ignored by critics and the public. He then tried his hand at prose fiction and attained a modest success with a charming novel about an aging scholar and bibliophile, *Le Crime de Sylvestre Bonnard* (1881; *The Crime of Sylvestre Bonnard*, 1890). With that novel, France discovered his own unique voice and style: a subtle blend of gently ironic, self-mocking tone with an understated, deceptively simple sentence structure. The novel, however, was conspicuously lacking in emotional power or depth and displayed no sense of aesthetically pleasing form.

It took another decade of painstaking experimentation before he solved these problems of fictional composition in his brilliant novel *Thaïs*. Drawing on a well-known medieval legend, France reimagined the story of the celebrated courtesan of Alexandria who was pursued by a pious monk bent on converting her to Christianity. Although the reader knows, from the start, the ironic outcome of the story (the monk falls in love with Thaïs, while Thaïs falls in love with Christ), the novel manages to enchant the reader with its subtle character portrayals, its quiet humor and decorous style, and above all, its disciplined management of form and pace. The contrast of the scandalous subject matter and the decorous style provides perhaps the greatest delight for the reader.

The success of *Thaïs* in 1890 marked the end of France's long apprenticeship and launched his literary career proper. For the next quarter of a century, he showed himself to be exceptionally inventive and versatile in using his highly polished writing style, his distinctive voice, and his newly developed sense of literary form. Collections of ingenious short stories alternated with full-length novels which were surprisingly varied in both matter and manner. He seemed committed to never repeating his successes and strove always to try new subjects, new forms, and new techniques. In an astonishingly short period of time, his achievements became so great as to have earned for him international renown and to have made him his country's most acclaimed writer. France continued to enjoy a high level of both critical and public acclaim for his work through the first decade of the twentieth century, including the publication, in 1912, of what is probably his finest novel, *Les Dieux ont soif* (*The Gods Are Athirst*, 1913). Thereafter, as though he had suddenly run out of creative energy, his career abruptly diminished, both in quality and in quantity, and he busied himself in his declining years with revising his writings for an edition of his collected works and with writing a fictionalized autobiography. After 1912, he seemed obsessed with his own past and unable to look to the future.

The heart of France's literary career, and his claim to a place in literary history, rests therefore primarily on the work he accomplished during that richly productive period between 1890, when *Thaïs* appeared, and 1912, when he published *The Gods Are Athirst*. What is particularly impressive about those years is the startling variety of his literary activity. In addition to seven novels and five collections of short stories, he published a volume of philosophical meditations, two volumes of polemical essays on political subjects, a historical study of the career of Joan of Arc, several volumes of collected literary criticism (originally published in periodicals), and two plays. He also wrote newspaper articles and delivered speeches as part of his political involvements and provided numerous prefaces for the work of young writers just beginning to write; the most notable was a laudatory preface he wrote for

Marcel Proust's first publication, a collection of stories and sketches entitled *Les Plaisirs et les jours* (1869; *Pleasures and Regrets*, 1948). France was, in short, the complete man of letters during that period of his life, trying his hand at all the genres recognized by the literary establishment and turning out a truly staggering quantity of published material.

Several novels and short stories stand out as landmark events in his career, marking new levels of achievement in his vocation as a storyteller. Perhaps his most imaginative use of the short-story form occurred in the delightful collection called *L'Étui de nacre* (1892; *Tales from a Mother of Pearl Casket*, 1896). The story entitled "Le Procurateur de Judée" is a tour de force of historical reconstruction, in which France depicts the biblical figure Pontius Pilate living in retirement in Sicily and reminiscing with a friend about his days as a Roman public official in Judea. The cleverly chosen point of view evokes a very different Judea from that depicted in the New Testament, and when the reader discovers, at the end, that Pilate has no recollection of his encounter with Jesus, he is struck with a revelation that calls into question the process of history and humanity's ability ever to recapture the past correctly.

Two years later, France published an apparently conventional love story which nevertheless managed to introduce, in an unobtrusive manner, the explosive concept of feminine independence. This novel, called *Le Lys rouge* (1894; *The Red Lily*, 1898), received scant attention when it appeared because it had few of the hallmarks of France's usual witty and ironic manner and seemed to be a routinely realistic psychological novel of no particular distinction. It has since, however, been recognized as a pioneering experiment with an important and daringly modern social theme and one of Anatole France's most original achievements.

The series of four novels published around the turn of the century, under the umbrella title of *L'Histoire contemporaine* (1897-1901; *Contemporary History*, 1910-1022), was another experimental work notable for at least two reasons: the creation of one of France's greatest characters, the philosopher Monsieur Bergeret, whose ironic wit animates each of the four volumes; and the concept of incorporating real contemporary events and personages into a fictional framework, converting the direct observation of public events into the basis for a unique kind of historical novel, in which the present is treated as already part of history. Although *Contemporary History* was originally widely read as popular, gossipy entertainment, it was later recognized as a serious experiment in fiction and influenced the development of such multivolume chronicle novels as Proust's *À la recherche du temps perdu* (1913-1927; *Remembrance of Things Past*, 1922-1931).

France's best-known short story, "Crainquebille," which appeared in *Crainquebille, Putois, Riquet, et plusieurs récits profitables* (1904; *Crainquebille, Putois, Riquet, and Other Profitable Tales*, 1915) and was subsequently made into a successful stage play, probably owed its initial fame to the perception that it was a clever allegory of the Dreyfus affair, since it concerned a humble pushcart merchant who is falsely accused of a crime. The passage of time, however, has allowed the connection to a specific event gradually to recede into the background, until "Crainquebille" could be recognized as the brilliant social satire it is, exposing the hypocrisy of the class structure and the corruption of the judicial process in all modern Western societies. Rather than a specific comment on the Dreyfus affair, "Crainquebille" was a universal plea for social justice and thereby an achievement of lasting importance to the short-story genre.

The most popular of France's writings, over the years, has probably been the satirical novel *L'Île des pingouins* (1908; *Penguin Island*, 1914). Its fame is deserved, if only because it displays the author's best literary talents: genial humor, clever invention, shrewd observation of human conduct, a delightfully witty style, and a pervasive sense of the melancholy ironies of history. There is no more Voltairean work in France's corpus, in the specific sense of an imaginatively comic way of revealing the seamy underside of human events. *Penguin Island* is a philosophical tale in the form of a burlesque of serious historiography.

Last, and surely best, in this series of France's most enduringly significant artistic accomplishments, is the remarkable historical novel *The Gods Are Athirst*, which so vividly evokes the atmosphere of the Reign of Terror in Paris during the French Revolution. In this work, a mature artist has created an unforgettable cast of characters and given his story a disciplined and harmonious form, resulting in one of the most penetrating and pessimistic analyses of the nature of revolutions ever written. It is perhaps fitting that the culminating masterpiece of France's career should combine so admirably the talents of the literary artist with those of the dedicated historian.

Bibliography

Primary
NOVELS: *Le Crime de Sylvestre Bonnard*, 1881 (*The Crime of Sylvestre Bonnard*, 1890); *Les Désirs de Jean Servien*, 1882 (*The Aspirations of Jean Servien*, 1912); *Thaïs*, 1890 (English translation, 1891); *La Rôtisserie de la Reine Pédauque*, 1893 (*At the Sign of the Reine Pédauque*, 1912); *Le Lys rouge*, 1894 (*The Red Lily*, 1898); *L'Histoire contemporaine*, 1897-1901 (*Contemporary History*, 1910-1922), includes *L'Orme du mail* (*The Elm Tree on the Mall*), *Le Mannequin d'osier* (*The Wicker Work Woman*), *L'Anneau d'amethyste* (*The Amethyst Ring*), and *Monsieur Bergeret à Paris* (*Monsieur Bergeret in Paris*); *Histoire comique*, 1903 (*A Mummer's Tale*, 1921); *L'Île des pingouins*, 1908 (*Penguin Island*, 1914); *Les Dieux ont soif*, 1912 (*The Gods Are Athirst*, 1913); *La Révolte des anges*, 1914 (*The Revolt of the Angels*, 1914).

SHORT FICTION: *Balthasar*, 1889 (English translation, 1909); *L'Étui de nacre*, 1892 (*Tales from a Mother of Pearl Casket*, 1896); *Le Puits de Sainte-Claire*, 1895 (*The Well of Saint Clare*, 1909); *Crainquebille, Putois, Riquet, et plusieurs autres récits profitables*, 1904 (*Crainquebille, Putois, Riquet, and Other Profitable Tales*, 1915); *Les Sept Femmes de la Barbe-Bleue*, 1909 (*The Seven Wives of Bluebeard*, 1920).

PLAYS: *Crainquebille*, 1905 (English translation, 1915); *La Comédie de celui qui épousa une femme muette*, 1908 (*The Man Who Married a Dumb Wife*, 1915).

NONFICTION: *Alfred de Vigny*, 1868; *La Vie littéraire*, 1888-1892 (5 volumes; *On Life and Letters*, 1911-1914); *Le Jardin d'Épicure*, 1894 (*The Garden of Epicurus*, 1908); *Vers les temps meilleurs*, 1906, 1949; *La Vie de Jeanne d'Arc*, 1908 (*The Life of Joan of Arc*, 1908); *Le Génie latin*, 1913 (*The Latin Genius*, 1924); *Sur la voie glorieuse*, 1915.

MISCELLANEOUS: *The Complete Works*, 1908-1928 (21 volumes); *Œuvres complètes*, 1925-1935 (25 volumes).

Secondary

Axelrad, Jacob. *Anatole France: A Life Without Illusions*. New York: Harper and Brothers, 1944. A readable biography, emphasizing France's influence as a social critic and partisan of justice. While the research is generally accurate, the point of view is overly sentimental and admiring and insufficiently critical and analytical.

Bresky, Dushan. *The Art of Anatole France*. The Hague: Mouton, 1969. A serious and careful attempt to dissect France's famous writing technique, using the tools of rhetorical criticism. The analysis is penetrating and helpful, if somewhat repetitious.

Chevalier, Haakon M. *The Ironic Temper: Anatole France and His Time*. New York: Oxford University Press, 1932. Knowledgeable and engagingly written, this book provides an excellent analysis of France's ironic outlook, set against a detailed portrait of the political climate in which he lived.

Jefferson, Carter. *Anatole France: The Politics of Skepticism*. New Brunswick, N.J.: Rutgers University Press, 1965. This study emphasizes the historical and political, rather than the literary, ideas of France and is especially informative on the complex and shifting political positions he took in the last two decades of his life.

Sachs, Murray, *Anatole France: The Short Stories*. London: Edward Arnold, 1974. A brief analysis focused on France's career as a writer of short stories. The primary aim of the study is to define and evaluate France's distinctive contribution to the evolution of the short story as a literary form.

Virtanen, Reino. *Anatole France*. New York: Twayne Publishers, 1968. Intended as a general introduction to the author's work, this volume is con-

cise, accurate, and sound in its evaluation of France's career and very helpful in its detailed analyses of the most important individual publications.
Walton, Loring Baker. *Anatole France and the Greek World*. Durham, N.C.:
Duke University Press, 1950. A thoroughly researched study of France's
knowledge of classical civilization, especially Greek culture, and of the use
he made of that knowledge in composing his own books.

Murray Sachs

1922

Literature
Jacinto Benavente y Martínez, Spain

Peace
Fridtjof Nansen, Norway

Physics
Niels Bohr, Denmark

Chemistry
Francis Aston, Great Britain

Physiology or Medicine
Archibald Hill, Great Britain
Otto Meyerhof, Germany

JACINTO BENAVENTE Y MARTÍNEZ
1922

Born: Madrid, Spain; August 12, 1866
Died: Madrid, Spain; July 14, 1954
Language: Spanish
Principal genre: Drama

A rare example of a born dramatist, Benavente portrayed the complexities of life in a faithful manner and an accessible form, creating comedies of character that mirror reality and are both modern and classical in spirit

The Award

Presentation

The Nobel Prize in Literature was presented to Jacinto Benavente y Martínez, *in absentia*, on December 10, 1922, by Per Hallström, chairman of the Nobel Committee of the Swedish Academy. The award presentation emphasized the direct, effortless manner in which Benavente's rich life experiences found their way into his theater and his marked preference for writing about the life of the upper classes. He was praised for displaying "unfailing tact and strict loyalty to the subject," for a writing style distinguished for its gracefulness, and for the ability to "reproduce the wealth and mobility of life, the play of characters, and the struggle between wills, in a way that comes as near truth as possible." His aim was not to harrow the spectator but to resolve conflicts from which the characters would emerge all the wiser.

Benavente brought to the Spanish stage the outside world of reality observed with clear, unbiased eyes. He resisted artifice, ideology, excessive theatricality, and other facile conventions to achieve tension. Instead, he allowed verisimilitude alone to create dramatic effect.

Hallström singled out for praise Benavente's comedies, at the same time serious and lighthearted, dismissing his more serious works as less significant. The address cited his comedies as examples of the author's "unlaboured wit and comic verve, his radiant good nature, and his grace." In closing, the Academy declared Benavente a worthy heir to the strong and prolific tradition of Spanish letters.

Nobel lecture

Benavente was unable to attend the award ceremony. He was traveling with a theatrical troupe on an extensive tour through South America when the prize was announced; this commitment made it impossible for him to return to Europe to accept the honor in person. The Count de Torata, Spain's ambassador to Sweden, accepted the prize on Benavente's behalf. The ambassador thanked the Academy in the name of the author and added that the Nobel Prize was a well-deserved honor, conferred not only on

Benavente and his native Spain but on all other Spanish-speaking countries of the globe as well.

Prior to the acceptance ceremony, Professor H. G. Söderbaum of the Academy remarked that even though "the business of the dramatist is to keep himself out of sight and to let nothing appear but his characters," he regretted that Benavente, following this dictum too closely, had failed to receive the Nobel award in person.

Critical reception

Benavente was traveling in Argentina when the Academy announced its choice. Local newspapers, and the press throughout the rest of Latin America, rejoiced in his selection. He was received everywhere with great enthusiasm and became an honored guest and frequent speaker at a variety of civil and academic functions. Before his return to Spain, Benavente visited New York, Boston, and Chicago, where his drama *La malquerida* (1913; *The Passion Flower*, 1917) was playing to enthusiastic audiences. The author's newly granted Nobel Prize undoubtedly added to his celebrity.

The North American press did not react with great interest to the announcement. *The New York Times* (November 10, 1922) devoted only a brief column to news of the award; the account gives a brief biographical sketch of the author, emphasizing his early interest in pantomime and acting, and concludes with the statement that some critics view Benavente as the most important figure of contemporary Spanish letters. A number of articles of a more academic nature appeared in the course of the following year, including one by Benavente himself in *The Yale Review* (October 23, 1923). Federico de Onís, the distinguished Spanish scholar who headed the Spanish department at Columbia University for a number of years, wrote an essay on Benavente for *The North American Review* (March, 1923). In this article, de Onís summarizes the highlights of Benavente's career, emphasizing his unique contribution to the Spanish stage in the early part of the century. In addition to praising Benavente for his role as reformer, de Onís singles out the playwright's ability to capture the foibles and follies of upper-middle-class Madrid society. While de Onís recognizes that Benavente might not be a favorite among contemporary Spanish intellectuals, the critic asserts that he has no doubt that Benavente's work "will be incorporated into the classic store of Spanish literature as the most original and valuable contribution to the drama of the day."

As de Onís makes clear, not all Benavente's fellow Spaniards appreciated his art and his success. The popular press in Spain hailed Benavente as a national treasure and a worthy and deserving recipient of the Nobel Prize. Upon his return home from his triumphant American tour in 1923, Benavente became the object of public adulation. *El Imparcial* (the impartial), an important Madrid newspaper, organized a banquet in his honor; the municipal administratión of Madrid declared him "favorite son," and King Alfonso XIII granted him the Great Cross of Alfonso the Wise, the country's highest official intellectual honor. Yet, as de Onís' above-cited article acknowledges, Benavente had his share of detractors in Spain; a small circle of politically committed intellectuals dismissed his achievements, citing the melodramatic excesses of some of his best-known works and the frivolity of much of his dramatic production. Ramón Pérez de Ayala stands out as the most consistent figure in this group of relentless critics.

Biography

Jacinto Benavente y Martínez was born on August 12, 1866, in Madrid, Spain. His father, Mariano Benavente, was a prominent and cultured Madrid pediatrician, with numerous contacts in the world of politics and literature. His mother was Venancia Martínez. The young Benavente, who spent long hours in his father's rich library, rapidly developed a special interest in drama, which was reinforced by frequent trips to the theater and the circus and the writing and staging of plays for the amusement of his playmates.

The young Benavente was an intelligent but undistinguished student, remaining in school mostly to please his father. He entered the University of Madrid to study engineering and then law, withdrawing permanently upon his father's death in 1885. Nineteen-year-old Jacinto was left a considerable sum of money, an inheritance that served to relieve him from any career or financial worries and freed him to devote himself to what he had always longed to do: reading, writing, and travel. He visited England, France, and Russia between 1885 and 1892.

During the early years of his career, Benavente wrote poetry and nonfiction and contributed to a number of journals and newspapers in Spain. His first dramatic success came in 1896, after the premiere of his *Gente conocida* (well-known people). A series of well-received comedies and dramas followed, and the playwright found himself enjoying popular acclaim in his native Spain and throughout Spanish-speaking America, where he traveled on a number of occasions. He eventually produced an impressive number of plays; most critics believe, however, that Benavente did his best work between the opening of *Gente conocida* and the outbreak of World War I.

During the Spanish Civil War (1936-1939), he lived in Valencia, where he expressed sympathy for the Republican cause. At the end of the war, when the Republicans were defeated and the armies of Francisco Franco assumed control of the country, the playwright openly supported the aims of the victors.

Benavente never married. He died in Madrid on July 14, 1954, shortly before his eighty-eighth birthday. His will left a third of the estate to Rosario Benavente Martínez de Casero, an illegitimate daughter acknowledged for the first time upon his death.

Literary Career

Jacinto Benavente y Martínez was a highly prolific playwright, true to the illustrious tradition of Spanish drama dating back to Lope de Vega and Pedro Calderón de la Barca in the sixteenth and seventeenth centuries. Benavente authored more than 170 theatrical pieces, and it was not uncommon for two or even three of his plays to be running in Madrid theaters during the same season.

Benavente often acknowledged the influence of his fellow Spaniard José Echegaray y Eizaguirre, recipient of the 1904 Nobel Prize in Literature. While it is difficult to argue against the writer's belief in such an influence, it must be pointed out that Benavente's greatest contribution to the Spanish stage—and the main reason that he was selected for the Nobel Prize—resulted from the younger playwright's rejection of the thematic choices and dramatic conventions institutionalized by his distinguished predecessor. Benavente might well have been inspired to pursue a theatrical career by the success of Echegaray's plays and the accompanying positive image of the playwright as a popular public figure. Yet thematically and stylistically, the two writers are quite different.

Benavente's own work represents a deliberate departure from the dramatic standards that Echegaray had popularized and that had been widely accepted by the same theatergoing public of the late nineteenth century who would eventually view Benavente's early efforts. In fact, Benavente's first two stage productions, *El nido ajeno* (1894; *Another's Nest*, 1932) and *Gente conocida*, were received with some uneasiness by audiences conditioned by Echegaray and other contemporary neo-Romantic playwrights. Benavente was clearly going against what was fashionable; his characters were judged too true to life, their speech too common, their movements too natural. Echegaray's theater, and nineteenth century Spanish drama in general, reflected the opposite qualities; contrived situations, poetic speech, and exaggerated movement. Benavente's style, therefore, conforms more easily to the literary principles of realism, best exemplified in Spain by the novels and plays of Benito Pérez Galdós, although the latter considered himself a social reformer while the former disavowed any such goals.

Theatergoers soon accepted Benavente's new style, and several of his works, such as *La noche del sábado* (1903; *Saturday Night*, 1918) and *Los malhechores del bien* (1905; *The Evil of Good*, 1916), became the rage of the Spanish stage in the first years of the twentieth century. What eventually attracted a popular following, and what had initially repelled that same public, was Benavente's accurate portrayal of the virtues and defects of society. In his works these qualities were represented for the first time in single, complex characters. Gone was the clear distinction between good and evil, light and darkness, virtue and vice, so popular throughout generations; Benavente's characters embody ambiguity, are capable of good as well as evil, are virtuous and vicious all at once. Also discarded were the prototypes, Everyman and Everywoman, in favor of specific individuals in situations where they must face unique choices.

The Benaventine corpus is enormous. This fact, together with the sense that Benavente's best plays all share the same qualities, has led critics and historians of literature to analyze his works by dividing them into broad categories rather than approaching them chronologically. As a consequence, some of his best-known works have been grouped under the rubric of realistic plays; most of these contain a strong satirical vein and depict a wide range of subjects, from sophisticated Madrid high society to rural types. Fantasy plays, romantic comedies, and psychological studies have also served as headings to catalog much of the rest of Benavente's huge output. While critics, historians of literature, and biographers do not always agree on the specific titles to be placed in each of these categories—and any single play might well fit under more than one—most Benaventine scholars concur regarding the most famous titles.

Benavente's second play, *Gente conocida*, is a good example of the author's acceptance of the literary principles of realism, splashed with a strong dosage of satire. This four-act drama exposes the deterioration of the Spanish *fin de siècle* aristocracy by effectively erasing any trace of distinction between a nobility of birth that is fast becoming obsolete and a new, wealthy class desiring to purchase its way into the titled upper class. Most of the characters in the play are manipulative and self-seeking. They do not display any virtue or moral quality that would justify their fiercely maintained sense of superiority over the rest of society. The only exception is the young heroine Angelita; in circumstances reminiscent of Henrik Ibsen's plots, she is able to resist the enormous pressures placed upon her and refuses to conform. In this play, as in several others dealing with Iberian society, such as *La comida de las fieras* (1898; food for wild beasts), *La gata de Ángora* (1900; the angora cat, published in the thirty-eight-volume collection *Teatro*, 1904-1931), and *La gobernadora* (1901; *The Governor's Wife*, 1918), Benavente satirizes the tastes and customs of a social class that, he believes, has lost its bearings and purpose yet refuses to relinquish its claim to privilege. In these works, the clash between reality and self-delusion is made evident and provides the dynamic impulse for the plays' action. Plots tend to be straightforward and light; their language is clear and incisive; character development and dramatic impact are generated by the cumulative effect of a series of scenes rather than by a single event or revelation.

Benavente's attacks, however, are not restricted to the upper class; Madrid middle-class behavior receives its share of attention, as does the Church, the provincial gentry, the peasantry, and even the circus. Benaventine satire is at its most effective, however, in *Los intereses creados* (1907; *The Bonds of Interest*, 1915), which is arguably his best work and one of only a handful of his dramas still read by students of Spanish literature. The often-comical action of the play takes place in an imaginary city of the seventeenth century where two adventurers arrive in search of food, shelter, and whatever else they might connive to get. In true picaresque fashion, Crispín, the more scheming of the two, plans for the pair to establish a series of relationships or bonds, all based on deceit, with a few of the city's residents. When he and his partner Leandro are finally exposed as the ne'er-do-wells they really are, Crispín wisely assures his partner that all will end well. Too many people have been entangled in their web; they will seek to protect their name, reputation, and self-interest rather than enforce the law or worry about principle and truth. It should be noted that Benavente himself often played Crispín on-stage; it was his favorite character.

The Passion Flower was a second great national and international success for Benavente. Set in rural Castile, the action revolves around the love of a stepfather for his stepdaughter, a fact that is only revealed at the end of the play when the wife/mother discovers the truth. It is considered one of his finest psychological studies in its perceptive, sensitive portrayal of different kinds of love. The play enjoyed great success in several cities of the United States, where it was performed during Benavente's 1923 visit.

By the second half of the 1910's, Benavente had established himself as a distinguished and popular playwright. After this time, the quality of his dramatic works would never rival his earlier successes. He continued to write plays, including an entire collection directed at children, and to add to his reputation as an accomplished literary figure outside the theater. He composed a collection of poetry, *Versos* (1893; poems), and the nonfiction *Cartas de mujeres* (1893; letters from women)—an early example of the author's fascination with women as characters. He served as editor of the journal *Vida literaria* (literary life) from 1901 to 1909 and was a weekly contributor to the Madrid newspaper *El Imparcial* from 1908 to 1912.

Always sensitive to criticism, Benavente vowed in 1920 never to write for the theater again. This pledge coincided with his decision to accompany a theatrical troupe on a tour of South America, where he eventually received news of the Nobel award in 1922. He abandoned his resolve in 1924 after his triumphant return to Spain, composing more than seventy new works in the next thirty years; in the year of his death, 1954, three new plays of his were being performed on Spanish stages.

Benavente's contributions to theater are evident. His forceful and prolific reaction against the sentimentality and artifice of the Spanish stage at the turn of the century served to reform and energize the art. The structure of his theater differed from his predecessors' in its simplicity and directness. His interest in social problems, his sharp social criticism, and his choice of characters, recognizable for their flaws as much as for their virtues, elevated the genre and challenged audiences. The hypocrisy of society—be it social, political, or religious—was exposed for all to see. It is evident that he provided his work with a façade of radicalism. He wrote about controversial topics such as corruption, infidelity, and incest, yet he never went beyond exposing their existence. This restraint prompted some of his less admiring critics to express open disappointment over the author's lack of a more forceful and clear political agenda. With justification, they accused the author of lacking a serious commitment to use theater as an instrument of social change; his collaboration with the Franco regime confirmed that he was, at heart, only a traditionalist.

Benavente's popularity has been diminishing slowly since the 1950's. Although he has been the subject of a small number of doctoral dissertations, he cannot be said to be a figure of continuing interest to readers and scholars. In awarding Benavente the Nobel Prize in Literature, the Swedish Academy rewarded him for his role as innovator of the Spanish stage rather than for his qualities as a writer with a universal voice. The prize itself helped Benavente to regain some of his early zeal and fame, but it did not succeed in securing for him a position as one of the leading figures of twentieth century Spanish letters.

Bibliography

Primary
SHORT FICTION: *Vilanos*, 1905.
PLAYS: *El nido ajeno*, 1894 (*Another's Nest*, 1932); *Gente conocida*, 1896; *La comida de las fieras*, 1898; *La gata de Ángora*, 1900; *La gobernadora*, 1901 (*The Governor's Wife*, 1918); *La noche del sábado*, 1903 (*Saturday Night*, 1918); *No fumadores*, 1904 (*No Smoking*, 1917); *Teatro*, 1904-1931 (38 volumes); *Los malhechores del bien*, 1905 (*The Evil of Good*, 1916); *Rosas de otoño*, 1905 (*Autumnal Roses*, 1919); *La princesa Bebé*, 1906 (*Princess Bebé*, 1918); *Los intereses creados*, 1907 (*The Bonds of Interest*, 1915); *El marido de su viuda*, 1908 (*His Widow's Husband*, 1917); *Señora ama*, 1908 (*A Lady*, 1924); *La escuela de las princesas*, 1909 (*The School for Princesses*, 1924); *El príncipe que todo lo aprendió en los libros*, 1909 (*The Prince Who Learned Everything Out of Books*, 1918); *La malquerida*, 1913 (*The Passion Flower*, 1917); *La ciudad alegre y confiada*, 1916; *Plays by Jacinto Benavente*, 1917-1924 (4 volumes); *Pepa Doncel*, 1928; *La melodía del jazz band*, 1931; *La moral del divorcio*, 1932; *El pan comido en la mano*, 1934; *La infanzona*, 1945; *Mater imperatrix*, 1950.
POETRY: *Versos*, 1893.
NONFICTION: *Cartas de mujeres*, 1893; *Teatro del pueblo*, 1909; *De sobremesa*, 1910-1916; *Conferencias*, 1924; *Recuerdos y olvidos: Memorias*, 1962.
TRANSLATIONS: *Don Juan*, 1897 (of Molière's *Dom Juan: Ou, Le Festin de Pierre*); *El rey Lear*, 1911 (of William Shakespeare's *King Lear*).
MISCELLANEOUS: *Obras completas*, 1952-1964 (11 volumes).

Secondary

Benavente, Jacinto. *Plays by Jacinto Benavente*. Translated by John Garrett
Underhill. 4 vols. New York: Charles Scribner's Sons, 1917-1925. Underhill, Benavente's translator, introduces each volume with an erudite and
admiring view of the playwright. Aside from wishing to enlighten the
reader about the artistry of Benavente, Underhill also seeks to respond to
what he considers unwarranted anti-Beneventine criticism, especially with
regard to the dramatist's lack of a social conscience.

Friedman, Edward. "The Thorns on the Roses: A Reading of Benavente's
Rosas de otoño." *International Journal of Women's Studies* 4 (1981): 168-
172. A feminist appraisal of one of Benavente's best plays, premiered in
1905. In it, a philandering husband threatens the stability and well-being of
his family. They are eventually spared only because of the wife's willingness
to sacrifice herself for their sake. Benavente's interest in and ability to portray female characters are dissected in this useful article.

Onís, Federico de. "Jacinto Benavente." *The North American Review* 217
(March, 1923): 357-364. This brief article, written shortly after the award
of the Nobel Prize to Benavente, is generally a sober tribute to the playwright by a distinguished academician. Emphasizes the fact that Benavente
had already achieved great fame at home at the time of the award, and
that the prize would scatter this well-deserved fame throughout the world.
De Onís also views Benavente as a serious writer who aims at a better
humanity and a juster world.

Peñuelas, Marcelino C. *Jacinto Benavente*. Translated by Kay Engler. New
York: Twayne Publishers, 1968. In an attempt to update Walter Starkie's
book (below), Peñuelas incorporates many of Starkie's conclusions, largely
accepts the categories into which the British writer divided Benavente's
work, and devotes serious attention to Benavente's best plays. This book
also gives some attention to his nondramatic literary works, although the
discussion is not especially enlightening. Aside from the obvious advantage
of having been written after the death of Benavente, with the insights that
can only come from hindsight, this book attempts to present a fairly objective analysis of Benavente as a social reformer; Peñuelas concludes that the
Nobel Prize winner was never able to overcome the prejudices of the privi-
leged class into which he was born.

Sheehan, Robert L. *Benavente and the Spanish Panorama, 1894-1954*.
Chapel Hill, N.C.: Estudios de Hispanófila, 1976. This study, the only
scholarly work on Benavente to appear in English in the 1970's, is a welcome addition in that it not only considers the aesthetic elements of the
Benaventine legacy but also examines the social and political climate in
which they developed. The author admires his subject and attempts to reconcile the divergent opinions expressed by two generations of critics.
Sheehan concludes that Benavente was a reformer rather than a revolu-

tionary, a patriot rather than a leftist or a rightist.

Starkie, Walter. "Benavente, the Winner of the Nobel Prize." *Contemporary Review* 123 (January, 1923): 93-100. One of only a handful of articles to appear in the English-language press following the announcement of Benavente's selection as Nobel laureate. The author, Great Britain's preeminent Benaventine scholar of the period, applauds the choice of the Swedish Academy and demonstrates why he believes that Benavente deserves the honor. Benavente's most successful plays receive a brief commentary.

_____. *Jacinto Benavente.* London: Oxford University Press, 1924. The standard English-language study of the work of Benavente. Although it only deals with the first half of the dramatist's career, it presents a serious and thorough analysis of Benavente's best plays by re-creating many details of plot and dialogue. The author asserts that Benavente was responsible for important innovations; he is compared, with good effect, to numerous important figures of European drama and is viewed as a precursor of important Continental trends. The author is less admiring of Benavente as a person; Starkie finds offensive the Spaniard's sympathies for the kaiser during World War I.

Underhill, John Garrett, ed. Introductions to *Plays by Jacinto Benavente.* 4 vols. New York: Charles Scribner's Sons, 1917-1925. Underhill, Benavente's translator into English, introduces each volume with an erudite and admiring view of the playwright. Aside from wishing to enlighten the reader about the artistry of Benavente, Underhill seeks to respond to what he considers unwarranted anti-Beneventine criticism. especially with regard to the dramatist's lack of a social conscience.

Clara Estow

1923

Literature
William Butler Yeats, Ireland

Peace
no award

Physics
Robert Millikan, United States

Chemistry
Fritz Pregl, Austria

Physiology or Medicine
Sir F. G. Banting, Canada
J. J. R. Macleod, Great Britain

WILLIAM BUTLER YEATS
1923

Born: Dublin, Ireland; June 13, 1865
Died: Cap Martin, France; January 28, 1939
Language: English
Principal genres: Poetry and drama

After mastering the late Romantic mode of poetry, Yeats transformed his
style and subject matter to become both a preeminent modern poet and a
national literary and cultural leader

The Award

Presentation

The Nobel Prize in Literature was presented to William Butler Yeats on
December 10, 1923, by Gustaf V Adolf, the King of Sweden. The presentation emphasized two contrasting aspects of Yeats's art, the private emotional
and lyrical elements and the public art which "expresses a people's spirit."
Yeats was at the forefront of the Irish cultural and literary revival and was
the founder of the Irish National Literary Society and the Abbey Theatre,
but he refused to allow his art to be subordinated to purely patriotic or nationalistic ends. He was fond of quoting John O'Leary's dictum: "There are
some things a man must not do to save a nation"; Yeats took that to mean
not writing sentimental or propagandistic poetry. He believed that one of his
aims as a poet and a man was to achieve a "Unity of Being" by reconciling
the opposing forces within him. In addition, he wished to transform his country by giving it the artistic models necessary to a "Unity of Culture" rather
than giving it a political program in verse.

Nobel lecture

Yeats's Nobel lecture was not on his poetry or on the historical or occult
concepts that were central to his thought. He chose to write on a more general and public topic for the occasion: "The Irish Dramatic Movement." In
large part, Yeats's lecture is devoted to a celebration of the role that others
played in this movement. He talks first about the literary situation in Dublin,
where a literary interest replaced a political one after the fall of Charles
Stewart Parnell in 1890. The literary scene was bleak at the time and the only
theater available had to be imported from England. Yeats and his chief
collaborator, Lady Augusta Gregory, decided to gather contributions and re-
cruit actors for a new theater.

The chief playwrights for the Abbey Theatre were Yeats, Lady Gregory,
and John Millington Synge. Yeats lavishes great praise on the others' plays
and little upon his own, but he does acknowledge that he was instrumental in

helping both become playwrights. He found Synge in Paris and urged him to go to the Aran Islands so that he might discover a life yet unexpressed in art. Moreover, Lady Gregory's plays were first staged as companion pieces to the short poetic plays of Yeats.

In addition to the artistic triumphs of the Abbey Theatre, Yeats mentions the controversies. Yeats's own *The Countess Cathleen* (1892) was denounced by a Catholic bishop as heretical, and Synge's *The Playboy of the Western World* (1907) caused a riot because of its unflattering portrayal of the Irish peasant. In both cases, Yeats presents the Abbey as standing in opposition to the forces of religious and political narrowness. His long-range view, however, is optimistic: *The Playboy of the Western World* may have been rudely greeted on its opening night, but "the Dublin audience . . . has long since accepted the play." The lecture ends with Yeats confidently looking to future triumphs of the Abbey Theatre. (The Abbey was, however, to take an un-Yeatsian direction in the years to follow: Sean O'Casey became its next great playwright with the production of *The Shadow of a Gunman* in 1923, and his naturalistic and unpoetic plays became the most popular in the Abbey repertory.)

Critical reception

The critical reception to the announcement that Yeats had won the Nobel Prize in Literature was generally favorable, but the commentators emphasized various reasons for the award. Some stressed the political context as the primary motivation of the Nobel Committee. Both the New York *Evening Post* and *The Washington Post* saw the award as a virtual recognition of the newly created Irish Free State. The *Evening Post* went so far as to state that "the Nobel directors have always shown a disposition to recognize representatives of literary nationalism."

A slightly different rationale was evoked by reports that stressed Yeats's position as a leader of the National Dramatic Society and the Irish National Literary Society. The *Providence Journal* saw the award as a recognition of Yeats as the leader of the Irish, or Celtic, Renaissance. In a similar comment, the New York *Evening Mail* focused on Yeats's role as the leader of a dramatic and national movement. The New York *World*, however, saw it as a retrospective award, since the movement he had created "has largely disintegrated. He himself has written his best work and Synge is dead."

A few journals of opinion saw the justification of the award for artistic rather than nationalistic reasons. The *Boston Evening Transcript* and *The Evening Telegram* (New York) praised Yeats for the lyrical and musical qualities in the early poems but made no mention of later developments and changes in Yeats's poetry. The only other source to stress the range of Yeats's achievement was *The New York Times*, which touched on Yeats's "numerous lyrical poems, essays, sketches, and works for the stage." They also acknowledged his place as the leader "of the new Irish nationalist school."

There may have been some truth to the charge that the award was primarily for political reasons; since politics is the one thing Yeats wished to avoid or ignore, it would be an ironic misemphasis of his achievement. More accurate is the recognition of Yeats as the leader of a national literary and cultural revival; that was what he set about to do and partially accomplished. Those who singled out only or primarily the early poems of Yeats as justification for the award failed to grasp his achievements as a poet and a playwright. If Yeats had written only the lyrical early poetry, he would not have received the Nobel Prize or changed the culture of his nation.

Biography

William Butler Yeats was born in Sandymount, a section of Dublin, in 1865, into a family that had a strong upper-middle-class Anglo-Irish background. Yeats's father, John Yeats, was a painter and devoted to a life in the arts. Yeats attended an art school for a time but found that his talent lay in poetry. He was also interested in the cultural revival that was just starting. It was during this period that Yeats met Maud Gonne; she was a committed Irish nationalist and revolutionary and, while Yeats loved her, he despised her involvement with politics.

From 1906 to 1912 Yeats was deeply involved in the activities of the Abbey Theatre and with Lady Gregory and John Millington Synge. The decade from 1914 to the awarding of the Nobel Prize in 1923 was a very full one. Yeats's personal life was easier; his friendship with Lady Gregory and his marriage to Georgie Hyde-Lees in 1917 gave his life an ease and stability that it had not had before. He still longed for Maud Gonne in his poems, but his wife gave him peace.

The years after he received the Nobel Prize were very productive. Yeats did not fade in old age; he wrote his finest book of poetry, *The Tower* (1928), and one of his greatest plays, *Purgatory* (1938), in his later years. Yeats's art became more complex and more modern during this period, as his poetry and drama reflected some of the historical concepts outlined in *A Vision*, a "meditation upon history" written with the aid of his wife, which he first published in 1925 and thoroughly revised for another edition in 1937.

Yeats's last years were turbulent; he had a Steinach operation (that is, a vasectomy) in Switzerland in the hope of renewing his sexual powers, and he suffered from various illnesses. His closest friends, Lady Gregory and Olivia Shakespear, died, and he felt isolated. He had to leave Ireland during the winter in search of warmer climates, and he spent less and less time in his homeland. He died on the Riviera on January 28, 1939.

Literary Career

Yeats began his literary career during the Pre-Raphaelite period, when the doctrine of art for art's sake was prominent. He was influenced by the writings and character of William Morris and such Romantics as Percy Bysshe Shelley and William Blake. There were other influences on Yeats; he was drawn to the recent translations of Irish myths by Standish O'Grady and the revival of the Gaelic language. Yeats did not choose between these two strands of influence but attempted to incorporate them into his character and art. His first major poem, "The Wanderings of Oisin," is late Romantic in its style, but it uses an Irish myth for its subject matter. In *Crossways* (1889), Yeats's first book of poems, he declares the aesthetic doctrine that "Words alone are certain good," but also includes ballads on Irish subjects in "The Ballad of Father O'Hart" and Irish myths in "The Madness of King Goll."

Yeats's aestheticism was evident in his subsequent books of poetry, but it took a slightly different form. Yeats became interested in the philosophy of Madame Blavatsky and the doctrine and practice of magic. *The Rose* (1893) uses some of this occult lore in such poems as "The Rose of the World." The number of Irish poems increased, and poems such as "Fergus and the Druid" and "Who Goes with Fergus?" make better use of the Irish material. *The Rose* includes one of Yeats's finest early lyrics, "The Lake Isle of Innisfree," which contrasts the barren and blighted city with the natural peace of the Lake Isle. The sound patterns of the poem are especially notable, as well as such visual images as "noon a purple glow." This collection also included "The Lamentation of the Old Pensioner," which touches on the important Yeatsian themes of old age and time.

Yeats was also writing many important plays for the Abbey Theatre at this time. His two most successful plays, *The Countess Cathleen* and *Cathleen ni Houlihan* (1902), had Irish subjects. *The Countess Cathleen* deals with Cathleen's selling her soul to the devil to buy back the souls of the peasants; she is then saved because, "The Light of Lights/ Looks always upon the motive, not the deed." This dubious theology disturbed some of the clergy, but it was successful in attracting an audience. *Cathleen ni Houlihan* was not controversial and pleased the patriots in Dublin with its evocation of the renewal of the land through revolution. Cathleen is, for most of the play, an old woman, but at the end she is described as having "the walk of a queen."

The next book of poetry Yeats published was *The Wind Among the Reeds* (1899). It contains some of Yeats's finest love poems for Maud Gonne. "The Lover Tells of the Rose in his Heart" contrasts "the wrong of unshapely things" with her "image that blossoms a rose in the deeps of my heart." The book also contains poems based on Irish folklore or myths, such as "The Host of the Air" and "The Song of Wandering Aengus." Both poems deal with the loss of something precious, a bride or a vision, that must be recaptured. At the conclusion of both poems, the speaker is left with an endless quest.

Yeats's next two books, *In the Seven Woods* (1903) and *The Green Helmet and Other Poems* (1910), are transitional; there are many poems to Maud Gonne, but they have an edge and bite to them. For example, "No Second Troy" celebrates Maud's beauty but also stresses her destructiveness: "Why, what could she have done, being what she is?/ Was there another Troy for her to burn?" There are also satirical poems on the reception of Synge's *The Playboy of the Western World* and topical poems on the difficulties involved with running a theater. Perhaps the strongest poem from this period is "Adam's Curse." It is both a recognition of the loss of love between Yeats and Maud Gonne and an analysis of poetic creation. In these poems, Maud Gonne has been placed within the context of the world; she is no longer all to him or isolated from experience.

The next book, *Responsibilities* (1914), is a watershed in Yeats's style and subject matter. His "responsibilities" to his ancestors and the future are defined in the opening and closing poems of the book. In between is a celebration of those who influenced him, including the "poets with whom I learned my trade," such as Lionel Johnson and Ernest Dowson in "The Grey Rock" and John O'Leary in "September 1913." The latter poem is especially effective in its contrast of those "who fumble in a greasy till" to the spirited O'Leary. Other memorable poems in the collection are the celebration of the aristocratic stance and the scorning of the middle-class view in "To a Wealthy Man" and "To a Shade," which is on the death and lack of recognition of Parnell. Perhaps the most complex poem is "The Cold Heaven," which reverses the reunion with the beloved in the afterlife portrayed in *The Rose*. Here, the lover is not united with his beloved; instead, the "ghost" is "sent/ Out naked on the roads."

The Wild Swans at Coole was published in 1917; an enlarged edition was published in 1919. It is one of Yeats's most moving collections. The title poem uses the swans as a symbol of the power of creation or of love, a power that the poet loses at the end of the poem "when I awake some day/ To find that they have flown away." There are three poems on the death of Robert Gregory, the only son of Lady Gregory. "In Memory of Major Robert Gregory" is one of the finest elegies in the language; it celebrates Gregory as a Renaissance man who dies at the height of his power and excellence. "The Fisherman" speaks of a change in style and audience as Yeats dedicates himself to write for an Irish peasant "one/ Poem maybe as cold/ And passionate as the dawn." "Ego Dominus Tuus" also deals with changes within Yeats. It is a dialogue between "Hic" and "Ille" or self and anti-self. Hic urges the poet to "find myself and not an image," but Ille is victorious as he calls upon the "anti-self" to "disclose/ All that I seek." Also notable is "The Phases of the Moon," which attempts, rather pedantically, to turn the system of *A Vision* into poetry.

Michael Robartes and the Dancer (1921) contains some of Yeats's most complex poems and some of his more direct commentary on the Irish situation. "Easter 1916" transforms the rebels of the Easter rebellion of 1916 into heroes and Yeats into a bard. It is a profoundly apolitical poem about a political event. Yeats makes the event and the people involved in it into myth, so that the event paradoxically can be called a "terrible beauty." "The Second Coming" speaks of a nightmarish historical period to come after the two-thousand-year cycle of Christianity comes to an end. Yeats leaves that coming terror undefined as he asks "And what rough beast, its hour come round at last,/ Slouches towards Bethlehem to be born?" "A Prayer for My Daughter" offers a different vision. Yeats asks that his young daughter be blessed with the aristocratic virtues of custom and ceremony as an antidote to an "opinionated mind."

The Tower was Yeats's first book of poems published after he won the Nobel Prize. It is filled with a surprising bitterness caused primarily by health problems. The first poem in the book, "Sailing to Byzantium," is a poem of escape from the processes of life, of "Whatever is begotten, born, and dies." Yeats counters this process with an eternal and unchanging work of art, the "golden bird" into which he transforms himself. The poems that follow do not touch on that escape but confront the problems of age and history. "Nineteen Hundred and Nineteen" is the most intense of these poems; it portrays a world of violence where former idealists are now "weasels fighting in a hole." Even works of art are destined to be destroyed, and the only solace the creator has is an aloof "solitude" in the midst of destruction. "Among School Children" continues this concept of destruction and expands it. Not only art but also love and affection are doomed to decay and destruction. Yeats, however, added a last stanza which transcends the apparent hopelessness by proposing the unity of all things. In that unity, there is no process or distinction between parts, so "How can we know the dancer from the dance?" In addition to this triumph over time and decay, the book ends with "All Souls' Night: Epilogue to 'A Vision,'" which also celebrates Yeats's control over the movements of history that he codified in *A Vision*. The poem ends with a unity of supposed opposites, a union of heaven and hell: "To where the damned have howled away their hearts,/ And where the blessed dance."

The Winding Stair and Other Poems (1933) was designed to alleviate some of the bitterness of *The Tower*. There are a number of poems in the book honoring Yeats's friends and collaborators of the past, such as "In Memory of Eva Gore-Booth and Con Markiewicz," "Coole Park, 1929," and "Coole Park and Ballylee, 1931." "Coole Park, 1929" is especially notable for its evocation of an aristocratic tradition in which "traveller, scholar, poet" are welcomed and flourish. The book also contains one of Yeats's greatest poems, "A Dialogue of Self and Soul." Like the dialogue of Hic and Ille in "Ego Dominus Tuus," the dialogue between "My Self" and "My Soul" is about opposites; "Soul" pleads an escape from "the crime of birth and death" while

"Self" is content to accept the "impure" and "live it all again/ And yet again. . . ." The "Self" is victorious at the end of the poem as it "cast[s] out remorse" and declares: "We are blest by everything,/ Everything we look upon is blest."

In *Words for Music Perhaps and Other Poems* (1932), the "Crazy Jane" poems celebrate the sexual urge and act. Crazy Jane, the speaker in these poems, refutes the narrow and conventional view of the Bishop. In "Crazy Jane Talks with the Bishop," the Bishop urges her to "Live in a heavenly mansion,/ Not in some foul sty." Crazy Jane, like the Self, pleads for unity, since "fair needs foul," and she posits yet another vision of Unity of Being in a reconciliation of opposites:

> But Love has pitched his mansion in
> The place of excrement;
> For nothing can be sole or whole
> That has not been rent.

The vision defeats the Bishop.

Yeats was writing plays during this period, but they were less important to his literary achievement than his poetry. There are, however, two plays that stand out: *The Resurrection* (1927) and *Purgatory*. *The Resurrection* takes the form of a debate by a Greek and a Hebrew over the death of Christ and His possible Resurrection. The Hebrew argues that Christ was only a man, while the Greek believes that he was a God and the body they buried was a mere "phantom." As the debate continues, Greek revelers celebrating Dionysius pass by; after a Syrian reports that the tomb is empty, however, the revelers change their chant to "God has arisen!" The play ends with the Greek commenting on what has taken place; the two-thousand-year cycle of Greek rationalism has been displaced by the Resurrection of Christ, a concept of the cycles of history that also can be found in "The Second Coming."

Purgatory is in the form of a Japanese Nō play, and once more the principle of recurrence is the major theme. The souls in purgatory must reenact the deeds committed in their lifetime until someone releases them. The main character in the play is an Old Man whose mother is doomed to repeat the scene of her sexual transgression with a groom that led to the conception of the Old Man. His attempt to release his mother leads instead to the reenactment of his own act of murder; earlier it had been the murder of his father, but now he kills his own son. At the end of the play, the Old Man asks God to "Appease/ The misery of the living and the remorse of the dead."

The last two books of poetry that Yeats published contain many of his strongest poems but lack the design and integrity evident in such earlier volumes as *The Tower*. One reason for this weakness is that *Last Poems and*

Plays (1940) was arranged and published after Yeats's death in 1939. *A Full Moon in March* was published in 1935 and contains only one important poem, "Supernatural Songs," which consists of twelve sections. The main speaker in the poem is Ribh, a Christian hermit who denounces Patrick's view of the Trinity as an abstraction, since "Natural and supernatural with the self-same ring are wed." In the last section, "Meru," a larger vision of man's nature and experience is posed in the repetition of the cycles of history.

Last Poems and Plays includes such brilliant poems as "Lapis Lazuli," "The Municipal Gallery Revisited," and "The Circus Animals' Desertion," as well as many undistinguished ones. "Lapis Lazuli" is another poem on the cycles of history and the attitude that is needed to confront such change, a "Gaiety transfiguring all that dread." "The Municipal Gallery Revisited" is reminiscent of Yeats's middle poems which celebrate his friends or attack his enemies. He singles out Synge and Lady Gregory for special praise and concludes: "Think where man's glory most begins and ends,/ And say my glory was I had such friends." "The Circus Animals' Desertion" is Yeats's attempt to summarize his career and to issue a defiant description of his last and greatest phase. After summing up those earlier periods, he touches on the ultimate cause of his art: "Now that my ladder's gone,/ I must lie down where all the ladders start,/ In the foul rag-and-bone shop of the heart."

The award of the Nobel Prize to Yeats in 1923 was certainly merited. Yeats not only had a distinguished career as a lyric poet and dramatist but also created and led the resurgence of a literature and a culture, an achievement that few Nobel Prize winners can claim. In addition, Yeats had, in essence, another poetic and dramatic career after he received the award. During his last years he wrote some of his most complex and powerful poems and plays.

Bibliography

Primary

SHORT FICTION: *John Sherman and Dhoya*, 1891, 1969; *The Celtic Twilight*, 1893; *The Secret Rose*, 1897; *The Tables of the Law; The Adoration of the Magi*, 1897; *Stories of Red Hanrahan*, 1904; *Mythologies*, 1959.

PLAYS: *The Countess Cathleen*, 1892; *The Land of Heart's Desire*, 1894; *Cathleen ni Houlihan*, 1902 (with Lady Augusta Gregory); *The Pot of Broth*, 1902 (with Lady Gregory); *The Hour-Glass*, 1903; *The King's Threshold*, 1903 (with Lady Gregory); *On Baile's Strand*, 1904; *Deirdre*, 1906 (with Lady Gregory); *The Shadowy Waters*, 1906; *The Unicorn from the Stars*, 1907 (with Lady Gregory); *The Golden Helmet*, 1908; *The Green Helmet*, 1910; *At the Hawk's Well*, 1916; *The Player Queen*, 1919; *The Only Jealousy of Emer*, 1919; *The Dreaming of the Bones*, 1919; *Calvary*, 1921; *Four Plays for Dancers*, 1921; *The Cat and the Moon*, 1924; *The Resurrection*, 1927; *The Words upon the Windowpane*, 1930; *The Collected Plays of W. B. Yeats*, 1934; *The King of the Great Clock Tower*, 1934; *A Full Moon* in March, 1934; *The Herne's Egg*, 1938; *Purgatory*, 1938; *The Death of Cuchulain*, 1939; *Variorum Edition of the Plays of W. B. Yeats*, 1966.

POETRY: *Mosada: A Dramatic Poem*, 1886; *Crossways*, 1889; *The Wanderings of Oisin and Other Poems*, 1889; *The Rose*, 1893; *The Wind Among the Reeds*, 1899; *In the Seven Woods*, 1903; *The Green Helmet and Other Poems*, 1910; *Responsibilities*, 1914; *Responsibilities and Other Poems*, 1916; *The Wild Swans at Coole*, 1917, 1919; *Michael Robartes and the Dancer*, 1921; *The Tower*, 1928; *Words for Music Perhaps and Other Poems*, 1932; *The Winding Stair and Other Poems*, 1933; *The Collected Poems of W. B. Yeats*, 1933, 1950; *A Full Moon in March*, 1935; *Last Poems and Plays*, 1940; *The Variorum Edition of the Poems of W. B. Yeats*, 1957; *W. B. Yeats: The Poems*, 1983; *The Poems: A New Edition*, 1984.

NONFICTION: *Ideas of Good and Evil*, 1903; *A Vision*, 1925, 1937; *Autobiographies*, 1927, 1955; *The Letters of W. B. Yeats*, 1954; *The Senate Speeches of W. B. Yeats*, 1960; *Essays and Introductions*, 1961; *Explorations*, 1962; *Ah, Sweet Dancer: W. B. Yeats—Margaret Ruddock, a Correspondence*, 1970; *Uncollected Prose by W. B. Yeats*, 1970, 1976 (2 volumes); *Memoirs*, 1972.

Secondary

Bloom, Harold. *Yeats*. Oxford: Oxford University Press, 1970. An erratic but occasionally enlightening book on the poetry of Yeats by a major critic.

Ellmann, Richard. *The Identity of Yeats*. New York: Oxford University Press, 1954. This early study of Yeats remains a useful introduction to Yeats's poetry and thought.

Henn, Thomas Rice. *The Lonely Tower: Studies in the Poetry of W. B. Yeats*. London: Methuen, 1950. An excellent discussion of the poetry, especially the later poems.

Hone, Joseph. *W. B. Yeats: 1865-1939*. London: Macmillan, 1943, rev. ed. 1962. This is the standard biography of Yeats, and it is filled with details about his life and the controversies that surrounded him.

Jeffares, A. Norman. *A Commentary on the Collected Poems of W. B. Yeats*. Stanford, Calif.: Stanford University, Press, 1968. Since Yeats alludes to many persons and events that are not immediately recognized by readers, this is an indispensable book. Jeffares also provides information about Yeats's esoteric theories.

Parkinson, Thomas. *W. B. Yeats: The Later Poetry*. Berkeley: University of California Press, 1964. An intensive study of the revisions Yeats made in the late poems.

Vendler, Helen. *Yeats's Vision and the Later Plays*. Cambridge, Mass.: Harvard University Press, 1963. A brilliant and forcefully written application of Yeats's thought to his plays.

Whitaker, Thomas R. *Swan and Shadow: Yeats's Dialogue with History*.

Chapel Hill: University of North Carolina Press, 1964. A difficult book to penetrate, but it is invaluable on Yeats's poetic use of history.

James Sullivan

1924

Literature
Władysław Reymont, Poland

Peace
no award

Physics
Karl Siegbahn, Sweden

Chemistry
no award

Physiology or Medicine
Willem Einthoven, Netherlands

WŁADYSŁAW REYMONT
1924

Born: Kobiele Wielkie, Poland; May 7, 1867
Died: Warsaw, Poland; December 5, 1925
Language: Polish
Principal genre: Fiction

Reymont's masterpiece, The Peasants, *a broadly conceived and powerful epic in which the drama of the Polish peasant is shown against the background of the seasons, is a hymn to life and attains universal significance*

The Award

Presentation

The announcement that Władysław Reymont had won the Nobel Prize in Literature was made on November 14, 1924. Since the official ceremony was not held because of the author's illness, Per Hallström, Chairman of the Nobel Committee of the Swedish Academy, prepared a critical essay in place of the presentation speech.

The essay points to the primacy of direct experience and to the epic sweep in Reymont's four-volume novel *Chłopi* (1904-1909; *The Peasants*, 1924-1925). Reymont rejects preconceived theories and describes the peasant as he knew him. Having assimilated Émile Zola's techniques of constructing novels, Reymont nevertheless transcends naturalism. In *The Peasants* Reymont is "naturalistic in method but epic in scope."

It is characteristic of the epic that its parts may portray struggle or suffering, yet the total impression is one of harmony and calm. No matter how shattering the experience, the individual remains "entire and simple and moves in *one* piece." It is this kind of plastic beauty and monumentality, the essay notes, that Reymont attains in *The Peasants*. While showing the weakness of his Polish peasant, Reymont also manages to portray his nobility and, above all, a "gleam of heroism" in his deep attachment to the soil. Contributing to the epic breadth of the novel are the compositional device of the cycle of seasons, the "typical validity" of the episodes, the "unity of style," and the "uncommon power and delight in color"—as well as the characterization, which at times attains the status of symbol. The essay concludes by noting the universality and the "distinctive and monumental shape" which Reymont's powerful epic contributes to literature.

Nobel lecture

Unable to attend the presentation ceremony in Stockholm, Reymont, like some of the previous recipients of the Nobel Prize, forwarded an autobiographical statement to the Committee. Discussing his early education, Reymont stresses the role that reading, as opposed to formal instruction, played in his development as a writer. Between the ages of six and twelve he read widely and voraciously both Polish and foreign literature in Polish translation. By the time he was nine, Reymont started writing poetry, while his passionate reading became a stimulus for a rich fantasy life. He writes, "I arranged the world according to my private use, looking at it through the poems I had devoured."

While Reymont's reading alienated him from everyday reality in his youth, it eventually led to his intellectual liberation and physical separation from the narrow and conservative outlook of his family. He suggests that his reading produced, in addition, a sense of dissatisfaction with himself and his immediate surroundings. Nor was he able to come to terms with his environment after he had left home and worked as a poorly paid minor official for the railway: "I could adapt myself neither to the mentality of those around me nor to the conditions of my existence." For four years, from twenty to twenty-four, Reymont engaged in a series of changing professions, but already at the age of twenty-two he made an irrevocable commitment to literature.

A major theme running through Reymont's description of his search for self and his quest to become a writer is the theme of suffering and privation. The hunger, solitude, torment, and misery which he experienced in those years were endurable only because of his dream to be a writer: "I had faith in the world and a thousand bold projects in my mind." Finally some of Reymont's stories were published. He reports that he felt an "unspeakable happiness" because he had finally found his way.

Yet Reymont's torments were not over. He moved to Warsaw and again suffered hunger and privation to the point where he considered suicide. He reports that as his newfound faith grew more profound so did his "fascination with annihilation." Finally he was able to attract the attention of the critics again, and starting in 1895 Reymont's career was on the rise. The importance that Reymont attached to the arduous road to achievement and the fact that he minimized the achievement itself are evident from the perfunctory manner in which he lists his major novels in the last paragraph of his statement to the committee.

Critical reception

The initial reactions to the announcement that Reymont had been awarded the Nobel Prize were mixed. Some responses, such as that of *The Times* of London (November 15), were entirely positive. Others registered surprise that a relatively unknown writer had been chosen. Still others directly or indirectly criticized the Nobel Committee's choice.

The article published in *The Saturday Review of Literature* (November 29) serves as a typical example. It contains elements that appeared in one form or another in many articles of the day. First, the reviewer refers to the obscurity of Reymont in literature, at least as far as the English-speaking world is concerned. Second, he compares Reymont to his better-known predecessor, Henryk Sienkiewicz, who won the Nobel Prize in 1905. In this connection the reviewer also mentions Stefan Żeromski, a contemporary who was also a candidate for the prize and who had his supporters both in Poland and in Sweden. Finally, he gives biographical information about Reymont as well as an analysis of *The Peasants* and other works.

Other critics who were less informed about Reymont's writings gave voice to their surprise at his selection in tones bordering on hostility. Thus the critic for *The New York Times* (November 16), after a few summary phrases in which Reymont is compared to Sienkiewicz, assumes a polemical tone. He asserts that the Nobel Committee "frowns upon rebels and pessimists." He argues that the typical profile of a writer selected for the prize is one who voices "traditional pieties," writes about peasants, and closely identifies with the aspirations of his people. He concludes that the reason that Poland is the only Slavic country represented in the history of Nobel Prize in Literature awards may result from the fact that the Committee bestows its prizes "as rewards for patriotism, or perhaps even for parochialism." Given the critic's predilection for rebels, as well as the fact that the last third of the article is devoted to deserving Russian writers, it is possible that the critic's discontent was motivated by political considerations.

The writer for the popular journal *The Outlook* (November 26) also registers his dissatisfaction with the fact that the Academy bestowed a prize "upon an author comparatively unknown." Much like his colleague from *The New York Times*, he finds it "odd" that while Poles had won twice, a Russian had never been awarded the Prize in Literature.

Some articles, such as that of *Time* magazine (December 1), were simply ambiguous in terms of their attitude to Reymont. Reviewing the recently published first volume of *The Peasants*, *Time* pronounces it "truly epic in its scope, a carefully worked, heroic pattern." On the other hand, the article is titled, rather disrespectfully, "Cows, Vodka, Acres, Potatoes, Soil, Love, Hate."

The second wave of responses to Reymont's Nobel Prize was much more positive and better informed. The overall purpose was to fill the gap in knowledge about the Polish writer. Such is an article in *The New York Times Book Review* (November 30), which to a great extent revokes the comments of the earlier article in *The New York Times*. The author frankly admits that little is known about Reymont in this country, "although his powerful genius has been widely recognized on the continent of Europe." By way of rectifying this situation he interviews Albert Morawski-Nawench, a lecturer at Columbia University, who was personally acquainted with Reymont and who responds warmly to him both as a personality and as an artist.

The *Literary Digest* (February 14, 1925) follows a similar strategy by quoting extensively from an article by Rupert Hughes (who had also met Reymont) published in February in the *International Book Review*. A few months later the *Literary Digest* (January 23, 1926) published a short sketch by Reymont in its pages.

Other articles published in 1925 fall into two categories. They either provide information about *The Peasants* and Reymont's other works or they review individual volumes of *The Peasants*, which were published in 1924 and 1925. In the latter category, a review by Joseph Wood Krutch in *The Nation* (January 21, 1925) is representative of the entirely positive responses; the first two volumes of *The Peasants* are described as "an amazing piece of architecture." In another, less than flattering appraisal, Edwin Bjorkman wrote in *The Literary Review* (January 24, 1925) that while *The Peasants* deserves high praise as a record of human existence, it is flawed artistically by its deliberate tone and its emphasis on detail.

Biography

Władysław Reymont was born on May 7, 1867, in Kobiele Wielkie, a small village in central Poland. His parents were Józef Rejment, a village organist, and Antonina Kupczyńska. Reymont had very little formal education. He was an autodidact. At the age of thirteen he was sent to live with his sister in Warsaw. Three years later he received a diploma from the Tailors' Guild. In 1884 Reymont was banished from Warsaw to his parents' house by the czarist authorities for political activity. In 1885 he ran away and joined a traveling actors' troupe for a year, and then engaged in a number of professions. He was a surveyor, store clerk, salesman, and journalist. For a few years he worked as a minor official for the railroad.

In 1893 Reymont published some journalistic pieces, but he was determined to be a creative writer. With this in mind he moved to Warsaw, where he quickly received critical recognition. His first novel, *Komediantka* (1896; *The Comedienne*, 1920), was published during that period.

Reymont had taken his first extensive trip abroad in 1894. Living and working outside Poland agreed with him, and he wrote his major works in France. The bulk of *The Peasants* was written in Paris, where Reymont moved with his wife, Aurelia, after their marriage in 1902. Reymont spent the years of World War I in Poland. After Poland attained independence, he resumed his travels and came to the United States in 1919 and again in 1920. In 1920 he purchased an estate in western Poland and settled there. Weakened by heart trouble in the last years of his life, Reymont died in Warsaw on December 5, 1925.

Literary Career

Reymont began his career as a writer in the mid-1890's and continued writing steadily for the next thirty years. He was a prolific writer, steadily producing at least twelve volumes of novels and an equal number of short stories. Reymont's evolution as a writer ran parallel to the literary movement in Poland known as "Young Poland" or "neo-Romanticism," which was introduced in the last decade of the nineteenth century and became the dominant force in Polish literature until Poland won its independence in 1918. Young Poland was part of the modernist movement sweeping Europe at the time, the early manifestations of which were Decadent and Symbolist poetry. In Polish literature this tendency represented a reaction against a group of writers (Bolesław Prus, Eliza Orzeszkowa, Henryk Sienkiewicz) called "positivists," whose critical-realist approach to literature was based on utilitarian principles in both individual and socioeconomic terms. In practice this meant educating the Polish masses, building a strong economic base in the partitioned parts of Poland, and abandoning romantic notions of national liberation movements which brought catastrophe to Poland in 1831 and 1863.

Reymont stayed aloof from the heated literary battles fought by his young contemporaries with the positivists at the turn of the century in Warsaw and Kraków. He did not share their commitment to an art for art's sake aesthetic or their transcendental philosophy, which Czesław Miłosz characterizes as a "contract" entered into by the artist with "the ineffable essence of reality." Reymont was much more in tune with the humanistic attitudes expressed by the positivists, as well as with their critical and down-to-earth description of social reality.

Nevertheless it cannot be said that Reymont was an adherent of positivism or that he was not affected by the new aesthetics of the modernists. Reymont can be characterized as a writer who looms large in the interstices between the two movements. He neither adhered to the specific literary and social program of action proposed by the former nor was indifferent to the new sensibility and the new literary style of Young Poland, especially as far as his stylistic impressionism, hyperbolized imagery, and rhythmic prose are concerned. In terms of outlook he was, additionally, strongly under the influence of Zola's naturalism. Yet ultimately, like the work of all artists of the first rank, his works are experiments with many literary approaches and styles and simultaneously reveal a style which is recognizably his own.

Reymont's literary debut came in the early 1890's, when he published some journalistic pieces in the journal *Głos* (the voice) in 1892 and 1893. When in 1893 Ignacy Matuszewski, one of Poland's leading critics, responded positively to Reymont's manuscripts, Reymont decided to go to Warsaw, "to conquer the world." A year later he attracted the attention of the public and the critics with his "Pielgrzymka do Jasnej Góry" (1894; pilgrimage to Jasna Góra). Combining history with an intensely personal response, this account of a yearly pilgrimage to the shrine of Częstochowa by a large mass of people suggested the manner in which Reymont was to portray reality in his future works.

The Comedienne and its sequel, *Fermenty* (1897; ferments), draw heavily on his experiences as an actor in a traveling troupe and his life in the provinces. Both volumes describe the experiences of Janka Orłowska, the "comedienne," in a traveling company. This is not a deep psychological study of Janka's disillusionment, her fall, and (in the sequel) her mental ferment as she readjusts to the uneventful provincial life which she tried to escape. Instead, Reymont chooses to highlight her experience and her moral dilemma by creating a series of lively, rapidly shifting, impressionistic scenes from the lives of provincial actors, which are contrasted in the second volume with a detailed description of the milieu in which she finds herself when she returns to the provinces.

In the same year that he published *Fermenty*, Reymont published a collection of short stories. The subject matter of *Spotkania* (1897; the meeting) is closely observed peasant life, which Reymont treated in a detached, naturalistic manner. The materialism in men's motives and their brutal struggle for existence can be seen in any story from the collection, such as "Śmierć" (death), in which the daughter lets her father freeze to death in a barn because she is dissatisfied by the inheritance that he has left for her. Human coarseness and inhumanity are shown in the story "Suka" (the bitch), where the cruelty of a woman to her child is contrasted to a bitch that saves her puppies. A more complex story from the collection is "Tomek Baran." In its depiction of hunger and poverty in the village, in its confrontation with the outside world, and, ultimately, in the solidarity of the village, the story anticipates themes that Reymont was to develop more fully in *The Peasants*.

In his next major work, *Ziemia obiecana* (1899, two volumes; *The Promised Land*, 1927), Reymont returned to the impressionistic manner that he used in *The Comedienne*, but here the social sweep and the cast of characters is more ambitious, the pace more nervous, and the impressionistic history more intense and emotionally charged. The title of the work is an ironic reference to the city of Lodz, which had undergone rapid expansion and industrialization in the second half of the nineteenth century. The narrative focus is on three characters—a German, a Pole, and a Jew—but their stories do not form the true structural center; they are merely the emanations of those forces which operate in the city. Focusing primarily on the textile industry, Reymont weaves an impressionistic tapestry of exploitation, greed, ruthlessness, and cruelty. The emotional tone of his descriptions, as well as the anti-urban tone of the work, the first in Polish literature, led the great Polish critic Julian Krzyżanowski to assert that Reymont looked at the city of Lodz not as a "modern sociologist" but as a "theologian, who regarded it as the work of Satan."

As if recoiling from the harsh realities of the city, Reymont returned to his earlier theme of the countryside, a task which was to consume him for a number of years. The result was his great epic of peasant life, a novel which Reymont saw as the work that he had been preparing himself for in all of his previous works. Translated into nearly every major language, it was first published in book form between 1904 and 1909 in four volumes: *Jesień* (1904; *Autumn*), *Zima* (1904; *Winter*), *Wiosna* (1906; *Spring*), and *Lato* (1909; *Summer*). As in *The Promised Land*, the plot does not play a major structural role. The love story in which the son Antek is pitted against his father for the affections of the latter's young wife is derived, as Jerzy Krzyzanowski notes, from *Phaedra* and adds an element of tragedy to the novel. The central focus of the novel, however, is not on individuals but on the peasants as a group. This is not only the Polish peasant but also the peasant as he has been from time immemorial, tied to the soil and submitting to the rhythm of the seasons.

In leisurely ethnographic detail Reymont shows the highly ritualized existence of the peasant from birth to death: his wise primitivism as well as his primitive cruelty and his attachment to the land, which is both loving and grasping. A major factor in the startlingly visual images evoked by Reymont is the manner in which he uses language. Its stately and occasionally hyperbolized tones correspond to the epic flow of the material depicted. In addition, Reymont not only renders the dialogue in a peasant dialect of central Poland but also uses a stylized peasant idiom in the narrative and descriptive passages.

Having depicted the village and the city in Poland, Reymont next turned his gaze backward to Polish history, thus following in the footsteps of his illustrious predecessor Henryk Sienkiewicz and his contemporary Stefan Żeromski. Reymont's historical novel *Rok 1794* (1913-1918, three volumes; the year 1794), a monumental work that took a number of years to complete, was published as a trilogy: *Ostatni sejm Rzeczpospolitej* (1913; the last diet of the republic), *Nil desperandum* (1916; never despair), and *Insurekcja* (1918; insurrection). It covers the eventful years in Polish history of 1793 and 1794 and focuses on both the country's betrayal by the Polish aristocracy and the heroic, popular insurrection under Tadeusz Kościuszko. While the trilogy has received modest praise for its mass scenes, the use of a rapid impressionistic style employed with such telling effect in *The Promised Land*, and some memorable passages, most critics see the work as one of Reymont's weaker efforts, one in which the self-taught writer does well but is ultimately overwhelmed by the complexity of the material.

The trilogy seemed to have drained some of Reymont's strength, as did his illness in the last few years of his life. While he still wrote occasional pieces and had great plans for writing a novel on Polish-Americans, after Poland had gained its independence he became more involved in the social and political life of the resurrected state. The Nobel Prize that he received toward the end of his life was a fitting tribute to this self-made man who had over a relatively brief life span traversed the path from an obscure Polish village to international fame.

310   *Nobel Prize*

Reymont was a renowned writer in his own country already in his lifetime, and he was rather well-known in Europe when he received the Nobel Prize. Yet it was the prize itself that brought Reymont true international fame. While he remains popular in his own country, some of his works have lapsed into obscurity. Such is the fate of his rather dated spiritualist works, many short stories which lie buried in his voluminous short story opus, and the novel *Rok 1794*. Nor are many of his novels read internationally with the intensity that they once were. One work, however, *The Peasants*, the work for which he specifically received the prize, remains a classic of world literature.

Bibliography

Primary

NOVELS: *Komediantka*, 1896 (*The Comedienne*, 1920); *Fermenty*, 1897; *Ziemia obiecana*, 1899 (2 volumes; *The Promised Land*, 1927); *Chłopi*, 1904-1909 (4 volumes; *The Peasants*, 1924-1925), includes *Jesień* (*Autumn*), *Zima* (*Winter*), *Wiosna* (*Spring*), and *Lato* (*Summer*); *Rok 1794*, 1913-1918 (3 volumes), includes *Ostatni sejm Rzeczpospolitej*, *Nil desperandum*, and *Insurekcja*; *Pisma*, 1921-1925, 1930-1932 (32 volumes).

SHORT FICTION: "Pielgrzymka do Jasnej Góry," 1894; *Spotkania*, 1897; "Lili," 1899; *Burza*, 1907; "Marzyciel," 1910; *Z ziemi chełmskiej*, 1910; *Za frontem*, 1919; "Bunt," 1924.

PLAY: *Za późno*, 1899.

NONFICTION: *Reymont we Francji: Listy do tłumacza "Chłopów" F. L. Schoella*, 1967 (letters); *Listy Władysława Stanisława Reymonta do brata*, 1969 (letters); *Reymont w Ameryce: Listy do Wojciecha Morawskiego*, 1970 (letters); *Miłość i katastrofa: Listy do Wandy Szczukowej*, 1978 (letters); *Listy do rodziny*, 1980 (letters).

MISCELLANEOUS: *Pisma*, 1921-1925, 1930-1932 (32 volumes).

Secondary

Borowy, Wacław. "Reymont." *The Slavonic and East European Review* 16 (January, 1938): 439-448. This brief article is a well-documented survey of Reymont's life and works. In its perception of Reymont's literary impressionism it moves away from standard interpretations of Reymont as a realist.

Kridl, Manfred. *A Survey of Polish Literature and Culture*. Translated by Olga Scherer-Virski. New York: Columbia University Press, 1956. A brief overview of Reymont's literary career. Emphasizes the structure and the language of Reymont's works. A brief excerpt from *The Peasants* is quoted and analyzed.

Krzyzanowski, Jerzy R. *Władysław Stanisław Reymont*. New York: Twayne Publishers, 1972. An excellent study of Reymont's life and works, analyzing all of his major and some of his minor works. The only book-length study available in English. Includes an extensive documentation and a bibliography of works in English.

Krzyżanowski, Julian. *A History of Polish Literature*. Translated by Doris Ronowicz. Warsaw: Polish Scientific Publishers, 1978. This definitive history of Polish literature is indispensable for its presentation of literary movements in Poland. The approach to Reymont is social and literary. Includes an excellent bibliography and illustrations.

Marble, Annie Russel. *The Nobel Prize Winners in Literature, 1901-1931*. New York: D. Appleton Co., 1932. The chapter devoted to Reymont and Henryk Sienkiewicz is a popular account. The discussion of Reymont's literary output is brief and impressionistic.

Miłosz, Czesław. *The History of Polish Literature*. London: Macmillan, 1969. A brief but penetrating account of Reymont's literary path. Especially good for its spirited descriptions of Reymont's contemporaries and literary movements. Contains a bibliography.

Jerzy Kolodziej

1925

Literature
George Bernard Shaw, Great Britain

Peace
Sir Austen Chamberlain, Great Britain
Charles G. Dawes, United States

Physics
James Franck, Germany
Gustav Hertz, Germany

Chemistry
Richard Zsigmondy, Austria

Physiology or Medicine
no award

GEORGE BERNARD SHAW
1925

Born: Dublin, Ireland; July 26, 1856
Died: Ayot St. Lawrence, England; November 2, 1950
Language: English
Principal genre: Drama

A dramatist who gave new life to the older radical tradition by putting its ideas brilliantly onstage, Shaw challenged every kind of conventional wisdom but managed to charm his audience with his wit, good humor, and wild extravagance

The Award

Presentation

The Nobel Prize in Literature for 1925 was presented by Per Hallström, Chairman of the Nobel Committee of the Swedish Academy, in early December, 1926. Hallström defended George Bernard Shaw against the suspicion that he was an insincere trickster and buffoon by pointing to his high seriousness of purpose and to the great consistency with which, over forty years, he had argued the case for his political and philosophical ideals. As a radical, he had championed both unpopular socioeconomic causes and the new aesthetic forms onstage of Henrik Ibsen and Richard Wagner. As a vigorous and self-confident rationalist, he had been a determined opponent of sentimentality and romanticism, and, from the beginning, his plays were unsparing satirical assaults on hypocrisy and prejudice. Despite the severity of his fundamental criticism of society's faults and his polemical combativeness, he had carried on his assault with great humaneness, generosity of spirit, and good humor, which made the bitterness of his attack palatable to his audience. His most recent work showed him to be at the height of his poetic talent. If his earlier historical plays seemed determined to stand all the received wisdom about the past on its head, in *Saint Joan* (1923) he had succeeded, without doing violence to history, in bringing to life a heroine for an age which was not remarkably favorable to heroism—an extraordinary triumph. Throughout his career he had used humor with great genius to support the deepest and noblest convictions of his conscience, making himself, as the French called him, the Molière of the twentieth century.

Nobel lecture

Shaw did not believe in prizes for literature. Indeed, he told his biographer, the American academic Archibald Henderson, that he thought the whole idea of giving prizes for work in fine arts was absurd and that the Nobel Prize selection process in particular was a lottery open to all who had achieved a modest degree of celebrity. This was said some time before Shaw was selected. As a rule, he turned down offers of honors and had declined to be knighted or considered for the even more prestigious Order of Merit. Nevertheless, when the Nobel Prize was tendered to him, he decided after some hesitation to accept, not without some teasing from Henderson. In his letter of acceptance to the Nobel Committee, however, Shaw declined to take the prize money—more than $40,000, a sizable sum at the time—as he said his writing provided him with quite a comfortable income. Since the prize could not be separated from the award of the money, Shaw suggested that a trust be established to support the translation into English and publication of works of Swedish literature.

Shaw did not attend the award ceremony. The prize was accepted on his behalf by the British Ambassador to Sweden, Sir Arthur Grant Duff, who noted his country's appreciation for the support to be provided to cultural relations between the two countries. It is fitting that the first publication carried out under the foundation's auspices was of four plays by August Strindberg.

Critical reception

Shaw was hardly plucked from obscurity by the award of the Nobel Prize, and no enormous amount of attention was paid to the event though it was duly reported in the newspapers. As Shaw was relentless and skillful in attracting public attention, and he was already world-famous in the 1920's, it would hardly have been possible for the award to have generated much more press coverage on him than he already had. The literary world was, however, rather surprised. As William Butler Yeats had won very recently, and there was a noticeable tendency, despite disclaimers to the contrary, to ensure a distribution of prizes among all the major literatures, it was not expected that someone writing in English would win again quite so soon. Further, there was an expectation that the next writer working in English likely to be honored would be Thomas Hardy.

Beyond those considerations, literary modernism had made a decided impact on the critical world by the mid-1920's. In the wake of Yeats, English literary standards and fashions were being reshaped by the critical work and writing of T. S. Eliot, Ezra Pound, Virginia Woolf, and James Joyce. It was not that any of those writers was about to be considered for a prize but that, in comparison to that company, Shaw might be dismissed by avant-garde critics as a hopeless relic of a bygone age, a writer of comic trifles, and a propagandist for outmoded social and economic doctrines. Lytton Strachey, for example, a reasonably shrewd observer of the cultural scene, though he admired Shaw's humor, thought that most of his plays were flatly out of date. The newer writers, busily creating a distinctive modern literature, were either reactionary in their politics or rather apolitical. Politics and social change were not at the center of modern literature. In contrast, as a political radical, Shaw was out of step and, on other terms, where he might have shared common ground with the newer writers, his reputation as a cultural iconoclast lay far behind him. His struggles with the Lord Chamberlain about the "obscene" character of *Mrs. Warren's Profession* (1893) paled in comparison with Joyce's difficulties in getting *Ulysses* (1922) into print.

If Shaw seemed to be out of date to the critics of the modern movement, in the middlebrow literary world he was a formidable figure. During World War I, his political views had, once again, antagonized many people, but at its end his career had revived most spectacularly, the fury at his lack of patriotism apparently forgotten. *Saint Joan* in particular was popular around the world, as well as an artistic triumph, and with Shaw riding the crest of such a sweeping success it is easy to see why the Nobel Committee offered him the prize, however unenthusiastic they (and his public) were about his socialist ideology. Not all of Shaw's serious ideas were a liability. His "vitalism," the idea of the "Life Force," was an important general current in the intellectual climate of the 1920's, as the subsequent Nobel Prize given to Henri Bergson seemed to testify. There remained many who resisted Shaw's charm, who dismissed his work as mere clowning, verbal posturing, and shameless self-promotion. Others saw it only as political propaganda, hence not literature.

In a cultural climate which was full of darkness and pessimism, it was possible to see in Shaw, despite many discordant notes, all the cheerful, buoyant optimism and confidence of the past age. To be sure, in reading Shaw as a cheerful idealist, both the Nobel Committee and the public underestimated or simply ignored the complexity of Shaw's response to the postwar world and, indeed, they turned a blind eye to his deepening despair, masked as always by the Shavian antic disposition. The Nobel Committee was trying to award the literary prize, under the terms of the original Nobel bequest, to the most distinguished work "of an idealist tendency," a task which soon became incompatible with awarding it to a writer of respectable talent. For once, the paradoxical character of his work and its deep ambiguities worked solidly in Shaw's favor.

Biography

George Bernard Shaw was born in Dublin on July 26, 1856, into a family on the margins of the Protestant establishment in Ireland. His father lost all of the family's money, and Shaw left school to work in a real estate office when he was fifteen. His mother moved to London to study singing, and in 1876, Shaw followed. He lived there, hand to mouth, for almost a decade, supported by his mother's income as a singing teacher. He began writing, and turned out five unsuccessful novels. In 1882 he heard Henry George speak, discovered socialism, and became a convert to its doctrine. He became a central figure in the newly created Fabian Society and a well-known speaker for radical causes, though he was still penniless.

In 1885 his friend William Archer secured for him regular work reviewing books, and in the next few years Shaw established himself as a successful cultural critic with a number of London newspapers and journals, covering art, music, and literature as well as theater. From 1895 to 1898 he was the drama critic of the influential *Saturday Review*, and his criticism and polemical journalism attracted considerable attention. He did not finish his own first play until 1892 and had great difficulty initially in getting his work produced. In 1898, at last enjoying some success onstage, he married Charlotte Payne-Townshend and gave up reviewing to devote himself to playwriting. He also began a seven-year stint as a member of local government in London.

In the twenty years before the outbreak of World War I, Shaw produced a steady stream of plays: witty comedies full of strong social criticism, which were quite popular despite the indifference of the public to his radical ideas. During the war, Shaw's outspoken criticism of national policy made him extremely unpopular. Despite this, in the half-dozen years after 1918, productions of *Heartbreak House* (1919), *Back to Methuselah* (1921), and *Saint Joan* capped his career, secured his reputation as one of the great playwrights of the century, and led to the reception of the Nobel Prize in his seventieth year.

Though Shaw lived on for almost a quarter of a century, writing continuously, his fame spread by countless productions and film versions of several of his plays, none of his later plays was nearly as successful. His wife died in 1943, and he, having outlived all of his contemporaries, died at home at Ayot St. Lawrence on November 2, 1950.

Literary Career

Shaw's unusually long and productive literary life spanned seven decades. He started his apprenticeship as a writer in 1876 when he tried his hand at writing novels. Over the next few years he produced five novels, two of which were published but were financially unsuccessful: *Cashel Byron's Profession* (1886) and *An Unsocial Socialist* (1887). The others appeared in print much later as literary curiosities, once Shaw's fame as a dramatist was well established. The early prose exhibits the later Shavian trademarks: witty and iconoclastic rejection of the received wisdom of the day, an underlying seriousness, a concern with social questions, and relatively little interest in purely literary or formal matters.

His career as a successful critic began in 1885 as a book reviewer on the *Pall Mall Gazette* and as art critic on *The World*. Later he worked on the newly founded *The Star* for several years, was music critic of *The World* from 1890 to 1894, and from 1895 to 1898, in his last job as a regular dramatic critic, he worked for Frank Harris on the *Saturday Review*, a vantage point of some importance in the London theater. As a critic he was a bold champion of Ibsenite social realism onstage and of Wagner's musical revolution in opera. During this period, in addition to editing and contributing an important piece to the first *Fabian Essays in Socialism* (1889), his lecture to the Fabian Society on Henrik Ibsen was published as *The Quintessence of Ibsenism* (1891), which was successful enough to go through several editions. The culmination of his music journalism, his study of Wagner's ring cycle, *The Perfect Wagnerite* (1898), was also widely read.

He was consistently a frank partisan of what was new and revolutionary in culture and a fierce opponent of the staid philistinism of the late Victorian world. In his campaign against the conventional sentimentality of the London theater in the 1890's he mounted a sharp polemical attack on its reigning actor-manager Sir Henry Irving. This, predictably, won for him few friends among the well established. In addition, Shaw's own socialist views were anathema to the middle-class theater audience. As a result, when he began writing plays himself, he had small hopes for commercial success.

In 1892 he gave the first of his plays, *Widowers' Houses*, which he had begun in 1885 in collaboration with Archer, to J. T. Grein, the daring and highly independent producer of experimental work. Aside from Grein's private production of that work and the production of another of his "unpleasant" plays, *Mrs. Warren's Profession*, Shaw was unable to have his work staged at first. His attacks on slum landlords and on landlords who profited from prostitution were regarded as indecent. The Lord Chamberlain's office, which exercised the state power of censorship on what might be said or portrayed onstage, blocked regular production of his early work, thus confirming to Shaw his view of the fundamental hypocrisy of respectable society which condemned whores but not those who rented them their hotel rooms.

Undiscouraged by censorship, he continued to write plays. His long practice as a public speaker had taught him something about securing the notice of an audience and then winning it over despite its initial suspicion or hostility. The strategies he developed in the 1880's and 1890's he maintained for the rest of his long career. He was uninhibited in his use of extravagant paradox and outrageous declaration, and he gave no quarter to the complacent assumptions of respectable people. Once he got the attention he sought, Shaw disarmed the infuriated response to what he was saying with laughter, using all the tricks of the comic writer, from piercing wit and sly satire to the most farcical slapstick.

Since production in the West End (London's Broadway) was improbable, and the "little theatre" movement to showcase the avant-garde was only beginning in England—much encouraged by his own critical writings—it was likely he would see his works in print before they were produced. (The Lord Chamberlain's office would not normally be able to block publication of a play, only its public performance.) As a result, Shaw felt free to make his political and social arguments at length—not only in his dialogue, and even in the unusually full stage directions, but also in the extensive prefaces he wrote to introduce them. This set a pattern he continued to the end of his career. The texts of all of his plays were eminently readable because he intended them to be read as well as performed.

Having seen that a straightforward didactic approach could not win an audience for his views, Shaw put his drama of ideas, then as now regarded by producers as theatrical poison, into the dominant conventional forms of the day—historical costume dramas, drawing-room romances, and even melodrama. Thus lightly disguised, they remained the vehicle for his own characteristically unconventional purposes. Those were, on the one hand, to overthrow the mindless sentimental romanticism of the well-made plays which constituted the bulk of the London theater and, on the other, to make the case for his own unorthodox views, which were strongly socialist and feminist and determinedly hostile to the hypocritical morality of bourgeois Great Britain. In short, he was both a political and a cultural radical who visibly enjoyed exposing the inconsistencies, contradictions, and outright foolishness of the prejudices of the day, while savaging its bad taste. While proper Victorians were quite naturally indignant at his mocking tone and readiness to jeer at all the solemn pieties which they held dear, his good-natured humor saved him from the lynch mob and eventually found for him a popular audience.

Shaw's "pleasant plays" began his march to success. His airy comedy *Arms and the Man* (1894), while no roaring triumph, was produced. *The Devil's Disciple* (1897), set in the American Revolution, did better but was a distinct hit in distant New York; it may have been popular because it satirized melodrama, however much laced with Shaw's paradoxical wit, or because it was itself a melodrama. These plays began to establish a broader audience for Shaw than the devotees of the little theatre could provide. Faithful to his own serious purposes, Shaw had not succumbed to the lure of popularity by softening his criticism of society, for both plays had a serious point, puncturing the romantic and heroic view of war.

In 1904 the actor-manager Harley Granville-Barker, who had first discovered Shaw when playing Marchbanks in *Candida: A Mystery* (1897), began, in association with J. E. Vedrenne, producing Shaw's work systematically in repertory at the Court Theatre. Over three brilliant seasons, Granville-Barker and Vedrenne produced eleven Shavian plays with the author's collaboration, including *Man and Superman* (1903), *Major Barbara* (1905), *Candida, John Bull's Other Island* (1904), and *You Never Can Tell* (1898). These highly acclaimed productions established Shaw as a playwright of the first rank, whatever the public believed about his ideas. In the next few years there was a similar consolidation of his reputation in the United States and on the European continent.

During World War I, although Shaw was not a pacifist and supported the

Allied cause against Germany, he continued to criticize the conflict as monstrous foolishness. This stance earned for him a reputation for being unpatriotic, and there were fierce denunciations of both his views and his character. At war's end his reputation recovered, despite lingering resentment, because within a few years he had produced two of his finest plays, *Heartbreak House* and *Saint Joan*, respectively a Chekhovian drawing-room comedy full of black despair at civilization sailing onto the rocks and a political tract about the competing claims of faith and the nation-state, posing as historical romance. *Saint Joan* was an enormous success and has been continuously popular since its first production. Shaw, the atheist and critic of war, seemed an unlikely champion for a Catholic saint-girl warrior, but Joan was much of a piece with the rest of his resourceful, energetic, and brave heroines—Candida, Cleopatra, Major Barbara, and the rest. It was this great burst of creative energy which won for Shaw his Nobel Prize.

Shaw continued to write prolifically in his later years, as he said, out of force of a lifetime's habit, though none of his later plays had any great success. Critics began to complain of his talkiness, though, on the whole, the critical literature on Shaw has been distinguished by its lack of consensus. In New York, the Teatre Guild, a major producing organization on Broadway, continued to mount productions of his work until the outbreak of World War II. In Great Britain the actor Barry Jackson began the Malvern Festival, dedicated to the production of Shaw's work, both old and new.

Shaw had become a living classic, with all the dangers that involved—the living writer entombed in his reputation. Shaw had too much vitality to allow himself to be interred in that fashion, and his natural impishness and lack of respect made it difficult to turn him into a monument while there was still breath in him. His opinions continued to be the source of outrage. In the 1930's, amid a shattering depression, he continued attacks on his own society for its failures. These were taken to be endorsements simultaneously of Soviet Communism and Fascism. After World War II was over, his egomania unabated, he continued to amuse himself and enrage worshippers of William Shakespeare by insisting on his own superiority as a playwright. Finally, though he had long resisted having films made of his plays, in his last years and after much negotiation, he allowed Gabriel Pascal to direct the films *Pygmalion* (1938), *Major Barbara* (1941), and *Caesar and Cleopatra* (1945), broadening even further Shaw's public.

Early in his career Shaw saw the first of his "pleasant plays," *Arms and the Man*, turned into the highly popular operetta *Der tapfere Soldat* (1908; *The Chocolate Soldier*, 1909), though he declined to have anything to do with the venture. Six years after his death, on the one hundredth anniversary of his birth, his comedy of manners and class transformation *Pygmalion* (first performed in 1913) had just been turned into the popular musical *My Fair Lady* (1956). It is part of Shaw's extraordinary strength as a dramatist that his material should have delighted so many, for such a long time, whether in the form he intended it, or as a film, or as a commercial musical. It is a part of his ultimate weakness as a propagandist that so little of his own purposes in writing have had any effect on his audiences.

As for the Nobel Prize, as is the case with many of the great writers who have received the prize, for Shaw it could be little more than acknowledgment of his artistic success. Shaw's failures and weaknesses as a writer and playwright notwithstanding, the twentieth century has not produced another writer of stage comedy who is his equal.

Bibliography

Primary

NOVELS: *Cashel Byron's Profession*, 1886; *An Unsocial Socialist*, 1887; *Love Among the Artists*, 1900; *The Irrational Knot*, 1905.

SHORT FICTION: *The Adventures of the Black Girl in Her Search for God*, 1932.

PLAYS: *Widowers' Houses*, 1892; *Mrs. Warren's Profession*, 1893; *The Philanderer*, 1893; *Arms and the Man*, 1894; *Candida: A Mystery*, 1897; *The Devil's Disciple*, 1897; *The Man of Destiny*, 1897; *You Never Can Tell*, 1898; *Captain Brassbound's Conversion*, 1900; *Caesar and Cleopatra*, 1901; *The Admirable Bashville*, 1903 (based on his novel *Cashel Byron's Profession*); *Man and Superman*, 1903; *How He Lied to Her Husband*, 1904; *John Bull's Other Island*, 1904; *Major Barbara*, 1905; *Passion, Poison, and Petrifaction*, 1905; *The Doctor's Dilemma*, 1906; *The Interlude at the Playhouse*, 1907 (playlet); *Getting Married*, 1908; *Press Cuttings*, 1909; *The Shewing Up of Blanco Posnet*, 1909; *The Fascinating Foundling*, 1909; *The Glimpse of Reality*, 1909; *The Dark Lady of the Sonnets*, 1910; *Misalliance*, 1910; *Fanny's First Play*, 1911; *Androcles and the Lion*, 1912; *Overruled*, 1912; *Pygmalion*, 1913; *Beauty's Duty*, 1913 (playlet); *Great Catherine*, 1913; *The Music Cure*, 1914; *The Inca of Perusalem*, 1916; *O'Flaherty, V.C.*, 1917; *Augustus Does His Bit*, 1917; *Annajanska, the Bolshevik Empress*, 1918; *Heartbreak House*, 1919; *Back to Methuselah*, 1921; *Jitta's Atonement*, 1923; *Saint Joan*, 1923; *The Apple Cart*, 1929; *Too True to Be Good*, 1932; *How These Doctors Love One Another!*, 1932 (playlet); *On the Rocks*, 1933; *Village Wooing*, 1934; *The Six Men of Calais*, 1934; *The Simpleton of the Unexpected Isles*, 1935; *Arthur and Acetone*, 1936; *The Millionairess*, 1936; *Cymbeline Refinished*, 1937 (adaptation of William Shakespeare's *Cymbeline*, act 5); *Geneva*, 1938; *In Good King Charles's Golden Days*, 1939; "The British Party System," 1944 (playlet); *Buoyant Billions*, 1947; *Shakes Versus Shaw*, 1949; *Far-fetched Fables*, 1950.

NONFICTION: *Fabian Essays in Socialism*, 1889 (editor); *The Quintessence of Ibsenism*, 1891; *The Perfect Wagnerite*, 1898; *The Common Sense of Muni-*

cipal *Trading*, 1904; *Dramatic Opinions and Essays*, 1907; *The Sanity of Art*, 1908; *Letters to Miss Alma Murray*, 1927; *The Intelligent Woman's Guide to Socialism and Capitalism*, 1928; *Ellen Terry and Shaw*, 1931; *Everybody's Political What's What*, 1944; *Sixteen Self Sketches*, 1949; *Correspondence Between George Bernard Shaw and Mrs. Patrick Campbell*, 1952; *Platform and Pulpit*, 1961; *Collected Letters, 1874-1897*, 1965; *Collected Letters, 1898-1910*, 1972; *The Nondramatic Literary Criticism of Bernard Shaw*, 1972; *Collected Letters, 1911-1925*, 1985.

Secondary
Bentley, Eric. *Bernard Shaw*. 2d ed. New York: New Directions, 1957. A brief, incisive critical study of Shaw by one of his principal American champions. The emphasis is on his role as a dramatist of ideas. There are separate chapters devoted to Shaw's views on political economy, "vitalism" (the Life Force), and his theories of drama. This second edition (the first was published in 1947) has additional material about his working relations with actors. Much of Bentley's other work about the modern theater is relevant; see his *The Dramatic Event* (1954).
Brustein, Robert. *The Theatre of Revolt*. Boston: Little, Brown and Co., 1964. A critical study of the master figures of the modern theater by one of the leading directors and producers of serious theater in the United States. Shaw is treated, in the chapter devoted to him, as a thoroughly modern dramatist and thinker and put in context with Ibsen, Strindberg, Anton Chekhov, Bertolt Brecht, Luigi Pirandello, Eugene O'Neill, and Jean Genet.
Chesterton, Gilbert Keith. *George Bernard Shaw*. 2d ed. London: J. Lane, 1935. No one could have been further from Shaw in his views than Chesterton, an archconservative and devout Catholic. Nevertheless, this early critical study has many shrewd and interesting things to say on the Shavian art. Like Shaw, Chesterton wrote against the grain of public opinion and was, therefore, an able deployer of charm and humor to overcome skepticism and win converts to his point of view. He could fully appreciate Shaw's skill at his own practices: They were gracious antagonists.
Ervine, St. John Greer. *Bernard Shaw: His Life, Work, and Friends*. New York: William Morrow and Co., 1956. A friend of Shaw for many years, though closer to Mrs. Shaw, Ervine was a fellow Irishman, writer, and sometime-manager of the Abbey Theatre. His biography provides a coherent and full review of the whole career. Despite the similarities in their backgrounds, Ervine was a conservative who could not abide Shaw's politics and unorthodox opinions. There was a current of hostility between them, though Shaw dealt with Ervine's disapproval with characteristic patience and courtesy.
Harris, Frank. *Bernard Shaw: An Unauthorized Biography*. New York:

Simon and Schuster, 1931. While this is a useful work, as Shaw had a hand in its composition (see Shaw's "sex credo" in chapter 17) and wrote a post-script for it, Harris is not reliable as a biographer. Harris did have a long association with Shaw going back to the 1890's, but this life of Shaw was written hurriedly because he needed the money badly. Despite Shaw's help, the work is colored by some petty jealousy.

Henderson, Archibald. *George Bernard Shaw: Man of the Century*. New York: Appleton-Century-Crofts, 1956. This is the third and final version of Henderson's long, disorganized, and generally indispensable life of Shaw. No other work provides as much information. Henderson, an American academic, took pains to cultivate Shaw and maintained a relationship with him from the turn of the century until Shaw died. The two earlier versions of this work—*Bernard Shaw: His Life and Work* (1911) and *Bernard Shaw: Playboy and Prophet* (1932)—still have some limited independent value. Henderson reworked them, cannibalizing each of the earlier books as he went along while dropping some bits of material. Also of some interest is *The Table Talk of G. B. Shaw* (1925), the best of which Henderson pillaged for the later biographies.

Kronenberger, Louis, ed. *George Bernard Shaw: A Critical Survey*. Cleveland: World Publishing Co., 1953. This is a convenient introduction to Shaw's critical reputation up to the time of his death provided by excerpts from contemporary criticism. Represented here are, among others, Edmund Wilson, Thomas Mann, W. H. Auden, Joseph Wood Krutch, George Jean Nathan, Jacques Barzun, Stark Young, John Mason Brown, Max Beerbohm, Ludwig Lewisohn, Eric Bentley, and G. K. Chesterton.

Laurence, Dan H. *Bernard Shaw: A Bibliography*. 2 vols. New York: Oxford University Press, 1983. A basic bibliography of work by and about Shaw based on the collections of Shaw manuscripts and printed material at the University of Texas and the holdings of the British Library, this exhaustive work is the starting place for any serious inquiry into Shaw's life and work.

S. J. Stearns

1926

Literature
Grazia Deledda, Italy

Peace
Aristide Briand, France
Gustav Stresemann, Germany

Physics
Jean-Baptiste Perrin, France

Chemistry
Theodor Svedberg, Sweden

Physiology or Medicine
Johannes Fibiger, Denmark

GRAZIA DELEDDA
1926

Born: Nuoro, Sardinia; September 27, 1871
Died: Rome, Italy; August 15, 1936
Language: Italian
Principal genre: Fiction

The novels and stories of Deledda are characterized by their strong sense of place and vivid depiction of the customs and beliefs of the Sardinian people, as well as the author's essential faith in the ability of humanity to persevere through hardships

The Award

Presentation

Henrik Schück, the president of the Nobel Foundation, presented the 1926 Nobel Prize in Literature to Grazia Deledda on November 10, 1927. His presentation speech focused on Deledda's vivid portrayal of the nature and customs of her native Sardinia. She has captured the savage beauty of the mountains surrounding the remote town of Nuoro and presented dispassionately and without moralizing the public sympathy toward bandits and the harsh justice of the vendetta. Her attention toward nature and primitive society stems from the Romantic movement's rejection of classical models and from Jean-Jacques Rousseau's interest in the natural state of man. Her predecessors in Italian literature include the regionalist writers of the nineteenth century, especially Giovanni Verga. Though Deledda eventually abandons her emphasis on specific locale, her writing still maintains its Sardinian character.

In their style and craftsmanship, Deledda's novels belong to the tradition of the classic narrative, although the composition is not always consistent and the transitions are sometimes hasty. Her virtues, however, far outweigh these flaws. She excels as a painter of nature, as a keen observer of primitive custom (almost rivaling Homer), and as a creator of figures both powerful and well-defined. By making these monumental figures credible, Deledda masterfully fuses idealism with realism.

The author stands apart from much of twentieth century literature in her refusal to promote a thesis or concentrate on a philosophical problem. Though she seems to be interested only in the past, Deledda still knows and responds to the present, showing an interest in and awareness of every aspect of human life. Her goal, she states, is to overcome the anguish of "life's slow death" by intensifying and enriching life's meaning. She sees and portrays people as they are, with all of their problems and failings, yet she still believes that humans can and should improve. The vision of life promoted in her novels is "serious and profound . . . with a religious cast." Though this vision is often sad or tragic, it is never pessimistic. In her love for life, Grazia Deledda fulfills Alfred Nobel's ideals for a writer—encouraging humanity with a moral strength.

Nobel lecture

Claiming an inability to make speeches, Deledda responded to the Swedish Academy in a typically self-effacing manner. In her brief remarks, she attributed the honor to Italy rather than to herself and then repeated an old Sardinian blessing, "spoken to friends and family on solemn occasions":

> Salute!
> Salute to the King of Sweden!
> Salute to the King of Italy!
> Salute to you all, ladies and gentlemen!
> *Viva* Sweden, *viva* Italy!

The brevity of the lecture illustrates Deledda's preference for the concrete over the abstract and reflects the absence of self-consciousness in the style and content of her novels. Indeed, little of her nonfiction prose is concerned with broad aesthetic questions.

Critical reception

Since 1907, but especially after the publication in 1920 of *La madre* (*The Mother*, 1923) and its rapid translation into most European languages, Grazia Deledda had placed among the top candidates for the Nobel Prize. The award for 1926 having been postponed for a year, in 1927 the Permanent Secretary of the Swedish Academy, Erik Axel Karlfeldt (himself a laureate in 1931), nominated Grazia Deledda, and this time she was elected—the second Italian and the second woman to have been so honored. The award came as little surprise to many Europeans, nor was Deledda herself unprepared. Most American and English readers, however, knew little of her work, only a few of her many novels having been translated into English—most notably *Dopo il divorzio* (1902; *After the Divorce*, 1905, republished as *Naufraghi in porto*, 1920), *Cenere* (1904; *Ashes*, 1908), and *The Mother*. The Italian critics generally acknowledged Deledda's merit, and Benito Mussolini paid her a special tribute at his official home; earlier he had named her to his Academy of Immortals.

Many of the American articles about the award praised Deledda's skill but acknowledged that most readers would be unfamiliar with her work. After several news briefs about the prizes, *The New York Times* published a feature article from Rome by Renzo Rendi in the December 18 edition of *The New York Times Book Review*. Like many other journalists, Rendi provides a lengthy biography of Deledda, including an account of the indignation of Deledda's family and townspeople at the publication of her first story (at age fifteen), a description of Sardinia, and a sketch of the author's parents and childhood. Renzi describes Deledda as a George Sand without the romanticism and comments on her similarity to Russian rather than French writers, a comparison that would prove frequent through the years.

Harry Hansen, in the *New York World*, also characterizes the exotic nature of Sardinian character and custom; he speaks highly of *The Mother* and of Deledda's typically Italian focus on motherhood. In her book review column in *Good Housekeeping*, Emily Newell Blair also singles out *The Mother* for its broad portrayal of human desires and sufferings. Suggesting that writers of Nobel Prize stature characteristically set forth their themes much more directly and clearly than do most writers, she goes on to contrast the sparse nature and simple story of *The Mother* to the lush countryside and ornate plots in the novels of Thomas Hardy. Blair then left-handedly praises *The Mother* as "absorbing and powerful for those to whom life is a textbook and humans are pitiful." An article that was reprinted in the review *The Outlook*, originally written for the Stockholm women's weekly *Idun* by Ellen Lundberg-Nyblom, praises Deledda for her vivid, realistic portrayal of Sardinian life, her epic style and concentrated dialogue, and her excellent, psychologically appropriate descriptions of landscape, but Lundberg-Nyblom also hints that Deledda's artistry is not as mature as that of earlier great novelists.

Far more negative is Ernest Boyd's article in the column "Literature Abroad" for the December 3, 1927, issue of the *Saturday Review of Literature*. Boyd maintains that the public bewilderment at the choice of Deledda is both a typical and a reasonable response, for the author is one of a series of obscure or mediocre writers who have won the Nobel Prize (interestingly, Boyd's list of such writers includes William Butler Yeats and George Bernard Shaw, as well as European writers whose work has been well-accepted in the English-speaking world). Boyd maintains that Deledda is a good but not great writer, and that the dearth of translations of her work into English is not unjustified. He provides a biography, but most of his article reviews the novels *Elias Portolu* (1903)—a novel he finds superior to *The Mother*—*Ashes*, and *Nostalgie*, 1905 (nostalgia). For Boyd, if the Nobel Committee wished to nominate an Italian, they should have chosen Gabriele D'Annunzio; if they had wanted to elect an Italian woman writer, others were just as deserving. Boyd concludes that Deledda's real parallel is with the American novelist Sarah Orne Jewett, for both are conscientious craftswomen writing in a minor genre, and both are unpretentious, vivid storytellers. Deledda's work, Boyd claims, is more regional than universal, but her works read better in translation, for the originals contain many stylistic flaws.

The *Edinburgh Review* article "The Novels of Grazia Deledda" in the April, 1928, issue is perhaps the most objective and informative review. It provides background and summaries for a number of novels, finding *The Mother* to be Deledda's highest achievement.

Biography

Grazia Cosima Deledda was born on September 27, 1871, in Nuoro, Sardinia, a town of about eight thousand inhabitants. Her father, Giovantonio Deledda, earned a diploma from the university in Cagliari and practiced law before turning to agriculture and the export business; he was also elected mayor three times. At forty, he married Chiscedda Cambosu, choosing a poor, beautiful young girl twenty years his junior over richer, more prominent women. His wife was illiterate but highly reputed for her embroidery, a craft which her daughter Grazia would adopt and continue into her later years.

Grazia Deledda was given a more thorough education than many Sardinian girls, but in Nuoro she could not continue formal schooling after the age of ten. Other than tutoring by relatives and teachers, she became an autodidact, reading widely and passionately both popular and serious literature, including such writers as Sir Walter Scott, Lord Byron, Heinrich Heine, Victor Hugo, Chateaubriand, Eugène Sue, Honoré de Balzac, Giosuè Carducci, Gabriele D'Annunzio, Giovanni Verga, Leo Tolstoy, Ivan Turgenev, and Fyodor Dostoevski. Deledda began writing early, but a number of family tragedies and crises, including the death of her father and the arrest of one of her brothers for stealing, left her in charge of the family olive press. She continued writing, and profits from her writing allowed her to travel.

At Cagliari in 1899, Deledda met Palmiro Madesani, a civil servant in the Ministry of Finance; soon they were engaged, and on January 11, 1900, they were married in Nuoro. Madesani was transferred to Rome, where the couple would live happily for the rest of their lives. Deledda devoted herself as much to maternal and domestic duties as to writing, though she wrote regularly and prolifically. The couple had two sons, Sardus in 1900 and Franz in 1904. They traveled and worked in Italy and France before finally settling in Rome; after 1911, Deledda did not return to Nuoro.

Shortly after winning the Nobel Prize in 1927, Deledda was found to have breast cancer, which gradually spread throughout her body. Having led a life marked by few remarkable events, either political or personal, Deledda died, after receiving last rites, on August 15, 1936, and was buried in Rome. At the request of citizens of Nuoro, her remains were transferred to a church near her hometown shortly after World War II.

Literary Career

At fifteen, Grazia Deledda published her first work, a short story, "Sangue Sardo" (Sardinian blood), in the Rome fashion magazine *Ultima moda*. This event stirred up controversy in her hometown and within her family, for many people objected to a young woman, particularly one without formal education, turning to a vocation dominated by men. Deledda continued writing, however, and soon established herself with writers and editors in Rome. She dedicated herself to steady writing, publishing an average of one book per year.

In her earliest works, Deledda reveals the influence of the romantic novel, with its emphasis on adventure and exaggerated plot devices. Having been fascinated since childhood by local customs, she began to concentrate more on the Sardinian land and people, particularly in such works as *Anime oneste* (1895; honest souls) and *La via del male* (1896; the way of evil). In 1894, Deledda published a study of Sardinian culture, *Tradizioni populari di Nuoro in Sardegna* (popular traditions of Nuoro in Sardinia). A frequent conflict in Deledda's novels stems from the inability of the native Sardinians to modify their customs and adjust to change. Often the customs of her characters are even older than Christianity and are based on ignorance and superstition. When these old beliefs come into conflict with the demands of the modern world, as they eventually must, the outcome is tragic.

As she moved away from standard adventure plots, Deledda began developing the conflict between the old and the new more maturely and in greater detail; the novels also became increasingly melancholy. Most of her greatest novels were written in the first two decades of the twentieth century. In *After the Divorce*, Deledda shows the tragic consequences of a relaxing of the Italian divorce laws. Constantino Ledda is mistakenly sent to prison for killing his uncle. Under a new divorce law, his wife, Giovanna, who is living in poverty, is able to remarry a landowner, in spite of objections from her relatives. Unfortunately, her new life is worse than her poverty, and now she is scorned by the villagers. After the real murderer confesses, Constantino returns to his village and begins a passionate but loveless affair with Giovanna. Unable to find happiness, he eventually kills Giovanna's cruel mother-in-law and is sentenced to hard labor in prison; Giovanna's life deteriorates still further. The novel shows that while the traditional prohibition of divorce had been inflexible and repressive, the new law fails to provide for the emotional needs of those whom it purports to liberate.

The almost certain failure of Deledda's protagonists to resolve the conflict between the old and the new gives her novels a sense of fatalism. Yet the public failure does not eliminate the obligation to act ethically, and this defeat often leads a character to seek a private expiation, typically through self-renunciation.

Elias Portolu, which Deledda completed during the first year of her marriage, is for some critics her greatest achievement. The young man, Elias, falls in love and has an affair with his brother's fiancée, who has a son from this affair. Contrite, Elias plans to become a priest, but then his brother dies. Though he could now marry his beloved, he cannot bring himself to do so.

Elias' own son by the affair dies, and he decides not to marry but to go through with his vows.

Deledda continued to write about Sardinia and its people even after she had left the area. Her works show a subtle development of character and a de-emphasis on dramatic plot devices, while retaining many of the same romantic conflicts. *Ashes*, which was made into a film in 1916 starring Eleanor Duse, further conveys the author's tragic outlook. A young Sardinian, the illegitimate son of a farmer, attends the University of Rome, but this education only serves to make him self-conscious and unhappy. Setting out to find his mother, he discovers that she is poor and wretched. Although ashamed, he takes care of her, but she dies, as if to relieve him of his burden. When he opens a bag she had placed around his neck, he finds only ashes.

After World War I, Deledda's work became even more intense and tragic, beginning with *Marianna Sirca* (1915), a story of Sicilian bandits. Deledda's best-known work outside Italy, *The Mother*, published in 1920, centers on conflicts of loyalty within a young priest who falls in love with a parishioner. When his mother threatens to expose him, he ends the affair, but his lover threatens to denounce him in church. At Mass, she finds herself unable to do so and then discovers the priest's mother, dead in her seat.

After 1921, Deledda began to concentrate more on the psychological states of her characters than on plot, as in *Il segreto dell'uomo solitario* (1921; the secret of the solitary man), and relied less on Sardinia as a setting. Her last novels have thinner, more allegorical plots and are often situated in undefined, atemporal settings, as in *Il paese del vento* (1931; the country of the wind). Deledda's posthumous novel, *Cosima* (1937), is her most clearly autobiographical work and one of her most mystical.

Deledda once stated that she wished to do for Sardinia what Tolstoy had done for Russia, and her emphasis on individuals caught up in tragic circumstances often beyond their control is reminiscent of the Russian novelists. She is often seen as a transitional figure, combining the form of the nineteenth century novel with the existential outlook of twentieth century fiction. What characterizes her fiction most distinctly is the author's passionate but objective concern for people caught up in fateful circumstances, a concern balanced by her expectation that they act as nobly as possible and with an awareness of their motives.

Grazia Deledda is still relatively unknown outside Italy and is mainly remembered for having won the Nobel Prize, though in her native country she is widely read and appreciated. Recent translations of her work and the feminist project of rediscovering neglected women writers may gain for her greater and longer-lasting recognition. Because of the traditional form of her works and the lack of a self-conscious concern with language, Deledda may not attract the attention of scholars concerned with literature that exhibits a more modern preoccupation with form, but for those critics and readers interested in the relationship between a writer's culture and philosophy, and between a character's historical circumstances and personal identity, Deledda's complex handling of setting and character should ensure for her a permanent place among esteemed twentieth century authors.

Bibliography
Primary

NOVELS: *Anime oneste*, 1895; *La via del male*, 1896; *Il tesoro*, 1897; *La giustizia*, 1899; *Il vecchio della montagna*, 1900; *Dopo il divorzio*, 1902 (*After the Divorce*, 1905; republished as *Naufraghi in porto*, 1920); *Elias Portolu*, 1903; *Cenere*, 1904 (*Ashes*, 1908); *Nostalgie*, 1905; *L'edera*, 1906; *L'ombra del passato*, 1907; *Il nostro padrone*, 1910; *Sino al confine*, 1910; *Nel deserto*, 1911; *Colombi e sparvieri*, 1912; *Canne al vento*, 1913; *Le colpe altrui*, 1914; *Marianna Sirca*, 1915; *L'incendio nell'oliveto*, 1918; *La madre*, 1920 (*The Mother*, 1923, 1974; also as *The Woman and the Priest*, 1922); *Il segreto dell'uomo solitario*, 1921; *Il Dio dei viventi*, 1922; *La danza della collana*, 1924; *La fuga in Egitto*, 1925; *Annalena Bilsini*, 1927; *Il vecchio e i fanciulli*, 1928; *Il dono di Natale*, 1930; *Il paese del vento*, 1931; *L'argine*, 1934; *La chiesa della solitudine*, 1936; *Cosima*, 1937; *Romanzi e novelle*, 1941-1969; *Opere scelte*, 1964; *Romanzi e novelle*, 1971.
SHORT FICTION: *Il giuochi della vita*, 1905; *Amori moderni*, 1907; *Chiaroscuro*, 1912; *Il fanciullo nascosto*, 1915; *Il ritorno del figlio*, *La bambina rubata*, 1919; *Cattive compagnie*, 1921; *Il flauto nel bosco*, 1923; *Il sigillo d'amore*, 1926; *La casa del poeta*, 1930; *La vigna sul mare*, 1932; *Soie d'estate*, 1933; *Il cedro del Libano*, 1939.
PLAY: *L'edera*, 1912 (with Camillo Antona-Traversi).
NONFICTION: *Tradizioni popolari di Nuoro in Sardegna*, 1894.

Secondary

Balducci, Carolyn. *A Self-Made Woman: Biography of Nobel Prize Winner Grazia Deledda*. Boston: Houghton Mifflin Co., 1975. The only book-length work in English devoted to Deledda, this biography is aimed primarily at young readers (junior high to high school age), but it is serious and well researched. Balducci bases many of the scenes in the book on Deledda's articles and autobiographical fiction, especially *Cosima* and *Il dono di Natale* (the Christmas gift). Contains a well-selected bibliography.
Gunzberg, Lynn M. "Ruralism, Folklore, and Grazia Deledda's Novels." *Modern Language Studies* 13 (Summer, 1983): 112-122. Gunzberg's scholarly monograph provides the general reader with helpful background on Deledda's treatment of rural life and her use of Sardinian folklore, as well as the thematic value of such material.
Lawrence, D. H. Preface to *The Mother*. Translated by Mary G. Steegmann. London: Jonathan Cape, 1928. Reprint. *Phoenix: The Posthumous Papers*

of D. H. Lawrence. Edited by Edward D. McDonald. New York: Viking Press, 1968. Though brief, this preface is important both for its historical value in helping to popularize the novel and for the insights it gives into both Deledda and Lawrence. Lawrence suggests that the interest of the book is not so much in plot, character, or theme but in its presentation of the instinctive life and the repression of sexuality by the mother's ambition.

Marble, Annie Russell. "Grazia Deledda." In *The Nobel Prize Winners in Literature: 1901-1931.* New York: D. Appleton and Co., 1925, rev. ed. 1932. Reprint. Freeport, N.Y.: Books for Libraries Press, 1969. This article provides a useful survey of American and Italian evaluations of Deledda during the 1920's. Marble raises the issue of the author's literary merit and, while acknowledging certain aesthetic shortcomings, suggests that Deledda's achievement is unique and significant.

Opfell, Olga S. "Sardinian Legend: Grazia Deledda." In *The Lady Laureates: Women Who Have Won the Nobel Prize.* Metuchen, N.J.: Scarecrow Press, 1978. Opfell's well-written article is one of the most succinct and useful surveys of Deledda's life and artistic themes. Objective but sympathetic, the article contains a brief bibliography of English and Italian resources, a discussion of women and the Nobel Prize, a time line from 1833 to 1977, and a general bibliography about the Nobel Prize.

Pacifici, Sergio. "Voices from the Provinces: Grazia Deledda and Marino Moretti." In *The Modern Italian Novel from Capuana to Tozzi.* Carbondale: Southern Illinois University Press, 1973. Pacifici's coverage of Deledda's major works is significant in that it abandons the traditional view that she is primarily a regionalist writer. He shows in a concise overview of the major novels that Deledda is concerned chiefly with universal themes stated in such conflicts as good versus evil, the temporal versus the eternal, and sensual love versus charity. An annotated bibliography provides a useful evaluation of both early and recent criticism.

Steven L. Hale